Date Due

Japanese People
and Politics

CHITOSHI YANAGA

Department of Political Science
Yale University

Japanese People
and Politics

John Wiley & Sons, Inc., New York

Chapman & Hall, Limited, London

To Galen Merriam Fisher

Preface

Japan was as quick to convince herself of the advantages of Western civilization as she was to realize the inevitability of reopening the country to commercial and diplomatic intercourse with the rest of the world. Consequently, she set out immediately to adopt voluntarily those features of the economic and political institutions of the West which could contribute toward the achievement of national security and prosperity.

In her resolute efforts to build a strong nation capable of preserving her independence and integrity, Japan adopted a constitutional form of government in 1889. Prompted by the urgency of building up national strength with the greatest possible speed, the leaders gave little thought, if any, to the establishment of individual freedom or democratic government. As a matter of fact, with rare exceptions, the leaders of the early Meiji government were inclined to look upon democracy as a system not conducive to the well-being or security of the nation and quite contrary to the traditional concepts and practice of government. This sort of attitude persisted until World War II. It was inevitable that although there were from time to time those who advocated democracy, conditions were not favorable for the establishment of democracy.

As an aftermath of defeat in World War II, however, the nation was confronted with the problem of democratization as well as stabilization of politics. At the same time, the urgency of achieving a viable economy brought into sharp focus the imperative need for greater efficiency in policy making and administration. Although the postwar Constitution which went into effect in 1947 was designed with a view to establishing a democratic system of government, it could not possibly be more than a blueprint of what still had to be achieved.

Japan's present political system represents a mixture as well as a juxtaposition of the traditional and the modern. In form and appearance it is obviously modern and Western; yet in its spirit and method of operation much of it remains traditional and Japanese. By analyzing the sociocultural ideas, attitudes, and behavior of the people, their economic needs as well as historical antecedents, and how they are reflected in, and are influencing, their management of national affairs, this work attempts to present as accurate and clear a picture as possible of the workings of Japanese politics and government.

Extensive use has been made of recent works of Japanese scholarship, mainly of the postwar period, that have not yet been crystalized into systematic works on Japanese politics and government. It was the good fortune of the author to be given the opportunity to observe Japanese politics in action at first hand in Tokyo at a most interesting transitional stage through a Fulbright Research Grant during the academic year 1955–1956. Some of the organizational changes in Japanese politics that took place after the manuscript was completed have been incorporated into the volume wherever they were of major significance. In the discussion and characterization of the political parties, however, no attempt was made to bring it up to the minute inasmuch as the understanding of the old party alignments before the mergers took place is necessary for the appraisal of the present two-party setup which is still a long way from a two-party system as understood in the Western democracies.

It would be impossible for the author to acknowledge his debt individually to all the scholars in the field, his colleagues, and students who have in various ways, directly and indirectly, contributed to the making of this volume. The author is particularly grateful to Professor Robert E. Ward of the University of Michigan for going through much of the manuscript while in preparation and offering valuable comments and suggestions. He wishes to express his thanks to Yale Univeristy and to Provost Edgar S. Furniss for a grant from the International Studies Fund, which made it possible for the author to visit several libraries including the Library of Congress in search of materials in the early stages of the preparation of the manuscript. Acknowledgment is also made to Mr. Sadayoshi Tanabe, Executive Director of the Tokyo Institute of Municipal Research and his staff for the assistance given the author in establishing necessary contacts and facilitating his research. The author wishes to thank Mrs. Lillian M. Harada for her painstaking work in the typing of the manuscript.

Saybrook College   CHITOSHI YANAGA
New Haven, Connecticut
and Tokyo.

August, 1956.

Contents

Introduction ——————

Emergence of Japan
as a Modern Power

Hardly had the twentieth century opened than the eyes of the world were turned upon a new power that had emerged in the Far East. By dint of unrelenting efforts Japan had succeeded in 1899 in throwing off the stigma of inequality which she had borne since the first treaties were concluded with the Western powers in 1858. Extraterritoriality, the label of inferiority, was gone even before Turkey had accomplished it. The following year, Japan joined the Western powers and participated in the Allied expeditionary force against the Boxers who had laid a seige on Peking. Two years later, in 1902, she startled the capitals of the world by concluding the Anglo-Japanese Alliance, the first bilateral alliance between a Western power and an Oriental nation. Far more startling to the world was the resounding military defeat she handed to Tsarist Russia in the Russo-Japanese War of 1904–05. At the end of World War I Japan had become one of the five great powers of the world.

How did Japan, virtually a hermit feudal nation for more than two centuries and isolated from the rest of the world, manage in so brief a space of time as less than fifty years to emerge from isolation, open its ports to foreign commerce, and proceed with extraordinary speed and thoroughness to equip herself with the productive techniques of the Western world? The world wondered and marveled at the amazing transformation which had been achieved in Japan with so little ado. "There is nothing in human history more astonishing" observed a distinguished English historian, "than the swiftness and success with which, in the course of a very few years, Japan discarded the forms of an ancient and admirable civilization under which she had lived contentedly for many centuries and by an extraordinary

1

effort of the national will adopted, and adapted to her own needs, a totally different system."[1] Another Englishman, a philosopher of renown, after a visit to Japan soon after World War I, was also deeply impressed by what he saw. "The modern Japanese nation is unique," observed Bertrand Russell, "not only in this age, but in the history of the world. It combines elements which most Europeans would have supposed totally incompatible, and it has realized an original plan to a degree hardly known in human affairs. The Japan which now exists is almost exactly that which was intended by the leaders of the Restoration."[2]

That the transformation of an Oriental feudal nation into a modern power occasioned disbelief as well as wonderment is quite understandable for what had been accomplished was quite without precedent or parallel. It involved in effect telescoping into mere decades the industrial revolution which had in Europe and America taken nearly two centuries to run its full natural course and transform the economic life of the West.

When the nation was confronted with the demands of the Western powers subsequent to the opening of the ports in the 1850's, the leaders quickly saw that the nation's independence and even survival were at stake. The choice lay between two alternatives: to be overwhelmed by the tide of nineteenth-century nationalism and expansionism of the West or to ride on its crest into the uncertain but hopeful and promising future. With little hesitation, they chose the latter course and the die was cast. It was imperative that the program of modernization be carried out with the utmost speed to bring the nation abreast with the advanced nations of Europe and America. Furthermore, it was apparent that simultaneous attacks had to be carried out on several fronts. Reorganization and centralization of government and administration, institution of compulsory education, establishment of national defense and compulsory military service, and, above all, mastery of Western techniques of production, finance, marketing, transportation, and communication were of the highest priority in view of the overriding urgency of building and shoring up national strength. Everything else was subordinate to this all-important goal. Animated by an unwavering singleness of purpose and devotion, the leaders faithfully followed their carefully worked out blueprint for a strong Japan. Time was of the essence and no

---

[1] Ramsay Muir, A Short History of the British Commonwealth, II, 617.

[2] The Problem of China (1922), p. 97. See also the author's article "The Meiji Restoration: an Example of the Adjustment of Cultural Patterns to a New Technology" in the 1943 Yearbook on Education (London).

attention was paid to anything which could possibly be regarded as frills in any sense.

To meet the demands of the new technology, it became apparent that obsolescent social ideas, attitudes, and practices would have to be discarded or modified. However, changes were not carried beyond the point of absolute necessity or absolute minimum needs. No serious attempts were made to radically change the traditional social structure or way of life. If any noticeable changes took place, they were certainly not the result of deliberate design but merely the unforeseen by-products which were perhaps not even thought of, much less anticipated.

The resulting synthesis of East and West was bound to be of a peculiar kind. Practically everything of the West that contributed to national efficiency was adopted and yet the traditional elements were left untouched so long as they did not constitute obstacles to modernization. What happened in the factories, for instance, was that while Western techniques of production were introduced, little or no change had taken place in the treatment of the workers. In the sphere of government and politics, Western forms were taken over avidly and enthusiastically, resulting in the extensive adoption of the formal structural and even, though to a lesser extent, the procedural features, while the spirit, ideas, and processes were left behind.

Western concepts of liberty and popular rights were espoused by political leaders as weapons in their fight against the government for popular participation. But they were seldom if ever thoroughly understood or applied even by the leaders inasmuch as they had been acquired largely out of context and without the benefit of the necessary environment of working institutions, practices, and processes. Traditional ideas and attitudes continued undisturbed to dominate the national thinking in spite of the remarkable scientific and technological advances which were made. Many of the old ideas were actually refurbished to serve the needs of the nation. And this was done most effectively perhaps in the molding of a new nationalism which the leaders felt must be equal to the task of coping with the surging nationalism of the nineteenth century world.

The inception of modern Japanese government goes back to 1889 when the nation was impelled more by external pressure than by internal needs to establish a constitution and a parliamentary government along Western lines. In this accelerated program of planned modernization of the nation's administrative organization, the primary though not the exclusive objective was the achievement of overall structural design such as would insure a maximum degree of efficiency and a rapid building up of national power both industrially and militarily. Inevitably the prime emphasis was on structural and functional modernization of the administrative machinery which affected only very slightly, if at all, the time-honored ideas and ideals of the people. Thus, it is patently clear that the Constitution of 1889 which clothed Japanese government in a Western garb, was not an instrument designed to secure to the individual his inalienable rights, if indeed the leaders conceived of such a principle at all, but rather a means of achieving national strength, security, prosperity, and international recognition.

The accelerated, unnatural, forced transformation of the nation from feudalism to a modern industrialized state was achieved at a heavy cost in the stresses and strains placed upon the people and in the violence that was done in various ways. Political institutions of the West were superimposed upon traditional Japanese sociocultural bases and operated without the benefit of traditions and experiences necessary for their success. In other words, although, in external appearances, Japanese government was as modern and Western as any in Europe or America, the concepts and attitudes, as well as the guiding principles which furnished the propulsive force of politics and government, bore little resemblance if any to those of the West. Nor could the behavior and reaction of the leaders as well as the body politic be anticipated, understood, or appraised in terms of Western behavior patterns.

What actually happened then was this: Western techniques of production along with the capitalistic system itself were adapted and developed without the benefit of such changes as Western society had undergone. Faced with the exigencies of the period, there was neither the inclination nor the time necessary for initiating and carrying through social reforms; the leaders concentrated their efforts on practical modernization limited largely to technological aspects and leaving social changes pretty much alone. The growth of capitalism took place under vastly different conditions, both politically and socially, giving rise to a different type.

The constitutional parliamentary system launched in 1890 thus operated in a singularly Japanese fashion. Westernization in the political sphere at best was little more than a superficial imitation of European and American institutions which had been transplanted only in so far as their structural features were concerned, and the adoption of Western political language or, rather, political nomenclature. The Japanese leaders did not wish to go much further in their modernization. This resulted in a multiplicity of façades which served to obscure if not conceal, especially for the casual or superficial observer, the traditional concepts and attitudes that were much too deeply rooted in the nation's past to be readily superseded by alien ideas and ways of doing things. In other words, Westernization which was carried out assiduously as part of the national program of modernization in the 1870's and 1880's without any compulsion from the outside, was never given the opportunity to undergo full and unrestricted development.

The forced modernization of the nation was inevitably accompanied by distortion, if not perversion, of values. For example, on the one hand there was an almost excessive emphasis on the good of the nation, that is, the national strength and prosperity, while on the other too little attention was paid to the well-being of the individual as a whole. The solution of problems which were producing the serious stresses and strains, as for example in the 1870's, was not worked out internally but sought and obtained in expansion. In this process attention was diverted from internal to external problems. The people, in spite of their own economic plight and oppressive restraints, deluded themselves into thinking that the prosperity of the nation was synonymous with their own individual prosperity.[3]

Japan's modernization actually plunged the nation from feudalism into an expansionist state without the benefit of a transitional period of bourgeois society which might have developed liberal tendencies. Although as a political organization feudalism was liquidated, its legacies were carried over into the new Japan. Rural conditions remained virtually unchanged. Capitalism developed by utilizing the legacies of feudalism and under the aegis of the government. The mercantile class not only did not develop into an opposing or liberalizing force against the absolutism of the government but collaborated with and was protected by it. What developed was actually state sponsored and protected capitalism of a highly political nature.

Monopolistic capitalism as it developed in Japan did not achieve the maximum efficiency for it depended greatly, perhaps almost too heavily, upon government support, politically and financially. Business and government became mutually dependent in national affairs and therefore necessary to each other not simply for economic reasons but also in a political way. This condition of mutual dependence continued, becoming stronger rather than weaker as the nation passed through political and economic crises.

[3] Fukutake Tadashi, *Nihon no Shakai*, p. 15.

Japan was admitted into the family of nations as an equal but only after she had won a victory in a war. She earned the distinction of being the first Asian nation to rid herself of the stigma of extra-territoriality by entering the arena of world politics in the 1890's. She became in fact a "Western power," if not in name. It was the successful war against Russia which ranked Japan as one of the major powers of the world. The two successful wars she fought gained for her the respect of Western powers to such an extent that her policy of expansion was given impetus. Her participation in World War I helped materially in the achievement of a position of leadership in Eastern Asia. Each advance she made in her expansion was the fruit of her efforts in modernization.

At the same time, both as part and consequence of World War I, there appeared within the country rumblings of dissatisfaction among the people which could not be ignored by the government and the political leaders. The Russian Revolution of 1917 made a strong impact on the workers as well as on the intellectuals. America's propaganda campaign to "make the world safe for democracy" also had a strong influence particularly among students, intellectuals, and professors with a liberal tendency. Unprecedented prosperity of wartime was soon followed by sudden recession and brought deep gloom to the nation. The great earthquake and fire of 1923 destroyed the greater part of Tokyo and Yokohama to add to the economic difficulties of the nation. Unemployment brought to the fore the proletarian movement and the Japanese people were exposed for the first time to the menace of communism.

Although in 1925 a universal manhood suffrage law went into effect enfranchising all the male population over 21 years old, the developments which ensued did not follow a liberal course. The activities of the leftist groups and particularly the Communists, coupled with unsatisfactory economic conditions which led finally to the panic of 1927, gave the rightist and reactionary elements the opportunity as well as the excuse to launch offensive operations both internally and externally.

Although the decade and a half from 1918 to 1932 is generally regarded as the period of responsible party government in Japan, it was far from the kind of responsible government that the British, for instance, understand and practice. However, it must be stated that, by comparison with what preceded and what followed, it represented the high-water mark of Japanese constitutional government. Yet because of the way in which power was wielded by the political parties, it was also a period of corruption.

The international developments of the 1920's contributed to the generation of an expansive spirit on the part of a great number of leaders. This was compounded of two ingredients, namely, the feeling that Japan's aspirations were being deliberately thwarted and that her right to live was being denied[4] by her neighbor, China, as well as by the Western powers, and the threat of Communism via China. Deterioration of economic conditions was viewed with alarm by the government because of the rapidly increasing population in the face of severe depression and unemployment. Thus for the first time the population problem became a major concern and a policy matter in national planning and politics. Consequently, the expansion policy from 1928 on reflected the sense of urgency resulting from the spectre of population pressure.

Economic nationalism and international competition gave impetus to the urge for expansion during the 1930's. Political power passed from the political parties to the military who shaped the policies both internal and international. The military sought the solution of internal problems through international action. At home, responsible party government disappeared and a totalitarian structure came into being with the complete abolition of the political parties. The ever mounting inconsistencies, incongruities, and maladjustments in the political and economic life of the nation reached alarming proportions and got out of hand and, aided by ultranationalism and the impasse in international relations, culminated in the Pacific War.

One of the most ambitious political experiments of all time was attempted by the Allied Powers immediately following Japan's surrender in 1945. This was in persuance of the provisions of the Potsdam Proclamation of July 26, 1945 to "remove all obstacles to the revival and strengthening of democratic tendencies among the Japanese people," and to establish "freedom of speech, of religion, and of thought, as well as respect for the fundamental human rights."

For a little over six and one-half years from September, 1945, through April, 1952, the Japanese people were governed under the authority of the Supreme Commander for the Allied Powers who exercised that authority through the existing government. The Allied initial postsurrender policy was designed to insure the development of Japan into a peaceful democratic nation, and to this end reforms were instituted in the political, economic, social, and cultural aspects of national life.

There is no doubt that the experiment was successful in a number

[4] Prime Minister Takashi Hara wrote an article which was translated and published as "Live and Let Live" in the early 1920's.

of respects.   However, it would be naïve to assume that in the brief
space of less than seven years the basic character, ideas, and attitudes
of the Japanese people, or their institutions or way of life, can be
altered so radically as to produce overnight a democratic system of
government.   To be sure, many of the undemocratic and militaristic
features of national life were suppressed if not liquidated, but traditional concepts and modes of thought and action which had been
nourished and nurtured through the centuries could not be eradicated
in spite of the purges that were carried out.   Democratic ideas and
processes were encouraged but always within the restrictive and
sometimes stultifying framework of military occupation.   During the
latter half of the period of occupation the exigencies of the international situation forced a noticeable shift in Allied policy.   Security
was given precedence over democratization which was now very much
in the background.   Even before the period of occupation came to
an end, the building up of the nation's defensive strength was begun
largely as a result of the outbreak of the Korean War.

The new Constitution guaranteed the fundamental rights of the
individual but the people did not really feel or appreciate the meaning of such rights and they are not yet in a position to assert them
effectively.   Agricultural land reform elevated the position of the
small farmer and yet neither the basic problem of miniscule farming
nor the conservative mentality of the agrarian population has been
affected in any way.   The labor laws have expanded the rights and
freedom of the worker but his livelihood is still insecure and he is not
in a position to be appreciative of such legal gains, nor can he carry
out the implementation of his rights.   The legal and constitutional
groundwork has been provided but does not yet rest on solid foundations.   Socially, economically, and politically, there is at best only
a precarious basis for the development of democracy.

It was quite natural that, when the Occupation ended and full
sovereignty was restored, a sort of reaction should set in to undo at
least in part what had been instituted by the Occupation.   Psychologically it was a natural reaction of revulsion against a pressure
under which the nation had been placed as a result of defeat.   In an
assertion of national self-respect even the more desirable Occupation-
sponsored reforms were bound to suffer.   Even the pro-American
government of Prime Minister Yoshida came out shortly after the
end of Occupation with the statement that one of the immediate
tasks of the nation was "to rectify the mistakes of the Occupation."

1 ——————————

The Japanese People

GEOGRAPHICAL SETTING OF JAPANESE POLITICS

What sort of geographical setting do the 89,000,000 Japanese have in which to work out their problems? Without a clear idea of this physical environment at the very outset, it would be difficult to grasp the full significance and implications of Japanese politics.

The Japanese archipelago comprising the four main islands of Honshu, Hokkaido, Kyushu, and Shikoku with numerous small islands is anchored off the northeastern coast of Asia. Its area of approximately 142,300 square miles is smaller than either Montana (145,878) or California (156,740). Located entirely in the temperate zone between 30° and 45° North Latitude, its climate is mild compared with that of neighboring countries like Korea and China. The mildness is due largely to insularity and the moderating influence of the warm ocean current, the Black Current (Kuroshio), and the seasonal winds. The latitudinal spread of temperature is roughly the equivalent of the Atlantic seaboard of the United States. The northernmost island, Hokkaido, corresponds to the New England states and the southern tip of the southernmost island, Kyushu, has the climate of northern Florida. The islands of Amami-Oshima which were returned to Japanese sovereignty in December, 1953, are actually covered with subtropical vegetation. Extreme climatic conditions are unknown but Japan abounds in earthquakes.

Because of its mountainous and volcanic nature, the country has a very limited arable land area which does not exceed 16 percent. The soil is only moderately fertile in the delta regions but actually

9

very poor elsewhere and it is only through the extensive use of chemical as well as organic fertilizers and intensive farming and multiple cropping that the agricultural productivity is maintained at a high level. There are no really large plains in the country. Rainfall is abundant and water is plentiful, especially in short streams, making it a valuable source for the development of hydroelectric power. Its disadvantage, however, is the relatively high humidity which obtains, giving discomfort especially in the summer. Weather changes and variations are marked and sudden, making forecasting extremely difficult and flying conditions hazardous. The long and highly indented coastline totaling some 17,000 miles, affords a large number of excellent harbors as well as beautiful inlets, bays, and promontories. Actually no place in the interior is as much as 150 miles from the nearest seacoast.

It would be impossible to assess fully and accurately the influence of geography on Japan through the two thousand years and more of her national development. For our purpose it will suffice merely to touch upon facts which are well established and generally accepted. The fact of insularity which is not unlike that of Great Britain has had a profound influence on her national character and development. The comparative physical isolation it afforded has enabled the nation to develop her own culture without being completely overshadowed and engulfed by Chinese civilization as in the case of Korea which is physically contiguous to China. It left the Japanese pretty much undisturbed to adopt and adapt selected elements of Chinese culture which they liked and felt would serve their needs, and at the same time to reject those which they did not care for. In due course alien elements were assimilated into Japanese culture so completely and in such a manner as to lose their original identity, frequently giving rise to products far different from and even superior to the original. National development was achieved without the disruptive effects of foreign invasions, assuring the undisturbed and full expression of native genius. Moreover, the nation was able to preserve its independence. Thanks to insularity, like Great Britain, Japan developed into one of the world's greatest maritime powers in the twentieth century. However, it was actually the paucity of raw materials coupled with the pitifully small area of arable land that forced the nation to turn to foreign trade out of the desperate need for survival. While there have been obvious advantages accruing from the fact of insularity, there have also been disadvantages. Perhaps the most serious disadvantage which has become increasingly recognized is the insularity of outlook and psychology of the people. It must be emphasized, however, that this was not necessarily a disadvantage for the greater part of Japanese history. It has become a disadvantage comparatively recently in the world of the twentieth century.

THE PEOPLE

Who are the real ancestors of the Japanese people? Where did they come from and how did the Japanese people come to be what they are? In spite of the advancements in the fields of anthropology, ethnology, ethnography, and archaeology, no light has been thrown on the mystery which surrounds the origin of the Japanese people. No conclusive or definitive evidences are available to determine when and how the original Japanese came to settle in the archipelago. However, of one thing there is no doubt whatever. Even at the dawn of history the Japanese people were already a mixed race and not of a single racial stock.

Without troubling ourselves with details as to the time, the sequence, or the size of the successive migrations into the archipelago, we can obtain a fairly satisfactory picture of the beginnings of the Japanese people. It is now generally accepted that the entire archipelago was already inhabited by the aborigines, the Ainu, in the neolithic period. As to where they came from and who they were, the mystery will probably never be solved. That they were of proto-Caucasoid origin is beyond doubt. During the ensuing eneolithic age, that is, the stone-iron age, the Mongoloid Tungusic people came over from the Asiatic mainland in several successive waves of migration, very likely by way of the Korean peninsula, some four thousand years or more ago, and began the conquest of the aboriginal inhabitants. Possessing a superior culture they soon overwhelmed the Ainu population both culturally and politically. To this proto-Japanese element was added the Ainu strain and subsequently the Malay strain of the island of Kyushu, the southernmost island of the archipelago which has been the home of the Hayato or Kumaso tribes. At a much later period came the migration of the Han people, or the proto-Chinese, and this continued down into the early stages of Japan's historic period, but numerically they constituted only a minor addition. Thus the Japanese people are of a very heterogeneous origin combining practically all the known major strains of the human race, namely, Caucasoid, Negroid, Mongoloid and all their variations, mixtures, and mutations. It is not entirely improbable on the basis of physical characteristics that can be discerned that at some point there even took place a slight infusion of Semitic strain. The Japanese people are thus the result of a process of extensive miscegenation which began in the prehistoric and protohistoric periods.

Because of the resemblances in their traits, temperaments, and even their achievements, the Japanese have been likened to some of the peoples of the West. They have been called variously the "Britons of the East," "Yankees of the Far East," and "Germans of East Asia." But such characterizations not only are misleading but actually constitute a hindrance to the accurate understanding of the Japanese people.

SOCIOCULTURAL FOUNDATIONS

In spite of ethnic heterogeneity in so far as the origins are concerned, after centuries of continuous assimilative process, there exists today striking cultural homogeneity which in many ways exceeds even that of the English people and certainly antedates it by many centuries. As a matter of fact, cultural homogeneity had been attained in Japan even before the English nation as such had actually taken shape. This remarkable homogeneity has been brought about by a common language, way of life, traditions, and customs, bolstered by a strong sense of kinship which is the product of centuries of isolated national development in the "tight little islands" unmolested by alien invasions and reenforced by actual inbreeding of centuries.

Cultural homogeneity produced a powerful sense of social solidarity, precluding the development of any kind of racial antipathy. The national habit established early in history of borrowing quite freely if not unrestrictedly from alien cultures, starting with the Korean and Chinese, developed into the practice of enthusiastically receiving foreign things, ideas, and even persons of different racial origins and cultures. Racism therefore has been unknown throughout her history and racial problems have never arisen in Japanese politics for racial groups have never existed to form a minority of any sort.

Religiosity has been one of the characteristics of the Japanese people though not to the same degree or in the same manner as, for example, in India. Religion has always had a strong and salutary effect on Japanese social and political ideas, attitudes, and developments. As a matter of fact, in the very beginning, no distinction was made between religion and government which were virtually synonymous. Even after a limited sort of distinction had been made between the two, no clear-cut separation could be effected. Religious tolerance bordering on indifference has been normal and traditional perhaps because of the predominance of polytheistic proclivities in the realm of religious life. Religious syncretism has been a notable feature of Japanese development as manifested particularly in the Shinto-Buddhist syncretism. Persecutions on purely religious grounds have been virtually unknown for they have taken place only when religion was exploited for political purposes and appeared as a threat to the political security of a regime. Religious wars such as Europe witnessed not infrequently are unknown.[1] Nor have there been any dangerous cleavages or divisions, either social or political, based on religious differences.

The advent of two alien religions, Buddhism in the sixth century and Christianity a thousand years later, in the sixteenth century, aroused no hostility. It must be pointed out, however, that Christianity in the 1890's provided an issue that was exploited politically by ultranationalists who branded the religion as un-Japanese; but there was no persecution of the Christians. On the political scene, there have never been clerical or anticlerical parties such as have been common throughout continental Europe and South America.

LANGUAGE AND LITERACY

Japan today has one of the highest rates of literacy in the world.[2] This was accomplished in a matter of only a few decades as part of the highly accelerated program of modernization launched in the 1870's. It was imperative for the success of the program. However, because of the emphasis placed on literacy per se rather than on the well-rounded education of the individual, and because of the purpose to which it was put, namely, indoctrination and regimentation, the benefits of literacy have not been entirely of the kind one expects in the Western democratic nations. Compulsory education after World War II was extended to nine years,[3] and a considerable shift in emphasis and goals has resulted.

The difficulty of mastering the written language has been a very serious drawback in the development of the youngsters though it is not generally regarded as such by the average Japanese.[4] The dif-

---

[1] The Shimabara Rebellion, 1637–1638, ostensibly a religious war, was in reality a political rebellion against the oppressive rule of the local daimyo. It was put down and its leadership exterminated because it was Christian.

[2] Literacy in Japan compares favorably with countries like Great Britain and the United States since the percentage is somewhere in the 90's. This places her far above the other countries of Asia most of which range between 20 and 30 percent.

[3] Formerly it was only six years.

[4] Educators, however, early recognized this and repeated attempts have been made to reduce the number of "characters" or "ideographs" to a manageable number. In 1947, the number of characters to be mastered during the period of compulsory education was reduced to 881.

ficulty of mastering the language is due to its complexity which is perhaps without parallel. There is no other language in the world which can equal Japanese in the multiplicity and complexity of pronunciation. A written character can be pronounced anywhere from two, which is the minimum, to perhaps six or seven different ways depending on the way it is combined with another character.[5] To further complicate matters, the elaborate system of honorifics requires fine distinction in the use of words according to the rank and status of the persons involved in conversation or communication. This feature, which recognizes the hierarchial relationships in the family and society, hinders the development of a feeling of equality.[6] Honorifics, however, are not confined to persons only; they apply to inanimate things as well.[7] It is doubtful if democratization can actually take place unless and until equality is achieved in the language, and class or sex distinctions are forgotten in the speech of the people.

Lack of preciseness in the speech of the people as well as the habit of indirection creates serious problems especially in politics. Speaking in vague generalities is quite normal and yet in some ways a great deal of precision and exactness of expression is expected. In poetic language, for instance, minute distinctions are made not so much for scientific accuracy as for aesthetic gratification. Early summer rain is known as *samidare* (or rain in the month of May). Spring rain is *harusame*. Monsoon rain is called *tsuyu* (dew-drops) or *baiu* (plum rain). The Japanese language is especially rich in nuances and double meanings, making it undoubtedly the world's best for play on words which could be exploited successfully for clever slogans in politics as well as in the entertainment field, but frequently the world's worst in getting the right meaning across.

CULTURAL PLURALISM AND TENSION

Through successive periods of history, the Japanese people have developed a national culture which has been the result of the mixture of elements both indigenous and alien. Japanese cultural development has been a successive series of importation and assimilation of elements of alien cultures which have in time produced a sort of

---

[5] Japanese belongs in the Ural-Altaic family of languages and is unrelated to Chinese. Its closest relatives are Korean and Ryukyuan. The Ural-Altaic family includes such languages as Finnish, Hungarian, Magyar, etc.

[6] There are more than twenty different forms of the first person pronoun.

[7] Triple-honorific is to be found in such a word as *omiotsuke* (soybean-paste soup).

synthesis and amalgam.   The juxtaposition of the old and new, of the indigenous and alien, of the East and the West in the ideas, attitudes, and sensibilities, modes of thought and action, and manner of living, is quite apparent.   Nowhere else in the world is there such a juxta-position.   Nowhere else does one find so much tension in the minds of a large proportion of the people, which is the result of the clash of the cultures of the East and West.   A duality in the mode of life as well as of thought exists for the urban population of the nation. As a result a schizophrenic or split personality is fast becoming almost a normal condition among the educated individuals, particularly those who have spent a considerable part of their lives abroad in the West.

THE IMPACT OF SCIENCE AND TECHNOLOGY

Much has been said about the lack of inventiveness of the Japanese. They have actually been labeled a nation of copiers or imitators who have not originated anything.   Only until very recently, this char-acterization persisted in the West in general except among men of science.   It is true that Japanese genius has been expressed histori-cally more in taking over something and making improvements and refinements on it rather than in creating something entirely new and unthought of before.   The earliest manifestation of this sort of genius is the invention of the *kana* or phonetic syllabary in the ninth century.

Willingness and eagerness to adopt Western technology which de-veloped in the eighteenth and nineteenth centuries largely through the medium of the Dutch language gained impetus after the opening of the country in the 1850's.   Since the late nineteenth century Japan has produced a number of scientists of high repute whose contributions have attracted the attention of the scientific world.[8] In such fields as seismology[9] oceanography, meteorology, astronomy, bacteriology,[10] anthropology, botany, biochemistry,[11] and physics, the contributions have been noteworthy.

[8] For nineteenth century scientific developments, see the author's *Japan Since Perry*, pp. 83–85.

[9] Dr. Bailey Willis, who was professor of geology at Stanford University and known to thousands of students as "Earthquake Willis," after his visit to the Orient in the late 1920's stated that the Japanese excelled all the other nationalities in the scientific research into the earth's disturbances.   *New York Times*, Feb. 21, 1949.   Dr. Aikitsu Tanakadate perfected the parallel motion seismograph and the spiral seismography for recording vertical motion caused by earthquakes.

[10] Dr. Shibasaburo Kitasato (1856–1931), one of the brilliant students who studied under Dr. Robert Koch in Berlin, founded the Tokyo Institute for In-fectious Diseases, gained international recognition by his study of the infectious agent of bubonic plague.   Dr. Hideyo Noguchi (1876–1928) of the Rockefeller Institute for Medical Research made valuable contributions through original re-

In the matter of inventiveness, Japanese culture was rated, as of 1911, on the same level with the Mediterranean and below the Teutonic countries.[12] Japan's rapid rise to that position was regarded as unparalleled even by any Western nation. Even at the time Japan was more in the lead in the Asiatic industrial picture than England was in the European. By the end of World War I, she had achieved the position of the world's third greatest naval and maritime power.

Between the two world wars Japanese technology made rapid strides. The development and effective utilization of the automatic power loom invented by Sakichi Toyoda revolutionized the Japanese textile industry to strengthen its position in international competition. By the early 1930's, it had succeeded in forging ahead of the British cotton industry, virtually forcing the Lancashire mills against the wall. Also in the 1930's, in the period immediately preceding World War II, Japan led the world in the production of synthetic fiber.

It was not until after World War II that advances in Japanese science and technology became widely known. Even before World War I, Dr. Hantaro Nagaoka had developed a theory of atomic structure, anticipating the discovery of the atomic nucleus.[13] In a similar manner, Dr. Hideki Yukawa in 1934 postulated on theoretical grounds the possible existence of particles of a mass (meson), intermediate between a proton and an electron.[14] For this contribution he was awarded a Nobel Prize in physics in 1949. This was the first time a Nobel Prize had been won by a Japanese and was a recognition by the world that Japanese science had come of age. In the period following World War II, even as industry was slowly recovering from the effects of war, technological advances were being made. The superior quality of products, notably in the field of optics, attracted widespread attention for it demonstrated the technical skill and know-how of the people.

Japan's position as the leading Asian nation in the field of scientific and technological development has been the result of the virtually

search on the spirochaetes and the cause of syphilis, made bacteria-free virus for smallpox vaccination, demonstrated the cause of Oroya fever, and gave his life to the cause of yellow fever research. See Gustav Eckstein, *Noguchi* (1931), for a detailed biography.

[11] Dr. Jokichi Takamine (1854–1922) isolated adrenalin and diastase. See A. Casiglioni, *A History of Medicine* (1947).

[12] Mark Jefferson, "The Geographic Distribution of Inventiveness," *Geographic Review* 19: 649–661. October, 1929.

[13] Seishi Kikuchi, "Scientific Research" in Hugh Borton (ed.), *Japan*, pp. 207–217.

[14] George A. Baitsell (ed.), *Science in Progress*, 7th series (1951), pp. 242–245.

insatiable curiosity of the educated for better ways of doing things and the absence of the attitude of contempt for physical exertion and manual work. The important role of science in the future of Japan has been given due recognition since World War II and scientific education is being pushed ahead vigorously. In 1954, the Diet approved appropriations for atomic research for the first time, realizing that not only the future of the nation but its very existence would depend upon scientific progress. Quite naturally the impact of science and technology has greatly intensified social and psychological tensions among the people and complicated the task of the leaders. The adjustments necessitated by scientific advances have imposed tremendous stresses and strains on the nation and these are reflected in every sphere of life, notably in the realm of politics. It is clear that Japanese political behavior especially on the international level has come to be influenced profoundly by technological advances and their keen awareness of their implications.

POLITICAL LITERACY AND INTEREST

In the period since World War II the general public in Japan has become aware of political problems and of the fact that youth and women have come to take a far greater interest in politics than ever before.[15] It is patent too that the voters have developed a degree of critical attitude toward politics and politicians that did not exist previously.[16] Instead of acting on impulse and group psychology which influenced them greatly heretofore, the people are now beginning to speak their minds in their own language and within the framework of their own experiences where political matters are concerned.[17] It has been said that the Yoshida government has given the nation a valuable political education by its actions. However, the existing state of political awareness and sophistication of the Japanese in general still leaves much to be desired when compared with what is found in the Western democracies.

It is a truism that a large proportion of the human race is obliged to work so hard in obtaining the necessities of life that little energy is left over for other purposes.[18] The overwhelming majority of the Japanese people fall in this category. Furthermore there is the weight of centuries which has developed a passivity in the individual,

[15] *Asahi*, August 24, 1953.
[16] Kyugoku Jun'ichi, "Seiji ishiki ni okeru zenshin to teitai," *Seijigaku Nempo*, 1953, p. 120.
[17] Kyodo Kenkyu, "Kokumin seikatsu to seiji ishiki," *Kaizo*, June, 1953, p. 91.
[18] Bertrand Russell, *Power*, p. 9.

who regards politics as none of his concern and quite outside of his ken. Traditionally, the ruling class had made it clear that the people had no right to even show an interest, much less meddle, in the affairs of the government. Politics, which has been synonymous with government, had traditionally been regarded as the special preserve of the government officials and was "out of bounds" for the people.

Today, politics to an average Japanese citizen is still quite remote, for it is "something that is taking place somewhere." Every action which takes place within the Diet building is obviously political action but he is not sure where else it is taking place. So far, only a small percentage of the voters has managed to tie together their everyday life and politics in a real and meaningful manner, to appreciate fully the stake they have in politics. Civic loyalty is still pretty much in an underdeveloped state. Political obligations are as yet only hazily realized.

Political ignorance is widespread and is largely attributable to the fact that political knowledge as a rule does not help primarily to further the individual aims of the ordinary voter, nor does it on the other hand help the individual to avoid unpleasant realities. At the time of the general election of 1949, the *Asahi* newspaper conducted a poll to ascertain how many actually knew that there was a provision for referendum of the judges of the Supreme Court. It revealed the surprising fact that only 30 percent knew while 70 percent were not aware of its existence.[19]

If the polls demonstrate the lack of political knowledge in a convincing manner, the undeveloped state of political sensitivity reflected is startling. In the matter of political know-how that is necessary for effective participation in politics the average voter has a great deal to learn. This learning process has to begin with the individual who must disabuse himself of the laissez faire attitude towards politics and abandon the traditional idea that government is best in the hands of officials who are not in any way controlled or supervised.

Aloofness towards politics goes back to the Confucian idea that the ruler was, by definition, virtuous and that he knew better than anyone else what was good for the people. Since the ruler's job was to rule, there was no need for the citizen to be concerned about the affairs of government which are the concern of the ruler and his officials. The weight of tradition must be removed before the people become convinced that they are the government and their voices must be heard.

[19] *Asahi*, January 10–13, 1949; 1950 *Asahi Yearbook*, p. 487.

If the people are to develop real concern in politics several things must happen. Thus far the real interests of the people have not been reflected in political alignments or politics in general. The people must come to feel they have a real stake in politics and government. Political leaders so far have not begun to carry on any systematic program of political education. Members of the Diet, for example, have done little to establish intimate contacts with their constituents. Only a very few have made the voters feel close to them; most of them do not extend their contacts beyond the influential persons in their election districts.

In political matters the Japanese have a strong tendency to think in highly abstract terms. As a matter of fact, their discussions are carried on in a political language which is quite removed from the language of everyday life.[20] This is particularly marked among the intellectuals whose ideas are far removed from the realities of the workaday world. Their ideas more often than not serve to rationalize their actions instead of motivating them.

Women have become participants in politics for the first time in history. Until the new Constitution went into effect they had been denied the franchise. Traditionally they had been relegated to an inferior and subordinate role in society though their power and influence in the home were always considerable.[21] Consequently they were not in the stream of public issues and discussions as were the men who have always been in touch with the market place.

With the granting of the franchise, women have been brought into the political arena as voters and active participants. However, because of the rather secluded life they had lived, their sudden entrance into politics was not preceded by a period of gradual preparation for the role they were given. Consequently, the first general election in which they participated was as much a reflection of their initial outburst of zeal and enthusiasm for their newly acquired right as of the understandable confusion occasioned by their inexperience. When the novelty of voting had worn off, and with many problems to occupy them, there occurred a noticeable decline in their enthusiasm and participation.

The political participation of women is a new development and

[20] Kyodo Kenkyu, "Kokumin seikatsu to seiji ishiki," *Kaizo*, June, 1953, pp. 90–91.

[21] Prior to contact with Chinese civilization and Buddhism and even for a considerable period thereafter, Japanese women enjoyed a very high position in society. Only with the advent of feudalism did women assume a subordinate position.

experiment suddenly instituted and as such it will be some time
before its full impact is felt upon the nation's politics. There is no
denying, however, that as a consequence a marked change has taken
place in the complexion of Japanese politics for something new has
been added to the body politic.

THE ECONOMIC IMPERATIVES OF JAPANESE POLITICS

The elementary fact of Japan's national life can be stated suc-
cinctly as "too many people on too little land." With a population
of 89,000,000 in an area of little over 142,000 square miles or about
the size of the state of Montana, the nation is virtually "bursting at
its seams." The population density per arable square mile of land
is the highest in the world, as can be seen in Table I.[22] This is due

TABLE I.   POPULATION DENSITY PER AVAILABLE SQUARE MILE OF
LAND

Japan	4285	India	709
Indonesia	1801	Italy	725
United Kingdom	1797	France	513
China	1318	U.S.S.R.	236
Germany	1308	United States	217
Pakistan	948		

to the fact that only 16 percent of her total land area is arable and
her population is increasing at the rate of over a million every year.

The Population Problem Research Institute of the Ministry of Welfare estimated that the increase in population will continue steadily
until 1990 when the peak will be reached at approximately 107,000,-
000. Thereafter, it will decline but probably remain stationary at
around 100,000,000. According to its estimates the population increase appears as shown in Table II. Thus the ever increasing pop-

TABLE II.   ESTIMATED RATE OF POPULATION INCREASE IN JAPAN

1955	89,427,000	1985	106,813,000
1960	93,222,000	1990	107,214,000
1965	96,149,000	1995	106,677,000
1970	99,331,000	2000	105,512,000
1975	102,558,000	2005	103,749,000
1980	105,228,000	2010	101,290,000

ulation and the pressure it exerts upon the nation in manifold ways
have had a vital bearing on Japanese politics since World War I, and

[22] Taken from the *Yearbook of Food and Agricultural Statistics, 1952 Population.*
Vol. VI, Part I.   Food and Agricultural Organization of the UN.

particularly in the late 1920's when population pressure came to be reflected in national policies as well as in the anxiety of the nation's leaders. The period since the end of World War II has seen the aggravation of the pressure, especially with the loss of 45 percent of her former land area. The world is now aware of the "explosive threat contained in Japan's population pressure."[23]

A problem which is inextricably tied with population is that of food. Because of the scarcity of land it has been impossible for the nation to achieve self-sufficiency in food in spite of the fact that nearly 50 percent of the population is engaged in agriculture. Upwards of 20 percent of the nation's food requirements must be met by imports. Thus Japan is a food deficit nation.[24]

In order to support a large population and insure a degree of national well-being, Japan decided on industrialization. However, because of the paucity of natural resources and raw materials for her industries, she has had to depend very heavily on outside sources for raw materials on the one hand and on foreign markets in which to sell her manufactured goods on the other. This condition has had far reaching consequences on her political developments both internally and externally.

The urgent and even desperate need for developing export industries was recognized by the government at a very early stage of industrialization and a system of protection and subsidy was established. In the process a very intimate and mutually dependent relationship developed between business and government which in time gave rise to monopolistic capitalism. A high concentration of economic power resulted as a natural consequence. Economic power was easily translated or converted into political power. At the same time, a condition developed whereby it was impossible to carry on profitable enterprise without government good will and support. In other words, the tycoons of Japanese business and industry achieved their success largely through their dependence on political power. Politics and economics had become inextricably enmeshed, inseparable and mutually interdependent. Economic power came to be highly concentrated in the course of national economic development.

[23] Julian Huxley, "Population and Human Destiny," *Harper's Magazine,* September, 1950, p. 41. Dr. Warren S. Thompson, Director of the Scripps Foundation for Research in Population Problems, recommended in his report to General MacArthur a birth control policy to cope with the problem of population pressure, but he was bitterly attacked by representatives of the Catholic Church.

[24] "Estimated Deficit of Food," *The Sangyo Keizai,* Overseas Edition, June 1, 1952, p. 8.

In the period of Allied Occupation following the end of World War II, as a means of accelerating the nation's democratization, a policy was instituted whereby the deconcentration of economic power was effectuated. But this policy came to an end soon after the nation regained full independence and sovereignty and without having changed radically the structure or problems of national economy.[25]

The primary problem of politics is now more than ever the achievement of viable national economy which must depend to an increasingly greater degree on international trade. This places Japanese politics inexorably at the mercy of international developments and external factors which are more often than not beyond national control. Even on the domestic scene, the overriding issues are economic. It is over economic issues that struggles for political power are waged and battles are won or lost. All other issues become secondary and supplementary in the face of dire economic necessity.

[25] Higuchi Hiromu, *Zaibatsu no Fukkatsu,* discusses the revival of the *zaibatsu.*

2

The Japanese
Political Heritage

Beliefs, concepts, and ideas which comprise the sum total of a nation's political heritage provide the solid foundation on which a political system is firmly based. Without due regard to these cherished ideas it would be impossible to gain an insight into the political attitudes, actions, and reactions as well as the hopes and aspirations of a people.

Of greatest pride to the Japanese body politic today is the fact that they have the oldest ruling house[1] in the world, antedating the British royal house by many centuries. Furthermore, there has been no other dynasty throughout the 2000 years and more of Japanese history. Neither has there been a bloody revolution or a foreign conquest to change substantially or mar the substance of Japanese polity during its entire national history. The strong belief that the Japanese polity is unique and lasting as expressed in the concept of the *kokutai* is still a basic factor in the thinking of the vast majority of the Japanese people who are convinced that the nation will endure forever. The core of this *kokutai* concept is the strong monarchical tradition which has been emphasized as a proud Japanese heritage to be preserved.

The earliest concept of government antedating Chinese influence was a theocratic one. This was essentially a Shinto development which made no distinction between religion and government. Rather, it identified government with religion. This identity is still preserved

[1] The possible exception may be the Ethiopian ruling house headed by Emperor Hailie Selassie.

23

in the Japanese language, though perhaps not so much in concept. The colloquial rendering of governance is *matsurigoto* or "matters of worship." Its concept is expressed by the term *"saisei itchi"* or the merging of government and religion. This was quite natural since governance consisted chiefly, if not exclusively, of rituals and prayers in ancestor worship and supplication for good crops, rain, and immunity from diseases and natural disasters.

THE CHINESE INFLUENCE

Noticeable, if not radical, changes began to take place once the country came under the influence of Chinese civilization which introduced Confucianism, Buddhism, and Taoism and Legalism as well as Chinese laws, administrative system, customs, and manners. The impact of China came to be felt strongly in the 7th and 8th centuries, resulting in innovations and greatly modified government structure. Centralization was carried out to an extent never known before. A bureaucracy in an urban setting emerged to form the court aristocracy which surrounded and supported the throne.

It is highly significant to see what the Japanese did not accept or adopt at this time, which was a period characterized by historians as one of Sinification and Sinophiles. The idea of revolution was curtly rejected as the Japanese were not interested in the "mandate of heaven" as the basis of monarchy,[2] and the Confucian emphasis on filial piety above loyalty was reversed to give loyalty precedence over filial piety. The theory of monarchy based on the virtuous ruler was strengthened by making the distinction between the ruler and the ruled permanent and immutable and the position of the ruler unsubvertible. The right to rule was made hereditary in the imperial family. Thus with the help of Shinto and Confucianism the Japanese monarchical tradition was strengthened beyond anything the Chinese had known. Thus, in time, virtue came to be accepted as the inherent quality of the ruler. The threefold function of government, as postulated in the Confucian theory of statecraft, namely, to increase the people, to enrich them, and to enlighten them, became the norm for the officials to follow. Examplary conduct to show the way and lead the people came to be expected of the officials. "To govern is to know" became a familiar Confucian precept.

[2] The change in the "mandate of heaven" in the exercise of sovereign powers by the ruler involved only a change in dynasty. In other words what has been termed revolution in Chinese history was no more than a change in the ruling house and not in the location of sovereignty. Thus there was no theory of revolution in China in the Western sense.

Bureaucracy was the direct result of inspiration from the Chinese administrative system. A civil service system was introduced with a considerable modification in the spirit as well as in the purpose for which it was used. In Japan it was designed to strengthen the aristocracy which was made the backbone of the monarchy, whereas in China it had been introduced to destroy the power of the aristocracy. Consequently, in Japan the civil service examination was open only to scions of the aristocracy and government officials of fairly high rank and not to sons of commoners or low-ranking officials. Even the university which was established exclusively as a training school for would-be officials was not open to commoners. A strong authoritarian tradition thus developed along with its concomittant system of hierarchy. Under the strong influence of Confucianism, a strong conservatism developed although it could never equal that of China or India where it became almost an ingrained cultural habit to look back to a "Golden Age" in the past. Japanese conservatism, however, while cherishing the past and its heritage has not prevented the people from looking ahead into the future for better and more promising developments.

THE FEUDAL HERITAGE

Much has been made of the assertion that there still remain in Japan powerful feudal influences. What is meant by this is that there are still forces at work which are definitely the legacies of the feudal system. Although there is always the danger of overdrawing the picture, it would be difficult to deny that the Japanese are still influenced by the ideas and practices which were powerful under the feudal system which lasted nearly seven centuries. Japan's historical development like that of any other country reflects both change and continuity. Furthermore, it should be stressed that Japan is actually less than a hundred years removed from feudalism. It would be ridiculous of course to attribute all the evils in Japan to the fact that there still exist relics or remnants of feudal concepts and methods. Some of the more desirable achievements of Japan in the last hundred years were possible as the sequel if not the contributions of feudalism.

Historically viewed, feudalism which emerged in the late twelfth century was a natural, inevitable development since the existing state of affairs demanded change. The corrupt, effete, and inefficient court aristocracy brought it on by their wanton disregard of the needs of the nation and utter neglect of government. The establishment of a feudal military regime restored order to the nation after a century or more of chaos and maladministration.

Government administration was placed on an efficient, simple, and respectable basis by the military. The overelaborate system of law and administration which had been borrowed from China had long since ceased to be effective and served only as a decorative effect in the imperial court dominated by the pleasure-seeking, degenerate nobility. This state of affairs was promptly changed and law and justice were established and administered with speed and fairness. A strong moral and religious tone was added to society where it did not exist previously. Piety became the basis of deep religiosity which permeated society for the first time.

It was quite natural that in a political order dominated by the military, there should develop a military code of ethics to regulate the conduct of its members. This code, which in time was systematized and came to be known as Bushido[3] or the "Way of the Warrior" and accepted by all classes of people, has had a profound influence on Japanese thinking and behavior not only during feudalism but even subsequent to the liquidation of the feudal system itself.

As a code of ethics, originally developed to meet the rigid requirements for the training and discipline of the samurai in feudal society, it consisted of moral precepts derived from Buddhism, particularly Zen Buddhism, Confucianism, and Shinto, and represented a synthesis. It emphasized courage, honor, fidelity, benevolence, decorum, frugality, reverence, and loyalty and filial piety as the requisites of the samurai class. The concept of loyalty to one's master as understood in Confucian ethics was developed under Bushido to its loftiest point as it became a norm of conduct for the samurai who made the supreme sacrifice without even a second thought. It was in this intense feeling of personal loyalty as reflected in the lord and vassal relationship of feudalism that patriotism and loyalty to the Emperor in recent times came to be firmly rooted. Even in the realm of politics today, personal loyalty of feudal origin can be seen in operation.

The precepts of Bushido have had widespread influence and have been responsible for the military tradition in Japanese life and the respect for the military as a self-abnegating class. This respect for the military has been so strong, except in the period immediately following the defeat in 1945 and also the 1920's, that there had developed almost a belief in the incorruptibility of the military. This of course was disproved during and before World War II. However, the myth was partly responsible for the rise of the military to power in the 1930's and for bringing the nation to the brink of utter destruction in the Pacific War.

[3] See Nitobe Inazo, *Bushido*, for an exposition.

It was under feudalism too that national consciousness began to take concrete shape. With the establishment of feudalism there began a trend away from Chinese ideas and institutions. This began with the abandonment of Sinified legal and administrative systems of the court aristocracy and the establishment of simple and practical devices and institutions which were not so impressive as the Chinese-derived ones but much more suited to the needs of the times and Japanese conditions. Even the mode of life became more Japanese; so did the literature and the arts of the nation.

The unsuccessful attempted invasions by the Mongols in 1274 and 1281 did more than anything else to awaken national consciousness. Out of these two experiences of successfully repulsing the would-be-invaders was developed the belief that Japan was under divine protection and therefore could not be conquered by invaders.[4]

The arrival of the first Europeans in 1542 occurred as the nation was coming out of a century of chaos produced by contending semi-independent "states" ruled over by powerful *daimyos* or feudal barons. It is possible that the arrival of the Portuguese had the effect of hastening the unification of Japan. The subsequent arrival of Francis Xavier and his Jesuit co-workers in 1549 stimulated Japanese political thinking and induced an awareness of the vigor and power of the West. The amazing success of the Jesuits in securing converts and the close cooperation between them and the Portuguese traders whose aggressiveness was not confined to commerce but was rapidly taking on political complexion led to a ban on Christianity.

It has been made unmistakably clear that the proscription of Christianity which went into effect completely in the 1630's was decided as the most effective means of keeping out religious and political ideas as well as actual political forces which posed a threat to the security of the regime, if not to the very existence of the nation. This is borne out by the fact that no ban was really placed on trade, pure and simple, without any ties with Christianity or politics, as the Dutch and the Chinese carried on, or on scientific knowledge. Christian literature was banned but books on anatomy, astronomy, mathematics, medicine, navigation, etc. were permitted. The seeds of modern nationalism were thus sown with the arrival of Europeans whose colonial and expansionist activities came to be known to the Japanese.

[4] On these two separate occasions, the Mongol armadas were destroyed by typhoons which came to the rescue of the Japanese who called them *kamikaze* or "divine wind." The idea of "kamikaze pilots" of the Pacific War is derived from these historical events.

Great activity was witnessed among classical scholars and Confucianists from the late seventeenth century on, contributing greatly to the stimulation of national sentiments and emphasis on ancient ideals. Confucian orthodoxy, which the feudal regime forced upon the nation, weakened as people began to question the legitimacy of the authority of the Shogunate. In no small measure did the Wang Yang Ming School of Confucianism contribute to the weakening of the orthodoxy imposed with the support of the Chu Hsi philosophy. Bold thinking and action were stressed by the exponents of the activist philosophy of Wang Yang Ming.

Rigid social class system established in the sixteenth century as a means of securing the power of the ruling feudal house of Tokugawa through the rigid fixing or freezing of the status quo helped to stabilize the political power situation. For two and a half centuries it preserved the regime but it could not do so indefinitely. However, the class consciousness and particularly the emphasis on status which the rigid social system generated were carried over into present day life as one of the more conspicuous feudal legacies.

That some sort of feudal influence should be carried over into the modern period after the end of feudalism itself was only natural. It was the samurai class and of quite low rank who were responsible for the overthrow of the feudal system. They were the ones who furnished the leadership of the new Japan. It was their ideas and policies which were put into effect in the building of a modern state. Yet they were unable to rid themselves completely of feudal ideas, ideals, and attitudes under which they had lived in spite of the many progressive ideas they acquired. Samurai influence on Japanese life and especially in the economic and political life of the nation has not been fully appreciated.

When the new Government was launched in 1868, one of the crucial problems which faced the nation was the rehabilitation of the samurai class whose usefulness was over with the end of feudalism and who now constituted the displaced class. In an attempt to speedily absorb them into gainful pursuits they were encouraged to go into every type of activity. A very large percentage went into government service.[5] In the early stages of development former samurai virtually monopolized the police. Even the schools were staffed largely by teachers of samurai background. Business and

---

[5] In 1872, of the officials in the national government, 87 percent were former samurai while in 1880, 74 percent of those in both the national and local governments were ex-samurai.

industry claimed a large percentage of those of samurai background. Even in the political parties leaders from samurai families predominated. In the case of the political association, (Risshisha) headed by Itagaki, which became the basis of the Liberty Party in 1881, the membership was exclusively of samurai background. It is not difficult to see that the strong influence of the ex-samurai came to be felt in every field and particularly as close relationship developed between government, business, and political parties. The personal ties, a sort of esprit de corps stemming from a common background and even a feeling of affinity served as a strong catalyst in the building of a new Japan.

INFLUENCES FROM THE WEST

The process of eclecticism which has always operated in Japanese national development was accelerated during the half century or more after the 1870's. It is this second phase of the impact of the West that is especially significant because legal, political, and economic ideas and institutions along with social ideas and theories came to be examined, adopted, and emulated in a strictly voluntary way without any external pressure being applied to the nation.

Legal and political ideas, legal codes, and administrative machinery were borrowed from the West, not from any single country but from various countries. For example, the Continental civil law system was adopted instead of the Anglo-Saxon common law system, the criminal code and the code of criminal procedure were patterned after the French models, the commercial code was based on that of Germany. The local government system and the police were German-inspired while the Court of Administrative Litigation was taken right out of the French judicial organization. The parliamentary system was borrowed from Great Britain while the national banking system was borrowed from the United States.

The educational system was at first based on the American but later changed over to the German model. In the field of defense the army was based on the French model but later changed over to the German while the navy shifted from the Dutch to English organization and training. It is interesting to see that in the post World War II period, the shift in practically every field has been to the American system. But this situation has been more the political consequence of defeat in a major war than a voluntary change.

Although it is not expected that adaptations of anything alien to a country could be completely and speedily carried out, the scope and speed of modernization achieved have been phenomenal, even if frequently some aspects could not be anything but superficial especially in the initial phases.

In political ideas and practices Westernization has not proceeded as far or as deeply as a casual observer of the political scene is wont to conclude especially when conclusions are based on what he perceives only physically. A visitor to the Diet will see the members dressed in Western clothes deliberating in a modern building of modified Arabic architecture and conducting themselves according to rules of procedure which are more likely than not based upon the rules of order employed in the Congress of the United States. He is impressed by the resemblance between them and the members of Congress.

The truth of the matter is that the resemblances are superficial at best. What goes on in the minds of the Japanese M.P.'s are quite different both in substance and in the process by which they take shape. In their ideas and their mode of thought and action they are still far more Japanese than meets the eye, in spite of their apparent Westernization. Moreover, many Western concepts and practices have been so greatly modified to serve their purpose that in some instances they have been changed beyond recognition, just as has been done, in the course of centuries, with the importations or borrowings from China, India, and other parts of the world.

It is undeniable that Westernization has gone very far where individuals are concerned, especially in their technological training. Those who are highly trained as engineers, chemists, physicists, or mathematicians are completely Western in their scientific methods and thinking within the fields of their professional competence. However, as human beings and members of a social group, their Westernization is negligible for they are quite naturally Japanese. There is no appreciable transfer of scientific thought and attitude over into the realm of social relations, attitudes, and standards.

Westernization then could be achieved only within, and to the extent tolerated by, the framework of social structure and traditional thought patterns. Consequently it has been more successful in borrowing the forms than the spirit or substance even where genuine and assiduous efforts have been made. Furthermore national aspirations and goals and political considerations have frequently served as effective brakes to Westernization.

The Western impact has been most evident and significant along material, scientific, and technological lines. Visible and appraisable effects have been largely in such matters as organization, procedures, production techniques, management, and finance, and very little in the nonmaterial and spiritual aspects of national life. To illustrate this in the military development: the most modern scientific weapons were adopted by the armed forces and effective organization was used as witnessed in the Pacific War, and yet scientific thinking so far as psychology was concerned was virtually undeveloped. For all the modern weapons used, what existed in the minds of the military was not twentieth century scientific warfare but feudal samurai psychology which was responsible for the suicidal banzai charges which contributed nothing toward winning the war, the Kamikaze attacks which were, at best, of dubious value, and such fantastic ideas as fighting with bamboo spears.

Thus the Japanese have mastered science and technology as well as many of the advanced nations of the West and better than a good many of the less advanced Western countries. But the social ideas, structure, and environment in which they have found application have not undergone sufficient changes to accommodate technological advances in a Western manner. This situation obtains because Japanese society has not really been subjected to penetrating stresses or upheavals such as would shake it to its very foundation. No foreign invader at any time foisted an alien culture upon the people. Nor has there been anything comparable to the Renaissance which altered the nature of Western society. Actually spiritual development in Japan was introverted to the extent that it was conditioned entirely by her own spiritual needs for centuries. Some segments of the Japanese people have at various times completely yielded to foreign influences, like the French who are particularly fond of ideas and are easily carried away, but the nation as a whole, like the English people, has remained conservative.[6]

Japanese political ideas are compounded of various and sundry ingredients, both ancient and modern, both Oriental and Occidental. Among the major ingredients are Buddhism, Confucianism, Shinto, and Western ideas including Christianity. Since the middle of the nineteenth century the Japanese have been exposed to all the "isms" that the world has known. All the doctrines, dogmas, theories, precepts, concepts, ideals, and ideas which gained currency in the West came to be known in varying degrees in the political, social, economic, philosophical, and religious spheres of knowledge and experience and

[6] See A. L. Lowell, *The Governments of France, Italy, and Germany*, pp. 47–48, for his contrasting characterization of the English and the French on their attitudes regarding new ideas and changes.

produced some converts and advocates. There is hardly any work of significance in a Western language published since the mid-19th century which has not been translated into Japanese.

Like all other states, the character of the Japanese state as a sovereign body was the product of a long successive series of historical events and development and has been in existence from the beginning of the seventh century if not earlier. The nature of the Japanese state remained unknown in the West for a long time and only imperfectly from the sixteenth century on to recent times.

It was in the latter half of the nineteenth century, especially when the nation began to remodel itself along Western lines preparatory to making a bid to join the Western state system, that it became a subject of interest and study. Until the late nineteenth century, developments were completely outside the Western state system and practically unaffected by its theory and practice.

In Japanese thinking a clear-cut distinction has not yet been established between state and society as in Western political thought. This is a condition which is quite common, if not normal, in Asia. Even in the West the distinction does not exist so clearly in some countries. Such distinction as has been made that society is the area of voluntary groups and voluntary effort while the state is the area of legal rules and of action under those rules[7] would not make much sense to the people except to those who are simply theorizing in the abstract. It is quite natural, therefore, that there has not been the separation between politics, economics, ethics, and religion.

Such concept as the *kokutai* must, in spite of its vagueness, embrace both society and the state for it is an all-embracing concept which takes in Japan in its entirety. Perhaps the vast vagueness and the mystic and spiritual connotation it has gives it the all-inclusiveness. No two persons can agree exactly on what the correct definition of *kokutai* is, if, indeed, there is one.

If we are to attempt a definition which would come close to satisfying the Japanese, we may accept the doctrine which was worked out by the political thinkers of the West among whom were Montesquieu, Burke, Hegel, and De Maistre, that the state is a spiritual organism, the result of historical growth and the embodiment of the collective experience of the nations and of all ages. Of course it must include the political as well as the other experiences. Furthermore, the political structure would have to be regarded as coextensive and even identical with the social structure. Needless to

---

[7] See Ernest Barker, *Principles of Political and Social Theory*, p. 77.

say, the Japanese concept of state is built upon the traditional Shinto-Confucian basis of a conspicuously moral nature. If the state could be regarded as the juridical personification of the nation in a sense, but not exclusively so, it would no doubt appeal to the Japanese. Such a definition as Harold Laski's, that the state is the "crowning-point of the modern social edifice, and it is in its supremacy over all other forms of social grouping that its special nature is to be found," and "a method of imposing principles of behavior by which men must regulate their lives," will sound quite acceptable even though it may be regarded as not going far enough.

The Japanese accept the government as a natural growth that is essential to the well-being of the nation. At no time have they developed the idea that government is a necessary evil and the less there is of it the better. Instead they have a concept which is just the opposite. The idea that what the government does is proper and beneficial is so firmly entrenched in the minds of the people that the burden of proof as a rule is on the people and not the government. The people therefore are more likely to not only tolerate but willingly delegate extensive discretionary powers to officials than would be the case in the Western democracies.

The Japanese tend to assign a far more extensive role to the government than Western political theory would countenance. However, so far as general objectives of the government are concerned, they are pretty much the same as in any other country. The primary and basic objectives are the nation's security and independence, economic prosperity which includes social security for the people, and the preservation of its cultural and spiritual values or, broadly stated, its time-honored way of life.

In the process of achieving these ends different instruments are used by the government, as, for example, admonition and exhortation, customs and traditions and even habits, myths and symbolism, consensus of public opinion and coercion in various forms.

An ideal government is one which can be realized only when reliance is placed both on good laws and good men. The Western emphasis on government of laws rather than of men is the product of the age which was responsible for the idea that government was a necessary evil. It was a theory born of the need of checking the tyranny of absolutism.

The Japanese ideal, as in the case of the Chinese which was based on Confucianism, has traditionally been the government of men on the assumption that if good men are running the affairs of government they will make good laws and achieve good administration thereby insuring the welfare of the nation. However, if the government is not in the hands of good men, good laws would be of no avail. Even if there are bad laws when good men are in the government it would still be possible to realize good administration. The emphasis is still on men rather than on laws, although the emphasis on laws is far greater than in the other countries of Asia. The ultimate is the rule of philosopher-statesmen.

Sovereignty is a term which, like many other words of Western origin, did not exist in the political vocabulary of the Japanese. It is difficult therefore to characterize the Japanese concept with precision. The concept to which this term has been applied is the authority and absolute power of the Emperor, not as it existed in history as a *de facto* situation but as it was idealized in the process of its legal establishment in the Meiji Constitution. It connoted the absolute and indisputable power and prerogatives of the sovereign. However, in the political language of the post World War II period, it has come to mean exactly what it does in the Western democracies, namely, popular sovereignty.

The Japanese do not regard laws as sacrosanct or permanent, but merely the temporary expression of policy or opinion of the government as to what is best at any given time. Law thus constitutes a convenient working embodiment of certain principles and policies.

LIBERALISM

In the second half of the nineteenth century the new Japanese intellectuals read avidly and enthusiastically the works of political economists and political philosophers of the West. Writings of Ricardo, Adam Smith, Jeremy Bentham, John Stuart Mill, Montesquieu, J. J. Rousseau, and Alexis de Tocqueville were practically devoured by the politically ambitious and the intellectuals of the early Meiji period especially in the 1870's and 1880's. Utilitarianism, economic liberalism, and laissez-faire were espoused. But there were serious limitations and obstacles which stood in the way of the development of true liberalism.

Always Japanese liberalism was subservient to the interests of the state and overshadowed by statism and could exist only to the extent tolerated or permitted by the state.[8] Furthermore, it was never based on individualism for this did not exist. Its fatal weakness lay in the fact that liberalism was adopted in form but not

[8] See Kawai Eijiro, *Jiyu Shugi no Yogo* (1948), pp. 108–112.

really in principle. This was largely the result of the eagerness to impress and convince the Western powers that Japan had risen to their level. It was not an adoption of its substance which was understood by the people and desired by them. Furthermore, it was made a weapon or instrument, a sort of expedient, of power struggle against the clan oligarchy.[9]

Japanese liberalism was developed in an abnormal and distorted form and overrated by those who wrote about it later without a careful study of the realities of the movement. Western liberalism as in transplanted Japan was devoid of philosophy and principles, stripped of liberty, and without economic liberalism.[10] If indeed there has begun a bourgeois revolution, the process has not been completed. To this fact may be partially attributed the presence of vestiges of strong authoritarianism if not absolutism as an element of politcal life.[11]

The Confucian canon of decorum is so firmly embedded in social life and consciousness it not only takes precedence over liberty but actually works to check it. To an individual it is normally more important to be proper and conforming than to be right according to his convictions. Confucianism, which served as an instrument of thought control throughout the greater part of Chinese history and during the Tokugawa period of Japanese history, was actually used by the Japanese government and individuals as an effective antidote to Western ideas, especially liberalism, in the last two decades of the nineteenth century, for some of the influential leaders deemed liberalism and democracy to be antithetical to *kokutai*. It must be emphasized, however, that in spite of unfavorable conditions a considerable number of individuals of liberal convictions appeared on the scene.

Liberty, equality, and fraternity which were borrowed from the French enjoyed tremendous popularity, but again what really happened was that most of the people were fascinated by the sound of the political slogan without being influenced by the substance of the ideas. In other words, while they were virtually shouted from the housetops and enjoyed wide currency, they did not actually develop into a vital force in the political life of the nation. To many, even today, liberty seems to connote something uncontrolled, undisciplined, licentious, and even uncivilized.

Equality was nonexistent in a class-ordered society such as Japan.

[9] *Ibid.*, pp. 108–112.
[10] *Ibid.*, pp. 114–115.
[11] Nakamura Akira, *Chishiki Kaikyu no Seijiteki Tachiba*, p. 173.

Conditions more conducive to the development of equality appear to have existed in primitive society before the introduction of Chinese civilization. However, for practically the entire span of Japan's historic period, inequality both in concept and practice has been the normal condition of society. The same thing can be said with respect to the equality of sexes.

Egalitarianism, therefore, is a Western contribution which has only very slowly developed in the face of traditional forces which still condition if not regulate social and political behavior. The inordinate respect and deference shown to individuals on the basis of age, rank, and status, and even occupation, as well as the particular relationships, make the road to equality a rough one indeed. Even the matter of equality of women, which has been legally established in the Constitution itself, can be realized only when the traditional forces have been liquidated or neutralized.

In the political ideas of the Japanese today, there is a conspicuous overlay of Western ideas on traditional concepts. At the same time there has also been a hybridization of ideas, political, economic, and social. In few areas of political activity is this characteristic so much in evidence as in the socialist movement. As a Western inspired movement it was completely Western in its ideological content. It was only natural that the theory of socialism should be superimposed upon Japanese ideological foundations resulting in an overlay without radically changing indigenous ideas. Wherever modifications took place in the ideas, the results were more in the nature of hybridization than of complete assimilation.

There has been since World War I a decided Marxian bias among Japanese intellectuals particularly in the universities. In the 1920's Marxism had completely captured the imagination of Japanese intellectuals.[12] Not only had it become intellectually fashionable to believe in Marxism, but anyone who did not show his understanding of as well as enthusiasm for it was regarded as lacking in intellectual capacity. This attitude stems from the fact that the Japanese have always shown a peculiar "weakness" or predilection for theory and for neat theoretical statements deductively arrived at. In the dialectical materialism offered by Marxism and the "scientific" reasoning it contained, they found a special irresistible fascination.

The Japanese have not developed a strong sense of contrast between the real and the ideal. This enables them to overlook the real by concentrating on the ideal. It is quite possible that the intel-

[12] K. Miki, "The China Affair and Japanese Thought," *Contemporary Japan*, March, 1938, p. 601.

lectuals indulged themselves increasingly in theoretical mental exercises as the door was closed on practical and empirical examination and study particularly of economic and political matters. As a matter of fact the government encouraged theoretical emphasis in political science so that the studies carried on by the scholars were almost all highly legalistic and theoretical. Constitutional law was a subject of exigetical study without any reference to politics or actual government. In the universities there were no courses on Japanese government and politics; instead there were courses on the Constitution.

America's intensive campaign "to make the world safe for democracy" during World War I stirred the imagination of students and produced unexpected repercussions in Japan.[13] War against Germany came to be regarded as a crusade against autocracy and the forces of tyranny which were symbolized by the Kaiser. The undreamed-of economic prosperity that was produced by the war was somehow associated with democracy and aided the popularity of democratic ideas and ideals. In this upsurge of democratic idealism, Professor Yoshino of Tokyo Imperial University was the leading exponent. Under his influence came scores of students who became exponents of liberalism and democracy and subsequently leaders of proletarian political movements.[14] Out of the student population of World War I and after came the leaders of the socialist movement. Some of them turned Communists soon after the Bolshevik Revolution of 1917 which had a tremendous impact in Japan.

Extreme vulnerability to boredom is one of the characteristics of the Japanese, notably among the educated and the intellectuals. This, combined with the intellectuals' special susceptibility to frustrations and their identification of their interests with those of the working class and the shifting of their mood from intense dedication to intense boredom, has undoubtedly contributed greatly to the appearance of radical ideas and movements in Japan.

NATURE OF JAPANESE POLITICS

It has been repeatedly said that Japanese political changes almost never assume clear-cut swings of the pendulum and that they are almost always blurred compromises.[15] There is a great deal of truth in such a characterization, for the Japanese may well agree with the

---

[13] For the awakening of the people, see the author's *Japan Since Perry*, pp. 467–488.

[14] For an account of student participation in the socialist movement, see Kikukawa Tadao, *Gakusei Shakai Undo Shi* (1947).

[15] W. H. Chamberlin, "Japan at War," *Foreign Affairs*, April, 1939, pp. 480–481.

French that the more the situation changes the more it remains the same, that there have been almost no radical reformers in history who have been successful, and that traditionally the ideal path for one to follow has been the middle way. Going to extremes has been frowned upon for not only does it introduce discord and conflict but it would be considered highly aberrant.

There have been reforms, renovations, and restorations but no revolutions in Japanese history. Actually the only type of revolution the Japanese are familiar with is the palace revolution which involves merely a change in the group in power either in a peaceful and almost imperceptible manner or in a coup d'etat. Political revolution in the Western sense involving a change in the location of sovereignty or an upheaval in social organization resulting in the destruction of the old order and the establishment of a new social order had never really occurred. Even a dynastic "revolution" is unknown in Japan. Taine's characterization of England[16] as a nation which lends itself to reform without yielding itself to revolution might well be applied to Japan.

The Japanese would unhesitatingly subscribe to the view held by Edmund Burke and John Morley[17] that politics is a series of expedients and compromises. They would endorse the idea that it is "the art of the possible" involving primarily the search for the *modus convivendi* for there is the need for adjustment of conflicting interests between the various groups and individuals of the community. But many of these adjustments are made in Japanese life outside of the political arena making the political process as such less visible and observable to the individual.

In the countries of the West like the United States, Great Britain, and France, talking politics is a normal part of the everyday activity of a citizen and there is always an open season on political questions. But in Japan, the average citizen is by habit and tradition so differently constituted that he is very reluctant to express himself in public on political questions. Political argument has not yet been accepted socially as a safety valve for individuals. It is frequently fraught with great danger for it may develop into something so violent that it may cause irreparable damage.

It may be said in general that greater political awareness and sophistication as well as zeal and determination are found among members of the Socialist and Communist parties than among those who belong to the conservative parties. This is largely the result of

[16] H. Taine, *Notes on England* (1872), p. 219.

[17] John Morley is said to have once quipped that politics is something like logic in that it is neither a science nor an art but a dodge.

greater emphasis by the radical parties on issues than on personalities.

The complexion of Japanese politics has been determined since the inception of constitutional government by international events and stimuli which shaped its economic structure. Today in the aftermath of World War II, the nation finds itself in the position of having to rely almost entirely on external factors for survival. It is not an exaggeration to say that the nation is at the mercy of international developments. Another complicating factor in Japan's politics is the inordinately intimate relationship of mutual interdependence which exists between capitalism and the government.

Perhaps as a result of the shock of defeat, observers of the political scene have commented, the Japanese sense of independence and self-reliance has weakened, reaching rock bottom, while cooperation between capital and labor has all but disappeared and politicians have become obsessed with glory and power, paying little attention to anything else.

3 ⸻

Japanese Political Behavior

Forces which condition and influence human behavior are so complex that it would not be possible to deal exhaustively with all the facets and relevant facts of the behavior of any people. However, since human behavior is essentially a response to environment and stimuli of all sorts, some insight into the behavior of individuals and groups such as the government and officials, political parties, its leaders and members, and the voters, could be gained by examining the general environment of politics.

Since the actions of individuals and groups are based more often than not on abstract concepts, images, and symbols rather than on direct and certain knowledge obtained empirically, the understanding of the emotional contents of culture becomes indispensable to the study of behavior. In the following pages, an attempt is made to find out something of the Japanese character and pattern of behavior which are the product of centuries of national, social, and political experience.

This simply means that the subject of scrutiny is really social behavior as it is manifested in the political sphere. In other words, it is substantially ordinary social behavior with political implications and consequences translated into political action which commands our attention. Since political behavior is determined by a whole complex of factors and motives which are not easy to identify or isolate and practically impossible to weigh or measure, we can merely attempt to see how it might be reflected in the sensitive spots of the political structure. This can be done only against the broad background of history, economic and social organization, geography and culture, plus a multitude of other factors.

More than any other industrialized nation of the world in the twentieth century, Japan shows a very pronounced dichotomy or duality in her national character, a "split personality" which is the consequence of her cultural development. There is a juxtaposition of the old and the new, Eastern and Western, traditional and modern, in all aspects of her national life. Furthermore, the opposite psychological tendencies which are present in various degrees everywhere have been accentuated by the rapid modernization and industrialization which were imposed upon the nation in the latter part of the nineteenth century. As a by-product of this forced speed up, ambivalence in the political sphere is perhaps more visible and acute in Japan than elsewhere.

JAPANESE CHARACTER

Sociopolitical Traits

ACTIVISM. An activist philosophy which permeates Japanese life places a high premium on action with the resultant neglect or minimization of thought or words. This stems from the energy and industry which have been traditional with the Japanese in their social environment. Although deep thought and meditation have always been stressed by Zen Buddhism in particular, this was never thinking in the Western sense but rather an exercise in introspection which did not involve intellectual exercise. The Japanese have thus developed more into doers than thinkers and have exhibited impatience and restiveness time and again in their history. Their national energy has overflowed into foreign lands more than once in the twentieth century. However, it is to be noted that for more than two centuries, from the 1630's to 1853, the nation's energy was contained within her borders under a rigidly enforced policy of seclusion. The English love of action finds its Asian counterpart in Japan. English love of action is reflected even in the names of warships such as Repulse, Resolute, Revenge, Adventure, and Dispatch. The Japanese too have named ships suggesting action, such as Flying Dragon, Divine Wind, Ocean Wind, and Snowstorm. Thus the man of action is the type respected universally in Japan and the respect is even greater if his action harmonizes with his words or ideas.

ASSIMILATIVENESS. Throughout history, the Japanese people have demonstrated their assimilative capacity. In fact, their entire national development of the last two thousand years has been a series of successive importations, adaptations, and assimilations of elements of foreign cultures. Their readiness to adopt on a large scale elements of Chinese civilization beginning with the sixth and seventh centuries of the Christian era, to borrow from the European countries in the sixteenth and seventeenth centuries, and to learn from America and other countries of the world in the nineteenth and twentieth centuries, demonstrates not only the absence of xenophobia and a sense of cultural superiority but also their capacity to borrow wisely. Yet this national trait has been the basis of the Western as well as the Chinese characterization of the Japanese as imitators and copyists who are incapable of originating or inventing anything. Actually, nothing which the Japanese borrowed from abroad remained in its original form, for invariably through their inventiveness and assimilative power they have produced something quite different and even original.[1]

Cultural tolerance and a strong eclecticism grew out of the Japanese experience of borrowing and assimilating foreign cultures. Alien races, alien institutions, skills, and religions were all welcomed from a very early period of national development. When Buddhism was introduced in the sixth century it met with no religious opposition. When Christianity was first introduced into Japan in 1549 by Francis Xavier, it was received with enthusiasm by the people and even the authorities. As a matter of fact, Xavier expressed amazement at the religious tolerance of the people.

One searches in vain for any historical evidence of racism or racial discrimination of a really serious nature. No doubt racial antipathy existed as between the aborigines of the islands and the newcomer-conquerors but this was more political than social. Racial hostility was resolved early in history with the merger of the existing racial strains and the achievement of social and cultural homogeneity. There was no foreign domination to develop internal political opposition into a racial struggle. While racial antipathy as such did not exist as a social attitude, antiforeignism was manifested in various ways after the arrival of the Europeans in the sixteenth century. However, a careful study of the antiforeign policy will show that it was always based on political considerations, particularly on the question of national security or national pride. During World War II, a program of anti-Semitism inspired by the Nazi regime was

---

[1] A Japanese nuclear physicist, Dr. Hideki Yukawa, whose entire scientific training was received in his own country, was one of the host of scientists whose originality contributed toward the final result. A study made just before World War I on inventiveness placed Japan's on the same level of achievement as that of the Mediterranean countries.

launched in Japan at the insistence of the Germans but it collapsed since the public simply did not respond.

If there has been any discrimination with respect to foreigners, it has been discrimination in their favor. Immigrants from Korea and China in the early period of history were given preferential treatment, particularly those who were scribes, tutors, artists, scholars, priests, and even artisans and craftsmen. The traditional attitude of respect and cooperation accorded foreigners and foreign cultures, which is deeply rooted in the Japanese psychological make-up, has made them into Xenophiles rather than Xenophobes.

AUTHORITARIANISM. Authoritarian proclivities are rather noticeable in Japanese life. While there are indigenous sources of this trait, it represents one of the distinct contributions of Chinese civilization. Through Confucian political philosophy which gave refinement and sophistication to their rather rudimentary political ideas and in-stitutions, the Japanese adopted and strengthened authoritarianism to fit their particular needs. The Confucian family system was made the cornerstone of the Japanese family structure, thus providing the basis of authoritarian rule within the family. In adopting Chinese ideas, some modifications were made, as for example the reversing of the concept of loyalty giving loyalty to the sovereign precedence over filial piety. Needless to say, Shinto and feudalism contributed decisively to the development of the authoritarian tradition. With a long bureaucratic tradition dating back to the seventh century A.D. the Japanese have had the political and social setting and climate conducive to the development of the authoritarian personality. Also, in the course of those centuries the people have become habituated to accepting officiousness on the part of the bureaucrats as a matter of course.

Without an understanding of the group orientation of the in-dividual in Japanese society, many aspects of their behavior would be unintelligible. Since the Japanese live in closely knit groups and in actual physical proximity, they are group-conscious almost to ex-cess; they think, act, and live as a group. The group always comes first whether it be the family, community, or nation. The group is everything, the individual as such is relatively unimportant and must always be subordinated. Group welfare takes precedence over in-dividual welfare. As a group they are strong and confident of them-selves but as individuals they are vulnerable. Conformity to the collective wish of a group or community becomes a powerful condi-tioning factor. Consequently community sanction is more awful and feared than ordinary legal sanction.

On this group consciousness is based the system of joint responsibility which has been the norm of social behavior. In feudal times,
a group of five families was held responsible jointly for everything
from tax collection to turning in a criminal and each family was held
responsible jointly for the actions of all the members. The concept
of joint responsibility simultaneously supports and is supported by the
ingrained habit of consultation (*sodan*) on every level of group life,
the family, the relatives, the neighborhood, the village, the town, the
city, and right on up to the nation, and in various spheres of activity,
business, government, political parties; in fact no facet of life is unaffected by it.

This group cohesiveness gives rise to clique politics or coterie
politics which very often gives rise to impersonal, anonymous exercise of authority. It could lead also to a certain kind of irresponsibility because, when everybody is responsible, it often turns out that
nobody is really responsible. Responsibility becomes so diffused
that it cannot be pinned down. This type of nondeliberate irresponsibility could create a situation where one of the group or someone
outside can actually function for the group without clear or definite
delegation of authority.

TRADITIONALISM. Deep-rooted conservatism underlies the Japanese
character. This is an aspect of strong traditionalism not unlike that
of the British. The Japanese cling tenaciously to age-old traditions
and love the "pomp and circumstance" surrounding their royalty,
ceremonies, and rituals of all sorts, honors, and ranks. When the
policy of Westernization seemed to be going too far in the late
nineteenth century the leaders feared that destroying tradition might
kill the very soul of Japanese civilization. Lest the craze for Westernization get completely out of hand, the government took steps to
counteract it. Among other things, it published a translation of
Edmund Burke's *Reflections on the French Revolution* which was an
antidote in England for the subversive philosophy of the French
Revolution.[2] Burke's ideas were helpful in restraining people from
indulging in excesses.

The average Japanese, more likely than not, tends to accept the
status quo and is content to leave things pretty much as they have
been in the past. This attitude is particularly strong among the rural
agrarian segment of the population. However, the workers in the
cities under the influence of the radical parties are showing their dis-

---

[2] Burke was a man after the heart of the Japanese conservatives for he detested
running roughshod over tradition.

satisfaction with the *status quo*. They are becoming less willing than the British workers to accept the class system although certainly they do not come anywhere near the American workers' unshakable belief that every kind of success and every form of advancement is open to them. In a poll conducted by a government agency in which 3,000 persons were asked if the story of the struggles and achievements of Hideyoshi, a person of the humblest origin who rose to fame and power, serves as an example for the youth for all time, 80 percent replied in the affirmative,[3] proving that the public believes firmly that rising above one's class and achieving success not only is legitimate but should be encouraged.

PRAGMATISM. There is pragmatism in Japanese life not unlike the Englishman's preference for the practical approach in dealing with problems and avoiding issues of theory or philosophy. This practical turn of mind, aided by impatience, often leads to action first and analyzing or rationalizing later. Japanese philosophy has concerned itself chiefly with ethics, especially social ethics and national morality. It is not difficult to see how Bentham's pragmatism and John Stuart Mill's utilitarianism appealed tremendously to the Japanese leaders of the early Meiji period like Fukuzawa Yukichi and Okuma Shigenobu.

If the Japanese fail to show any evidence of distrust of logic as reflected in the English character, they most certainly do not share the French belief in the peculiar efficacy of logic or doctrines in dealing with social and political realities, nor do they evince mystic faith in human reason. Compromise is a normal way of life to the Japanese. Theirs is a highly practical and empirical approach to life and its problems. Their preoccupation has been with the art of getting along in the world. Discipline, then, becomes a necessary and integral part of the art of living. There is no stigma attached to compromise for it does not carry the connotation that it does in some of the countries of the West, namely, the sacrificing of one's principles in the process. It is the belief that if principles stand in the way of harmonious human relationship between individuals or groups, they should be either set aside or modified, that really provides the justification for compromise. In a pragmatic approach, compromise is accepted as a necessary social and political *modus vivendi*. Irreconcilable disagreements become impossible even though bargaining and haggling may be an inevitable part of compromise.

[3] Hayashi Chikio, "Kokuminsei no ichimen," *Asahi*, July 3, 1953. This article is based on the study made by the Statistical Institute of the Ministry of Education.

Making mutual concessions becomes an accepted mode of reaching an agreement. Shunning of litigation and settling matters out of court have been a customary procedure based not so much on distrust of the judiciary as on the desire to demonstrate their ability to compose differences as human beings in the time-honored method of meeting half-way. At times, of course, the obsessive desire for harmony is carried too far at the expense of the democratic process.

Moderation is highly prized while extremism is abhorred. A down-to-earth attitude and approach are preferred to pretentious, high-sounding proposals in the solution of problems. Noticeable also is the attitude of bowing to the inevitable, which is basically a philosophy of life which has helped the people to give in to powerful forces, especially of nature, in order to increase their chances of survival. This yielding, as a tree does in the face of a strong wind, has developed the resiliency of the people without becoming fatalistic to the extent of assuming a "do-nothing" attitude, as for instance in Taoism of China or Hinduism of India. As manifested in the political sphere, this attitude of bowing to the irresistible has developed, over a period of centuries of feudalism, into passivity, if not indifference, on the part of the majority of the people. But in spite of this attitude of resignation there are not infrequently outbursts of criticism or lampooning of authority.[4]

LAW-ABIDING ATTITUDE. Love of order for which the Englishman is noted finds its Asian counterpart in Japan. This is rooted in the social system and maintained by the almost ingrained attitude of respect for law and authority resulting from centuries of habituation and conditioning. Traditionally, the respect for and trust in government on the part of the people have been great, perhaps inordinately, so that direct criticism of the government was unthinkable until comparatively recent times.[5] The Confucian idea that the sovereign had to be virtuous to hold the "Mandate of Heaven" to rule over the land and people went through a process of perversion and distortion at the hands of officials both in China and Japan so that it came to imply that the ruler by reason of his position was virtuous and that the government too was virtuous, unimpeachable, and unassailable. While the attitude is changing, the average individual is likely to take the government's word as against that of a private citizen without second thought, for in his mind the government is wise and knows

[4] Hidaka Rokuro, *Nihonjin no Shiso to Ishiki*, pp. 6–7.

[5] When the feudal authorities banned criticism of the government, the ingenuity of the people found a way for they lampooned the government indirectly and subtly in satires and even in "scribblings on the walls."

what is best. This traditional respect for the ruler and the concept of the dignity of the ruler, hence the government, and the depreciating of the people, make government endorsement of any privately sponsored community undertaking or fund-raising campaign necessary in insuring its success. However, the frequent scandals in which the Diet and the government have been involved have done a great deal to convince the people that neither the government nor the officials can be so virtuous or infallible as they had been made to believe.

It should be emphasized, however, that the Japanese have demonstrated that they can be rebellious and defiant under certain conditions and situations. The peasant uprisings of the Tokugawa period, while not political in nature, nevertheless show that when conditions become unbearable the people are fully capable of resisting authority and revolting against the government. The series of uprisings in the 1880's in the Kanto and Tohoku regions were definitely politically inspired and aimed at the government. In 1918, the skyrocketing price of rice caused a nation-wide flare-up of rice riots which got out of control and caused the downfall of the Terauchi government. Even today there is evidence of latent patriot-martyr spirit (*ronin* or *soshi* spirit) which could come to the surface in a crisis and give rise to political bullies who can be exploited to the detriment of orderly democratic processes of government. To brand the Japanese people as completely docile and incapable of indignation and explosion is to misread history and ignore their potential that is on "the other side of the coin." Obedience to authority is not entirely blind and can be expected only under normal conditions and only up to a point, the point of combustion or explosion.

The respect for authority is reflected also in nongovernmental spheres such as in organizations of all kinds, business firms, industrial plants, community activities, and also in the family. Respect for age is conspicuously demonstrated both in government and in nongovernmental spheres. Age is revered for it represents experience, maturity, mellowness, and wisdom as opposed to immaturity, lack of experience, and brashness of youth. If precedence cannot be established by normal means, it is always age which becomes the decisive factor. Before World War II, there was a provision in the election law which stipulated that when two candidates for office were tied with equal number of votes, the older of the two shall be declared elected. In politics as in other activities of Japanese life, due reverence for age is expected as a matter of course.

INSULAR PSYCHOLOGY. For years now the Japanese have been conscious of the fact that they are conditioned by a narrow, "insular psychology" which has been a serious weakness in their national character and development. That there have been insular outlook and viewpoint in Japanese thinking and action no one can deny, any more than the English can fail to recognize that they too have something similar which Barbara Ward has termed the "neurotic self-attention" of "insularity."[6] While the Japanese may succeed in modifying their insular psychology to some extent, it would be impossible to undo the effects of it or to liquidate it completely, for much that is good in their culture and national character is both the cause and the effect of it.

Physical containment in their native islands for two thousand years and more without any invasion from the outside or even a large influx of immigrants has given the people a habit of concentration on and preoccupation in their own national affairs. Even more responsible for turning their attention in upon themselves was the more than two centuries of seclusion from the rest of the world. It was a policy of calculated aloofness for the purpose of insuring national security. All the while the people were completely absorbed in their own affairs in their tight little islands. This developed in Japan the kind of introspective attitude which led to the habit of thinking and acting alone and enjoying it. When the nation was reopened to world intercourse in the middle of the nineteenth century, the government and its leaders found it very difficult to think and plan within a broader framework of international relations. Even in the twentieth century they failed to develop adequately a global sense which would enable them to perceive the world-wide implications of the national policies. Nor have they been able to plan their policies with sufficiently broad international outlook. Undoubtedly this has been due largely to the fact that they had no experience until the twentieth century in developing policies in concert and in close coordination with other powers. Separate independent action had been the more normal procedure until very recently.

Turned inwardly upon themselves, this insular psychology has produced the effect of emphasizing parochialism, as, for instance, the emphasis on geographic origins, that is, prefectural and home town affinities as the basis of intimacy in social and political relationships. The preoccupation with internal developments and problems forced the strengthening of kinship feeling as well as nepotism. It increased pettiness, jealousy, suspicion, and distrust, traits which had been fostered by feudalism which encouraged provincialism and local pride. Domestic provincialism was carried to the point of condoning

6 "British Insularity," *N.Y. Times Magazine*, February 15, 1953, p. 9.

shameless behavior if one were outside of one's own province.[7]   On the other hand, it contributed mightily to the development of social solidarity and national consciousness.   Accentuated undoubtedly by the condition of insularity is a kind of inferiority complex on the part of the Japanese which shows up in international relations.   It has been reflected in their defensive attitude particularly since the nineteenth century when extensive contacts were established with the West.   This attitude, mistaken for a superiority complex, conditioned Japan's actions in the twentieth century on the international scene.

KINSHIP FEELING.   One of the consequences of isolation from the rest of the world was a highly developed sense of kinship which obtains among the people, a feeling which actually transcends the bounds of verifiable consanguinity.   Beginning with the family, it embraces the neighborhood especially in the rural areas where a single hamlet is bound by a strong tie, or memory, of kinship.   The village tutelary deity in the local Shinto shrine is regarded as the common ancestor of the families living there.[8]   An entire local community therefore can actually behave as a group of persons all related to one another.   This feeling of kinship has been extended to the whole nation whenever there has been a need for bolstering national unity. The idea that the whole nation is one large family with the emperor as the father at the head of all the Japanese people is a symbolic representation, to be sure, but it is more than that.   Such a strong sense of consanguinity can develop only in a closely knit social fabric of a nation which has developed in geographic isolation for centuries due to its insularity.

This feeling of kinship, aided by favorable environmental factors has turned the people into simple, open, frank, and credulous folk to whom privacy of the type which developed in the West was unknown.   Even their dwellings are constructed in a manner which permits little privacy if any.   There is no trace of prudishness in the traditional cultural pattern.   The people have not developed anything resembling the Puritan tradition which is the Calvinistic English contribution to the Western world.   They are relatively free of inhibitions as such, though discipline has imposed on them a certain degree of reserve and restraint which prevent them from parading emotions in public.   Even a public display of affection is frowned upon and no one would dare betray his sorrow.   Distrust and suspicion were attitudes which developed during the period of feudalism.

[7] It was felt that it was perfectly all right to commit *faux pas* while one was traveling, outside his own province or home town, where he was not known.

[8] See the section on village life in John F. Embree, *The Japanese Nation.*

Actually they had to be fostered within the political system, even in such everyday matters as fire prevention and theft prevention.[9]

PERSONALIZATION. The Japanese have developed what is virtually a cult of personality of which the habit of personalization is a part. They actually indulge in the idealization of personality. The ideal of the "virtuous," able, selfless, fearless, benevolent, and righteous personality which is largely based on Confucian ideas looms large in the popular mind and the strong inclination toward "hero worship" tends to overshadow other considerations. As a result, the people simply cannot detach political issues from personalities and examine them on their merits. They look at the men instead of their ideas or the issues and conclude that the politics of a good man must be good politics.[10] This is just the opposite of what obtains in the Western democracies, such as the United States, Great Britain, and France, where for the most part issues take precedence over personalities. In the matter of emphasis on personality the Japanese attitude is much closer to that of Latin America where it is said that the history of politics can be told largely if not wholly, on the basis of personalities. A government official feels his loyalty directly to the person of his superior and is more sensitive to his wishes than to the duties and responsibilities of his office. The party faithful is loyal first to the leader and only secondarily to the principles and policies for which his party stands. Thus the overwhelming emphasis on personalities and personal considerations in Japanese politics provides one of the major problems in the firm establishment of the democratic process.

It is on personal loyalty that the institution of "bossism" in Japanese politics is firmly based. Without it bossism not only would be weaker but would be of a different nature. Personalization has contributed immensely to the informalization of many phases of the political process. Negotiations are carried on informally behind the scenes in very unofficial places such as the well-known teahouses. Coterie politics, which utilizes informal groups of friends in decision making, is also a part and parcel of the highly personalized psychology and behavior of the people.

STATUS CONSCIOUSNESS. In spite of the fact that the feudal class system was legally abolished more than eighty years ago, its traces have not yet disappeared completely. It exists today in the form of

[9] The saying: "When you see a flame, think of it as a fire; when you see a person (stranger), think of him as a thief," was a practical precautionary warning against fire for people living in highly combustible dwellings, and against robbery and thievery.

[10] H. Sassa, "Our Public Opinion," *Contemporary Japan*, March, 1937, p. 547.

status-consciousness. Behavior is still regulated by one's awareness of the status he has in society. There is much more to the concept of "station in life" than meets the eye for it is deep-rooted in the psychology of the people. It is reflected in the etiquette and in the language that is used.[11]

Mode of Thought and Expression

An analysis of the Japanese mode of thought and expression at once reveals a complexity the like of which is not found in any country of the West. Generally speaking, the substance of Japanese thought process and expression is made up of three main ingredients, the Western European, Chinese-Confucian, and indigenous Japanese, which were mixed in varying proportions within the population. It is impossible to suggest a quantitative or qualitative evaluation of each of these ingredients with regard to social or political behavior but an attempt at a descriptive or explanatory analysis would be useful.

The first of these ingredients, comprising Western European intellectual contributions, came into the country in the mid-nineteenth century to provide a leaven to the nation that had just emerged from isolation and was embarking on the program of Westernization. Among other things such elements as Protestantism, humanism, and socialism opened the minds and eyes of the Japanese. But quite understandably only the educated, and particularly the leaders in government and the intellectuals, were affected by Western thought. This stream of Western European ideas left the masses untouched and while the educated class took to the ideas they were not always successful in assimilating them. What developed was a lush growth, on the surface, of Western ideas which failed to send roots down deeply into the soil of traditionalism.

The second element was Confucianism which had been developing for centuries particularly during the last two hundred and fifty years of feudalism under the Tokugawa Shogunate (1603–1868). It was the political philosophy adopted by the ruling class and imposed upon the populace in the form of "public morality" through the newly established educational system. Its principles were clearly enunciated in the Imperial Rescript on Education promulgated in 1890 to provide the foundation of national morality which conditioned the thought and action of the people.

For the overwhelming majority of the people left to their own

[11] See the discussion on language in Chapter 1.

natural inclinations, it was the indigenous mode of thought and expression. Much more realistic, flexible, resilient, and adaptable than the rigid Confucian pattern, it has conditioned the behavior of all the people. It is a mode born of down-to-earth common sense and wisdom acquired through the practical experience of living. But as a force in the thought life of the nation, it has been lost in the actual process of life. Consequently it has become more a way of life than a mode of thought.[12]

LANGUAGE. Language offers one of the most fruitful sources for the study of a people's mode of thought and expression. There is no such problem of multiplicity of language in Japan as exists in other countries of Asia. No other major Asian country has the linguistic unity that Japan possesses. Although there are slight local variations in the vernacular, a standard language of universal currency is used and understood throughout the country by the 89,000,000 inhabitants. Since language developed in the arena of everyday life for very practical purposes, it reveals and reflects various facets of social life, customs, and organization of the people. It is the mirror which reflects the social ideas and attitudes of a people. Consequently, a careful study of the language in action, particularly in a country like Japan, can provide numerous explanations of the behavior of the people.

Quite by accident, and not by design, Japanese as it exists today is one of the most difficult languages to master,[13] but at the same time the most interesting because of its complexity. To the indigenous language which had no writing, the Chinese character was applied but with resultant complications which were altogether unanticipated. Chinese pronunciation of the characters was adopted but with the inevitable result of inaccurate transference of sound to the Japanese ear, giving only an imperfect Japanese approximation of Chinese sounds. At the same time all the Japanese terms which existed only in spoken form were equated to the Chinese characters, giving rise to two or more different pronunciations for every character imported. Practically every word can be expressed in at least two different ways, the original Japanese and the Sinified Japanese which are usually compounds. In the sixteenth and seventeenth centuries European words, especially Portuguese and Dutch, came into the language again with Japanized pronunciations, and finally in the nine-

---

[12] Hidaka Rokuro, Sasaki Ayao, and others, *Nihonjin no Shiso to Ishiki*, pp. 3–8.

[13] Ridiculous as it may sound, during the Pacific War one view had it that the Japanese language was deliberately made difficult to give Japan an advantage in time of war.

teenth and twentieth centuries English, German, and French words were incorporated into the language. While the polyglot make-up of the vocabulary makes the language interesting and demonstrates the assimilative power of Japanese culture, it is not actually the characteristic which makes its mastery so difficult.

What adds color as well as difficulty to the language is the class and sex distinctions which have been incorporated into it with its elaborate system of honorifics providing for the numerous status gradations of pronouns such as is unequaled by any other language. Furthermore, the language is replete with nuances, onomatopoeic expressions, double meanings, tones and overtones, and endowed with the quality of vagueness and imprecision but also of poetic beauty and fluidity.

Perhaps no language in the world is better suited for play on words. Circumlocution along with the disregard for accuracy and the striving for rhetorical effect have been at once the cause and the effect of the language. The language itself is definitely not conducive to exactness of expression. Nor have the users consciously striven for such preciseness. This can be a serious disadvantage but it cannot be denied that it can be useful for propaganda purposes.[14]

INEXPRESSIVENESS. Despite the fact that the language is quite adequate for full expression and even eloquence, inexpressiveness has traditionally been one of the conspicuous characteristics of the people. From the earliest period of history, the people seem to have prided themselves in the fact that theirs was a "nation of few words." As a vehicle of expression, action has always been preferred to words. In fact, more often than not, action has preceded words. Especially in international relations this has been true partly because the Japanese themselves have always felt that they have not been and never will be understood. Loquacity has always appeared abhorrent and the natural tendency has been to distrust eloquence. "Beautiful words lack sincerity" is a Chinese saying which the Japanese really took to heart. Loquacity has been equated with disputatiousness as well as insincerity and even emptiness. "Empty vessels make the most sound" has been their belief. Talking is boasting and is contrary to the attitude of humility which is so highly valued.

---

[14] During the Pacific War, for example, the information section of Imperial Headquarters used to report to the nation periodically the "annihilation" of the American fleet in the sea battles, to the amusement of those on the outside. In their usage, annihilation can be in various degrees ranging all the way from partial to complete annihilation, because of the loose and inexact sense in which words are employed.

Elocution has not been part of the traditional training of the Japanese until very recently. Public speaking as such has been known less than a hundred years.[15] Even the present-day Japanese is not adequately taught or trained in self-expression and is not accustomed to voicing his own personal ideas. The average Japanese is inept at expressing clearly and conveying to other people his views and feelings. He lacks the art of informal give-and-take in discussions which has become a normal part of an individual's training in Western countries. Moreover, self-restraint in speech is still considered a necessary part of good taste and proper behavior. Then too, individual views or opinions are of small consequence; they are important only when seconded by others. Since the end of World War II, however, the people have developed the habit of expressing their views quite freely.

INEXACTITUDE. Exactitude or accuracy has never been one of the major demands of Japanese social life. Preciseness, by their standards of social conduct, is often regarded as rudeness and is offensive to them.[16] To say too clearly what one means is to underestimate the listener's intelligence and power of comprehension and constitutes an act of discourtesy, if not an insult. This rule of conduct is reflected in life, art, and in literary dialectics. In other words, vagueness of expression exists by design and in response to the demands of social etiquette. Too great a clarity or exactness is frequently regarded with suspicion, an attitude not unlike the English distrust of logic. A Japanese is not disturbed by contradictions in logic for he does not set much store by logic. The pronounced tendency on the part of most people to avoid any semblance of narrow partisanship leads them instinctively to take a vague, noncommittal attitude even on hotly debated issues in which they may be emotionally involved. In accentuated form, this tendency can easily appear, especially in public affairs, as a kind of evasiveness.

The habit of exactness has not really taken firm hold in Japan yet. The notion and practice of scientific accuracy are still new and of recent origin. Newspapers still reports blandly of a meeting which was attended by "approximately 1274 persons." Still relatively undeveloped is the relentless drive to pursue the truth as in the West. In social relations the pursuit of truth is abandoned if there is the slightest chance that it might impair harmony or satisfactory existing relationships. Even punctuality is not regarded as a virtue in strictly

---

[15] Fukuzawa Yukichi first introduced the art of public speaking to Japan in his school, the Keio English School, in the 1860's shortly after he returned from his visit to the United States in 1860.

[16] H. Sassa, "Our Public Opinion," *Contemporary Japan*, March, 1937, p. 556.

social matters although especially in business, industry, and science, maximum possible accuracy, exactitude, and punctuality are now insisted upon.

INDIRECTION. The direct approach, especially the blunt, point-blank method which is generally accepted in most Western countries is seldom, if ever, used in either social or business relations. Even in politics, it is resorted to rarely and only under dire circumstances and where the ordinary method of indirection is inappropriate or ineffective. In the context of Japanese society, the indirect method works more efficiently and without causing embarrassment to any except to those ubiquitous intermediaries or "go-betweens" whose job it is to serve as shock-absorbers or more accurately "embarrassment-absorbers." When transactions are carried on by means of go-betweens it is less noticeable, bargaining can go on much more satisfactorily, and, most important of all, should the negotiations fall through, the blame for the failure can be pinned upon the intermediary and neither of the negotiating parties need suffer a loss of face. Of course, there are drawbacks to this method of negotiating which militates against one party and works to the advantage of the other, but this sort of risk cannot be eliminated regardless of the methods used. The technique of indirection is so congenial and convenient to those who are accustomed to it and is so much a part of the way of life that it can not easily be replaced by a more direct method.

ABSTRACT, NONCATEGORICAL THINKING. Conspicuously reflected in the mode of thought of the Japanese is a strong preference for a priori methods especially in dealing with abstract ideas and ideals. Their fondness for the deductive method leads the intellectuals especially to prefer the theoretical approach in fields like politics and economics. This proclivity has been responsible for the popularity of Marxist thinking. Even the man in the street strongly tends to think in very abstract terms when dealing with politics, and in an abstract language unrelated to his own experiences.[17] This is undoubtedly a feudal heritage, at least in part, which had even been encouraged under the totalitarian political structure of the late 1930's and during World War II. Consequently, until after the war there were almost no empirical studies of significance in the fields of government and politics.

Noncategorical thinking has been traditional and normal in Japan. Categories are not clearly established and things are never neatly divided or classified into simple opposites as black and white, or

---

[17] Kyodo Kenkyu, "Kokumin seikatsu to seiji ishiki," *Kaizo*, June, 1953, p. 89.

right and wrong, or good and bad. There must always be something in between and again something between the in-betweens. In
their behavior, there are no irreconcilable opposites. There is always
room for, as well as the means for, achieving compromise. Instead
of categorization there exists a very blurred distinction. Good is
not clearly demarcated from bad. Right and wrong are not as clear
as black and white. Everything is relative; nothing is absolute.
Even values are relative; even moral values are not absolute.

The concept of sin is quite different from what obtains in the
West. To begin with, there is no concept of original sin or the "fall
of man." It is social sin rather than moral sin with which the
Japanese are concerned, for it is the transgression of the social
code which is the more serious of the two. Individual sin is
something almost alien to their way of life. There exists a wide area
of tolerance within which the concept of sin as understood in the
West does not operate.

EMOTIONAL DRIVES. There would be very little substance left in
any civilization if the emotional forces and elements were removed
from it. In fact, civilization could hardly exist without the propelling
force of emotion. In the countries of the Far East, pride in their
spirituality and, especially in Japan, the emotional content of life are
very high. However, in the case of the Japanese, emotive expression
is governed by rules of propriety when not actually suppressed. One
way in which it is normally manifested is as a popular cult of aes-
theticism[18] which places a high value on the appreciation or enjoyment of beauty in nature, life, and art. Emotional expression in art,
drama, music, dance, and poetry has a place in the everyday life of
the people and is by no means confined to the professionals. The
mode of emotional expression of the Japanese has been colored
strangely by a kind of effeminate sentimentalism at times.

Emotional expression in public, however, is another matter for
their rigid rules of social conduct have required the suppression of
feelings. Like the English the Japanese are extremely chary of expressing emotion individually. Yet group or social expression is approved in sports or in the reverence of the Emperor. In kabuki
drama, for instance, where there is a scene which touches the heart-
strings of the audience it is quite proper for a man to shed tears
freely though he absolutely may not weep at the death of his loved
ones. On the other hand, if he has failed in discharging his duty,
even on the field of battle, he can shed "masculine" tears of morti-

---

[18] Ruth Benedict, *The Chrysanthemum and the Sword*, p. 2.

fication. The misconception that the Japanese are devoid of emotion has resulted from the fact that they do not easily show emotion in public. Outwardly composed and calm, a man nevertheless carries within himself the makings of emotional outbursts in which only the time and place are the governing conditions. The concealment of anxiety and grief is as natural as the control of one's temper and not unlike the Englishman's phlegm. But behind such rigid control lies a stronger emotion than behind the habitual outbursts of passion of a more volatile people. Repressed emotions must and do find safety valves for indirect externalization in humor, sports, fine arts, and literature.

Beneath the rather solid surface of stoicism is found the sentimental, emotional make-up of the Japanese which shows up so clearly once the barrier is penetrated. When the lid of self-control and discipline is lifted the impulsive nature comes to the fore. It is this emotional trait that sustains the various practices and institutions, their social and political and economic activities, and makes them vulnerable to emotional appeals, didacticism, indoctrination, symbols, and myths.

The strong religiosity of the Japanese, though not the intense, all-pervasive force that it is in India, is sustained also by their emotional nature. Religion[19] along with art, drama, music, and poetry affords the people a socially approved outlet for emotional expression. Moreover, religion has, in Japan's national development, actually served to satisfy the aesthetic needs as much as the piety of the people.

Politics has for some time now provided the Japanese with a legitimate arena as an outlet for the emotions not only of the representatives but of the public as well. As an alternative to violence, it is serving a useful function as a safety valve. If political actions are to carry the force of conviction and determination, one can hardly deny an amplitude of emotion to the body politic. The release of emotion is often necessary to clear the atmosphere in politics but it can lead to violent clashes particularly when reason takes the back seat and moderation is forgotten in the heat of argument, as frequently happens on the floor of the Diet.

Since the individual is ever conscious of what society in general thinks of him or his actions and is constantly thinking in terms of approbation or disapprobation, he develops hypersensitivity along with self-consciousness. While his constant emphasis on, and re-

---

[19] Edwin O. Reischauer, *The United States and Japan*, pp. 125–133.

iteration of, his unworthiness and how little he has to offer to others are part of social etiquette which emphasizes the respect he is showing, such a practice cannot help but strengthen the impression of self-depreciation and subservience if not inferiority.

The universal characterization of the Japanese which is widely accepted is that they are a very proud and sensitive people. Yet, in reality, they are not much more sensitive or proud than any other people in the world. The Japanese, it is true, are highly sensitive to adverse opinion or criticism, expressed or implied, and easily take offense. They are equally sensitive to praise and appreciation. Their sensitivity underlies their strong desire to be accepted and be well thought of by others. On the international scene these attitudes are even more poignantly reflected. Any slight, slur, or discriminatory act has been strongly resented as an affront to national honor.[20] This has been due largely to the inferior diplomatic status to which she was relegated and the uphill struggle she had to carry on before she could achieve a status of equality in the family of nations. In dealing with the nations of the West, Japan had to conduct herself with the eyes of the whole world upon her.

SENSE OF OBLIGATION. Perhaps no other emotional force in Japanese society is as powerful and propulsive as that which inheres in the sense of obligation or indebtedness which is known as *on*. From the cradle to the grave, this emotional force, in all its variations and manifestations, propels the individual in his actions. Life is an endless succession of favors received for which repayment must be made with diligence. The social behavior of the people becomes unintelligible without adequate consideration of this peculiarly Japanese concept and practice. The fabric of society is thus woven with the warp and woof of mutual and reciprocal indebtedness and obligations. Obligations bind the individual to individuals and groups in a tight web of relationships which ignore individual rights and desires. What exists is a hierarchy of obligations beginning at the top with loyalty to the emperor and the state, to society at large, to the family as manifested in filial piety, to one's superiors, teachers, friends, in-laws, and even to subordinates and servants.

The moment an individual is born, he is indebted and beholden to the country of his birth. When his schooling begins, he becomes indebted to his teachers and he is not allowed to forget this fact the

---

[20] Japanese pride was hurt by such incidents as the Three Power Intervention of 1895, San Francisco School Board Incident of 1906, denial of the racial equality clause in the League of Nations charter, denial of naval parity in the Washington Conference of 1921–22, and the Exclusion Act of 1924.

rest of his life. Then, when he takes his place in society as one of its useful members, he finds that the scope of his indebtedness has increased tremendously for now he is indebted to his employer or superior official as well as to a host of others. An individual is thus destined to spend all his life reciprocating the favors he has received or trying to repay the debts he has incurred, fully aware that it would be impossible for him to repay all the obligations either quantitatively or qualitatively. The final ledger of obligations is never balanced. It is patently clear to a Japanese that fulfilling one's obligations is the supreme task in life, and as such, it becomes the basic condition of behavior.

Traditionally loyalty to the state and the emperor has been at the very top of the hierarchy of obligations. In feudal times, the primary loyalty was to one's lord and only indirectly and secondarily did loyalty reach the emperor if at all. But in the nineteenth century, this obligation was transformed into absolute loyalty to the Emperor who became the personification of the state. This was achieved in the Imperial Rescript on Education (1890) and the Rescript to the Soldiers and Sailors (1882). Although the obligations to the family and to the state are unlimited, the latter take precedence over the former. In China, filial piety or family loyalty always took precedence over loyalty to the emperor but when the Japanese took over from her continental neighbor the political philosophy of Confucianism, they reversed the order while rejecting completely the idea of revolution.

Filial piety is a form of repaying the heavy burden of obligation to one's parents and is one of the very first lessons a child learns in life. On this obligation the authority of the parents is firmly based, especially that of the father who is the head of the family. Filial piety is loyalty to the family and as such is of a primary nature. Aside from the two principal loyalties there exist a myriad of loyalties which determine the behavior of individuals.

GIRI. The whole gamut of human obligational relationships is included in the concept of *giri* which is all-embracing in its implications. No facet of life could exist outside it. Everybody must and does move within its orbit. Merely to give all the different connotations the word conveys to a Japanese would be an impossible task. It means duty, justice, honor, face, decency, respectability, courtesy, charity, humanity, love, circumstance, gratitude, claim.[21]

[21] See Ruth Benedict, *The Chrysanthemum and the Sword*, pp. 114–176, for a detailed discussion of *on* and *giri*. An interesting "Schematic Table of Japanese Obligations and Their Reciprocals" is given on p. 116.

Giri is an all-pervading force in the behavior of all classes of people and in all walks of life: the prime minister, the official, the politician, the businessman, financier, industrialist, intellectual, student, parent, the factory worker, and the farmer. Although the complexities and ambivalences of *giri* must be taken into account, it operates because of the universal need for respecting and expressing "human feelings" (*ninjo*) in social life that exists in closely knit communities. There can be no *giri* in a Robinson Crusoe existence for it can only be maintained vis-à-vis society. It can therefore be interpreted as the "ways of society," which at one and the same time can mean "the demands of custom," "social courtesy or decency," and "the shackles of convention." The sanctions of *giri* are to be found in society in the mores, customs, and folkways, and not in the laws.

The obsessive behavior regarding honor or "face" is inextricably tied in with the demands of *giri*. In a negative sense it operates to prevent shame or disgrace to one's name, while in a positive sense it becomes a desire for fame and prestige. In feudal society, loss of honor either by insult, dereliction of duty, failure, or cowardice called for vendetta or suicide, both of which are forms of redressing a wrong or a disgrace. There was also another way out of such dishonor, namely, renouncing the world by taking the tonsure and leading a cloistered life in a Buddhist monastery. While these methods are no longer employed in their original forms, the spirit of vengeance or retaliation is still very much in evidence especially in the political sphere.

Suicide, the most extreme form of aggressive action that a Japanese can resort to, has been a part of the operational code of *giri*. Not only is it condoned but in the Tokugawa period it was even glorified in literature for those who committed suicide in romantic love pacts. There has never been any stigma of cowardice attached to suicide. On the contrary the act has been regarded as the final demonstration of a man's courage and determination.[22] Properly carried out, it will remove the stigma or disgrace attached to a person's name. It serves as an apology to atone for one's failure, as a protest to induce a change of heart in someone thereby changing a course of action, or as a final desperate method of winning an argument in a controversy. Used as a threat, it has effectively forestalled, prevented, or induced action. To commit suicide to avoid the disgrace of capture by the enemy has been a common practice since feudal times. Suicide has often been an alternative to destroying

[22] *Ibid.*, pp. 166–168.

others. Sometimes, suicide is even demanded as a challenge to one's sincerity.[23]

CURIOSITY. Curiosity has been one of the conspicuous attributes of the people which has profoundly affected their social and political behavior and achievements in various fields of national endeavor. Insatiable at times, their curiosity, coupled with the strong desire to learn, has been responsible for the rapid strides they have taken in modernization and industrialization, enabling them to achieve the position of one of the major powers of the world and to become the first Asian nation to take its place alongside the advanced nations of the West. The scientific and technological advances made in the last seventy-five years may be attributed to the impelling drive for information, knowledge, and know-how. This trait underlies their predilection for something new, something different, something interesting, and something useful.

In their social milieu, curiosity is manifested in various ways and is aided and abetted by existing social conditions and attitudes. Because of the primary social relations in the communities, practically all the goings-on are known to everybody. Gossiping about individuals and families is an acceptable social pastime and everyone practices it. Moreover, town-talk serves as the preventive of boredom where excitements occur only rarely, if ever. The love of gossip is reflected in the political gossip columns of the daily papers which are read avidly by the people.

LOVE OF PLEASURE. In view of the rigid requirements of an ethical code which demands heavy repayment of obligations and drastic renunciations, it is quite surprising to find that it is so accommodating to the pleasures of the five senses.[24] The Japanese have been traditionally fun-loving people. They love conviviality. Few peoples in the world can boast of such a continuous round of festivals and festivities throughout the year as the Japanese. Enjoyment of life's pleasures is considered legitimate and necessary. Consequently there is little moralizing in their enjoyment of pleasure. As a matter of fact they do not divide pleasures into spiritual and sensual categories; nor do they attempt to identify the spirit or soul as good and the flesh as evil. Consequently, there are no evil pleasures which are to be avoided.

Love of pleasure is reflected in the behavior of businessmen, poli-

[23] This was done in the verbal duel which was fought on the floor of the Diet between Minister of War Terauchi Hisaichi and Saito Takao, member of the House of Representatives in the 1930's.

[24] Ruth Benedict, *op. cit.*, pp. 177–194.

ticians, officials, and others who do not hesitate to mix business and pleasure, using places of pleasure even for serious transactions. A teahouse is not considered inappropriate or undignified for deliberations and decision making on matters of business and industry or government policy. It is this desire for pleasure which is being satiated in part in the elaborate receptions and entertainments which government officials hold frequently at the expense of the taxpayers. Every government department has a sizeable amount set aside in its budget for entertainment purposes, a practice which is unknown in the United States, for instance. Business firms make it a regular practice to give lavish entertainments. This has a very contagious effect on the government for officials have intimate connections with businessmen.

THE IRRATIONAL AND THE UNCONSCIOUS. Human beings all too often say that they want one thing and really want its opposite, not because they are hypocrites but because the human mind has a way of disguising the clear purposes of its own thought and action. We are not the rational creatures that we think we are, and we do not know ourselves.[25] Consequently, the irrational and the unconscious in social life assume a much greater importance than we are accustomed to recognizing. Irrational emotional forces are responsible for the paradoxes of history as well as the ambivalences and aberrations of individuals and groups in social and political life. Furthermore, the fact that in Japan as elsewhere social values represent an accumulation of values uncritically and emotionally accepted by society from time to time, adds to the difficulty of analyzing individual and group behavior.

One of the most important forces which determines the behavior of a social group is its spiritual and emotional training and background. In general, the spiritual bond which holds human groups together consists of three elements, namely, traditions, interests, and ideals. Tradition looks to the past from which the collective heritage of the group is derived but must condition the present and shape the future. The interests of the group deal primarily with the present needs although they must be projected into the future and are affected inevitably to some extent by the past. Ideals are more for the future achievement but they influence behavior in the present.

These three ingredients, then, hold together and activate human groups. Two of these, traditions and ideals, are abstract emotional forces while only one, the interests, can be regarded as meeting the

[25] R. F. M. Durbin, *The Politics of Democratic Socialism* (1940), quoted in Snyder, *Roots of Political Behavior*, pp. 43–44.

practical and concrete needs of the group. From this, it is clear why myths and symbols of all sorts come to have such powerful influence in social and political life especially when the power of imagination is fully utilized to glorify the past and the nation's heritage and rouse the people to a definite course of action.

Like other peoples, the Japanese have had their share of myths. In the political realm these have been powerful indeed, for some of the myths have come down from prehistoric times. The nation possesses as systematic a political mythology as can be found anywhere in the world. Among the myths best known in the West were those of the divinity of the emperor and of the nation's invincibility, both of which were powerful forces in Japan's development. They appeared plausible to the populace since, although they were based largely on hope and wishful thinking, if not actual distortion, they were at the same time related to historical facts.[26]

The Japanese have also accumulated a wealth of political symbols which are steeped in emotional significance. The oldest of these is the "Three Divine Treasures," the imperial regalia regarded as the symbol of the emperor's sovereignty. They consist of a mirror, a sword, and a curved comma-shaped bead, the possession of which is regarded as prima facie evidence of the emperor's right to rule. There are also the national heroes many of whom have been deified by Shinto and enshrined in the national consciousness of the people.[27] Half or more of the national holidays were of a political nature and many of the popular festivals have a very strong political flavor, even though they may be folk festivals. There is no paucity of music which can stir up strong pride for the motherland as well as patriotic martial spirit. The sword as a symbol of justice, Mount Fuji of the eternal and incomparable majesty, and the cherry blossom of the Japanese spirit, have been celebrated in art and literature. The flag and the national anthem, both of which were adopted only after the reopening of relations with the West in the middle of the nineteenth

[26] The myth of invincibility was based on the defeat of the Mongol invasions of 1274 and 1281 which was achieved through divine assistance in the form of perfectly-timed typhoons which were called "divine wind" (*kamikaze*) together with such historical facts as the defeat of China in 1894–1895 and the defeat of Russia in 1904–05 which furnished a plausible basis for the wishful thinking that Japan will never be defeated because she had never been defeated in a war.

[27] For a comprehensive discussion, see D. C. Holtom, *Modern Japan and Shinto Nationalism*.

[28] The national anthem has proved more effective in emotionally stirring up the individual. The rising-sun flag actually does not carry the symbolic power to the Japanese that the Stars and Stripes does to an American, perhaps because it has

century, have been powerful symbols of unity.[28] Military parades and naval reviews were held frequently in the past in order to stir the patriotism of the people. Court ceremonies and rituals serve as powerful mobilizers of national emotion.

JAPANESE SOCIETY: ITS STRUCTURE AND RELATIONSHIPS

Japanese society is a tight web of relationships with the emperor at its epicenter as the centripetal force, pulling all the individuals toward it from all directions. Within this web of relationships, the individual is rigorously self-disciplined and knows exactly what his place is and how he is to behave. But once he gets outside of this web, he not only loses his social bearings but even feels released from the bond of normal obligations and loses restraint as well as responsibility.[29]

The Family

The family as the primary unit and basic organization of social regulation has always played an important role in Japanese society. A hierarchical family system within an extremely rigid, stratified society continued down into the second half of the nineteenth century. Status in the family and social life were determined at birth and each individual was trained and educated to fit into his little niche and the prescribed way of life in an authoritarian atmosphere.[30]

Each individual assumed his proper station in life and understood the social mechanism thoroughly. His status or place in society was determined by a combination of several factors including his position in the family, his economic condition, age, sex, occupation, and marital status. His status governed not only his behavior and language but even the dwelling and clothing he was entitled to use. His position in the family hierarchy was based upon sex, generation, and primogeniture.[31] Equality did not exist in the family or society since the social order was built upon a hierarchial system. In this status-ordered social organization everyone had to behave in a manner in keeping with his station in life.

While changes have taken place in the family system in the last fifty years, its importance as the primary social unit and basic organization of social regulation has not diminished greatly. It is still the

---

no connection with a stirring historical event such as Francis Scott Key witnessed and put into verse.

[29] Frank Gibney, *Five Gentlemen of Japan*, goes into this problem.

[30] The best treatment of the place of the family in Japanese society is Kawashima Takeyoshi, *Nihon Shakai no Kazokuteki Kosei*.

[31] Kawashima Takeyoshi, *Nihon no Shakai to Seikatsu Ishiki*, p. 57.

basic social unit and a form of private "government" which continues to make its impress upon Japanese character and personality, industrial and business behavior, military psychology, and the attitude of the farmers and laborers. Although the family's hold on the individual has decreased somewhat it is still the locus of social life and politics as well, and even business is strongly influenced by it.

The individual family is presided over by its head who is usually the father and the representative of his ancestors. His word is law for he has the authority to run the family affairs and has control over all the members. "There are four things to fear in this world," a Japanese saying goes, "and they are the earthquake, thunder, fire, and father." To preserve the family line and its honor is his most important duty and obligation to his ancestors. Thus, the primary function of the family is to preserve and conserve, not to innovate, change, or destroy. Small wonder then that the family system itself should be the bulwark of conservatism, socially and politically. Rural families in particular are the strongholds of conservatism in the country. It has been demonstrated that many individuals who give support to progressive or radical political programs more often than not switch over to the conservative parties upon assuming the headship of a family, and even inherit the political party preferences of their fathers especially when they become candidates for office in an election.

The Neighborhood

The smallest group of neighbors on the most intimate terms in a local community consists ordinarily of five or six families. There is a custom of long standing which requires a family moving into a community to call on all the immediate neighbors, that is, families on both flanks and the three across the street, to pay their respects in order to be accepted by the neighbors as one of them. During World War II, the government made use of these neighborhood groups, which had been in existence as neighborhood associations and known as *tonari-gumi*, for administrative purposes. Orders, instructions, and notices from above, and even rationing, were handled through these neighborhood associations. This was a simple matter because there were already the pre-existing informal neighborhood groupings in every community.

The Hamlet

In physical and geographic terms, the largest social unit within which intimate relations could exist is the hamlet made up of a cluster of families living closely together. This is the largest circle of

first-name intimacy and a large proportion of the inhabitants are related and perhaps all of them would be if their relationship were
carefully checked back several generations.[32]   This is the group
which has its local tutelary deity that is regarded as its common
ancestor.   There is not only a feeling of kinship but also a remarkable
homogeneity of ideas, outlook, and attitude especially in the rural
areas.   The hamlet association was the rural organization so effectively used by the government during the war.   Its urban counterpart was the block association.   The urban equivalent of the hamlet
is the city block but, except for the administrative purposes to which
they are put, the two are entirely different.   There is no feeling of
kinship for there is not even the remotest kind of blood relationship
holding the inhabitants together.   Except for the friendly acquaintance established within the five or six families living closely together
there is not the intimacy that exists in a hamlet.

The Village

Several hamlets usually form a village which is an administrative
rather than a social unit.   The village leaders are simultaneously the
leading citizens of the hamlets because the primary basis of prestige
lies in the hamlet.   The influential leaders are men either of wealth
or of wisdom who enjoy positions of prestige and respect.   Among
them are the doctors, teachers, and old families of wealth, especially
those who can boast of having produced the village heads in the
feudal days.   These influential men are the spokesmen or representatives of the village in its dealings with the outside whether it be
with the government or the parties.

The Town, City, County, and Prefecture

Even the village, strictly speaking, is no longer an effective social
unit.   The town, city, county, and prefecture are much too large to
be considered anything but administrative units.   However, they continue to furnish the sentimental basis of associations.   The feeling of
affinity or intimacy among people from the same village, city, county,
or even prefecture is quite noticeable.   Psychologically, it is one of
the stronger bonds which exist even in politics.   Where there are a
sufficient number of people residing, as in the nation's capital or in
some foreign country, associations are formed on the basis of the

[32] In a great many of these hamlets only a few family names are in use, indicating that there is close consanguinal relationship.

prefectures from which they come.[33]   Under the old system, intimacy among the Diet members was greatest among those who came from the same prefecture because groupings were on the basis of prefecture rather than of parties.

Community Social Structure

During the Tokugawa period, social structure or the class system was predicated upon three major considerations, namely, economic or political function, economic standing, or the possession of wealth and family status.   There were four large social categories or classes of people with the military (samurai) at the top, followed by the farmers (peasants), artisans, and merchants.   Within each of these classes were further gradations according to family status and the possession of wealth.   Such minute and elaborate distinctions as existed during the feudal period no longer obtain but it would be unrealistic to think that class divisions vanished with the end of the feudal system in the nineteenth century.

Class divisions and class organization do exist in Japan just as they do in English society and elsewhere.   However, they are no longer based on functions.   Economic status or possession of wealth has superseded function and has become the most common basis of class division though it is certainly not the only one.   There is still a great deal of emphasis placed on family status according to the length of residence in a community, possession of historically famous ancestors or lineage, or meritorious service rendered in the past as evidenced in rank or decorations received.   Lines between classes are no longer rigidly drawn and it has been possible for individuals to climb over and across these obstacles since both wealth and position can now be more easily achieved than in former times.   Moreover, politics affords the opportunity to ambitious and capable persons to overcome the disadvantage of obscure family status, lack of wealth, and low position.   Through education, it has become possible for a bright and able person from a poor family to achieve a position of importance in government, business, or industry.

Following the usual method, Japanese society can be divided into three general classes: upper, middle, and lower.   In a general way, it is possible to say that the most accurate indices for classification would be educational level, profession or occupation, and income.

[33] Among the Japanese residents in the United States there were associations of people from Yamaguchi, Hiroshima, Fukuoka, Kumamoto and other prefectures which were organized primarily for social purposes.

Of course, these different classes have their social norms which determine the way they live and behave, particularly in such matters as eating, dressing, talking, thinking, and playing.

Social Relationships

No matter how odd, how peculiar, how stultifying, immoral, or even reprehensible from the viewpoint of some other national ideas or mores, existing social relationships will be approved, valued, and preserved by a people if they are born into and brought up in them and taught them as right, proper, and decent. Nothing that outsiders may say or do can alter these practices noticeably especially when they are emotionally based and deeply rooted in the traditional culture of the people.

Social relationships in Japan are based on the recognition of a hierarchy which is less rigid today than it was not so long ago. However, they are still based firmly on the five cardinal human relationships of Confucianism which the Japanese adopted thirteen centuries or more ago. These relationships are exemplified in those of master and servant, father and son, older brother and younger brother, husband and wife, and friend and friend. The only relationship which might possibly include the idea of equality is the last named. However, even in this relationship, equality is an incidental rather than a chief factor. All the other relationships are those between unequals, that is, superior and inferior involving subordination and subservience. Authority (position and rank), age, and sex, are the elements which determine the superior-inferior relationship. Within this large framework fall practically all the infinite variations of relationships and obligations among which may be included the teacher-pupil, predecessor-successor, junior-senior, *oyabun-kobun*, master-apprentice, and in-law relationships. All these relationships and obligations are carried over into economic and political activities. It can be said that practically every successful politician, bureaucrat, financier, businessman, or industrialist owes his achievement to the advantageous working of one or more of these relationships.

SOCIAL, ECONOMIC, GEOGRAPHIC BONDS IN SOCIETY

The Family Tie

Of all the bonds which hold people together in Japan, the strongest is still the family tie. This tie which is either consanguineous or marital is seen in operation just as effectively in the political as in the economic spheres though perhaps less conspicuously in political

activities. In business no attempt is made to minimize the role of
family tie for the great fortunes of the nation have been family
centered and their multifarious activities have usually carried the
family name. All but one of the "Big Five" of the zaibatsu have used
their family names conspicuously in their industrial, commercial, and
financial activities.[34]

While in politics the family tie is less conspicuous as compared
with business, it is nevertheless a powerful factor. Marrying into
the right family and acquiring either affluence or influence or both,
has been regarded as a sure way to success in business, finance, or
government, and even in politics. Many a successful career in government, politics, or business has been the result of a fortunate marital tie.[35] The desire to keep wealth in the family operates strongly
everywhere but particularly in Japan where it is perhaps more intense
because of the family system. Consequently, by marrying into a
wealthy family or by marrying a son or daughter into a wealthy family, it becomes possible to insure financial backing for one's business
or political activities.

Nepotism is a natural by-product of the family system. Consequently, it is more common in a society whose structure rests solidly
on the family system. In business it is recognized universally but in
politics it is frowned upon, especially in the Western democracies
where the family system as such does not exist. In Japan the practice
is perhaps not as conspicuous as it is in some of the other Asian
countries but it does exist to a far greater extent than in many a
Western country.

The School Tie

In government, one of the strongest bonds is the old school tie.
To most people, claiming the same alma mater and having gone
through the same ordeals and tribulations as well as the pleasant

[34] Mitsui, Sumitomo, Yasuda, and Okura are family names known to all while
only Iwasaki has always used the business name of Mitsubishi ("three diamonds")
which is the family crest.

[35] Kato Takaaki and Shidehara Kijuro, both of whom achieved the highest
political position of prime minister, married into the Iwasaki family (Mitsubishi).
Prime Minister Yoshida, who in 1953 formed a government for the fifth time, began
his career as an adopted son of a wealthy childless family and later became the
son-in-law of the eminent and influential statesman, Makino Nobuaki, by marrying
his daughter. He thus acquired both affluence and influence. His own daughter
then married a wealthy coal magnate thereby adding considerably to his affluence
though indirectly. See Natori Giichi, *Seizaikaijin no Meiun,* for the marital
relationships of financiers and politicians.

experiences of youth can often mean a great deal more than simply an accidental consanguineous or marital tie. The school tie gives rise to a kind of esprit de corps which makes possible a special clique made up of graduates of the same university. By far the most numerous and influential clique in the government service including the diplomatic service has been the group of graduates of Tokyo University. In the beginning, graduates of private universities were virtually excluded from the government's higher civil service and the diplomatic service because the clique made it a point to keep out the graduates of other universities and particularly the private universities.

These cliques were not confined simply to civilian university graduates in government service. They were found among the graduates of service academies, particularly the military and naval academies. Among the graduates of these schools, subcliques were formed on the basis of class or the year of graduation and also on the basis later of whether or not they attended the service colleges, that is, the war college and the naval college. School tie loyalty or esprit de corps worked among other university graduates too. Keio University graduates were influential in the business world while Waseda University graduates distinguished themselves in the field of journalism and practical politics for a long time.

Since the end of World War II considerable changes have taken place. School tie loyalty has not diminished but the virtual monopoly which the graduates of prewar imperial universities, now government universities, enjoyed in government civil service has been broken though they are still numerically superior. At the same time the graduates of Tokyo University have gone into politics in such large numbers that they have far outstripped the graduates of Waseda University.

Home Town Affinity

The fact of common geographic background has been a very strong basis of intimacy and close cooperation especially if individuals were brought up in the same community with similar or identical experiences and schooling during childhood and early youth. The history of the early Meiji period abounds in such friendships. It is doubtful if the arduous work of putting the new Meiji government on its feet could have been achieved without this type of home town affinity and friendships. At the same time, however, it is this sort of affinity combined with the school tie loyalty and esprit de corps that has given rise to cliques and coterie politics as well as to the oligarchic clan government of the Meiji period.

BEHAVIOR PATTERNS

It would be extremely difficult, if not impossible, to identify and isolate behavior patterns of the different classes. In their general cultural and social behavior patterns all the classes have a great deal in common. Consequently any attempt to establish clear-cut distinctions would end in failure except on the very practical functional level. What makes the task doubly difficult is the fact that the division into upper, middle, and lower classes is valid only in the most general way. It cannot be foolproof, for there is much more in common between the lower upper class and the upper middle class than the two extremities of either the upper or middle classes. Similarly there is a great deal more in common between the lower middle class and the upper lower class than between the two extremities of any single class. In other words, the overlapping marginal areas of the different classes make accurate categorization of behavior patterns extremely hazardous.

Nevertheless, it is necessary to have a general idea of what these three classes are like and how they are composed. The upper class embraces the wealthy landowners, the capitalists, and the high level managers of huge enterprises. Families connected with big business including the zaibatsu fall in this category. Perhaps not more than two or three percent of the people can be included in this class. That they represent the wealthiest class in society is self-evident. It is quite apparent too that they are conservative in their social and economic views and attitudes and advocate policies which protect and advance their interests. In this respect they are quite homogeneous.

There has been a tremendous growth of middle class in Japan with the progress of industrialization. This was an integral part of the basic economic changes brought about in the structure of capitalism. The growing technical-scientific needs of industry and the increasing complexity of production and distribution have increased rapidly the numbers of technical and managerial employees. Planning, regulation, and control within industry itself have expanded the staff personnel. Expansion in the economic functions of government and of public services has multiplied the number of persons employed as well as the variety of activities and services necessary. In spite of the size and the contribution they make to national life, theirs is a still small voice in national affairs as compared with the upper class.

The middle class comprises a large segment of society[36] and forms

[36] Kawai Eijiro, *Jiyu Shugi no Yogo,* p. 119.

the backbone of the nation as taxpayers. However, there exists a high degree of heterogeneity among the members in their ideas, attitudes, educational levels, incomes, and the functions they perform in society. Included in this class are the white-collar workers or salaried persons ranging all the way from minor clerks and sales persons to owners of small and medium business and industrial enterprises, technicians, scientists, teachers, government officials, lawyers, doctors, journalists, writers, actors, musicians, librarians, accountants, clergymen, and social workers. Educationally they range all the way from those who have only compulsory education and a couple of years of secondary schooling up to professional training on the postgraduate and advanced research level. All the intellectuals regardless of the type of activity they engage in belong here. In this class are to be found the shapers and molders of public opinion and the architects of ideology. Thus, ideologically they can be spread over the entire range of the political spectrum. There are those to the left, to the right, and in the middle; there are those who are imbued with Western ideas and those who are steeped only in conservative Confucian ideas. So far as income is concerned, there are those who make less than some in the lower class. Perhaps it is not too far from the truth, even in Japan, to say that the middle class after all is only a state of mind.[37] Actually, no one has gone to the trouble of finding out precisely the proportion of people who belong to the middle class.[38] As an intermediate group which is relatively unorganized politically, it does not receive the attention it should from the political parties and is courted only at election time.[39]

The lower class is made up of the working classes which live by their labor in the fields, factories, mines, forests, and on the seas. They include both the unskilled and semiskilled workers but not the skilled ones who belong more properly in the lower middle class. There is a noticeable homogeneity in almost every respect as com-

[37] It was found that the largest percentage (79.6%) of American professional men and big-businessmen considered themselves as belonging to the middle class, while a far smaller percentage (65%) of small-businessmen and white-collar workers included themselves in the middle class. Richard Centers, *The Psychology of Social Classes* (1940), pp. 76–77.

[38] In 1948, the British Institute of Public Opinion conducted a poll and it was found that 47 percent of the people polled regarded themselves as middle class and 46 percent considered themselves as belonging in the working class. *News Chronicle*, April 29, 1949, quoted in Roy Lewis and Angus Maude, *The English Middle Classes*, p. 9.

[39] The Japanese use the term *chukanso*, or intermediate, in-between stratum or class to denote the middle class.

pared with the middle class. However, there is considerable difference between the urban factory worker and the rural farm worker, the former appearing quite radical by comparison with the latter who is very conservative. Actually even the urban factory workers are conservative for it is really their leadership that is radical and the leadership comes not from the lower class but from the middle class.

As has already been suggested, the most meaningful approach to the examination of behavior patterns seems to be on a functional basis. By this method there is a far better chance of bringing out the differences which are found in the behavior patterns. Since our primary concern is politics, it would seem that we ought to begin with the politicians. But a careful scrutiny of the Japanese political scene will reveal clearly the fact that the practicing politicians have not yet established a behavior pattern sufficiently typical of the group. Although politicians are known for their opportunism, expediential proclivities, compromising, and vulnerability to the lure of power and influence, their behavior pattern is actually the composite of the different professional or functional groups which are represented in practical politics. There are roughly five of these functional groups: the bureaucrats, businessmen (also financiers and industrialists), intellectuals (professionals), military men, and workers (farm and factory).

Bureaucrats

All sorts of adjectives have been employed to characterize bureaucratic behavior, among which are tradition-bound, inflexible, formal, secretive, arrogant, inefficient, cliquish, colorless, unimaginative, narrow and circumscribed in their outlook, and unresponsive if not utterly impervious to new currents of thought as well as to new popular demands. All these and many other characterizations are oversimplifications but they do furnish a clue to their behavior pattern and are not entirely without basis. It must be remembered that their training, background, and the functions they perform make them what they are. It would be necessary to go back to about 1870 and trace the history of the development of the bureaucracy to thoroughly analyze Japanese bureaucratic behavior. But this is not the place for such a detailed discussion.[40]

It is true that a government official does not have to be individualistic. As a matter of fact individualism is frowned upon. As long as

[40] An excellent discussion of the origins of modern bureaucracy in Japan is Sakata Yoshio, "Nihon ni okeru kindai kanryo no hassei," *Jimbun Gakuho* (Kyoto University), III, pp. 1–26, 1953.

the bureaucrat performs his routine work accurately and carries out the orders of his superiors faithfully, his service is considered satisfactory.   The modern bureaucrat is a lineal descendant of the feudal retainer who discharged his duties to his master with undeviating loyalty and diligence.[41]   In performing his duties, the bureaucrat must faithfully follow precedent and well-established procedures and practices and avoid innovations as much as possible if he is to be safe.   It would suffice and be better to follow orders from above than to try to carry out one's own ideas or convictions.   Time takes care of his salary, promotion, and pension.   All he needs to do is to bide his time and his turn will come.   Because he occupies a position of authority, he deludes himself into thinking that he is privileged and superior to the people and loses sight of the fact that he has interests in common with the working class.

Bureaucrats are deliberately inefficient since it is felt that high efficiency actually contributes to insecurity.   Not only would man power be reduced through efficiency but it would even stir up resentment within the bureaucracy itself.   Bureaucrats tend to expand rather than contract their activities, giving rise to interdepartmental jurisdictional disputes as well as to intense competition in their efforts to capture bigger budget allocations.   It is a matter of record that the highest percentage of government officials comes from the rural agricultural families and their ideas bear the conservative rural coloring, particularly of the rural land-owning class.   Furthermore the education of the bureaucrats which takes place for the most part in the government universities, particularly in Tokyo University, has always been strongly of the German jurisprudential type characterized by elaborate conceptualism and German bureaucratism.   Thus they are molded into a single pattern with a standard viewpoint and technical legal knowledge as well as the awareness of their privileged position.   The examination they take requires little more than the memorizing of the contents of the six legal codes.[42]   Unlike the British civil service the examination pays little attention to the general education of the candidates.

The civil service tends to recruit those whose thoughts and ambitions do not turn naturally to politics.   Interest in politics develops later, however, as they reach the higher echelons from which many go

[41] Nakamura Akira, *Chishiki Kaikyu no Seijiteki Tachiba,* pp. 150–170 is an excellent treatment of the bureaucrat.

[42] The *Roppo Zensho,* a collection of these six codes, has been known for generations as the bible of university students preparing for the higher civil service examination, the passing of which is necessary for appointment in the government.

into politics or into the higher managerial positions in business, finance, and industry. The flow of talents from government to business and industry is quite constant because the knowledge and experience of former high-level bureaucrats are very valuable and marketable.

Japanese bureaucracy has, in one way or another, always been involved in politics from the very outset. More bureaucrats have been prime ministers than have members of any other group since the beginning of parliamentary government in the country. There has never been a single businessman or industrialist to head a government. Since the end of World War II, it has become practically necessary for a bureaucrat to become a politician if he wants to be a cabinet minister, a post which every university educated bureaucrat aspires to attain. Under the old system, it was not necessary for cabinet ministers to be members of the Diet but under the new Constitution half of them must be members of parliament. This virtually forces the ambitious individuals in the higher echelons of the bureaucracy to be politically minded.

Big Business

Since Japanese politics operates within the framework of capitalism and under a system of mutually interdependent relationship between government and business, it is affected at many points by the behavior of big business. At times it is not so easy to know whether business subserves government or vice versa. In its historical development, big business was the creature of the government and the zaibatsu could not have come into being or grown without the government's initiative and aegis. As a matter of fact, modern capitalism itself was established in Japan by the government as an instrument of national policy. Even after it was firmly established business and industry always looked to the government for help whenever they were in need of any assistance. Consequently big business developed the habit of relying heavily on the government, assuming an attitude of subservience whenever necessary but always with the feeling that the government owed such a support. Monopolistic capitalism could not have developed without government protection and favors of all sorts. Inasmuch as it has looked to the government for help, big business has always shown deference to the government. However, at the same time, it employs every means at its disposal to make its influence felt on the government and more often than not has its way. True to the mercantile spirit, big business is calculating in its moves, planning shrewdly every step to derive the greatest possible advantage. Its behavior has been and is governed, first and last, by the profit motive and self-interest.   It assumes that what is good for business is good for the government and the country.

Big business has an esprit de corps all its own and works to safeguard its own interests in spite of the fact that within itself it may be harassed by divisive forces.   Through cartel agreements, for instance, which it has succeeded in reviving in the postwar period, it has strengthened its position enormously.   Big business has its own pressure groups but it is not content to rely on them entirely.   It sends its representatives into the parties where they hold important positions; it has men looking out for its interests in the Diet; and it has representatives in the Cabinet where its interests are protected and advanced.   Vitally interested in, and alert to, the political situation and developments, big business is sensitively aware that its security and prosperity depend on the good will and support of the government.   It is no mere coincidence therefore that the capitalists together with the landowner class gave the necessary support to the political parties from the beginning.   As a matter of fact, without their backing, parties could not have been launched and continued successfully.

Big business, however, has not yet developed to any appreciable extent the concept of public responsibility or philanthropy.   There is not the feeling of responsibility to the public at large that exists in the Western democracies.   This is perhaps attributable in a large measure to the fact that the family spirit dominates the thinking of the business leaders.   Business assumes the attitude that it will sell to anyone who wants to buy and can pay.   It is not overly concerned with anything but the immediate consequences which would redound to its own benefit.   Beyond its own interests it is not likely to go, particularly in such matters as the impact on international politics. This is illlustrated clearly, for instance, in the continued clamor on the part of business for the lowering of the bars against trade with Communist China.

The Military Mind

The Japanese military mentality has tended toward that of the quasi-intellectual, if not pseudo-intellectual, with a type of thought structure combining rationalism and irrationalism as well as radicalism and conservatism.   In a sense it can be regarded as a modified and modernized version of the feudal samurai pattern of thought and behavior.   While it no longer reflects samurai ideology in its pristine form, there is enough of it in evidence.   This has been due at least in part to the fact that the bulk of the officer and noncommissioned officer classes in the armed forces came from the middle or lower middle class which includes small landowners, small independent farmers, and small shopkeepers from rural areas and small towns which are, unlike the urban centers, the strongholds of conservatism where samurai ideals are still respected. The modern military man is a samurai who has been trained in the technological aspects of modern warfare but who has not yet freed himself from the old concepts and precepts of the feudal days. He can fly a plane, man a tank, fire automatic weapons as well as an American, but he has yet to adjust himself to the ways of modern scientific warfare. In other words, he is still pretty much a feudal warrior who has at his disposal modern weapons and equipment and is capable of banzai charges and other methods which are just as outmoded but which reflect the spirit of old Japan.

Because of an extremely circumscribed view and training the prewar Japanese military mind was practically devoid of real understanding of even the most elementary sort of economic or political problems. Since the military man is conditioned to reacting only to orders from above and also to issuing orders to which he expects obedience, compliance, and execution without question, his action is founded on a superior-subordinate relationship. Action more often is on an *ad hoc* basis, one thing at a time, with rarely any plans for a follow-up. This was clearly demonstrated at the time of the February 26 incident in 1936. At the same time there is a conspicuous lack of the ability to improvise, or suddenly on short notice to change the course of action which had been carefully mapped out in advance. There is also a one-track-mindedness which does not permit an over-all view or consideration of the various ramifications of problems or peripheral aspects of a problem. Naïveté and simplicity have been reflected time and again by the military particularly in dealing with complex political and economic problems.

In ideology, the military tends to be conservative and reactionary although at times it has exhibited radicalism of unusual variety. These traits are not conducive to the development of flexibility or the philosophy of compromise or give-and-take so necessary in politics. Tōjō admitted during the Tokyo War Crimes trial that the military were not sophisticated in the ways of politics and that they were not politicians.[43]

Intellectuals

That segment of the middle class which goes by the name of intelligentsia is far from homogeneous for it includes among others such professionals as doctors, health officials, lawyers, government

[43] Nihon Gaiko Gakkai, *Taiheiyo Senso Gen'in Ron,* pp. 102–103.

officials, inventors, and technicians who are trained in scientific, technical, legal, and administrative skills but are quite different in their outlook, attitudes, mode of thought from those whose activities are more in the nature of emotional and intellectual exercises such as professors, scholars, authors, religious and social workers. However, certain generalizations would apply to these intellectuals.

In general it may be said that intellectuals are detached and remote from the actual developments in the social environment and although they are the forerunners of new ideas they fail to really assimilate and make them a part of their intellectual equipment. On the whole they have tended to be very theoretical and abstract, having acquired their knowledge, for the most part, without the benefit of empirical methods. Japanese intellectuals are known for their strong Marxist bias, the pristine, theoretical, bookish brand of Marxism unrelated to operational Communism. They are conceptually disorganized and divided within themselves largely as a consequence of the disorderly juxtaposition of Western ideas and their own traditional ideas. The attitude of these intellectuals is one of passivity, negativism, and contemplative inaction. Not a few of them take refuge in activities which are removed entirely from the social realities and live in daydreams. Another group tries to find escape in an attempt to transplant at home the sort of life they enjoyed so much while abroad. There is also a new type of intellectuals who rose from the ranks of the working class to become labor leaders.

Intellectuals have demonstrated that by and large, by temperament and by training, they are not suited for careers in the hurly-burly of politics either as party leaders or elective office holders. But there is quite another reason for their being limited to partial participation in politics. With the possible exception of lawyers, their functions cannot easily be delegated to or performed by substitutes the way those of businessmen and industrialists can, especially in the higher echelons. Intellectuals have to do their own work of thinking, writing, or research in making their living. However, their services have been sought especially as consultants and advisers in the education of the public, as "brain trusters" to give advice to those in power, and also as executives and secretaries in labor unions and political parties. They have been particularly effective in their function of political criticism and sparking movements aimed at the achievement of social reforms and democracy.

The intellectuals have been particularly effective in bestirring the public to action through criticisms, protests, memorials, and representations, and even by needling the government into action. Professors, students, writers, and journalists have left indelible marks on the course of political development and not infrequently have shaped the political forces. Their effectiveness in stirring up public opinion is exemplified in the success of the seven Tokyo University professors who virtually forced the government to quit wavering and make up its mind to go to war with Russia in 1904. The leadership in the movement for democracy by Professor Yoshino Sakuzo in 1917 is a demonstration of the decisive role played by an intellectual. But the part played by the numerous intellectuals in the social democratic movement of the 1920's is convincing proof of the valuable contributions made to the beginning of the process of political maturation.

Quasi-Intellectuals

There is a borderline or marginal group, which lies between the intellectuals proper and the working class, that has come to be known as the quasi-intellectuals,[44] a term used by Professor Maruyama Masao of Tokyo University who regards this group as the social backbone of the Japanese fascist movement.[45] Included in this are small factory owners, factory foremen, building contractors, retail store owners, master-carpenters, small landowners, independent farmers, elementary school teachers, village and town office employees, lower echelon government workers, and Buddhist and Shinto priests. This group which is regarded as a part of the middle class actually constitutes the backbone of the nation and, as distinguished from the intellectuals, forms the activist element which can be readily stimulated into action. It assumes the initiative in their respective spheres of everyday activity in the shops, factories, schools, and other places of work in a paternalistic way, influencing and controlling the thought and personality development of those who work for or under them.

The ideological impact of the powers-that-be reaches the masses after passing through this group of quasi-intellectuals whose bias and interpretation are transmitted as a matter of course. Although the group acquires information and knowledge of a fragmentary and

[44] See Hidaka Rokuro, *Nihonjin no Shiso to Ishiki,* pp. 66–67.

[45] A similar conclusion is reached by Dr. Else Brunswik who states: "Totalitarian movements have had a special appeal to the lower middle class. Members of this class are typically authoritarian. They exaggerate their idealization of their own and their depreciation of alien groups; they have a primitive attitude toward outsiders." Else Brunswik, "A Study of Prejudice in Children," *Human Relations,* vol. I (1948), pp. 295–306.

incomplete sort through the mass media of communication, they are the relatively well-informed individuals in their communities and are the ones who express some sort of opinion on every political, economic, and social problem. Socially this group is integrated with the working class, but culturally it forms the bottom layer of the intellectual group. It is conservative, reactionary, retrogressive, highly patriotic, and even ultranationalistic.[46] It is from this group that the ultranationalists of the 1930's came. The participants in the May 15, 1932 incident in which Premier Inukai was assassinated and the February 26, 1936, incident in which Premier Okada barely escaped but several others were assassinated were from this group. This is the group which has produced the noncommissioned officers of the armed forces, the police officers, the lowest echelon of government officials, and the elementary school teachers. In fact, it has been the hotbed of extremism.[47] Significantly and oddly enough, this group has not really developed a mind of its own; instead, it has been manipulated and controlled from above.

The Working Class

In Japan, both the factory and mine workers are recruits from the rural farm community. In the mining industry the laborers are at the most only three generations removed from the rural villages of their origin. The factory workers are only two generations removed at most. The largest percentage of factory workers is made up of those who recently left the farms, and a great many of them still move back and forth between the farm and the factory seasonally. Consequently, although there is a noticeable difference between a farm worker and a factory worker in the type of labor they perform, their ideas and attitudes and even their problems are basically the same. Although this group has traditionally been the most docile, it has begun to bestir itself very noticeably since the end of World War II, as a result of the development of labor unions and attendant political activities.

POLITICAL MOTIVATION

Generalizations about the motives of those who go into politics can serve a useful purpose but there are obvious limitations. It is always difficult to determine what factors have been the most decisive. Many individuals find themselves in politics not as the result of forethought and planning but quite accidentally and unintention-

[46] Tanaka Sogoro, *Nihon no Seito*, pp. 27–28.
[47] Nakamura Akira, *Chishiki Kaikyu no Seijiteki Tachiba*, p. 177.

ally. This is particularly true in Japan where few people ever start with the idea of making a career out of politics, as frequently happens in the United States. Politics does not yet have the lure it has in some other countries.[48] The average person does not care to be a politician, for the profession of politics still is not considered to be on the same high level as science, medicine, teaching, or business. Even the legal profession has a long way to go before it can command the respect of the average person who is usually suspicious of lawyers who have not altogether lived down the shyster reputation acquired in the early days. But politicians are regarded as low as, if not several notches lower than, the lawyers in the eyes of the man in the street. This is bound to change, of course, but only slowly, just as the profession of acting came to be respected only in recent years. In the period following World War II, however, politics has become a stepping stone to success for ambitious young officials as well as to party men, and the desire to hold public office has become widespread though not yet universal.

Chance seems to play a very important part in getting people into politics, as for example having friends or family friends in the game. Among the leaders of the radical parties there are a large number who became interested in social and labor problems during college days when they participated actively in the extremely popular campus study-discussion groups led by professors. Others got into politics via the labor movement in which they have worked up to the position of leadership. Regardless of the way in which they got in, almost without exception, they have all discovered the fascination of politics. A prominent politician confessed that he "likes politics better than eating" and that politics has become part of his very fiber and existence after having gone through ten elections.[49] Something similar seems to have happened to former Prime Minister Yoshida who took over rather hesitantly, if not reluctantly, the presidency of the Liberal Party when Hatoyama was purged and forced to give up the position. Later when Hatoyama was depurged and wanted to repossess the presidency, Yoshida refused to relinquish it. When the Diet passed a no-confidence resolution in March, 1953, for having called a Diet member a "stupid fool" for persistent quizzing

---

[48] Frank R. Kent, in discussing American politics, says that "it has its lure for the highest and the lowest and the gate is ajar for all. It means honor and glory to some, power and prestige to others, opportunity for public service to a few, a chance to enrich themselves to more, a living to most." *Political Behavior*, p. 229.

[49] Mizutani Chosaburo, "Seikai no katasumi no beddo ni," *Seikai Orai*, March, 1953, pp. 8–10.

of the Prime Minister, Yoshida dissolved the House and demonstrated clearly to the public that he was determined to hang on tenaciously to the premiership and to the party presidency as well.

The annals of Japanese politics are full of interesting cases of reluctant, confused novices stepping into the political arena for the first time, full of doubts and fears, and developing after years of experience into seasoned veterans thoroughly versed in political strategy and stratagems, who are not happy unless they are right in the thick of political battles.   This is undoubtedly the result of having tasted power and found its exercise pleasant and gratifying.

For Japanese politicians and men in public life, the most impelling force which drives them is their vaulting ambition to achieve glory and honor resulting from the education and indoctrination to which they have been subjected.   There is a popular saying that when a tiger dies he leaves his skin behind but man leaves his name.   Even a man like General Tanaka, who had already distinguished himself as a military man, was motivated by the desire for fame and glory in his behavior and action as prime minister and president of the Seiyukai party in the late 1920's.   Since the way to achieve glory is to obtain power,[50] politics becomes the major vehicle for the acquisition and exercise of power.   Prestige, approbation, pleasure, ease, and affluence can be the rewards.   Like many other peoples, and particularly the French, the Japanese are obsessed by the desire to be cabinet ministers.   It is this almost pathological craving for a ministerial post more than anything else that makes politicians, and even bureaucrats, eager to become members of the Diet. Membership in the Diet is looked upon by most politicians as merely a stepping stone to a post in the cabinet and ultimately the premiership. Once a person has actually served as a minister he can forever thereafter be identified as such and regarded as having the privileges and prestige of the post, in much the same way that senators, judges, and generals in the United States are always known and even addressed as such long after their services have actually terminated.

Position and prestige attainable through politics normally cannot be maintained in style unless political power is employed in a manner that will enable the politician to achieve, maintain, and increase affluence.   Consequently a substantial degree of wealth or economic security becomes a strongly desirable, if not indispensable, condition in the life of a politician.   The personal drive for power is kept alive, if not increased, by a politician out of the need to insure his own

---

[50] Bertrand Russell points out that, as a rule, the easiest way to obtain glory is to obtain power. *Power*, p. 11.

preservation; he soon finds that security is a precarious affair and feels that he must acquire more power to secure that which he has obtained. Thus the perpetual and restless desire of power after power continues on indefinitely.

Politicians who look at politics primarily as an opportunity for public service are still few and far between. The average politician will not easily or willingly sacrifice his career in the public interest; nor is he overly concerned about principles or the means he employs to attain his goals. Practically all of them are in politics as a means directly or indirectly of realizing a life of greater affluence, influence, prestige, and honor. Some remain in politics and work up into the inner core of the party leadership while many leave to enter, or return to, the professions of their choice, taking along with them whatever honor, prestige, or influence they acquired while "politicking." The lure of public office is no less to businessmen, bankers, and lawyers who are comfortably well off in a financial way.

POLITICAL MODUS OPERANDI

Modes of action in politics are essentially methods which are used in society as a whole, though perhaps employed with a degree of refinement and even subtlety at times but with ruthless vigor and nakedness at other times. They are no more, no less, than the situational manifestation of the social traits of a people in action in the rough-and-tumble of politics, where frequently the best as well as the worst in people is put on exhibition. The immunity which the lawmakers enjoy on the floor of the Diet no doubt has contributed at least in part to the generally unrestrained behavior that is quite frequently on display, in full view of the public.

Group or consensus action having been more the norm in Japanese social behavior for centuries left little, if any, room for individualistic behavior which is regarded as subversive to the closely knit social fabric, particularly to the family system. The people show a natural propensity for consulting one another on anything that is important or cannot easily be decided by an individual. This gives rise inevitably to the practice as well as the psychology of joint responsibility. It also produces a system in which there is a plenitude of advisers and consultants in every type of activity involving decision making of some sort. Hardly any group worthy of the name would ever think of operating without advisers; public and private organizations in the villages, towns, municipalities, national government departments, professional associations, and economic organizations must all have their advisers and consultants.

Indirection is the method which is used universally, although in the nations of the West it is the direct method that is normally preferred and used more frequently. In Asian, particularly East Asian, countries the indirect method is favored over the direct approach. It is more to the liking of the Japanese people and is used constantly by everyone. Even in the mode of expression, it is the vague, roundabout manner of "beating around the bush" that is acceptable rather than the blunt point-blank approach. An integral part of the technique of indirection is the intricate system of intermediary or go-between which is employed in social, economic, and political affairs. Almost no negotiation is ever begun without the use of an intermediary in some form or other. If a go-between is not used in initiating a negotiation, one is certainly brought in at some stage of progress. This is a necessary safeguard against the loss of face which is such a serious matter that it is scrupulously avoided where humanly possible. It is a practice which has made possible the rise of the go-betweens, fixers, wirepullers, and influence peddlers of all sorts in Japanese politics. These behind-the-scene operators go by various names, the most common being *kuromaku, sakushi,* or *kaoyaku.* Political bosses are able to operate effectively and thrive because of the extensive use of indirection which helps to preserve anonymity to a remarkable degree. Hidden power, or anonymous responsibility as it is called, is a kind of political irresponsibility which can and does stem from this system to the detriment of the democratic process.

Although indirection is the accepted method under normal conditions, direct action comes to the fore when normal channels of action are either closed or deemed to be too cumbersome or ineffective to produce the desired results. Direct action is definitely a deviation from the accepted norm of behavior by an individual or a part of a group which acts on its own responsibility and initiative even though it is a contravention of the rules of society. However, it is usually condoned by the public if the motivation is laudable. Direct action is drastic but it is not aberrant behavior in terms of the existing social framework and it carries with it a sort of social, if not legal, sanction. Certain forms of direct action were not only condoned but even encouraged by the feudal authorities during the Tokugawa period in the name of honor. It was looked upon as an acceptable substitute for justice. Direct action has been regarded more or less as a method of breaking through the rigid formalities of the feudal social and political procedure. Moreover, it had the tacit sanction of "the end justifies the means" philosophy which has been common in Japan and other Asian countries. Direct action is resorted to now, as in the past, with full awareness of its consequences.

Accommodation

Consultation, the normal procedure in the decision-making process, enables one to poll views informally and obtain in advance a consensus in social and political matters to aid in the adoption of the best possible course of action. This is actually a phase of accommodation which is an indispensable method of operation in a closely knit social organization where constant efforts are necessary to preserve harmony by preventing and resolving clashes. When clashes occur, compromises are achieved through some sort of mediation or even arbitration which are part and parcel of Japanese social life.

A very high degree of social cohesion or solidarity obtains in Japanese life.[51] However, the people all subject themselves voluntarily to strict self-discipline and self-restraint in order to minimize social conflicts. Their obsession for harmony has been exploited frequently for political purposes. It is this attitude which underlies the practice of stressing acceptability as the decisive criterion in the choice of political leaders. This has the effect invariably of narrowing down the choice to the least objectionable, rather than the most desirable, person. An acceptable candidate in politics within the social framework would be regarded as a man with personality and stature who is impartial and moderate, a man who has few enemies, if any, and is a harmonizing influence in bringing together various competing factions. He may not necessarily be the best man from the point of view of ability, efficiency, intelligence, or astuteness.

An appeal to moderation is very effective in resolving conflicts and the government as well as other groups have invoked it time and again to bring divided factions together. Combined with an appeal to unity and solidarity and supported with such a question as, "What would the world think of such behavior?," it has never failed to work in times of national emergency. Because of high sensitivity to situational realism, the people are quick to recognize the futility of struggling against any force that is beyond control and cannot be successfully coped with, and they accommodate themselves to the inevitable without much ado. There is, interestingly enough, still a strong reluctance to insist on legal rights against one another or to carry disputes into the courts for fear that they would have to bear

[51] Yanagida Kunio, "Japan's Social Solidarity," *Contemporary Japan* (1934–35), 3: 388–97.

the stigma of not being able to adjust and settle their differences the way accommodating human beings ought to.

Conversion

Of all the techniques familiar to the Japanese, conversion is probably most frequently and successfully employed in every conceivable activity and particularly in politics. Moral suasion is an unusually potent weapon in the hands of a people who thrive on moralizing. The obsession for unanimity in decision making which is an aspect of their love of harmony frequently works in a curious way when applied to concrete situations. Whenever possible, which is practically all the time, decisions are made final only when unanimity is obtained even though it is forced and may actually be more in form than in spirit and substance. But that does not matter. Technically there may be dissenters, but as long as they do not register opposition it is quite enough to satisfy the passion for unanimity. Or if it is a small group, the majority will work on the dissenting minority until they are "converted" to the majority point of view either by moral suasion or even veiled threats.

Conversion has been achieved traditionally through example and exhortation which are part of the Confucian way which has not yet gone out of style altogether. Exhortation is still used though perhaps not nearly as much as it used to be. The two most powerful techniques which are being used most consistently and effectively today are education and propaganda. These methods were adopted at the beginning of the Meiji period when the nation embarked upon a carefully planned program of modernization. During the 1930's in particular, they were employed with telling effect by ultranationalists and the militarists because of the special vulnerability of the people to emotional appeals based largely on political myths and powerful symbols. Regimentation of the populace has been a rather simple task for those in control of the educational system and the mass media of communication.

Coercion

No government or political organization can function without resort to coercion in some form. However, the form it takes may not be recognized at times. Here we shall touch upon a few of the more important coercive techniques employed by individuals and groups in political activities to keep the individuals in line and under control.

Ridicule is one of the most potent social weapons in community life. To be laughed at is far more painful to an individual who feels the pangs of shame than the mere payment of a monetary fine which does not attract any widespread attention and may not even be noticed by the community. Another method which is commonly used is rejection which exists on various levels and with varying severity. A useless, wayward, prodigal son is expelled, disowned, or disinherited by a father who is head of the family. The family or the individual that has outraged the community may be subjected to ostracism (*mura hachibu*) by the joint decision of the entire village. A member of a party can be read out of it for intransigence or disloyalty. In its most extreme form, coercion in politics could take the form of assassination which is not legally sanctioned but not infrequently is morally condoned. This is understandable in the light of feudal practices and even in the light of nineteenth-century European attitudes. The celebrated nineteenth-century Swiss political scientist, J. K. Bluntschli, believed that murder was admissible in politics when it was not committed for base and personal motives but for the lasting security and prosperity of society and when it was necessary to that end.[52] This was almost exactly the reasoning used by the defense in the trial of the participants in the attempted coup d'état in the 1930's when ultranationalists were resorting to direct action. The public showed strong sympathy for those on trial because of their protestation of high motive, namely, the desire to save the nation from the corruptive forces at work.

There is another very frequently used method which is nonviolent in nature. Its effectiveness lies in "ignoring" or refusal to take cognizance of a fact in social and political life. It carries the implication that, whatever it is, it is not worth even the slightest attention. It is also based on the attitude that only fools respond to the provocations or proposals of a fool. *Mokusatsu* may be a refusal to accept a protest, proposal, advice, or even an ultimatum. In effect, it could be snobbery or insult coldly calculated to unnerve or disconcert the victim.

[52] Bendetto Croce, *Politics and Morals*, p. 88.

4

Dynamics of
Japanese Politics

Whether we agree with Lord Acton that power is evil, degrading, and demoralizing, or with Charles E. Merriam that political power is important for the individual personality and for the social group,[1] the fact remains that it has always existed in society in all ages and in all places and will continue to operate. Force is an ever present element in society. Every man and woman uses one or more forms (force of mind, force of body, and force of wealth) to obtain dominion over others, to live more securely, and to satisfy his or her desires. A political power situation inevitably "arises from the need of some form of equilibrium, adjustment, *modus vivendi* between the various groups and individuals of the community"[2] and exists as an admixture of coercion and cooperation.

The attitude toward power manifested by individuals has varied greatly from place to place and from time to time. Neither Hobbes nor Machiavelli found the manifestation of power obnoxious for they considered it to be a perfectly natural drive common to all men. But the sensibilities of men like Henry Adams and Lord Acton were outraged beyond repair, leading them to disavow power as an unmitigated evil and retreat from it completely. The problem of politics today is that of controlling power by keeping its operation within reasonable bounds and by channeling and utilizing the power drive for constructive ends, for, as Bertrand Russell has indicated, man

[1] Charles E. Merriam, *Political Power* (1950), p. 10.
[2] *Ibid.*, p. 21.

is driven by desires which are essentially boundless and insatiable and chief among them are the desires for power and glory.[3]

Even if we may not go as far as Merriam that "no single factor in life will be more important than the composition and incidence of political power, and no task more urgent than the understanding and utilization of a force whose mastery may mean light or darkness for individuals and for civilization,"[4] we recognize the impelling need of focusing our attention on the nature, source, and manifestation of political power. We are aware, however, of the impossibility of measuring power relationships. Only a general delineation may be attempted successfully.

JAPANESE APPROACH TO POLITICS

It has been pointed out that the American approach to politics is still largely legal, formal, structural, and mechanical, with the main emphasis on legal forms rather than on social or economic realities and on political machinery rather than on functional aspects.[5] Among the politicians in the United States there is still an overwhelming preponderance of lawyers. The predominant influence of lawyers in American politics has provided the world's foremost example of government by lawyers.[6] This accounts largely for the legalistic bent of the members of Congress in their attitude and actions on both foreign and domestic policies.

Japanese politics have been conditioned much more directly by economic and social realities and have been relatively unaffected by legalistic and mechanistic concepts of government. This is reflected in the fact that there are more businessmen and industrialists than lawyers among the politicians. Business and industry send their representatives into the inner circles of the parties and furnish funds for political activities, particularly election funds. There is little of the *sub rosa* variety of political activities, for much of the struggle for power now goes on in full public view. The pattern of Japanese politics is a simple one. Politicians with their followers (supporters) confront one another in the struggle for power and fight or make peace after shrewdly calculating the profit or loss in every situation.[7]

While the Japanese approach to politics tends definitely toward

[3] Bertrand Russell, *Power*, p. 9.

[4] Merriam, *op. cit.*, p. 144.

[5] William G. Carleton, "Are We Politically Adolescent?," *The American Scholar*, Winter, 1946–1947.

[6] E. Schattschneider, *Party Government*, pp. 11–12.

[7] Maeda, Tamon, "Seito no naifun," *Asahi*, February 25, 1953.

the practical and utilitarian, it lacks the mellowness or the political genius of the English, for politics in the Western sense is such a new game to the Japanese that they have not yet mastered it as well as Western sports like baseball at which they are now quite adept. Since politics is not only new but also alien and Western in origin, the ground rules have not yet been firmly established. As a consequence the political "free-for-all" with no holds barred is common and occasions little surprise. This is in sharp contrast to the elaborate rules governing social relations which regulate their behavior. While the ideal of compromise is held high and practiced quite successfully in social relations, it cannot be said truthfully that the same condition obtains in the political sphere as yet.

The Japanese approach seems to lie somewhere between the English and the French. It was English political genius that perfected the parliamentary form of government and gave it to the world. Yet it remained for Montesquieu, a Frenchman, to crystallize the tenets of English political philosophy and define the principle of separation of powers. What seems to appeal most strongly to the Japanese is neither a highly practical approach nor a very theoretical approach but a middle ground or a combination of both. Yet while they speak of agreement in principle, they find it difficult to devise satisfactory working arrangements. However, in this respect, they usually do not go to such extremes as the French among whom divergencies of views are so great and irreconcilable that they are forever seeking formulas which in turn are loaded down with qualifications and reservations.

If, as it has been said, France comes closer to being governed by intellectuals[8] than any other country, Japan is governed by businessmen, industrialists, and financiers, and those who represent their ideas and interests. Only in the Socialist and Communist parties do intellectuals really enjoy the prestige and carry the weight commensurate with their social position. In Japanese politics there is no tendency as in France to overindulge in the luxury of thinking for themselves as individuals even at the expense of national unity. Since there exists no highly developed taste for philosophical disputation, politics is not burdened with intense intellectual activity of the sort which encourages quibbling over almost imperceptible shades or divergences of opinion.

[8] The French love of the intellectual is reflected in their unshakable faith in rationalism which is tantamount to a cult of reason and also in the names they give to warships, such as Diderot, Voltaire, and Condorcet. See M. Demiashkevich, *The National Mind*, pp. 188, 190.

The French seem to be hampered by an inability to readily organize in politics[9] because a Frenchman is a rabid individualist who lives for himself, not for the body politic, and abhors everything which might seem like discipline or restraint.[10] The Japanese find that their difficulty is overorganization and the multiplicity of political organizations. Shifts in party membership and splintering of parties are occurring constantly in Japan. But these shifts and splinters are not caused by the intensity of political beliefs and sentiments but by the intensity of personal feeling and loyalty to a leader. Intensity of political sentiment precludes the development of real political issues in France where politicians, who are more theoretical than practical, are inclined to pursue an ideal and reluctant to give up any part of it for the sake of attaining the things which lie within their reach.[11] Friendly compromise and cooperation between opposing political parties rarely occur in France.[12] In contrast, an Englishman's tenacity of purpose is tempered by a readiness to admit reasonable compromise. In other words, obstinate resistance happily exists side by side with his aptitude for compromise.

In Japan real political issues rarely develop because the politicians are preoccupied with personal relationships to the practical disregard of issues, and not because of a relentless and uncompromising pursuit of an ideal with the "all or nothing" attitude of the French. In the matter of compromise they come closer to the English than to the French.

In general, a Frenchman is quite likely to arrive at the comprehension of a thing by means of classification and by the deductive method while an Englishman depends on the inductive method by the sheer accumulation of a mass of facts and evidences.[13] A Japanese is predisposed by tradition and training more toward the deductive method but not completely so. The political leaders, and even the people in general, show definite preference for the exercise of common sense, relying on the accumulated and proven wisdom of the race rather than on all sorts of magic formulas, utopian ideas, and panaceas. But the Robinson Crusoe type of resourcefulness and self-reliance which exemplifies the English national character has yet to develop in the management of practical affairs in Japan.

[9] A. L. Lowell, *Governments of France, Italy and Germany,* pp. 82–83.

[10] René Sedillot, "Why Frenchmen Don't Pay Taxes," *New York Times,* Magazine Section, September 6, 1953, p. 14.

[11] A. L. Lowell, *op. cit.,* p. 81.

[12] M. Demiashkevich, *op. cit.,* pp. 243–244.

[13] H. Taine, *Notes on England* (1872), p. 307.

In contrast to the average Englishman's instinctive abhorrence of violent methods in political and economic struggle,[14] the Japanese, not having had the political experience and maturity of the English, would tolerate and condone a considerable degree of violence. They are not averse to a good fight even on the floor of the Diet, as witnessed in the melee of June, 1954, which was deplored by the press. Although assassinations have not taken place since the mid-1930's, they cannot be regarded as having been abandoned entirely.

It would not be possible for a Japanese politician to be elected to office on the basis of eloquence as in France because the people do not place such inordinate value on the ability to speak and are not easily carried away by brilliant oratory. They have more in common with the English in their distrust and suspicion of a glib tongue. A scoundrel is more likely than not to be extremely eloquent for in the Japanese mind eloquence is not equated with truth and sincerity but with their opposites. They elect a public man, as the Germans used to, on moral solidity and philosophical attitudes and are not interested in or influenced by looks or oratory. As with the English, there is also an innate shyness, a cultural trait, which does not make the Japanese brilliant and effortless conversationalists like the French. Also like the English, they do not know how to amuse themselves by means of conversation.[15]

Japanese politics has never suffered from anything like the rationalism of the French who are inclined to believe that reason is the only reliable regulator of life.[16] The Frenchman's exaggerated belief in the unfailing efficacy of formulas is reflected in the attitude of the French masses who show faith in the power of the leaders to solve intricate problems by a simple rationalistic formula, especially if it possesses the deceptive appearance of quasi-mathematical neatness and exactitude.[17] Such a cult of reason is unknown to the Japanese. Any attitude even resembling intellectualism on the part of a politician would be resented, much as an exhibition of cleverness, "brain," or "high-brow" by any public man is deplored in English politics.[18] Lucidity and logic as such do not necessarily constitute political or even social assets any more than they do in England. Japanese con-

---

[14] For example, the first attempt in English history to use the weapon of general strike by the Labor Party on May 3, 1926, failed because of the Englishman's dislike for violence.

[15] H. Taine, *op. cit.*, p. 321.

[16] M. Demiashkevich, *op. cit.*, p. 182.

[17] E. Faure, *The Spirit of the Forms*, p. 120.

[18] M. Demiashkevich, *op. cit.*, p. 148.

versation, like that of the English, is notable for reserve, subtle reticences, and evasive circumlocutions.

Although they have been trying for some time now, the Japanese have not yet developed such a high degree of skill in the manner of presenting things. The French, of course, show consummate skill in devising political formulas and slogans with tremendous appeal and although a politician's actions are soon forgotten, a phrase made by him or about him often becomes a part of him.[19] Their fondness for slogans goes back at least to the French Revolution when the great triad "Liberty, Equality, Fraternity" was coined. Japanese politicians will very likely never equal the French, but they have shown a great fondness for slogans though not necessarily for formulas.

CATEGORICAL IMPERATIVES: THE FORCES OF POLITICS

Independence

It is a truism that the indispensable *sine qua non* of the state are land, people, and sovereignty. The continued existence of the state depends on the preservation of all these three elements none of which is dispensable. It is in the course of the preservation of national life that the driving forces of politics are generated. These forces make up the sum total of the political, social, economic, and psychocultural needs of the nation.

Independence, or territorial integrity, which is motivated by the strongest of human instincts, the instinct of self-preservation, must be jealously guarded. Japan's fear for her safety and independence was never so strongly felt as in the middle of the nineteenth century when the nation was reopened to the world in the face of the strong nationalism and expansionist trend of the West. Her fear of Western aggression was inspired by what was taking place in China, her great neighbor, during and after the Opium War. Both the antiforeign and pro-Western elements in the country were strong proponents of Japan's independence but they differed on the question of what policy to pursue. The former believed in keeping out the foreigners. The latter who were the progressives believed that the adoption of Western civilization was an inevitable as well as an urgent condition not only for the preservation of independence but for national progress as well.

The view which held that the renovation of Japanese society through the adoption of the desirable features of Western civilization was imperative prevailed, and modernization on a national scale was

[19] M. Demiashkevich, *op. cit.*, p. 234.

undertaken, resulting in the adoption of the capitalistic system as well as the production techniques of the West, in order to insure the nation's survival. The national goal was to meet the Western powers on equal footing and to cope with the problems resulting from the relations with them. Internal developments and politics were geared to this all-important goal of preserving national independence and achieving equality with the West.

Once the task of modernizing and strengthening the country was achieved, fear for national security rapidly receded into the background. The growing strength and confidence of the new nation gave rise to expansion which led inexorably to a world war from which she could not emerge victorious. Thus a whole century after her reopening, as the result of her defeat in World War II and subsequent military occupation of the country and the polarization of the world into two powerful opposing forces, Japan once again is impelled by fear for her safety.

No nation can hold itself together for long without self-respect or national pride based upon a heritage worthy of preservation and cultivation along with a record of achievements. Something of uniqueness must be found in the nation's past to bolster national pride. The Japanese have discovered it in their concept of *kokutai*, or national polity, which embraces and symbolizes all that is glorious in the nation's past, that can be cherished as their proud heritage. Although the term was used frequently even before 1868, in rescripts, decrees, and public documents of other types, it was not a legal concept; it was used rather in an historical, ethical sense.[20] It was on this that both nationalism and patriotism were firmly based and nourished. It was in the concept of *kokutai* that the aspirations, hopes, and fears of the nation were inextricably tied together and the uniqueness of the nation stressed and glorified.

Independence would be hollow and without real meaning until and unless a nation enjoyed equality, not merely in name but in fact as well. For decades, the Japanese leaders fought for equality which they won at least legally in 1899. But the struggle to achieve real equality continued thereafter, only to be interrupted by the outbreak of the Pacific War. The struggle for equality, though in a somewhat different sense, is once more the national goal in the period of post-World War II. The lack of a feeling of equality on the part of the Japanese leaders was reflected in their inferiority complex, which was not so identified by them but was overcompensated for by the ideas and actions of the military and ultranationalists of the 1930's.

[20] Minobe Tatsukichi, *Shin Kempo Gairon* (supplemented by Miyazawa Toshiyoshi), pp. 1–2 (preface).

Not the least of the problems confronted by the nation is its security against external as well as internal dangers. The problem was initially met squarely with the setting up of a national defense system in the 1870's and for the next three quarters of a century Japan was able to provide completely for her own self-defense. With the defeat in 1945, however, she was stripped completely of her military force. But the outbreak of the Korean War in 1950 started her back on the path to remilitarization rather reluctantly. Thus, since 1952, the political picture in Japan has been colored by the question of rearmament and once more military problems have become one of the major issues of national politics which will undoubtedly have a profound influence on the future course Japan will follow.

Economic Viability

The fact that economic well-being is essential to the security and independence of a nation needs no elaborate argument. As a "have not" nation in the age of industrialization, the problem of national economic viability has been the greatest headache to Japan. The very limited land area and the paucity of natural resources, particularly the essential raw materials for an industrialized economy, have been the source of national anxiety particularly in the face of rapidly mounting population pressure.

It was the population pressure, which first began to attract the attention of the Japanese government as well as the outside world toward the close of the decade following World War I, which served as the basis of the expansionist policies of the military in the 1930's.[21] Dr. Warren S. Thompson is convinced that "as long as there is a basis for a growing feeling within a nation that it is being made to suffer unjust hardships as compared with more fortunate peoples, it will not be difficult to arouse a strong sentiment favoring aggressive action."[22] Today it still constitutes one of the dangerous and explosive factors of Japanese politics.[23] During the 1930's, which was a

[21] G. D. H. Cole in his *Introduction to Economic History 1750–1950* (1952) has this to say regarding Japan's expansion: "With a narrow and infertile territory and a rapidly growing population, Japan felt even more strongly than the Western countries the impulsion towards a policy of militant imperialist expansion." (p. 108)

[22] Warren S. Thompson, "The Need for a Population Policy in Japan," *American Sociological Review*, XV (February 1950), p. 32.

[23] Warren S. Thompson, the eminent American authority on population problems, believes that "population pressure contributes to the heightening of international tension and may be considered a potential cause of war." See "The Need for a Population Policy in Japan," *American Sociological Review*, XV (February 1950), pp. 25–33.

decade of strong economic nationalism throughout the world, there was advocacy among the Japanese for fair and unobstructed access to the world's raw materials and markets, if not the equitable distribution of the world's resources.

Now in the post-World War II era, the Japanese nation is confronted with economic problems of unprecedented magnitude. As a consequence of defeat, she found herself economically prostrate with the greater part of her industrial capacity destroyed and all of her colonies lost, reducing her territory to about 55 percent of what it was formerly. Unable to stand on her own economic feet, she has been maintaning herself largely with economic assistance from the outside, chiefly from the United States. What must be achieved by the nation is the ability to support herself without depending upon outside economic assistance.

From a purely domestic point of view, the gravity of the nation's economic plight has pushed economic problems to the very forefront of politics. Nothing of importance exists today in the realm of politics which is not economic in nature. On the domestic front, there are numerous serious economic problems which are crying for solution. Security and independence along with the stabilization of national livelihood, which are predominantly economic in nature, have been of greatest concern to the people. They provided the key issues in the general elections of October, 1952, and April, 1953.

There is the pressing need for a more equitable distribution of wealth as well as opportunities, although the masses have not yet risen in revolt against existing conditions. It has become clearer than ever that the urgent task of Japanese politics is to bring about such a change without any catastrophic consequences. This task is an extremely difficult one but it must be tackled with determination and without delay.

Mounting Popular Demand for Participation in the Exercise of Political Power

There is no cleavage of any kind within the nation over the urgent need to achieve a sound and viable national economy. On the issue of national prosperity the nation is united as one. It is with regard to the question of how this prosperity should be spread out and what means should be used to achieve such a distribution that conflicts arise in Japanese politics. The strong desire for profit by business and industry frequently comes in direct conflict with those who are determined to push policies which would result in a more equitable distribution of the nation's wealth and in the raising of the standard of living for all.

The extension of the suffrage in Japan's political development was a slow and gradual process which reflected the struggle between those who would limit the participation of individuals in politics on the basis of material possessions and those who advocated the broadest possible base for political decisions. Although legally the broadest possible base for politics has already been provided for in the new Constitution, extensive participation by the people in political decisions has not yet been achieved. And before this happens there will take place in the arena of practical politics skirmishes and clashes of all sorts. Political stability which is much needed will remain unachieved until the gap which exists between the constitutional and legal provisions and political reality is closed.

It is from the process of meeting these three impelling needs discussed above that the principal driving forces of Japanese politics are generated. These imperatives have provided the background against which issues have been raised and fought over in the incessant contest for the control of political power.

STRUGGLE FOR POWER

Politics is an unceasing and continual process in which the social needs of both individuals and groups are translated into public policy. As such, it is a substitute for force and a method of living and working together in peace in the face of diversities and conflicts which are ever present in the community. With individuals and groups seeking to exercise government power or to influence those who exercise such power, it is quite natural to find that "tensions and emergencies are of the essence of politics."[24]

In the incessant struggle for power, the "political situation is a moving equilibrium, a continuous reintegration or reorganization of changing factors, working not only from within but also from without the group."[25] The political situation is vastly complicated by rivalries and conflicts arising from the clash of interests. Regional differences not only in economic needs but in the temperamental make-up of the people have been the cause of misunderstanding and resentment. Cleavages among industrialists arise from the difference in their specialization. Competition creates tension among corporations engaged in similar enterprises. Political parties find themselves at

[24] Charles E. Merriam, *The Role of Politics in Social Change*, p. 36.
[25] *Ibid.*, p. 104.

loggerheads in their contest to capture government power. Families are pitted against families in the relentless pursuit of power and prestige. Struggle for power is manifested in multifarious ways: capital *v.* labor, government *v.* business, government *v.* labor, the Diet *v.* government, bureaucracy *v.* the Diet. At the same time a vertical struggle for power is going on in each and every one of these groups. It is out of these complex power relationships and struggles that politics emerges. In the struggle for power the clashes are not so much over principles, goals, or substance as over the method, scope, timing, and personalities involved. Consequently there is agreement in principle as regards what needs to be done but disagreement regarding when, how, who, and how far.

Power Structure

Social power is the capacity to control the behavior of others either directly by fiat (order) or indirectly by the manipulation of available means. Status and property are two of the more conspicuous sources of power since they determine who shall hold the reins of political power.[26] But there are other sources such as office or position (party leaders, union officials, bureaucrats, executives, managers), knowledge (specialists, scientists, intellectuals), and personality.

It is a relatively simple matter to see how political power is distributed formally or legally since government is clearly set forth in the constitution and the laws of a nation. The formal instruments of power include the government or Cabinet, the Diet, political parties, and the bureaucracy. It hardly needs to be emphasized that the form of government may or may not truly reveal the distribution of power. Furthermore, it is clear that all power cannot be constitutionalized and, even if it were possible, it would not be desirable to do so if dynamic changes and growth and creative human achievements are not to be obstructed. Consequently, a great deal, if not a major part, of the power struggle is carried on outside the Diet, the political parties, and even the government.

In nearly all societies today there is a more or less privileged group or "ruling class" (*shihaiso*) which, regardless of the form of state, exercises power out of proportion to its numbers. The laws reveal where the government power resides, while the economic system shows the repository of political power. The former is legalized government power and the latter is informal political power. It is the informal power structure, which is difficult to delineate, that can provide the real key to the understanding of politics in action.

[26] R. M. MacIver, *Web of Government*, p. 94.

In spite of the adoption of a new Constitution in 1947, there has been no fundamental change in the distribution of political power in Japan. The power structure remains essentially the same as the forces at work have not changed. Human institutions are affected and modified by the forces which are exerted upon them internally and externally just as the shape, form, and development of a tree are the combined result of the forces at work, such as sunlight, wind, rain, soil, temperature, and what man or animals do to it.

Groups having considerable power over others have been the landowners, financiers, industrialists, and businessmen. This continues to be the case but there has been an increasing tendency among the workers to challenge the existing state of affairs. It has become quite evident that the managerial class and the technical experts have come to wield influence in recent years. With a higher state of technological development, there has resulted in Japan a greater concentration of political power.

Informal Organizations for Power

Economic power is the root of political power. Economics is therefore as much an instrument of politics as politics is a tool of economics. It is well known that various private groups by using economic pressure do more than any public organ to determine what the government and the public could or may do, not only in the realm of politics but even in our thoughts, tastes, and habits. In other words, they constantly exert power over the behavior patterns of a people. Economic power is translated into social power and thence into political power. Any social system reveals itself as a struggle for the control of economic power since those who possess that power are able in the measure of their possession to make their wants effective. Effective organization thus becomes the crux of this power struggle.

CAPITALIST GROUPS. With the coming of the industrial revolution, economics began to dominate the general environment and overshadow other aspects of life. There emerged a new elite of mercantile and industrial magnates. As a result, statesmanship began to react and respond to the environment of big business.

In Japan, business came to hold an important place in the power situation toward the close of the nineteenth century. Ever since, the business group has been intimately associated with the political management groups, resulting in a periodic interchange of personnel. Their concentrated economic power, especially with the growth of monopolistic capitalism, made them influential in the newer methods of effective political campaigning, in the control of the press, and even in the cruder and more direct forms of outright corruption of lawmakers and even officials. If it can be said, as it has been, that most governments act in the image of great businessmen, the Japanese political scene is dominated by the financiers who wield the greatest power in determining policy.

So far as the general public is concerned, the Japan Chamber of Commerce and Industry is undoubtedly the best known. As a nonpartisan organization, its avowed purpose is to promote the development and improvement of commerce and industry and contribute toward the advancement of the general social welfare. It is the Japanese counterpart of the Chamber of Commerce of the United States. Practically every city of more than 50,000 has its local chamber of commerce which is a constituent member of the national organization in Tokyo.[27]

Without doubt the most powerful economic body is the Federation of Economic Organizations,[28] which as the name implies is a federation of business, industrial, and financial associations. The Japan Federation of Employers' Associations (Nihon Keieisha Dantai Remmei) representing the employers' point of view, wields great influence in the realm of employer-employee relations. The Japan Management Association (Keizai Doyukai) is the fourth major body representing business interests. These are the "big four" of Japanese economic associations which by combining their resources can translate economic power more effectively into political power than all other organizations put together. It is through these economic organizations that business and financial interests apply pressure on the government and political parties. They are in the position to make the government listen to their views. This they do periodically by reacting to political changes and government policies and actions, or by transmitting their views directly and formally to the government or in informal discussion with the Prime Minister and the key cabinet ministers. Their policy proposals receive prompt attention and more often than not are adopted by the government. Heads of these organizations confer with government and party leaders, apply pressures, mediate, intercede, and perform a variety of functions of a political nature. They intercede even in the internal disputes of a political party.

[27] As of September 1, 1953, there were local chambers in 154 cities.

[28] The Keizai Dantai Rengokai has no counterpart in American economic associations since its scope is more extensive than the National Association of Manufacturers.

Business and trade associations exist in every conceivable type of economic activity, organized on the basis of type as well as geography, but they ordinarily do not play such an important role inasmuch as they do not even enter the picture in the relationship of business and government.[29] From time to time *ad hoc* organizations are set up to promote trade such as the Association to Promote Trade with Red China.

Economic interests even in the Western countries today do not enjoy as much freedom and independence within the state as they did in the nineteenth century. In spite of the power of business, financial, and industrial interests, they have been quite dependent upon politics, and Japan is no exception. In the process of translating economic power into political power, a struggle of varying intensity is taking place continuously and incessantly on ever shifting battlegrounds, though most of the actions are not visible to the public. However, there is a high degree of understanding and cooperation between the government and business, since a preponderant percentage of the business leaders especially in managerial positions come from the universities with the same training behind them as the civil service, namely, law training, and they represent a very similar outlook and viewpoint.

ORGANIZED LABOR. Labor unions have only recently become a factor in politics but when compared with Great Britain or the United States they are still in the early stages of development. It is only since World War II that labor has achieved a position of some influence. Consequently it is a long way from becoming a formidable force. Because of its newness and immaturity as well as lack of leadership, it has not reached the point of constructive participation in politics. Nevertheless its activities in politics have been conspicuous. The Left Wing Socialist Party was actually the instrument of the General Council of Japanese Labor Unions (Nihon Rodo Kumiai Sohyogikai) or Sohyo.

Before the war, the labor movement had suffered from the suppression policy of the government and the internal strife and weakness of its unions resulting in constant splitting. The suppression of the labor movement began in 1924 with the promulgation of the

[29] There are a few exceptions, however, among these may be mentioned the Japan Foreign Trade Association (Nihon Boeki Kyokai) Council of Financial Organizations (Kinyu Dantai Kyogikai), National Federation of Bankers Associations (Zenkoku Ginko Kyokai Rengokai), Japan Coal Association, Japan Steel Federation, Japan Shipowners' Association, Japan Shipbuilding Industry Association, Japan Mining Association.

Peace Preservation Law and continued vigorously in the 1930's, culminating in the dissolution of the Japan General Federation of Labor (Nihon Rodo Sodomei) in 1940 and the labor movement disappeared. In its place, the government set up the Japan Industrial Patriotic Association (Dai Nihon Sangyo Hokokukai) and developed it into a patriotic movement for its own purpose during the war.

The end of World War II brought the labor movement back to life as it was the policy of the Allied Powers to strengthen the position of labor as a means of encouraging democratic development. Labor unions mushroomed overnight after October 5, 1945.[30] Before the year was over, 855 unions had been formed with a total membership of approximately 600,000, far exceeding the prewar peak of union membership. The growth of the union membership in the next half decade was unprecedented in the history of the labor movement not only of Japan but of the world as well. The all-time record was achieved in March, 1949, when the total number of unions reached 36,507 with an aggregate membership of 6,896,208.[31] In this newly revived labor union movement, intellectuals and white-collar workers joined wholeheartedly and in force to provide knowledge and leadership for the movement in the confused postwar society. Actually the inflation had lowered the income of these classes to the level of the workers with whom they united. Government and public officials too organized themselves to strengthen their position vis-à-vis the government.

Decline in the labor movement set in visibly in 1949 with the shift in the Occupation policy which began to emphasize the building up of national economy and national strength. This resulted inevitably and naturally in de-emphasizing, if not abandoning, democratization and instead emphasizing every possible increase in production. Labor was forced into assuming a defensive position as government pressure was increased.

If the decline in the labor movement was inevitable it was because of the conditions under which it began and developed. The initiative, inspiration, and energy for democratization of which it was an integral part had all come from the outside. Since the movement was launched from above, with the necessary force and support also coming from above, there was little need or opportunity to develop within the unions themselves the kind of membership and leadership necessary for carrying on under their own power. Furthermore,

[30] Japan Seamen's Union, which was the largest before the war, was the first to re-emerge as a labor union.

[31] Suehiro Izutaro, *Nihon Rodo Kumiai Undoshi*, pp. 173–174.

since the movement flourished because of the weakness of capitalist and management groups, it was destined to recede in the face of the revival and increasing strength of capital and management and the normalization of capital-labor relationship.[32]

Like unions everywhere, the Japanese unions have as their goal the improvement of the social and economic positions and conditions of the working class which constitute their membership. Their political activities have been directed at the capitalist groups whose control over politics has been direct and powerful. It is quite natural therefore that they should affiliate themselves with those parties drawn largely from the working class, namely, the Socialist Party and the Communist Party.

Although the unions vigorously carry on their political activities, it is chiefly the leaders who are directly participating in political action. In other words, the close relationship between labor unions and political parties is largely, if not exclusively, a tie-up between the union leadership and the party leadership. There is a large chasm between the masses or rank-and-file membership and the political parties. This condition is responsible for the fact that, while the unions shout the overthrow of the reactionary conservative regime in power, the members continue to vote for conservative parties because of the existing geographic or personal bonds which are stronger than the party ties.[33]

FARMERS. In Japan's development, the farmers have at no time assumed a position of importance comparable to, or even anywhere near, that of those in the United States or France. Until only a few years ago, they were not even a factor in politics in spite of the fact that they were the taxpayers who bore the brunt of the burden in every age and in such major programs as the industrialization of the nation in the latter part of the nineteenth century. The development of agriculture, unlike that of the United States, was not based upon independent farmers who were freeholders at the same time and therefore had a powerful voice in local self-government. Consequently there has not developed in Japan a powerful political element comparable to the farm bloc fully capable of asserting its own rights. In spite of the fact that nearly half of the gainfully employed are farmers, as contrasted with not much more than 10 percent in the United States, their political power position is negligible when compared with American farmers. Politicians make no attempt to woo

[32] Sumitani Mikio, "Taishu undo ni okeru hiyaku to renzoku," *Seijigaku Nempo*, 1953, pp. 89–107.

[33] *Ibid.*, p. 104. See also Okochi Kazuo, *Nihon no Rodo Kumiai*.

the farm votes. The feudal concept of the usefulness of the peasants did not include respect for them as individuals. Since it was only their productive function that was valued, they had been the ex- ploited and downtrodden. As a result of centuries of indoctrination under the feudal regime, they developed a frame of mind and attitude which may be characterized as resignation to the existing state of affairs, evasion of realities, dependence and reliance on others, and self-defense. Because of powerful traditionalism, they adhere te- naciously to the family beyond which they are not accustomed to ex- tend their thinking in their everyday life. They find it difficult to appraise problems beyond the village level. Only as members of the smaller social and economic units can their thinking and action become feasible.

The rural scene is dominated by the landowners instead of the farmers. For the greater part of Japan's history, especially under feudalism, landowners exercised power and influence. Throughout the period of feudalism, they were, at the top, landowning feudal lords and, in the localities, village headmen. Even after the feudal system was liquidated, mayors of towns and village heads more often than not came from the landowning class whose influence continued undiminished in the modern industrial age.

The farmers organized themselves for the first time after World War I in order to improve their lot, particularly in an effort to bring down the tenancy fees. In this struggle against the landlords, many of whom had turned into capitalists residing in the cities and invest- ing their income in industrial activities, the farmers joined forces with the urban industrial workers. Farmers' unions and labor unions formed political parties which preserved the identity of both in the names, such as the Farmer-Labor Party and Labor-Farmer Party. Some of them supported the Socialist parties.

There is nothing comparable to the American Farm Bureau Federa- tion, the National Grange, or the National Farmers Union, which are so familiar on the American political scene. Most of the organiza- tions which were created for the benefit of the farmers were either government organized or supported or both. Consequently, they were unable to develop into organizations which could oppose and influence the government in its policy making.

Although the farmers have experienced in the postwar period the strength of organization, they are still held back by the conservative forces and habits which are the legacies of feudalism. Furthermore the agricultural land reform instituted under the Occupation in- creased the number of farmers who own land. Ownership of land has made them quite conservative. This has resulted in the drifting away of the farmers from the activities of the industrial workers.

PROFESSIONAL GROUPS. As one would expect to find everywhere the Japanese have their professional associations. The most effectively organized and functioning are the doctors and lawyers. Of necessity every professional group has its association, but not every one is active politically. Although the teachers are not active through their professional associations, since the end of World War II they have been carrying on aggressive political action through their labor union, the Japan Teachers' Union, which has a membership of over a half million and is the largest constituent member of the leftist General Council of Labor Unions (Sohyo) of over 3,000,000 members.

Although the Japan Medical Association is influential in policy making in the field of medicine, it is perhaps not as powerful as its American counterpart. In over-all policy making, the Japan Bar Association probably plays more nearly the role of influence that is played by its American counterpart. However, in the appointment of judges, it does not have the recommendatory power that the American Bar Association enjoys.

Professional societies in fields other than law and medicine are much less likely to exert pressure or influence upon policy making except in matters directly within their competence, leaving general social policies pretty much to others to handle. This is particularly true of learned societies which are averse to discussing policy questions, preferring to concern themselves chiefly if not exclusively with serious academic problems and researches. The possible exceptions are writers whose influence is great, perhaps exceeding that of the same class in the United States.

PATRIOTIC AND SERVICE ORGANIZATIONS In the decade of the 1930's patriotic societies of all kinds and the veterans' organization constituted a force of overwhelming power when mobilized by the military and ultranationalistic groups. Here was a propelling force which transcended specific interests and was employed particularly against the political parties and big business, both of which were condemned as the primary, if not the sole, cause of the plight in which the whole nation found itself in the wake of world-wide economic depression.

The largest of this type of organization was the Imperial Reservists' Association which embraced in its nationwide membership all those who had served in the armed forces. Membership in this government-subsidized but army-supervised organization was automatic and, with a local chapter in every village and hamlet, its impact on national thinking and action was great indeed, since there was no other competing veterans' organization.[34]　It performed the functions of a civic association in the social life of the community while at the same time it gave assistance in employment problems.　Its members were the "legionnaires" who were always present on patriotic occasions such as parades and other public functions.　Although the Imperial Reservists' Association was disbanded by the Occupation, a new organization has reappeared as the Japan Veterans' Association.

In addition to the all-inclusive veterans' organization, there were separate officers' groups for the army and navy which were designed to look after their welfare by promoting friendship, furnishing assistance and convenience such as would be provided by a combination of army and navy hotel, commissary, credit union, library, and convention and banquet hall.[35]　Included in their regular activities were the holding of lectures, the publication of the association's periodical as well as books, and the study of military and naval science. Through these organizations and activities considerable influence was exerted on the public.

Ultranationalistic societies which flourished in the 1930's endeavored to pressure the government and the public into accepting their views and policies in national affairs.　The best known in the West was the Black Dragon Society (Kokuryukai) which was only one of a score of such organizations all of which were banned by the Occupation in 1946.[36]　Although they were branded secret societies by the West, the existence and activities were quite well known to the Japanese themselves.　Similar organizations have reappeared in the period following the restoration of full sovereignty in 1952.

The Japan Red Cross Society which was founded in 1890 is a humanitarian organization which in spite of its active use in war has remained nonpolitical and neutral in its activities.　Consequently, it has exercised tremendous influence in both domestic and international affairs.　It has been active in the repatriation of Japanese from Communist China and the U.S.S.R. and consequently it carries prestige unsurpassed by any other organization.　Even the government is moved by it.

TECHNIQUES AND INSTRUMENTS OF POWER

In the struggle for power all sorts of methods are used; there is endless variety in the means available.　Violence in the form of phys-

[34] Its membership ran into the millions.

[35] Kaikosha for army officers and Suikosha for navy officers.

[36] For a complete list of 27 organizations which were disbanded, see Supreme Commander for the Allied Powers, *Political Reorientation of Japan*, pp. 480–481.

ical coercion such as purge or liquidation has been used if and when threats were ineffective. Political parties still use thugs or *soshi* (political strongmen) to beat up the opposition, a relic of the feudal days when they were regularly employed. More frequently, economic power or money power is employed. Reward or punishment by granting or withholding money is always very effective and more refined than violence. There is always the danger that this might develop into bribery and corruption, for in the past even the government resorted to bribery to win elections. Nonmaterial rewards and punishments in the form of grant or denial of honor in rank and title have been particularly effective in Japanese politics and will continue to be so in the future. The use of myths and the manipulation of symbols, words (slogans), associations, and customs have been fully exploited in government and politics.

All these methods have been used singly or in various combinations by various organizations, including even the agencies of government, to overcome or resolve differences and frictions within as well as in relations with others.

Increasingly in the struggle for political power, effective use is being made of the weapons of group influence among which must be included propaganda, electioneering, and lobbying. The first two of these have to do with the conversion of the electorate if not the entire public, but the third deals only with the lawmakers and the government and is therefore directed at the government and the legislative assemblies on various levels. Needless to say these weapons are employed by all groups which are engaged in political activities.

Pressure Groups

Pressure groups (*atsuryoku dantai*) as known in the United States are a relatively new development in Japanese politics. This has been due largely to the fact that the need for such organizations had not been felt because of different conditions. American lobbyists rest their right to influence legislation upon Article I of the Constitution which permits people "to petition the Government for redress of grievances" and their activities are strictly regulated. Japanese lobbying has been carried on informally with even the political parties maintaining their separate lobbying in the Diet. Since Diet members are bound by the decision of the party caucus, they are less vulnerable to lobbying as such. Since it is quite easy for outsiders to attend the committee meetings of the Diet, representatives of interest groups sit in to listen to the deliberations. Their mere presence can cramp the style and stifle discussions and free expression. Committee mem-

bers often direct their utterances to the gallery and the representatives of special interests and of the government.[37]　And yet lobbies
have not developed into anything as strong as those in the United
States.　When compared to the French lobbies which have been
characterized as insidious by comparison with the American, the
Japanese lobbies are quite undeveloped and virtually innocuous and
will remain so for some time.　Furthermore, there seems to be no
sinister connotation attached to lobbying even in the popular mind.

Business and industry, labor, agriculture, medicine, law, and other
interests maintain their lobbying activities through their pressure
groups.　However, aside from these interest groups there are other
organizations which carry on activities designed to influence legislation or appropriations.　Among them are associations formed by
governors, by mayors, by speakers of legislative assemblies from the
prefectural to the village level.　There are *ad hoc* groups like the one
for the promotion of trade with Communist China.　In addition to
these traditionally recognized pressure groups, there exist those which
are not intended to be, but in reality serve as, such.　The quasi-
judicial administrative commissions and committees belong in this
category and perform the very valuable function of pressuring the
government into providing necessary legislation.

Indirect lobbying is employed along with overt demonstration by
various interest groups.　Business is more likely to use the former
method with a high degree of refinement and *savoir-faire*.　Labor,
however, readily resorts to demonstrations of all sorts including the
strike which is its most powerful weapon.　Some pressure groups
have actually pitched tents and camped right outside of the Diet
building to make their demands or protests known not only to the
lawmakers but also to the nation and public at large.　"Grass roots"
lobbying such as is considered the most effective form in American
politics has not developed in Japanese politics.　This is due largely
to the fact that campaigns to stir the "grass roots" into action are
ineffective because the local electorate is so easily controlled by the
political bosses.

The healthy growth of pressure groups capable of influencing legislation for the good of various interest groups is essential to the healthy
and democratic development of Japanese politics.[38]　This is not only
a desirable but a necessary condition, especially because of the predominant power and influence of the bureaucracy in the face of
which only the powerful vested interests have been able to make their

[37] *Seikai Orai*, March, 1953, p. 112.
[38] Royama Masamichi, "Atsuryoku dantai no igi to genkai," *Horitsu Jiho*, XXV
(January, 1953), pp. 3–7.

desires known in policy making and legislation. The urgency of the condition stated above becomes even more apparent when one realizes that, even in a democracy, the political parties alone are unable to represent all the various interests within the nation. Interest representation becomes a *sine qua non* and indispensable in the democratization of the administrative process. Lobbying when kept in the open is an essential adjunct to the legislative process. The weakness or failures of the administrative commissions in Japan can be attributed in great part to the undeveloped state of pressure groups and inadequacy of the training of their leaders.[39]

The Invisible Force of Japanese Politics: The Manipulators (Kuromaku)

Japanese politics has been characterized by behind-the-scene activities of intermediaries, fixers, and manipulators who have been known variously as *kuromaku* (wirepuller), *kagemusha* (general's double), or *sakushi* (schemer or tactician). Not infrequently the actors on the political stage have moved according to the promptings and wire-pulling of these political prompters, managers, and deal-makers and danced to their tunes. Some of the most skillful and resourceful operators, tacticians, schemers in politics have been relatively obscure personalities who operated behind the scenes. Transfer of political power was effected time and again like a business transaction with the *kuromaku* as go-betweens. These invisible operators established contacts and connections, and made necessary arrangements for political deals and compromises. Constitutional parliamentary government was thus carried on perhaps more often than not in the privacy of a teahouse or reception room rather than in public view. Not infrequently the *kuromaku* functioned as the agent and broker in important political deals which decided who should form the government. The use of intermediaries in politics is but a transfer of the old established standard social procedure of employing go-betweens in marriage as well as in business deals where there is the need of saving face in the event of failure, as well as a person to do the necessary leg work and assume the blame should anything go awry, and even attempt to patch up matters.

The term *kuromaku* actually came into being in the 1890's when there was invisible government in effect. General Yamagata utilized the Genro (Elder Statesmen) system to manipulate the Matsukata Cabinet. Yamagata may thus be credited with the institution of invisible government in modern Japanese politics by functioning as a wirepuller behind the scenes.[40]

[39] *Ibid.*, p. 8.
[40] Okuma Shigenobu, "Nihon no Seito," *Meiji Kensei Keizai Shiron,* p. 143.

One of the best known *sakushi* in the recent history of Japanese politics was Koizumi Sakutaro who began his career as a journalist and achieved both wealth and prestige.[41] In practically every major political change of the 1920's, Koizumi had a hand. He was instrumental in making Takahashi resign his peerage to become the President of the Seiyukai Party in 1921, to lead the movement to preserve constitutional government thereby forcing out the Kiyoura Cabinet. It was also he who succeeded in getting General Tanaka into the presidency of the Seiyukai Party in 1925.[42]

Kuromaku and *sakushi* are invariably men of passion, zeal, emotion, and convictions, who love adventure, action, and negotiations and are vigorous operators. Since they must operate behind the scenes the most successful ones are persons who do not crave the limelight. Although well-known public figures have functioned as such at times, their function has been a natural one which is accepted by politicians and by society as a whole. Anyone in politics who serves as a go-between, intermediary, fixer, arranger, liaison, or mediator can be regarded as a *kuromaku*. Even an *alter ego* or confidant of the prime minister has been so regarded if he operates informally behind the scenes without any official position. Consequently there have been any number of such individuals in recent Japanese politics.[43] Some have actually enjoyed the confidence of prime ministers, and this to such an extent that they were entrusted with matters which were not even revealed to the ministers' confidential secretaries.

The Boss System

Bossism permeates Japanese politics and constitutes a powerful force because its roots lie deep in the feudal past and it is based on the Confucian precepts of loyalty to one's parents, superiors, masters,

[41] Early in his youth, Koizumi resolved that he would make money so that he could become a member of the Diet. He unsuccessfully tried speculation in rice but achieved success with a weekly economic journal, *Keizai Shimbun*. He then established a printing business, Sankyosha, which turned into a money-maker. When he worked on the *Jiyu Shimbun*, the *Liberal* Party organ in Tokyo from about 1894, Kotoku Denjiro was also working on it. The friendship that developed between the two continued in spite of Kotoku's veering to the left in political ideology. Koizumi helped to supplement Kotoku's living expenses and, when the latter was executed for high treason in 1911, he attended the wake of his friend, and for twenty years thereafter he contributed toward the living expenses of Kotoku's widow.

[42] Baba Tsunego, *Gendai Jimbutsu Hyoron*, pp. 184–187.

[43] Persons known to have been *kuromaku* include among others Izawa Takio, Mori Kaku, Goto Ryutaro, Akita Kiyoshi, Toyama Mitsuru, Miura Goro, and Hoshi Toru. It would be impossible to compile a complete list, of course.

teachers, employers, and benefactors. Its conceptual basis is Confucian and its operational code feudal and it is supported by the power of money. Consequently the system is feudalistic in both psychology and methods employed, with certain modern refinements.

Japanese political bosses have not achieved, at least in the popular mind, the kind of notoriety associated with names like Boss Tweed of Tammany Hall, Hague of Jersey City, Pendergast of Kansas City, Kelly of Chicago, Penrose of Pennsylvania, Long of Louisiana, and others. There are at least two reasons for this. In the first place, the Confucian basis of the boss-henchman relationship has a certain attractiveness about it, in emotional content especially, with loyalty and obedience the prominent features. In the second place, Japanese politics has not had its counterpart of the "age of muckrakers" such as American politics has passed through.

The boss system as a method of control based on the *oyabun-kobun* relationship is in operation in some form in practically all major segments of Japanese society. It is a system based upon simulated patrimonial principles in which persons in authority assume obligations of protecting and looking after the welfare of their subordinates much as foster parents do, and the subordinates reciprocate with personal loyalty based on their feeling of duty and obligation. In the feudal period, this relationship was highly developed in the craft guilds and all sorts of apprenticeship systems.

In the underworld there are gangs of hoodlums and racketeers extorting protection money. The gambling syndicates are controlled by the *oyabun* in each district. Even thieves, robbers, and thugs honor the system and its operational code. In legally sanctioned spheres of activity, an association dominated by an *oyabun* controlled the licensing and operation of tiny open-air "street-stalls" or shops in the large cities. Even business firms are organized virtually on the basis of *oyabun-kobun* ethics, stressing loyalty and obedience to the superior-subordinate or senior-junior relationship. Evidences of a modified boss system can be found reflected in the hierarchical setup within the government bureaucracy, the political parties, the Diet, the judiciary, and college and university faculties. Even within the various professional classes, such as lawyers, medical practitioners, engineers, musicians, actors, the same condition prevails. Interestingly enough, the ubiquitous boss system and its inescapability were "discovered" by the General Headquarters of the Supreme Commander for the Allied Powers.

Especially in rural society, landlord-tenant relations and employer-employee relations in local industries and forestry are patterned on the *oyabun-kobun* system of relations. In the building trade, mining, and industrial labor, the system is conspicuous.[44]

In the rural villages, the bosses who are landowners, or enterprise owners who are at the same time employers, have set up organizations which are not unlike the Communist cells and they sit on them, thus controlling local politics. There are prefectural assemblies, especially in Western Honshu, with more than half of the members under the control of such bosses.

There has been a decided increase in the number of boss politicians since World War II. This is a consequence of the naked fact that not only are the financial needs of the parties and politicians greater now, but also their fate is determined and controlled by the power of money. Members of the Diet are unable to live on their pay. They need money to keep in touch and in good relationship with the voters in their constituencies. Such conditions favor the emergence of boss politicians in the parties. Actually most of the bosses wield power strictly on a materialistic basis. In other words, obedience or control is based on pecuniary relationship. Actually the bond which ties the henchmen to the boss is not of principles, issues, or even personality, but simply money with which loyalty is purchased. Threats are used by the bosses to keep the voters in line and to force them to do as they are told. In the 1953 general election campaign, threats used included possible boycott of shops, exile from the town, and loss of employment to those who campaigned for clean elections.[45] Much less frequently than in the United States, favors are done by local bosses. A person of influence especially in the rural community is a natural candidate for boss, since he is capable of representing the community (as *kaoyaku*) in relationships and dealings with the outside. He functions as the adviser (*sodanyaku*) or consultant in local matters and also as intermediary (*sewayaku*) and organizer.

[44] For a detailed study of the boss system in labor, see Iwao Ishino and John W. Bennett's study entitled *The Japanese Labor Boss System* (1952) which was published by the Ohio State University Research Foundation as Report No. 3 of Project 483.

[45] *Asahi*, Evening Edition, April 7, 1953, "Senkyo to fujinso no ugoki wo miru."

5 ⎯⎯⎯⎯⎯⎯⎯

Constitutional Development

and Structure

CONSTITUTIONAL HISTORY

Japan's constitutional development may be divided into three stages, with feudalism occupying the center of political activities during its most formative period. These three stages of development are the prefeudal period extending from the dawn of history to 1185 A.D., the feudal period from 1185 to 1868, and the postfeudal period since 1868. A brief consideration of the various changes which took place in the different periods is necessary as a background and setting of past and present Japanese politics and government.

The earlier half of the prefeudal period was one of indigenous, primitive, political organization based on the patriarchal clan system. Political power was in the hands of clan chieftains who held sway over different parts of the country. Although the institution of the emperor was fairly well established, the sovereign's power was neither direct nor absolute. His authority was indirectly exercised through the clan chiefs and not always accepted without question. This condition of diffused political power continued until 645 A.D.

The second and final stage of prefeudal development began in 645 A.D. and continued until the establishment of feudalism in 1185. This was the period in which political power was taken away from the clan chiefs and imperial authority was established. The Great Reform of 645 which initiated changes designed to strengthen the nation was inspired by the great neighbor, China, which, under the T'ang dynasty, was resplendent to a degree that dazzled the Japanese leaders who were intent upon the task not merely of establishing

113

firmly the authority of the Emperor but of strengthening the nation in order to win the respect of China. The planning and execution of the reforms and innovations were put in the hands of scholar officials all of whom were well versed in Chinese institutions, thought, and literature. Most of them had actually spent years of study in China. A great many, if not all, of them were enamored of Chinese culture. Consequently what took place at first was an almost indiscriminate borrowing, resulting in a virtual Sinification of ideas, institutions, customs, and costumes, and particularly legal codes.

Although the Great Reform did not begin until 645 A.D., the process of change had actually started at the beginning of the century. It was Prince Shotoku, the regent, who took the first steps leading to the adoption of Chinese ideas and institutions. In 604 A.D., he adopted the Chinese calendar which had been introduced only two years before. What is far more important was the promulgation, in the same year, of the Constitution of Seventeen Articles which is inseparably connected with his name. That this represented a tremendously important event in the political development of Japan cannot be doubted. The document represents the first Japanese attempt at a written law, meant to be a fundamental law of the land so far as the conduct of government administration was concerned. It laid down for the governing officials ethico-political rules of conduct based upon Buddhist, Confucian, and Shinto ideas. The principles and precepts embodied were a fusion or synthesis of legalism and moral suasion.

Prince Shotoku was also intent on placing Japan on a basis of equality with China as soon as possible. With this objective in mind, he dispatched for the first time in 607 A.D. an envoy who was not only a native born Japanese but a relative of the imperial family. Up to this time naturalized aliens had been employed not only to draft diplomatic correspondence but also to serve as envoys to represent the imperial court.

THE ESTABLISHMENT OF MONARCHICAL TRADITION: THE GREAT
REFORM OF 645 A.D.

A transformation unprecedented in the history of the nation was achieved by the leaders who had been awed and inspired by the splendor and grandeur of China's civilization. It took well over a half century for the reforms to come to complete fruition. It was not until the year 710 A.D. that the results were visible in the form of the first permanent capital at Nara laid out exactly like the Chinese capital of the T'ang dynasty at Ch'angan.

A central government was set up under a bureaucracy with court ranks and an elaborate system of legal codes all based on Chinese models. The new aristocracy of court nobles superseded the clan chiefs of the patriarchal system. Centralization, which was regarded by the Japanese leaders to be the secret of China's strength and prosperity, became the goal of the new political system.

As part of the centralization of political power which involved the reduction and destruction of the power of the clans, weapons were confiscated and provincial and district governors were appointed and dispatched to different parts of the country which had previously been under the control of the clans. Land holdings of the clans and members of the imperial family were taken away and a nationalized land system was introduced. Military organization was established and the command of the emperor was made direct. A tax system was reinstituted and strengthened.

The establishment of a strong monarchical principle was the chief goal of the leaders of the Great Reform. Both Confucianism and Shinto were used to bolster the imperial authority. In the new governmental organization, Shinto worship was actually given precedence over mere administrative matters. Worship was regarded as the most important business of the State. Under the new system the position of the emperor was greatly enhanced for he legally combined in himself a threefold function as the high priest of the nation, the ruler exercising sovereign power over the land and people, and the commander in chief of the nation's military.

To bring about the centralization of administration, a civil service system was imported from China with certain modifications. A national university was founded at the capital to serve as a training school for the scions of the court aristocracy. At the same time there were established in the outlying areas provincial schools which were on a level lower than the university, for the training of sons of district governors who aspired to official life.

The eighth and ninth centuries represented the height of Chinese influence on Japanese political and legal institutions. By the tenth century it began to wane as the indigenous elements came to the fore. The elaborate legal codes and political institutions from China were unequal to the task of coping with internal developments. Conditions developed which were not to be solved easily by methods that worked successfully in China. The land system broke down completely and private estates and manors emerged. As disorder increased in the outlying areas far removed from the capital, it became necessary particularly for the owners and managers of the private manors to have their own troops to protect their properties.

After a period of nearly a century of chaos and fighting, peace and order were finally restored. But the usefulness of the court aristocracy was now at an end. In its place appeared a feudal system under the domination of the military which lasted for nearly seven centuries, leaving a deep impress upon the character of the people and their ideas, institutions, and behavior.

FEUDALISM, A NEW POLITICAL STRUCTURE: ECLIPSE OF THE EMPEROR

Decentralized Feudalism

The political structure which was raised by the middle-class rural military gentry was poles away from the elaborate system set up by the effete urban civilian court aristocracy. The new rule by the military was characterized by vigor and simplicity of administration. Private property was firmly established and justice was carried out with the utmost speed and impartiality. In striking contrast to the inefficient and ineffective administration of the court aristocracy that it superseded, government now became a serious business. Laws were simplified and made the effective instruments of governance instead of an elaborate set of rules which was more decorative than practical in the aristocratic age. The legal framework and basis of feudalism were provided in the Code of Joei (1232 A.D.), the effectiveness of which continued right down into the Tokugawa period (1600–1868). Lord and vassal relationship was stressed to the point of elevating and extolling loyalty to one's master as the highest virtue, for which no sacrifice was too great. This was no doubt necessary at first under a decentralized feudalism which continued until the beginning of the seventeenth century. In spite of the organizational weakness of the decentralized political structure, it was able to withstand and repulse the Mongol invasions on two separate occasions in the last quarter of the 13th century.

Centralized Feudalism

A century of bloody, intermittent, internecine warfare brought the four centuries of decentralized feudal system to an end in the late sixteenth century. No man in Japanese history planned more carefully or worked more patiently, with foresight and acumen as well as craft and cunning, for the achievement of supreme political power and the preservation in perpetuity of that power in his family than Ieyasu, the founder of the Tokugawa house. His efforts were crowned with success to the extent of preserving power in the family for more than two and a half centuries, notwithstanding several incompetent successors who only by the grace of the gods occupied the post of Shogun.

The highly centralized political structure of feudalism under the Tokugawa regime was simplicity itself so far as the administrative organization was concerned. The devices and techniques employed within the framework of administration, however, had the effect of giving complexity to the actual operation of government.

Rigid control of all classes by keeping them in their proper places and not permitting them to intermingle or intermarry served for a considerable length of time to stabilize power relationships within the feudal structure. Yet this very policy, though eminently successful in preserving peace, in the long run produced rigidity and inflexibility, brought about stagnation, and rendered the military class impotent, ineffective, anomalous, and parasitical.

In spite of the national policy of isolation enforced for more than two centuries and the rigid system of class distinctions, the inexorable forces of change within and the pressures from without brought about the collapse of feudalism. When the American Commodore Matthew C. Perry arrived in Japan in the summer of 1853, the feudal regime was already tottering but managed to survive the shock of the Western impact for another fifteen years. The liquidation of feudalism was the necessary prerequisite to the emergence of a new Japan able to cope with new problems and particularly to live and survive in a world in which the Western nations held sway. It was a peaceful change-over accomplished without bloodshed, and perhaps the fact that it was achieved without destruction was responsible for the transmission to a new age the legacies of feudalism against which there had developed no strong revulsion. On the contrary some of the ideas and ideals were deliberately preserved and in some instances even refurbished and re-enforced to be utilized effectively in the modernization of the nation.

EMERGENCE OF A NEW JAPAN: THE MEIJI RESTORATION, 1868

With the demise of feudalism the way was cleared for a new political structure which was to receive the inspiration and impetus as well as the necessary nourishment for growth from the countries of the West. Ever since the seventh century Japanese political ideas and institutions had been under Chinese influence in varying degrees. From the middle of the nineteenth century Chinese influence all but disappeared and was now superseded by Western influence. The Charter Oath of Five Articles promulgated in 1868 by the young

Emperor Meiji who was then only fifteen years old, charted the course for the new Japan to follow. In setting forth the principles and providing the basis on which national politics should be formulated, it provided as follows:

1. Deliberative assemblies shall be established and all matters be decided by public opinion.

2. The whole nation shall unite as one in carrying out the administration of the affairs of state.

3. Every person shall be given the opportunity to pursue a calling of his choice.

4. Absurd customs and usages of the past shall be discarded and justice shall be based on the laws of heaven and earth.

5. Wisdom and knowledge shall be sought all over the world in order to establish firmly the foundations of the Empire.

It was the period of two decades which followed the Charter Oath of Five Articles and ended with the drafting of the Constitution that was the most crucial in determining not only the fate of the nation but also the form of government that was to be adopted. This was an interlude, a transition stage, between feudalism and constitutionalism which was dominated by a small oligarchy under an interim system of absolute monarchy. Opposition was intense against the oligarchically-run absolute monarchy with Emperor Meiji, who was then a minor, as its head. The populace was neither friendly nor sympathetic. On the contrary they were reluctant to go along with the new government. Feeling of insecurity as well as fear permeated the entire nation. The first decade therefore had to be devoted to the task of putting down peasant uprisings and political revolts in addition to beating down obstructive opposition within the government itself. Constructive work in the setting up of efficient governmental organization could not be undertaken without serious distraction until 1878 when the Satsuma Rebellion was put down as the last futile attempt to use force against the government.

In the second half of the preparliamentary period, the political parties emerged and the serious work of launching a representative form of government under a constitution was begun. It was decided by the government in 1881 that the national assembly would be convoked in 1890. Almost on the heels of the announcement which came on October 12, the first political party, the Liberal Party (Jiyuto), was launched on October 29 followed by the Constitutional Progressive Party (Rikken Kaishinto) on March 15, 1882. Only four days later, on March 19, the Constitutional Imperial Party (Rikken Teiseito) appeared. All the parties concentrated their energies on influencing the substance of the Constitution, each one intent on making its views prevail.

Ito Hirobumi who was entrusted with the task of studying the constitutional systems of the West, left for Europe in the spring of 1882 on an eighteen-month trip. After visiting Europe—France, Germany, and Austria—he returned in August, 1883. He had spent the longest part of his European sojourn in Germany where he became an admirer of Bismarck[1] and the Prussian bureaucratic system, and heard lectures by Professors Rudolph Gneist and Lorenz von Stein. In March, 1884, he set up the Bureau for the Study of the Constitution in the Ministry of Imperial Household and the work of drafting the constitution was begun under his direction. For two years preliminary research was carried on and the actual work of drafting was begun in 1886 and completed in 1888.

The members of the drafting committee under Ito were Ito Miyoji, Inoue Tsuyoshi, and Kaneko Kentaro. The committee carried on the work on the little island of Natsushima off Yokosuka where they lived in isolation, out of contact with even their families. Absolute secrecy was maintained to prevent any premature publicity which might lead to obstruction and delay if not failure of their work. Two foreign authorities were consulted for their advice, Dr. Herman Roessler, a German professor of constitutional law at the Tokyo Imperial University, and Sir Francis Taylor Piggot, a British diplomat.

In the same year that he set up the Bureau for the Study of the Constitution, Ito created a new system of peerage patterned after the Prussian model. This was obviously a political move and a bid for the support of the newly created peers. The following year, 1885, saw the institution of the cabinet system, antedating parliamentary government by a half decade.[2] Upon Ito fell the honor of becoming the first Prime Minister (Minister President) under the new cabinet system of government. In the meantime a modern civil service system was established by Ito to form the solid foundation for a new and strong bureaucracy which could give him support. It was decided that a special body of statesmen was necessary to deliberate upon the completed draft of the new Constitution. There was no

[1] He became such an ardent admirer of Bismarck that he affected the Chancellor's ways, even to such details as smoking a cigar.

[2] The Cabinet which came into being on December 23, 1885 was made up of the Prime Minister and the Ministers of the following 8 departments: Home Affairs, Finance, Foreign Affairs, Army, Navy, Justice, Agriculture and Commerce, Communications and Education. There was in addition the Minister of Imperial Household who was outside of the Cabinet.

representative body then in existence to go over the document. Thus in 1888 the Privy Council was created for the purpose of deliberating upon and approving the Constitution. On February 11, 1889, the Constitution was promulgated by Emperor Meiji amidst the rejoicing of the entire nation. The much desired goal of constitutional government was thus achieved.

THE NATURE OF THE MEIJI CONSTITUTION

The political struggle which culminated in the Meiji Constitution was not waged for the purpose of arresting the power of the sovereign, for no such need existed. Nor was it begun to secure and insure the rights of liberty to the individual, for there was no widespread demand for them. Rather, it was an integral part of the movement to create a strong national government which was the most immediate need of the nation at the time. What the Japanese leaders were looking for was not the substance of the ideas and principles to be incorporated in the fundamental law of the land but the form and language in which to express and embody them. Actually what was done was to clothe Japanese ideas in Western garb and to set up the kind of governmental machinery which would meet with the approval of the West and at the same time could best serve urgent national needs. The Prussian Constitution, which was eagerly studied by the Japanese, did not provide the basis of the Meiji Constitution but it served to reassure them that what they wanted in their constitution was feasible and practicable and could be incorporated in a document within the framework of Western constitutionalism, could be drafted as an instrument to insure national independence and prosperity. Inescapable, however, was a dichotomy, namely, the modernization of the administrative machinery on the one hand and the enhancement of the ancient monarchical tradition on the other. The traditional monarchical concept in its refurbished form was thus clearly expressed in Article I which stated, "The Empire of Japan shall be reigned over and governed by a line of Emperors unbroken for ages eternal," and in Article III which provided that "the Emperor is sacred and inviolable." There is no doubt whatever that an emperor-centric state was the goal of the constitution makers.

It has been emphasized that, unlike the Magna Carta, the Constitution was not a document extracted from the ruler. Instead it was a grant by the Emperor at a time when the need for it was not generally felt by the people. It was a necessary and not a premature document so far as the political exigencies of the nation were concerned. It was needed to bring stability to domestic politics. But it was even more imperative so far as Japan's bid for equality with the Western nations was concerned. Western powers were not willing to concede equality to Japan or even to negotiate treaty revision until and unless she had demonstrated to the world that she had become a "civilized" nation with a constitution and a "Western" system of law.

The Bill of Rights was incorporated into the Constitution because it had to conform to Western practice and form. However, all the provisions were qualified by the expression, "within the limits of law." It is obvious that the granting of political and civil rights and the insuring of the dignity of the individual were only remotely and vaguely in the minds of the leaders if at all. What was foremost and of overriding importance in their minds was a strong Japan able to stand up to the West and safeguard herself from both internal and external dangers.

There were only 76 articles in the Meiji Constitution, making it one of the briefest constitutions in modern history. It was the belief of the framers, and especially of Ito, that a constitution should contain only fundamental principles and should not be filled with details. Ito believed that it should be eternal and not require periodic revisions and amendments to meet changing conditions and needs. During the 58 years of its existence, it was never amended.[3] A rather lavish praise was heaped on the Japanese by Professor Frank J. Goodnow when he said that "the fact that the Japanese Constitution has been practically unamended during the twenty-seven years of its life is a tribute both to the ability of those who drafted it, and to the political genius of the people who are governed by it."[4]

GOVERNMENT STRUCTURE UNDER THE MEIJI CONSTITUTION

At least in theory and in a rather superficial way the principle of separation of powers was worked out. However, the separation was more apparent than real especially in its actual functioning. The executive branch was all powerful in practice, especially with the absolute power of the Emperor behind it. The legislative branch was com-

[3] In the summer of 1889 Kaneko showed the Constitution to United States Secretary of State James G. Blaine, who was favorably impressed by the inclusion of only fundamental principles and exclusion of details, its flexibility, and the absence of the provision for the impeachment of Cabinet ministers. Kaneko Kentaro, "Teikoku kempo no seishin kiso," in *Nihon Seishinshi Koza,* IV, pp. 10–12.

[4] A statement in the Preface to his *Principles of Constitutional Government,* (1916).

pletely overshadowed by the executive and had become little more than a rubber stamp.

Strong monarchical principles were quite noticeable in the governmental structure. Initiative in constitutional amendment was reserved exclusively to the Emperor. He had the power to issue ordinances, both regular and emergency, and the power unconditionally to declare war, make peace, and conclude a treaty. As his highest advisory body, there was the Privy Council. In addition there was the extraconstitutional, extralegal body of advisors known as the Elder Statesmen (Genro) to shield as well as to strengthen the institution and the person of the Emperor.

The legislative branch was organized as a bicameral system with the House of Representatives composed entirely of members elected directly by the people, and the House of Peers consisting of princes of the blood and higher grades of peerage enjoying life tenure while the members representing the lower grades of peers and the highest taxpayers were chosen from their own ranks. The remaining membership consisted of appointees recommended by the government in recognition of their meritorious services to the nation.

The judicial branch was in effect an arm of the executive branch and without the independence enjoyed by it under the new Constitution. Moreover, the doctrine of judicial review was completely absent. A separate administrative court was provided to take care of adjudication involving administrative action just as in the French system. An indispensable element of Anglo-Saxon law, the *habeas corpus*, was unknown.

A distinctive feature of the government was the position of quasi-independence which the military enjoyed.[5] This was based on the ordinance power of the Emperor and not on any constitutional, or even statutory, provision as has been erroneously assumed by writers. The right of direct access to the Emperor enjoyed by the military was responsible for its rise to power and control of national affairs in the 1930's and led to the Pacific War in 1941.[6] Under the Meiji Constitution there was no provision for the responsibility of the Cabinet to the Diet, nor was there any system of impeachment of Cabinet ministers. The government could be checked or stymied only from within the executive branch itself, as, for example, the

[5] The existence of such an arrangement under the Prussian and German systems provided the justification for the Japanese military in adopting it.

[6] For a discussion of the quasi-independent position of the military, see the author's "The Military and the Government in Japan," *American Political Science Review*, XXXV (June, 1941), pp. 529–539.

Privy Council, the Elder Statesmen, and the military functioning not as a part of the Cabinet but as the power of supreme military command.

The Meiji Constitution worked well in serving the needs of the new Japan, especially in helping to achieve the goals set forth at the time of its adoption. Needless to say, it had to operate primarily though not exclusively within the framework of Japanese experience and be geared to Japanese aspirations. The machinery and mechanics of the constitutional system were visibly Western. This had caused the West to delude itself into concluding that Japan had become thoroughly Westernized. Yet the ideas, attitudes, spirit, and methods which operated them were Japanese, though never clearly perceived as such by the casual observer. Undoubtedly the Meiji Constitution would have continued in force until the present had it not been for the defeat Japan suffered in the Pacific War of World War II.

ATTEMPT AT THE DEMOCRATIZATION OF JAPAN

Japan's acceptance in August of the terms of the Potsdam Declaration of July 26, 1945, brought World War II to its conclusion in so far as the fighting was concerned. But the task of remolding Japan into a peaceful and democratic nation as stipulated at Potsdam was begun in earnest when the shooting ended. Demilitarization and democratization were the twin cornerstones on which a new political structure was to be raised in the defeated nation by the victorious Allied Power.[7] It was clearly recognized at the very outset by the Supreme Commander for the Allied Powers that constitutional revision was the *sine qua non* of the kind of political reform necessary to achieve the goals envisaged in the Potsdam Declaration and incorporated also in the United States Initial Postsurrender Policy for Japan.[8] The thinking which dominated the Japanese leaders at the time, however, was that the necessary reforms could be instituted without any constitutional revision.[9] This fact does not necessarily imply that the idea of constitutional revision was not existent in any segment of the nation. Reflecting a sense of urgency, the Supreme

---

[7] It was stipulated in Paragraph 10 of the Potsdam Declaration that "the Japanese Government shall remove all obstacles to the revival and strengthening of democratic tendencies among the Japanese people. Freedom of speech, of religion, and of thought, as well as respect for the fundamental human rights shall be established."

[8] Supreme Commander for the Allied Powers, *Political Reorientation of Japan*, p. 90.

[9] Sato Isao, *Kempo Kaisei no Keika* (1948), pp. 31–32.

Commander conveyed to the Japanese Government on several occasions during the first few months of the Occupation his concern in the matter of creating a new political order.

It was in mid-October that General MacArthur pointedly advised Prime Minister Shidehara who had just formed a new government that the reforms which Japan must undertake would "unquestionably involve the revision of the Constitution."[10]   As a consequence the government set up the Committee for the Investigation of Constitutional Problems.[11]

Once the work of constitutional revision was begun, various groups, especially political parties, came forth with several proposals, a situation quite reminiscent of the 1880's, the period immediately preceding the adoption of the Meiji Constitution.[12]   After three months of work the Matsumoto Constitution Committee came up with a draft which left the basic nature of the Japanese state unchanged and the emperor system retained intact.   The Matsumoto draft submitted on February 1, 1946,[13] was promptly rejected as unsatisfactory and the Supreme Commander decided that the most effective method of instructing the Japanese Government in the nature and application of the basic principles would be to prepare a draft constitution.[14]   Accordingly the Government Section of SCAP with utmost speed completed a draft constitution on February 10 and two days later submitted it to the Japanese Government for their guidance.   That this "was received with a distinct sense of shock"[15] is putting it mildly, for it was the hope of the Shidehara Government that the Matsumoto proposals might be made the basis of discussion and compromise in order that at least a part of the old system might be salvaged.   However, the Cabinet was quick to see that nothing short of thorough-going revision would be acceptable and set out to produce a draft.   This was completed on March 4 and two days later was approved by the Cabinet and an Imperial Rescript announced the adoption of the

---

[10] SCAP, *Political Orientation of Japan*, p. 91.

[11] Dr. Joji Matsumoto was appointed head of the Committee of seventeen of whom three were advisers and outstanding authorities on constitutional law.   It is interesting to note that at least six, including the Chairman, were law professors past or present.   See SCAP, *Political Reorientation of Japan*, p. 603.

[12] *Ibid.*, pp. 96–98.   The greatest problem which confronted everyone concerned with constitutional revision was the question of national polity, (*kokutai*), a peculiarly Japanese concept which at best is amorphous but extensive and practically all inclusive in its connotations.

[13] Department of State, *The Far Eastern Commission*, pp. 45–46.

[14] *Ibid.*, p. 102.

[15] SCAP, p. 106.

draft. Altogether the revision process involved four drafts[16] before it was submitted for approval to the Diet where amendments were made before its final adoption.[17] The new Constitution was promulgated on November 3, the birthday of Emperor Meiji, and took effect six months later on May 3, 1947.

THE NATURE OF THE NEW CONSTITUTION

That the new Constitution was inspired by democratic, if not American, political philosophy is beyond a shadow of doubt. The preamble to the Constitution reminds the reader of the ideas and language of such historic American documents as the Declaration of Independence, the Federalist Papers, the Preamble to the Constitution, the Gettysburg Address, and even the Atlantic Charter. The initiative came from the Americans too. It is also clear that the document was based upon the American-made draft submitted for the guidance of the Japanese Government. The political reform envisaged in the Constitution went much farther than the Japanese themselves were willing to go at the time, that is, before they felt, and resigned themselves to, the unforeseen pressure.

It represented a new departure, a thorough liberalization in political thinking. In fact, it went much farther in some respects than Americans themselves would have been willing to go if they were to reform their own institutions at home. The revision undertaking was a venture even for Americans and a political experiment of considerable scope and magnitude at least in its conception.

Perhaps the most conspicuous characteristic of the new Constitution is the simple colloquial style in which it is written making it easily understood by everyone. The stilted semicourtly, legal, and even somewhat feudal language in which the old Constitution was couched is gone, leaving no trace of it. This fact would be of considerable help in conditioning behavior conducive to a democratic way.

Unprecedented was the incorporation of a provision for the renunciation of war as an instrument of national policy, a feature which was deemed, by a not inconsiderable number of students of government, as somewhat visionary and unrealistic, if not actually utopian,

---

[16] All four drafts are to be found in SCAP, *Political Reorientation of Japan*, pp. 625–655.

[17] On August 24, 1946, the House of Representatives adopted the new Constitution by a vote of 421 to 8. The House of Peers adopted it by a vote of 298 to 2 with a few minor changes. The final version was approved in the lower House on October 7 by a vote of 342 to 5. The Privy Council, in a special session attended by the Emperor, approved it on October 29.

in a world which has not succeeded in renouncing force in one form or another in international or even internal relations.

The clear and unequivocal statement that sovereignty resided in the people was something entirely new and even revolutionary in concept which was added to the political thought of the Japanese. So was the concept of the Emperor as only the symbol of the state and the unity of the nation. The recognition and establishment of the principle of respect for the dignity of the individual were a distinct innovation under a new political order.

Respect for the dignity of the individual is firmly established in the new Constitution with ample safeguards for insuring civil and political rights. The Bill of Rights which forms an integral and prominent part of the new document provides the rights and freedoms which are guaranteed to the individual without any qualification whatever. This is in striking contrast to the "bill of rights" of the Meiji Constitution. Women have been given equality for the first time.

Legislative supremacy is established as a principle, making the Diet the supreme organ of the state. This places the legislative branch above the executive branch and makes it the sole lawmaking organ. The power to amend the Constitution is vested in the Diet. The government or the cabinet is now held responsible and answerable to the Diet. Unlike the old Constitution, the cabinet system is now provided for. Separation of powers has been introduced and checks and balances exist for the first time. The independence of the judiciary is a fact now in sharp contrast to the condition which obtained under the old system. Moreover, there has been introduced for the first time the doctrine of judicial review.

The emperor, under the new political system, became a mere symbol, divested of political power. At the same time, the imperial household was brought under the control of the Diet. Laws regulating it are enacted by the Diet like any other law and the expenditures of the imperial family must be appropriated by the legislature. This represents a radical change from the old system under which the imperial household was independent of the government and beyond the reach of the power of the Diet.

The new Constitution which consists of eleven chapters and 103 articles is a slightly longer document than the Meiji Constitution and quite naturally contains more detailed provisions. Despite the fact that it is as democratic as any constitution can be, it does not represent a documentation of what already exists in Japan as *fait accompli*. Rather, it is largely a blueprint of what is hoped to be achieved. Needless to say, what can and will be achieved will be determined by the traditions, customs, and usages most familiar to the Japanese people and not merely by the words and phrases which express the ideas and ideals of democracy which are in the Constitution.

Since the regaining of complete independence and political sovereignty, discussions have been going on regarding the question of constitutional revision. It was quite natural that, however desirable the new Constitution, there should be a feeling that sooner or later changes should be made if for no other reason than to bolster national self-respect. Even the government, for political as well as other reasons, began to make it known that it was necessary to "rectify" some of the too hastily introduced reforms as well as the mistakes and excesses of the Occupation. The question of constitutional revision, however, has revolved chiefly around Article 9 providing for the renunciation of war forever as a sovereign right. It is virtually a foregone conclusion that some revisions will be effectuated in the near future and it is not unlikely that a thorough overhauling might be attempted.

BASIC FEATURES OF THE NEW GOVERNMENTAL SYSTEM

What has resulted is a curious mixture of the American presidential system and the British system of responsible parliamentary government with the features of the latter more in evidence. It was decided, and correctly, by those who were responsible for the SCAP draft that the British system was more suitable for the Japanese.[18] Legislative supremacy, therefore, was adopted but in actual operation this principle is far from established. A bicameral legislature was finally adopted although at first the Supreme Commander favored a unicameral body.

A cabinet system rooted firmly in the Diet provides the administrative arm of the nation. In actual practice the government has dominated the legislative branch. The system of checks and balances exists at least in theory but is certainly not in effective operation.

Although a degree of decentralization was worked out, it did not change the structure of the government which has been unitary in nature with the prefectures serving only as administrative units of the central government. The system of elective governors of course did not elevate the position of the prefecture to a semiautonomous unit such as is found in a federal system. Although the police was partly

[18] SCAP, *Political Orientation of Japan*, p. 102.

decentralized, after the war, a centralized system was reinstituted in 1954.[19] Within the new political framework are found such democratic devices as referendum and recall which have actually been tried out. Impeachment of Cabinet ministers is now provided for but it still remains to be applied.

As for the actual distribution of political power, no radical changes have taken place under the new Constitution. Formally, political power is exercised by (1) the Government and the bureaucracy, (2) the parliament, and (3) the political parties. Informally and indirectly many groups in varying degrees share in the exercise of political power. Among them must be included business, landowners, professionals and intellectuals, and laborers and farmers.

[19] In 1954, the law to renationalize the police system was passed by the Diet.

6

The Emperor:

The Nation's Symbol

and Rallying Point

THE EMPEROR AS A SYMBOL

The Emperor has been and still is the living symbol of the nation's history, heritage, and achievements, of all that is glorious in the nation's past and present, of its continuity and durability. He is the incarnation of history and religion. In his person are epitomized the nation's hopes, aspirations, and promise. He is the spiritual anchor, the moral rudder, and the political gyroscope that insure the safety and steadiness of the course of the ship of state. As a symbol he is enshrined in the hearts of the people who attribute everything good to his virtue.[1]

In looking for the unique in their history, the Japanese have been wont to point to the fact that there has been but a single line of rulers for the two thousand years of national existence. No nation on earth today, they believe, can boast of a reigning house which has come down in "lineal succession unbroken for ages eternal." The present ruler, Emperor Hirohito, is officially the 124th in the line of succession in the family. Because there has been only one dynasty, the imperial house to this day has no family name.[2] To most

[1] This has not always been so for it is a relatively recent development which accompanied Japan's emergence as a modern power in the nineteenth century.

[2] The Emperor has only one name, the given name, Hirohito. But his personal name is used only for the record since no one really calls him by that name, not even his own Empress. The people refer to him as His Majesty (Heika). He has no nickname or abbreviations of his given name. All these practices differ

Japanese, the imperial line will continue indefinitely and perhaps forever, "coeval with heaven and earth."

There is no family in Japan today older than the imperial house. This is emphasized and contrasted with other countries, such as England where many a peer is more anciently British than the royal family which began in 1714 when George I, a Hanoverian, became the first monarch of the present ruling house of Windsor.[3] However, there are many points of resemblance between the Japanese emperor and the British monarch. Among them the most noticeable are the symbolic role which they occupy and the attitude of reverence and affection shown by the people toward them. It is believed firmly that the imperial family more than anything else in the nation gives uniqueness to the Japanese concept of *kokutai* or "national polity" and distinguishes Japan from all the other countries of the world.

The reverence for the Emperor is almost unbelievable especially to those who have not witnessed its manifestation at first hand. Furthermore, it is unfathomable since it is an emotional and practically a religious manifestation. Perhaps the British alone of the Western peoples today can come closest to understanding the Japanese attitude toward the sovereign.

There is little doubt that, like the English, the Japanese adore their nation by giving full adoration to the Throne. As with the British, the monarchical institution provides the great centripetal force and the national rite by which all the people, except for the Communists and perhaps some extreme Socialists, are bound together regardless of social class, economic station, or even political creed.[4] The Emperor is necessary emotionally to the Japanese just as the Crown is to the Britons.

In political life, especially on the national level, the most powerful force is sentiment and the most effective motives for sentiment are symbols. Japan, like any other nation, cannot exist without the sentiment of loyalty which nearly always is affixed to a symbol. The throne thus is the most powerful living symbol of the unity and solidarity of the Japanese nation and as such makes possible un-

---

greatly from those of the British. King George VI for instance was Albert Frederick Arthur George Windsor and "Bertie" to his family.

[3] The present Queen Elizabeth II is the fortieth in line of succession from William, the Conqueror who, in 1066 led his successful invasion into the British Isles to establish the house of Normandy. In the ensuing centuries the Plantagenets, Tudors, and Stuarts followed and it was in 1714 that the House of Hanover (Windsor) was founded.

[4] See M. Demashevich, *National Mind*, p. 104.

swerving loyalty as well as affectionate reverence toward the imperial family. Every occasion is therefore effectively used to foster such a feeling by providing an opportunity for the externalization of emotions just as is done by the English.[5]

Only recently in a survey made by the United Nations Educational and Cultural Organization, it was found that 74 percent of the youth of postwar Japan strongly "believe the Emperor remains, at the very least, the symbol of the nation, not only on paper, but in the hearts and minds of the people."[6] This came as a revelation to many in the Western nations in view of the fact that the Emperor, in his New Year's Message to the people on January 1, 1946, had denied any attribute of divinity. The efforts of the Occupation authorities to humanize the Emperor and remold the institution into something resembling the British monarchy were successful but not necessarily in the sense some people had anticipated. What actually happened was not the "devaluation" but rather the enhancement of the position and person of the Emperor. Before 1946, he was too sacred to even look at, and was inaccessible. But under the new Constitution he appeared among the people not only within their direct gaze but even shaking hands with them. Moreover, the Imperial Palace was thrown open to the public, enabling the people to enter the compound to wish the Emperor well on New Year's Day[7] and on his birthday.

Although a great deal had been made of the divinity of the Emperor, it was the Western nations, rather than the Japanese people, who took it literally. For very few Japanese, if any, ever regarded the Emperor as divine in the sense in which the West interpreted the term.[8] While it could be regarded as an oversimplification, the divinity of the Japanese ruler was not very different from that of the Roman emperors.[9]

The word *kami* in Japanese, which became equated with God in

---

[5] *Ibid.,* p. 103.

[6] UNESCO, *Courier,* August–September, 1954, pp. 12–35. See also Hugh H. Smythe and Masaharu Watanabe, "Japanese Popular Attitudes Toward the Emperor," *Pacific Affairs,* Dec., 1953, pp. 335–344.

[7] As one of the more than 300,000 persons who thronged the Imperial Palace on January 2, 1956, the author observed at firsthand the enthusiastic shouts of banzai by the assembled crowd when the Emperor and Empress made their appearance and the feeling of affection that was manifested.

[8] Even in English and American usage, the term divine carries several connotations other than God in the Christian theological sense.

[9] According to the Roman concept, the emperor was the descendant of divine ancestors who would after death join his forebearers in the apotheosis. See Lily Ross Taylor, *The Divinity of the Roman Emperor,* p. 181.

the Christian sense, was and still is a synonym for "above," "superior," "hair," "paper," "authority," "government," and "deity." Even the least educated peasant knows that the Emperor is mortal and is subject to the same afflictions of flesh as ordinary people. That the concept of divinity was deliberately refurbished and modernized in the late nineteenth century by the political leaders of the nation to further unity and instill loyalty and unquestioning obedience to authority there is not the slightest doubt. The leaders of the Meiji period fostered the idea that the Emperor was sacred and inviolable. This strengthening of the monarchical tradition in the Constitution of 1889 was but a means to an end, namely, the strengthening of the nation. But the emergence of the emperor system was the result of the close cooperation of the capitalists, militarists, bureaucrats, and politicians. In the course of the power struggles which were waged, attempts were made by groups to control the emperor system in order to exploit to their own advantage the symbolic value as well as the real powers inherent in the system.

The imperial family is the cynosure of the nation and is the object of the adulation and affection of the people. In it the people see the ideal family life which is to be emulated. Almost instinctively the people extend their family feeling and affection to the perpetual first family, sharing its every joy and sorrow. Shortly after the present emperor ascended the throne in 1925 the whole nation prayed and waited anxiously for the birth of an heir. Three times the nation waited for a crown prince but in vain. The fourth time, in 1933, the rejoicing of the whole nation knew no bounds when Crown Prince Akihito was born. Thereafter, the nation kept careful watch over the growth of the infant prince, followed him through childhood and adolescence. When, at the age of 18, he was proclaimed Heir Apparent, there was great rejoicing throughout the nation.[10] As he approached majority, the people began to show concern over the selection of his fiancée. When the Crown Prince traveled abroad in 1953 to attend as the Emperor's representative the coronation of Queen Elizabeth II, the Japanese public listened to radio broadcasts and scanned the papers for every bit of news that could be found regarding his doings.

It is not on joyous occasions alone that the nation's eyes and thoughts turn to the imperial family. In fact, in times of crisis, especially in the hour of sorrow, the nation feels even more strongly the ties that bind the people to the ruling house. During the fatal

[10] This ceremony which took place on November 10, 1952, was on the occasion of his coming of age.

illness of Emperor Meiji in 1911–1912, as he lay near death, the whole nation prayed. Hundreds of people came to the Imperial Palace Plaza and remained there for days praying for his recovery, refusing to go away.[11] When he died, the whole nation grieved as one family. This sort of quiet demonstration of loyalty and affection finds its counterpart in England.[12]

The symbolic role of the Emperor is brought out most vividly and dramatically through ceremonials of all sorts. Ritual and pageantry uplift the people on great occasions with the remembrance of their past and the timelessness of their institutions and give them a sense of stability as well as pride. Deep emotional significance is seen in the Japanese enthronement ceremony as in the British coronation. The accession of the Japanese Emperor has no exact counterpart in the world. The Emperor in complete solitude participates in a solemn religious ceremony of communion with the spirits of his ancestors in the inner sanctum, the holy of holies, of the ancient imperial palace at Kyoto. Here he takes a solemn oath to his ancestors, the substance of which remains unknown to others. This is followed by the enthronement ceremony.

Enthronement too is carried out in an ancient atmosphere of primitive simplicity and in utmost privacy. Unlike the British coronation, it is not a public function. The Emperor merely reports his accession to his ancestral spirits. His oath differs from that of the British sovereigns in that it is to the spirits of his ancestors and predecessors and not to any living persons. By comparison with the British coronation such as that of Queen Elizabeth II which was held on June 2, 1953, amid ancient ceremony and medieval pomp and witnessed by Britain's elite, the Japanese enthronement ceremony is almost colorless but is fraught with deep spiritual significance. There is neither crown nor scepter nor anointing with oil. The ceremony itself is without pomp and splendor but the occasion has an immensely powerful emotional and patriotic impact on the whole nation.

The symbolic role of the Japanese emperor may be more readily appreciated by a close examination of what Prime Minister Winston Churchill said in Ottawa in January 1952 with regard to the meaning of the British Crown:

[11] W. E. Griffis, *The Mikado*, p. 23.

[12] A similar attitude was witnessed in the winter and spring of 1929 when King George V lay dangerously ill in Buckingham Palace. Mixed groups patiently waited for the posting of the bulletins describing his condition, at the main gates of the Palace, under the cold humid winter sky.

On the whole it is wise in human affairs, and in the government of men, to separate pomp from power. Under the long constitutional monarchy established over centuries of Britain and of the Commonwealth, the King reigns but does not govern. If a great battle is lost, Parliament and people can turn out the Government. If a great battle is won, the crowds cheer the King. Thus while the ordinary struggles, turmoils and inevitable errors of healthy democratic government proceed, there is established upon an unchallenged pedestal the title, deeds and achievements of all the realms.

THE EMPEROR AS AN ORGAN OF STATE

In the period between the two World Wars a bitter controversy raged over the question as to whether or not the Emperor was an organ of State. At first the controversy was confined chiefly if not exclusively to the academic world, that is, among the specialists on the Japanese constitution. In the 1930's it was carried over into the political arena where it was bitterly fought as a political issue revolving around "the clarification of national polity."

The origin of the controversy goes back to the eve of World War I when Professors Uesugi and Minobe were friendly colleagues on the Law Faculty of Tokyo Imperial University but whose constitutional views were poles apart. The former occupied the chair of Japanese Constitutional Law and the latter the chair of Comparative Law and Administrative Law. The former was the exponent of the divine right of the Emperor while the latter was a firm believer in the institution of the Emperor as an organ of State. The former approached the subject matter with mysticism and highly charged emotionalism which had the effect of creating the relationship of a fiery prophet and patriot-founder of a religion and followers between him and his students. In contrast the latter approached the subject as a scholar with cool objectivity.

The controversy created no serious problems until the mid-1930's when the ultranationalists and reactionaries raised the cry of "clarification of national polity" in a move to destroy the organ theory of the Emperor which the Emperor himself had subscribed to personally although the fact had not been divulged to the general public. The Emperor did not feel that the organ theory in any way impaired the dignity of the imperial house.[13] Professor Minobe was denounced by the militarists and extreme rightist groups as a traitor and threatened that his life was in danger. The pressure which extremists, both civilian and military, applied on the government forced the authorities to take steps, at first more to prevent violence than to placate

[13] Ozaki Shiro, *Tenno Kikansetsu*, pp. 14, 58.

them. The army itself was split into opposing factions in a power struggle with the line drawn between the moderates and those who upheld the theory of divine right, not because the Emperor believed in it, which he did not, but in order that they might use it to their advantage as a propaganda weapon in their effort to win over public opinion to their side.[14]

Unable to resist the tremendous pressure brought to bear upon it by the military, the Okada government issued a statement on October 15, 1935, that sovereignty resided in the Emperor and that the so-called organ theory of the Emperor was utterly in conflict with the national polity (*kokutai*) and must therefore be rejected. A political judgment was thus rendered, banning the organ theory of the Emperor which Professor Minobe had held and expounded since 1913; his voice was silenced and the publication and sale of his books on the constitution were prohibited.[15] Because of the pressure of public opinion and the unfavorable atmosphere in the Diet, he was forced to resign his membership in the House of Peers which had been given him through imperial appointment in recognition of his valuable services to the nation as a scholar.

It is now a matter of record that the disastrous defeat suffered by Japan in the Pacific War was brought on by the military who exploited the Emperor institution. Its inevitable consequence was the liquidation of the military through the achievement of as complete a demilitarization as had ever been attempted anywhere. With the purging of the nation of the ultranationalist organizations, the support for the divine-right theory of the Emperor collapsed.

In the 1930's, particularly around 1935, the Emperor was already aware of the defiant attitude of the army which ignored his wishes while loudly proclaiming its opposition to the organ theory and giving lip service to the theory of divine right and complete sovereignty of the Emperor. During the war, the Emperor was deliberately kept from learning the truth about the war's progress.[16] The arbitrary and high-handed attitude of the military prior to and during the Pacific War was not to the Emperor's liking. In the imperial conference

[14] *Ibid.*, p. 62.

[15] The books of Professor Minobe which were proscribed were: *Outline of the Constitution* (Kempo Satsuyo), *Commentary on the Constitution* (Chikujo Kempo Seigi), and *Basic Principles of the Japanese Constitution* (Nihon Kempo no Kihon Shugi).

[16] Hosokawa Morisada, *Joho Tenno ni Tassezu* (1953) is a diary kept by the author consisting of memoranda on political information and views gathered specially for submission to Prince Takamatsu, a younger brother of the Emperor.

preceding the surrender, the Emperor spoke firmly and chidingly to the military emphasizing his determination to spare the nation of further unnecessary suffering. He then personally assumed the risk and responsibility of informing the nation of the decision to surrender on August 15, 1954. Only a few months later, the Emperor decided to strengthen the ties between the Throne and the people by repudiating the mystic concept of the Emperor which had been exploited by the reactionary elements. This took the form of the momentous New Year's Day Rescript of 1946. This pronouncement, in effect, was tantamount to the revival of the organ theory which was banned in 1935 and the vindication of Professor Minobe's constitutional views.

THE EMPEROR AS AN INSTITUTION

A careful examination of the position of the Emperor in history reveals that its real significance is to be found in the role he played as a symbol rather than as the actual wielder of political power. Throughout most of Japanese history he was the ceremonial head of the state performing all the ceremonial functions. This was true particularly during the nearly seven centuries of feudalism and even during the period of the supremacy of the Fujiwara family in the tenth and eleventh centuries. Conferring of honors, court ceremonies and rituals were his functions, leaving him entirely uninvolved in matters of actual government.

Through history, he remained partly by choice and partly by circumstances steadfastly aloof from the exercise of power in his position as ruler. Since the Emperor seldom, if ever, exercised power as the real ruler of the nation, he has never been feared or opposed either by the common people or by the powerful military leaders and the aristocracy. In surviving the vicissitudes of history, the Emperor has come to be accepted as the one sure symbol of continuity and stability of the nation. Undoubtedly it is one of the most enduring political institutions the world has seen.

It was not until the seventeenth and eighteenth centuries when the Emperor both as an institution and person was overshadowed by the shogun, the *de facto* ruler of Japan, that the sentiment of loyalty to the Emperor actually developed. When strong pressures from the outside world came to be felt by the nation after its reopening to Western intercourse in the middle of the nineteenth century, the urgent need to build up a strong nation prompted the leaders to strengthen the monarchy to an extent never before achieved.

The Emperor became the epicenter of the social and emotional life of the nation and the apex of the pyramid of political structure.

Theoretically he was made the source and possessor of absolute sovereignty but in practice he was carefully protected from the trouble of exercising it. All his decisions were made for him by those who surrounded him. However, he sometimes expressed his views though not in public or known to the public.[17]

While the Constitution of 1889 gave him absolute power, not once did he exercise that power on his own initiative. He acted always and only on the advice of his ministers. He was therefore spared the possibility of making errors of omission or commission. The responsibility was always that of the minister or ministers. The sanctity and blamelessness of the Emperor could be and were preserved.

Even more than the British monarch, it can be said that the Japanese Emperor reigns but does not rule. As the father of the people, and the rallying point of the whole nation, he has been powerful as a moral force. As the personification and symbol of the nation, its unity, and heritage, he does not express any shading of political opinion in public. Rather, he transcends party considerations and party struggles and does not become a part of the machinery of party government, for he represents and symbolizes the whole nation and not a segment, a faction, or a party. He does not function as a referee or umpire or a counterpoise but is automatically a harmonizer and unifier. Because the Emperor does not involve himself in partisanship of any sort, he is able to exert tremendous influence at times. He is in a position to give admonition, encouragement, or warning as the occasion arises without actually involving himself as a mediator.[18]

THE EMPEROR UNDER THE NEW CONSTITUTION

In his New Year's Day Rescript to the nation on January 7, 1946, Emperor Hirohito declared that the ties between him and his people "have always stood upon mutual trust and affection" and not "upon

[17] After seeing Foreign Minister Matsuoka on May 8, 1941, shortly after he returned from his trip to Europe where he had concluded the Soviet-Japanese Non-Aggression Pact, the Emperor expressed his view to Lord Keeper of the Privy Seal that perhaps it might be well to replace Matsuoka because of his militant attitude which had shaken the Emperor's confidence in him. Konoe Fumimaro, *Heiwa e no Doryoku*, p. 49.

[18] The British monarch, within the limits of strict impartiality, played a mediating role in a political crisis, as for instance in connection with the Parliament Act of 1911, over Home Rule in 1914, and in the financial crisis of 1931. L. S. Amery, *Thoughts on the Constitution*, pp. 5–6. There is nothing comparable to the above instances so far as the Japanese emperor is concerned. Queen Victoria frequently intervened by expressing objections to appointments. Such interventions are unknown in Japanese government.

mere legends and myths," nor are they "predicated on the false conception that the Emperor is divine and that the Japanese people are
superior to other races and destined to rule the world."[19]   The Japanese people were stirred by the declaration which appeared in the
newspapers throughout the country on an otherwise peaceful New
Year morning.   There had not been the slightest inkling in advance
that the momentous declaration was forthcoming and the nation was
taken by surprise.   Although few people if any believed in the divinity of the Emperor, no one had actually dared to act or express himself publicly on the matter.   However, the declaration let the bars
down, making the people feel much closer to the Emperor.   This
Rescript was a clear repudiation of the notion inculcated in the minds
of the Japanese by the ultranationalists that they were a chosen people with a divine mission to rule Asia, if not the world.   The Emperor called on the nation to unite firmly in its resolve to face the
present ordeal and to see civilization consistently in peace "so that
a bright future will be realized not only for Japan but for the whole
of humanity."   He appealed to the people to utilize the strong love
of the family and love of country which they have, in working toward
love of mankind.[20]

In the newspapers, for the first time there appeared pictures of the
Emperor in civilian clothes and in company with the Empress and
their children.   This was as unprecedented as the New Year's Day
Rescript itself.   Formerly, the only pictures seen by the public were
those of the Emperor in either a military uniform or an ancient ceremonial costume.

When the new Constitution took effect in May, 1947, the process
of "humanizing" and popularizing the Emperor was greatly accelerated.   The Emperor made personal appearances everywhere even at
places which were formerly thought unfit for the imperial presence.
He visited mines, entered the shafts and spoke to the miners, visited
factories and farms, and attended baseball games and other events
with the Empress.[21]   He has even attended a movie in one of the
regular movie theaters in Tokyo.   On his tours to various parts of

[19] The quotation is from the translation which appeared in the *New York Times*,
January 1, 1946.
[20] The Emperor's Rescript was in substance the reaffirmation of the principles of
the Charter Oath of Five Articles which was proclaimed by his grandfather,
Emperor Meiji, in 1868.
[21] Formerly the Emperor visited only a few places, and on very special occasions
such as the commencement exercises of Tokyo Imperial University and under very
official circumstances.

the country he met and spoke to individuals in the crowds welcoming him. Not being accustomed to meeting the public, the Emperor at first was obviously ill at ease and even at a loss to find the proper words to use. It was a novel experience for the people to meet their ruler face to face, which they had never done before, but they liked it. Once the Emperor became accustomed to the new ways, he enjoyed the freedom from restrictions and guarded seclusion which had been imposed on him. Meeting ordinary people and seeing them just as they are in their everyday life and sensing their attitude toward him made his position more meaningful.

In spite of the great progress achieved in making the imperial family a part of Japanese life, it will be quite some time before anything comparable to the pragmatism of the British monarchy can develop. British rulers were killed on the battlefield, murdered in dungeons, beheaded, crowned and uncrowned, exiled, imprisoned as mad, they married commoners and did things which ordinary Britons did. But while few of the things which have happened to British rulers have happened to Japanese emperors too, they have been carefully shielded from various external influences.

Living members of the British royal family have done almost everything an ordinary individual does without stigma or censure in any way. They have worked as traveling salesmen, advertized cosmetics, danced the cancan, married commoners, and even had Nazi in-laws. Yet nobody thought these things unusual, undignified, or derogatory. The Japanese royalty has not yet had sufficient time nor the favorable conditions to become pragmatic in its activities to the same extent. However, the initial steps have been taken in such a direction for fifty-one members of eleven families related to the imperial house gave up their royal status in 1947.

The Role of the Emperor

The change which has been effected with regard to the role and position of the Emperor is so basic that there no longer is an emperor system such as existed under the old Constitution.[22] The Emperor was sacred and inviolable and as head of the state he combined in himself all the powers of the state, legislative, executive, and judicial. Constitutionally, though merely theoretically, he held unlimited power. But in practice he never did exercise such power or even take the initiative in decision making. His decisions were

[22] Yokota Kisaburo, *Tenno Sei,* p. 110. This view is taken also by Professor Nambara Shigeru and Sasaki Soichi.

always based on the recommendations of his ministers. Consequently, in practical politics in the struggle for power, groups and
individuals vied with one another to maneuver themselves into a
position which would enable them to wield power in his name. As
we have already seen, the greater the mysticism surrounding the Emperor, the more easily was the system exploitable.

Under the new postwar Constitution which became effective in
1947, the Emperor is no longer the chief of state or the representative
of the nation. He has become merely the symbol of the state and the
unity of the people, deriving his position from the will of the people
in whom sovereignty now resides. This means in effect that legally,
if the majority of the people so desire, the institution of the Emperor
can be abolished.[23] He no longer possesses any power of government for he has ceased to be the fountainhead of power which he
was formerly. He performs only such acts in matters of state as
are provided for in the Constitution but he must secure the advice
and approval of the Cabinet. For these acts which he performs, the
Cabinet, and not he, is responsible.

In other words, he has been relegated to the position of performing
only ceremonial functions which normally comprise but a part of the
over-all functions of a chief of state with governmental powers.
Among these acts which are specifically enumerated in the Constitution are (1) the appointment of the Prime Minister designated by
the Diet; (2) the appointment of the Chief Justice of the Supreme
Court as designated by the Cabinet; (3) the promulgation of constitutional amendments, laws, treaties, and cabinet orders; (4) proclamation of general election of the members of the Diet; (5) convocation of the Diet at which he gives a brief speech opening the
session; (6) dissolution of the House of Representatives; (7) receiving foreign ambassadors and ministers; (8) attestation of instruments of ratification and other diplomatic documents as provided for
by laws; (9) attestation of the appointment and dismissal of Ministers
of State and other officials, and of full powers and credentials of
Ambassadors and Ministers; (10) awarding of honors; (11) attestation of general and special amnesty, commutation of punishment,
reprieve and restoration of rights; and (12) performance of ceremonial functions. In the performance of his acts, the Emperor may
delegate the function as may be provided by law. This is in sharp
contrast to the powers with which the Emperor was vested under
the Meiji Constitution. He was the supreme spiritual and religious

[23] *Ibid.*, p. 70.

leader of the nation by virtue of his position as the high priest of Shinto, the political head of state in whom sovereignty resided, and the commander in chief of the armed forces of the nation in which capacity he functioned independently of his position as the political head. Thus he combined in himself three distinct roles: ecclesiastical or spiritual, political, and military.

It is quite evident that, now more than ever, the Emperor reigns but does not govern. His power is practically nil, compared with that of the British monarch who plays a very definite role in the governmental process. While the British monarch has the right to be consulted by the Prime Minister, to encourage certain courses of action and to warn against others, the Japanese ruler has none of these rights. However, he is provided with information by Cabinet ministers on what is going on. He does not call a party leader to form a government, he simply performs the ceremony of appointing a Prime Minister who has already been formally selected by the Diet. He has no power to refuse a dissolution of the Diet such as the British monarch enjoys as a prerogative. Needless to say, the Emperor cannot vote. Nor can he express any shading of political opinion in public. He cannot actually intervene to influence important decisions. His moral influence however is still considerable and he is not a figurehead by any means. The relegation of the Emperor constitutionally to the position of symbol seems quite drastic, but in the light of history it is not unnatural or unreasonable and certainly does not do violence to the institution. For the emperors never personally concerned themselves with government or exercised powers of government. Instead they delegated those powers to officials close to them, and served rather as a spiritual and moral guiding force.[24]

The right to succession to the throne remains in the imperial family and the order of succession is according to the practice established under the old system after 1868. Primogeniture is the rule with succession running through the male line despite the fact that in early Japanese history there were a number of empresses who ruled in their own right, a development which has not been duplicated in any other major Asian country. A provision for regency exists in accordance with the Imperial House Law.

Imperial household affairs and finances, which under the old Constitution were independent of and completely outside the control of the government, have been brought under the jurisdiction of the Diet.

[24] Takagi Yasaka, "Kempo kaiseian ni taisuru shusei shian." *Chuo Koron*, July, 1946.

The financial needs of the Imperial household are provided by appropriations subject to the approval of the Diet.[25]

Furthermore, the greater part of the extensive property holdings of the imperial family was transferred to the State, reducing the Emperor's private property to only a fraction of what it used to be and making it taxable just as is the private property of an individual citizen.[26]   These and other changes in the economic position of the imperial household reduced immeasurably the role and influence of the Emperor in the Japanese economy, which were formerly very considerable.   The scope of the royalty was reduced noticeably by decreasing, if not eliminating, the possibility of economic dependence on the imperial family on the part of its close relatives.   Until 1946, the then existing eleven princely families, by virtue of their close blood relationship to the imperial family, enjoyed special status and privileges which were revoked in 1946.   Many of those who were within the circle of royalty voluntarily gave up their status and privileges and became for practical purposes commoners and went into the various occupations and professions.   Princesses including even the Emperor's daughter have married commoners.   By 1953 only the three houses of the Emperor's brothers were included in the category of royal families.[27]   Since titles of nobility were abolished under the new Constitution the remaining eleven former princely families are not even titled.

Popular Attitute Toward the Emperor

It was the firm belief of Prince Ito, the "Father of the Meiji Constitution," that the Emperor is absolutely beyond criticism in any manner or form and that he should not be subjected to irreverent discussion or derogatory comment.   This conviction was the basis for Article III which provided: "The Emperor is sacred and inviolable." From this provision stemmed lèse-majesté, an offense violating the dignity of the ruler.   Under the new Constitution lèse-majesté has been abolished.   However, the attitude of reverence toward the Emperor continues much in the same manner as before.   It is the old attitude which is still restraining the government as well as the public from using the likeness of the Emperor on paper money or postage stamps, a practice which has long been accepted in Western countries without anyone even suspecting that it might impair the dignity of the sovereign or president so honored.   There are, however, those

[25] Imperial Household Economic Law promulgated on January 15, 1947.
[26] Tanaka Sogoro, *Tenno no Kenkyu*, pp. 298–304.
[27] The families of Princes Chichibu, Takamatsu, and Mikasa.

who feel that the use of the Emperor's picture on stamps and other widely used items in everyday life will "humanize" the Emperor and increase popular affection for him.[28]

The loss of governmental power by the Emperor does not seem to have detracted one bit from his dignity.   On the contrary his position as a moral and spiritual force has been actually enhanced.   The adoration of the people now seems to be greater than ever because of, rather than in spite of, the "humanization" which has been achieved. Under the old Constitution, he could have said, if he chose to, like Louis XIV of France, "*L'état c'est moi.*"   Today even under the new Constitution, so far as the popular attitude is concerned, in a symbolic sense at least the Emperor may still be regarded as the State.

[28] In the "Letters from the People" column in the influential Tokyo newspaper *Asahi,* there appeared a letter on March 14, 1954, urging the postal authorities to issue stamps with the Emperor's picture on it, citing the success of a commemorative stamp issued in New Zealand on the occasion of Queen Elizabeth's visit.

7

The Prime Minister
and His Cabinet

HISTORY OF THE CABINET SYSTEM

The Cabinet system in Japan came into existence for the first time by imperial ordinance in December, 1885.[1] Unlike the evolution of parliamentary government in Great Britain where the cabinet was the last element to be established,[2] the Japanese development was reversed. The setting up of the Cabinet antedated the promulgation of the Constitution by four years and the opening of parliament, that is the Diet, by a full half decade. In December, 1889, ten months after the promulgation of the Constitution, a revised cabinet law went into effect with some modifications but this was actually the sanctioning of the system, as it was initiated in 1885, under the Meiji Constitution. This was accomplished by an imperial ordinance[3] rather than by statutory enactment of the Diet which was yet to open. With necessary modifications from time to time, the system continued until 1947 when the new Constitution went into effect.

Thus it was an extraconstitutional system, as in the United States,

---

[1] Imperial proclamation No. 69 of 1885 created the nine administrative departments which became the Cabinet. They were Home Affairs, Foreign Affairs, War, Navy, Justice, Education, Agriculture and Commerce, and Communications, each to be headed by a minister of state. The position of Prime Minister was created and Ito became the first presiding officer of the Cabinet.

[2] In Britain it was the last element to be added to the three which already existed, the electorate, the political parties, and the Parliament, thereby giving the final touch to the representative system. With it the system of parliamentary government assumed its final, though not perfect, form.

[3] Imperial Ordinance No. 135 of 1889.

144

Great Britain, and France, for there was no provision for such a body in the Constitution itself. Even the term "cabinet" was not to be found in the Constitution. The only possible hint was in Article 55 which stated that the Ministers shall give advice to the Emperor and be responsible for it.[4] This was by no means unusual since in Great Britain it was not until 1900 that the word "cabinet" appeared for the first time, on the notice paper of the House of Commons and although there is an oblique reference to it in the Ministers of the Crown Act of 1937, the Cabinet as such still has no statutory existence.[5] The ministers under the old Constitution advised the Emperor individually and separately and not as a body collectively responsible to the Emperor. Furthermore, the Prime Minister was not really the chief who had the power to control the group; he was only the moderator of a group of equals.[6] Consequently the Cabinet was not a strong executive organ.

There were also several other factors which contributed to the weakness of the Cabinet under the old system. More than once the Privy Council[7] proved to be the bane of existence for the Prime Minister. Even the House of Peers could and did not hesitate to make the effective functioning of the Cabinet impossible. However, the greatest stumbling block was the army which from 1900 on had the power to make or break the Cabinet.[8] There was also the problem of the executive size of the Cabinet[9] which made it unwieldly and well-nigh impossible for it not to get out of hand. Finally, there was the natural but unfortunate degeneration of Cabinet ministers into mere administrative heads of departments.[10] Because of the weakness of the Cabinet system as well as the multiplicity of political parties it was very easy to overthrow a government.[11] This is no longer the

[4] Article 55 reads: "The respective ministers of state shall give their advice to the Emperor, and, be responsible for it. All laws, imperial ordinances and imperial rescripts, of whatever kind, that relate to the affairs of state, require the countersignature of a minister of state."

[5] L. S. Amery, *Thoughts on the Constitution,* p. 1 *footnote.*

[6] Yamazaki Tansho, *Naikaku Ron,* pp. 245–265.

[7] *Ibid.,* pp. 225–239.

[8] See the article by the author, "The Military and the Government in Japan," *American Political Science Review,* XXXV, June, 1941, pp. 529–539, for the position of virtual independence the Japanese military enjoyed.

[9] Yamazaki, *op. cit.,* pp. 265–275.

[10] Yamazaki, *op. cit.,* pp. 276–280.

[11] In the sixty-year period from 1885 to 1945, forty-one cabinets were formed out of which twenty collapsed because of internal difficulties or weaknesses while only three fell because of attacks by the Diet. These were the third Katsura Cabinet in 1913, the Kiyoura Cabinet in 1924 and the Hayashi Cabinet in 1937.

case with the postwar Cabinet system which has an entirely different basis giving it the strength and unity it never possessed under the old system.

NATURE OF THE CABINET

Under the Constitution of 1947 the Japanese government comes very close to that of Great Britain in operation, if not so much in spirit. We can therefore get a clear idea of its nature in the definition given by W. I. Jennings, that the government is a "body of party politicians selected from among the members of that party or group of parties which has a majority in the House of Commons. By this operation the operations of government and legislative are integrated."[12]

It is quite evident that the Cabinet is the central directing instrument of government in administration and in legislation. It has supreme control of the national executive in accordance with the policy set forth by the Diet. It is constantly coordinating administrative action and delimiting the power of the various departments of the government. In short, it governs the country. To a considerable degree, it even exercises control over the Diet. This is in sharp contrast to the French Cabinet which is so pitifully weak that it cannot give political stability to the country. In legislation, it outlines a program much in the manner that the executive branch in the United States does. Legislative proposals both from within and without are sanctioned by the Cabinet. In other words, it controls the final determination of the policy to be submitted to the Diet. Thus, the Cabinet constitutes the starting point and mainspring of action in the management of national affairs. In the concentration of power and in the decisive action it possesses, the Japanese Cabinet comes nearer to that of Great Britain than of the United States.

At least in its constitutional framework, Japan has been provided with responsible government. The responsibility of the Cabinet is not merely towards the majority in the Diet but also to the wider interests of the nation as a whole. As members of the Diet Cabinet ministers are responsible to that body as a whole and to the nation for the effective functioning of the parliamentary process by the maintenance of full and free discussion of every aspect of government policy. While the responsibility of the Cabinet is unmistakably clear, the dual role of its members has not been fully appreciated. For more often they are conscious only of their role as officials in the exec-

[12] W. I. Jennings, *Cabinet Government*, p. 20. See also L. S. Amery, *Thoughts on the Constitution*, pp. 70–71.

utive branch. This is quite understandable, though rather lamentable, since the Japanese political tradition, having developed under and having known only monarchy, favored a strong executive, both in concept and practice under the influence of Confucian statecraft and ethics.

As has happened everywhere, in Japan too, the constant expansion of the spheres of activity and the increasing burden of government make it impossible for the Cabinet to give adequate attention to every problem. Consequently, much of the work of the Cabinet has had to be delegated to the lower echelons of subcabinet level and bureaus.

CABINET FUNCTIONS AND ORGANIZATION

By virtue of Article 65, the Cabinet is constitutionally the highest organ of executive power. It is not, as in Britain, a meeting of "His Majesty's confidential advisers" with the function of advising the monarch.[13] It does not have a monopoly of executive power for it does not exercise it exclusively. For example, there is the Board of Audit which exercises executive power and yet is independent and beyond the control of the Cabinet.

Included in the executive functions of the Cabinet as a body are (1) the making of great political decisions and (2) initiating vital policies. All major decisions of policy must be those of the Cabinet as a whole. In other words, they must be supported or rejected by every single member of the body. For every decision of the Cabinet each member is absolutely and irrevocably responsible. This principle of joint responsibility of Ministers which did not exist under the old system is predicated on the principle of absolute responsibility of every member. If there is any dissenter or intransigent, he must either resign or risk a dismissal by the Prime Minister.

In spite of the constitutional provision that the Diet is the highest organ of state power, and is the sole lawmaking organ of the State,[14] the initiative in legislation rests with the Cabinet, as in Great Britain. Executive leadership in legislation is a fact even in the United States since most of the important legislation is drafted in the White House and executive agencies. In Japan, the Cabinet has the task of initiating, designing, and working out the details of almost all important legislation.

It is not possible to gather what the functions of any organ are by merely examining the constitutional provisions. This is particularly

---

[13] Jennings, *op. cit.*, p. 71.

[14] Article 41 reads: "The Diet shall be the highest organ of state power, and shall be the sole law-making organ of the State."

true in the case of the Cabinet whose functions are complex and variegated. However, on the basis of the Constitution, it is possible to list the various functions with which it is charged.

1. Submit bills to the Diet. (Article 72)
2. Report on general national affairs and foreign relations to the Diet. (Article 72)
3. Exercise control and supervision over various administrative branches. (Article 72)
4. Administer the law faithfully and conduct affairs of State. (Article 73)
5. Prepare and submit a budget to the Diet for each fiscal year. (Articles 73, 86)
6. Manage foreign affairs, negotiate and conclude treaties. (Article 73)
7. Issue cabinet orders to execute the provisions of the Constitution and of the law. (Article 73)
8. Administer the civil service. (Article 73)
9. Decide on general amnesty, special amnesty, commutation of punishment, reprieve, and restoration of rights. (Article 73)
10. Attach signatures to all laws and cabinet orders. (Article 74)
11. Decide whenever necessary to convoke an extraordinary session of the Diet. (Article 58)
12. Convoke the House of Councillors in emergency session when the House of Representatives has been dissolved. (Article 54)
13. Designate the Chief Judge of the Supreme Court and appoint all other judges. (Articles 7, 79, 80)
14. Advise the dissolution of the House of Representatives. (Article 7)
15. Advise of proclamation of general election of the members of the Diet. (Article 7)
16. Advise the convocation of the Diet. (Article 7)
17. Make payments from the reserve fund in the budget for unforeseen deficiencies and get subsequent Diet approval. (Article 87)
18. Submit to the Diet final accounts of expenditures and revenues along with the statement of audit prepared by the Board of Audit. (Article 90)
19. Report at regular intervals and at least once a year to the Diet and the people on the state of national finances. (Article 91)

Inasmuch as the Cabinet is based on the Diet and functions effectively only with the support of the majority of its members, it determines the national policies in the name of that majority. Since that majority owes its existence to the people who elected the members, the Cabinet must heed public opinion. But at the same time the government must lead public opinion and, once it has decided upon its policies, it must push its legislative program through the Diet. Thus while endeavoring to harmonize national policies with public opinion, it has to formulate policies to be submitted to the

Diet for enactment into law.[15] When the policies are enacted into law, the Cabinet is entrusted with their execution.

It is quite clear by now that the executive power in practice, if not in theory, plays a decisive role in legislation by making a political decision as to what policies are to be adopted and how they are to be formulated so that they will be acceptable and feasible as legislation. It is the planning of a legislative program that takes up the greater part of the time and energy of the government and calls for the best minds and the highest statesmanship. The administrative function of the government, particularly the day-to-day operation of administrative departments and agencies, can be reduced pretty much to routine and does not require as much imagination or ingenuity as the political problems involved in high-level policy making and decision making.

Organization of the Cabinet

The Office of the Prime Minister is the nerve center and operational matrix of the government which is headed by the Prime Minister himself. He has control over the office and the auxiliary boards attached to it. The administrative managing director of the office is the Director of the Cabinet Secretariat who sometimes occupies a Cabinet post and is assisted by two deputy directors. It is the Cabinet Secretariat which manages the general affairs of the cabinet and serves as an auxiliary organ to the Prime Minister and the Cabinet. It fixes items on the agenda of the meeting of the Cabinet. Next in importance, or perhaps of equal importance in certain ways, is the Director of the Cabinet Bureau of Legislation who is responsible for giving legal advice and opinion to the Prime Minister and the Cabinet on the drafting of legislative bills and administrative orders and for carrying on research and study in both domestic (municipal) and international law and their interpretation and application. These two directors form the brain trust in the exercise of governmental power and in assisting in the translation of political power into governmental power.

The work of the Office of the Prime Minister is carried on by the several bureaus into which it is divided, namely, the Bureaus of Legislation, Statistics, Pensions, and Decorations. There are, in addition to and outside of the Office of the Prime Minister, a number of Boards and Commissions which function as its auxiliary organs in investigating, planning, and policy recommending, as well as in ad-

[15] Royama Masamichi (ed.), *Shin Kempo Koza,* II, pp. 348.

ministering those agencies under the direct control of the Prime Minister.[16]

At present there are eleven administrative departments, the same number as in the United States. Before World War II there was a time when there were thirteen departments, but compared with Great Britain or France the number has been relatively small. There is no priority ranking of the departments on the basis of either importance or date of establishment as in the United States. The organization of the administrative departments follows the same pattern. A department or ministry is headed by the Minister who is assisted by the Vice-Minister, who is a career man and is the real administrator, and by a Parliamentary Vice-Minister, a party man who serves as the liaison between the department and the Diet. Each ministry is subdivided into bureaus which number anywhere from four to nine depending on the scope of administrative matters it handles.[17] As a rule the bureaus are further subdivided into sections which constitute the lowest level of departmental organization. Not infrequently, however, there is an intermediate level which may be translated as a division (*bu*) which comes between the bureau and the section. Some of the ministries have in addition, institutes both of the research and training types, while all of them have attached bureaus as well as committees and commissions.

[16] As of September 1, 1953, there were the following:
  a. Seven boards
    1. Economic Policy (Deliberation) Board
    2. Administrative Management Board
    3. National Security Board
    4. Local Self-Government Board
    5. Hokkaido Development Board
    6. Procurement Board
    7. Imperial Household Affairs Board
  b. Three commissions
    1. National Public Safety Commission
    2. Fair Trade Commission
    3. Land Adjustment Commission
  c. Two central administrative headquarters
    1. National Rural Police Headquarters
    2. National Fire Defense Headquarters
[17] Number of bureaus in the various ministries:

Legal Affairs	9	International Trade and Industry	9
Foreign Affairs	8	Transportation	7
Finance	8	Postal Affairs	6
Education	6	Labor	5
Welfare	9	Construction	5
Agriculture and Forestry	5		

The Ministry Secretariat is charged with the important managerial and housekeeping functions of running the department smoothly. Among other things, it handles the following matters:

1. Confidential business.
2. Custody of Minister's and Ministry's seals.
3. Appointment, dismissal, promotion, and training of personnel.
4. Study and planning of the organization and operation of the department.
5. Examination, coordination, and adjustment of the administrative activities within the department's jurisdiction.
6. Examination of legislative bills and other documents.
7. Receiving, sending, compiling, and preserving of public documents.
8. Preparation of studies and statistics pertaining to the department's administrative activities, collecting of materials, distribution of printed matter and publishing.
9. Fiscal affairs including budget and final accounts.
10. Custody of department's property and equipment.
11. Management of health and welfare facilities for departmental personnel.

THE PRIME MINISTER

The position of Prime Minister is specifically provided for in the Constitution. This is in contrast to what obtains in Great Britain where constitutionally there is no office of Prime Minister.[18] Since there is no salary attached to the office, it is customary for the British Prime Minister to take some other office simultaneously, usually the First Lord of the Treasury, to be remunerated for his services.[19]

By virtue of the dual position he holds, the Prime Minister is the most powerful political leader in the nation, holding a position similar to that of the British Prime Minister whose powers are always great, and in an emergency not inferior to those of a dictator.[20] As chief executive, he is the head of the government. He is also the administrative head of the Premier's Office. As leader of the party he commands the support of the strongest party, more often than not, with a majority in the Diet. With his seat in the Diet he is the directly elected representative of the people and one of the nation's lawmakers. The Prime Minister is thus entrusted with the supreme political leadership of the nation and is answerable to the Diet and

[18] In Great Britain the existence of a Prime Minister was recognized for the first time in 1878 in a public document, the Treaty of Berlin, and later in the *Court Circular* of 1900, and mentioned for the first time in a statute when the Chequers Trust was constituted in 1917. L. S. Amery, *Thoughts on the Constitution*, p. 1 *footnotes.*

[19] W. I. Jennings, *Cabinet Government*, p. 71.
[20] L. S. Amery, *Thoughts on the Constitution*, p. 73.

ultimately to the people.   This was, indeed, not the case under the old system.

Powers

The Prime Minister derives his great power from his constitutional position of chief executive and undisputed head of the administration.   If the Cabinet may be compared to a board of directors or an executive committee, he is its powerful chairman.   As head of the Cabinet, he represents the executive body internally and externally. He calls the meetings of the Cabinet and presides over the proceedings, holding a tight rein over the members.   He controls and supervises its various and sundry administrative activities.   As the Cabinet representative, he reports to the Diet on general national affairs and foreign relations.

He is vested with the power to appoint all the Ministers of State who will sit on his cabinet and designates one of them to be the Vice Premier.[21]   As in Great Britain, the Prime Minister's power of appointment is a personal authority which he exercises as he wishes. The result is that he picks close personal and political friends not infrequently giving rise to more than just a semblance of "cronyism." However, the truth of the matter is that even the Prime Minister does not have complete freedom to make appointments in disregard of party and other demands.   Along with the power of appointment, the Prime Minister has the unquestioned and absolute power to remove any cabinet member at his pleasure.   This power of removal has been demonstrated convincingly and dramatically on two separate occasions since the Constitution of 1947 went into effect.[22]   He also has the power to reshuffle and reconstitute his cabinet any time he wishes to change its composition in order to meet the demands of political exigencies or for the sake of efficiency.   This power was dramatically demonstrated for example in July, 1951, when all the members of the Yoshida Cabinet submitted their resignation to enable the Premier to effect a large scale reorganization to prepare for the forthcoming peace treaty.   It is also reflected in the frequency with

[21] This power is derived from Article 9 of the Law of the Cabinet (Naikakuho) which enables the Premier to designate one of the ministers as Vice Premier to be acting Premier in his absence.   The first time this was put into practice was on June 1, 1947, when Prime Minister Katayama designated Ashida as Vice Premier.

[22] Prime Minister Katayama dismissed Agriculture and Forestry Minister Hirano in November, 1947.   This was the first time this particular power was exercised and created considerable furor, but not on a legal basis since Article 68 of the Constitution is clear and definite.   The next time it was exercised by Premier Yoshida who removed Agriculture and Forestry Minister Hirokawa in March, 1953.

which reshuffling has taken place in the period since the new Constitution took effect.[23]   There is another power which the head of the cabinet possesses.   He has the power to prevent legal action being taken against the Ministers of State during their tenure of office Article 75).   All these powers which did not exist formerly but were advocated, became a reality under the Constitution of 1947, giving unity and strength to the Cabinet and making the principle of joint responsibility feasible.

We have already seen how the Prime Minister has to perform a dual role, one part of which is clearly defined legally, as the head of government.   But the less clearly and, in fact, barely defined is the political role.   In this role, he must insure harmony among his Ministers of State and lead the cabinet as a unified body, for should there be discord which impairs its harmony and prevents its functioning as a unified whole, it must collapse.   In case the Prime Minister happens to be the leader of the party in power, he must lead it with skill and tact.   If it happens to be a coalition of several parties, he must be able to maintain the coalition by effective leadership.   He must direct the activities of the government and maintain the kind of relationship with the Diet which will enable him to continue to enjoy the confidence especially of the House of Representatives.   Finally, he must meet with all sorts of representatives and delegations on important problems and study them carefully and thoroughly and utilize party meetings and every other opportunity available to lead public opinion.[24]

Qualifications of a Prime Minister

Qualifications for any office can be stated easily enough since they are usually mere specifications.   However, unlike the problem of building a house or procuring certain commodities, in the selection of a prime minister or a cabinet minister all the specifications cannot be met as a builder would an architect's blueprint.   There are two categories of qualifications, the legal and the political.   The legal requirement is that he must be a member of the Diet and that he must be a civilian.   Since the Constitution merely stipulates membership in the Diet, it must be interpreted as membership in either House.   However, in practice, the prime ministers so far have all come from the

---

[23] Prime Minister Yoshida holds the record in the number of cabinet ministers he has appointed.   Such turnover is unthinkable in Great Britain or the United States.   Even to political observers in Japan it appeared much too frequent and capricious.

[24] Royama Masamichi (ed.), *Shin Kempo Koza*, II, pp. 353–354.

House of Representatives and probably will continue to do so.[25] Understandably the political requirements are the more difficult of the two to fulfill. He must be the leader of the party which commands an absolute majority in the House of Representatives. Or else he must be the leader of a party which, lacking a majority, has the support of other parties to be able to form a coalition government. There is another qualification of great importance. He must be *persona grata* and completely acceptable to the economic organizations (or business interests) and have sufficient contacts with them. Needless to say, he must, above all, possess the necessary qualities of leadership.

Actually there have been all sorts of prime ministers, ranging from the able and effective to the completely ineffectual. Some have been little more than chairman of a committee concerned primarily, if not only, with securing the greatest possible measure of agreement among more forceful colleagues. Not a few were manipulated by those behind the scenes. Others have been those determined to get their own way and have succeeded in attaining their objectives.

Designation and Appointment of the Prime Minister

Since a ship of state without a captain is not only inconceivable but extremely perilous, the first order of business when a new Diet convenes is the designation of a prime minister. This has the highest priority, taking precedence over other matters on the agenda. This does not mean, however, that the selection of the Speaker or the acceptance of the resignation of a member should not precede the selection of a premier.[26] Such matters are actually in the nature of preparatory steps preliminary to getting the Diet organized for effective functioning and cannot be regarded as items of business.

The Japanese method of selecting the head of the government is essentially that which obtains in Great Britain. However, in Britain no formal designation procedure is required; the leader of the majority party is summoned by the King or Queen and is asked to form a government. In Japan there is no custom such as exists in France where the man most responsible for bringing down a government is given the first chance to form a new one.[27] Rather, the custom which

[25] There is not yet in existence an established rule or practice requiring that the Prime Minister must be in the Lower House as there has been in Great Britain since 1923.

[26] Yamazaki Tansho, *Naikaku Ron*, p. 313.

[27] Since Pierre Mendès-France was the man most responsible for the fall of the government, he was asked by President Coty to form a new government. This he did after he was approved by an overwhelming vote by the Assembly on June 17, 1954.

is now quite well established requires that the man who forms a government must be the leader of the strongest party, which commands a majority or plurality of the seats in the Diet.

So far as procedure is concerned, two distinct steps are involved in the designation of the Prime Minister by the Diet. In the first step, ballots are used to select the person to be designated. If any candidate receives the majority of those present, he is declared the Diet's choice for designation. If, however, no one receives a majority, the first- and second-place winners are selected for the final run-off election. In the event of a tie, the winner is chosen by lot. In the second step, a resolution of formal designation of the successful candidate is presented and voted upon. The same procedure takes place in both houses. In the event that the disagreement between the two houses in the conference committee cannot be resolved, the action of the House of Representatives takes precedence over that of the House of Councillors and becomes the decision of the Diet.[28] This actually occurred in March, 1948, when Prime Minister Ashida won over his rival, Yoshida. The candidate who has been officially designated by the Diet becomes Prime Minister upon formal appointment by the Emperor.[29] Needless to say the Emperor's act is a ceremonial formality which is automatic and perfunctory for he has no power to refuse to perform it.

How the Premier Was Chosen Under the Meiji Constitution

Under the Meiji Constitution the appointment of the Prime Minister was strictly a matter of imperial prerogative. There was no condition imposed as to whether he should be a party man or a party leader. Until 1898, there was actually a deliberate effort on the part of those who had the power of recommendation to keep party men out of the picture. However, for the smooth operation of the government, it became necessary to secure the cooperation and support of the Diet and the practice of selecting the leader of the majority party came into existence and was in effect for a time. Yet until 1918 when a commoner, Hara, became Prime Minister, it was impossible for a person to be recommended for the position without the

[28] This is one of the reasons why the Prime Minister, as a matter of practical politics, would have to come from the Lower House whose support he must have. No party leader who feels that he would have a chance to form a government would seek election to the Upper House and thereby lessen his chance.

[29] In France the Prime Minister who is designated by the President has to be approved by the majority of the 628-member Assembly before he can form a government.

blessings of the Elder Statesmen and other influential persons close to the Throne. This meant, in effect, that he had to have family background, high official position, and some sort of clan connections, that is, connections with the influential clans of Choshu or Satsuma.[30] It is interesting to note that there has been only one instance of a Prime Minister who was actually a prince of the blood and closely related to the Emperor.[31] The selection of a premier was a very simple procedure in the beginning. In 1898, the Elder Statesmen, an informal group of distinguished statesmen of the early Meiji period, were called upon by the Emperor to recommend a new premier.[32] So far as is known, this became the precedent for the procedure in which the informal, extralegal, extraconstitutional body known as Genro, or Elder Statesmen, decided who should form the next government. The Emperor summoned the person recommended and commanded him to form a government. This practice continued until the late 1930's when there remained only one Genro, Prince Saionji, who was firm in his belief that a new method of selecting a premier was due.

Although it was not until 1940 that the last of the Genro passed away, a method had been adopted by the second half of the 1930's. The Lord Keeper of the Privy Seal assumed the responsibility of recommending a premier after consultation with the President of the Privy Council, Minister of the Imperial Household, and the ex-Premiers who came to be known as the *jushin*. This method continued right to the end of the war in 1945.[33]

Professional Backgrounds Represented by Prime Ministers

The premiership has always been the ultimate goal of the politically ambitious. In Japanese political circles, a politician is not regarded as a really great success unless he attains the premiership, just as

[30] The lack of such background and connections was the chief reason for Hara being by-passed several times for the premiership which he finally attained in 1918.

[31] This unprecedented event took place a few days after surrender on August 17, 1945 when the Higashikuni government was formed.

[32] Yanaga, Chitoshi, *Japan Since Perry*, p. 219.

[33] Following the resignation of the Koiso Cabinet in April, 1945, the Lord Keeper of the Privy Seal Kido called a meeting of the ex-Premiers which was attended by Okada, Hirota, Hiranuma, Konoe, Wakatsuki, Tojo, and President of the Privy Council Suzuki. After meeting on April 5 and 6, Baron Suzuki was selected as the candidate for the premiership and on April 6 the Emperor summoned him to the palace and commanded him to form a government.

military men do not consider themselves successful until and unless they attain the rank of full general. But the majority of the people do not yet share the view that the position represents the ultimate in achievement. Youngsters are not told that everyone has a chance to become a premier some day. Yet the premiership is more easily within reach of the Japanese youngster than the presidency is of the American youngster.[34] However, attaining the premiership is not as easy as in France where, as ex-Premier Georges Bidault once remarked, there are forty million potential premiers.

An analysis of the professional backgrounds of the prime ministers reveals the startling fact that the military profession has predominated. The role played by the military in the pre-World War II period was overwhelming. That they contributed decisively to the weakening, stifling, and final demise of parliamentary government is beyond doubt and is borne out statistically. Of the thirty prime ministers from 1885 until 1945, from Prince Ito to Prince Higashikuni inclusive, sixteen or more than half were military men, the army providing eleven and the navy five.[35] Almost without exception, these men were unable or unwilling to understand the role of political parties in parliamentary government and they showed antipathy toward normal healthy political processes.[36] Nor were they able to see the problems of the nation in the broad context of over-all national needs and capacities as well as international relations. Their training militated against their effective functioning in a position which required political skill as much as administrative know-how.

[34] In a period of 70 years, 1885–1954, there have been 51 governments and 34 prime ministers, whereas in the United States there have been 33 presidents in a period of 165 years (1789–1954).

[35] The Army's contribution were Generals Kuroda, Yamagata, Katsura, Terauchi, Tanaka, Hayashi, Abe, Tojo, Koiso, Suzuki, and Higashikuni, while the navy offered Admirals Yamamoto, Kato, Saito, Okada, and Yonai. It must be added that one, General Tanaka, was actually President of the Seiyukai when he became Prime Minister. However, although he was legally the leader of the majority party, he was never able to think or act like a party man. He was a military man always and to the very last.

[36] That the governments headed by military men were held in very low esteem by political observers and commentators can be seen in the characterization of the Terauchi (1916–18), second Yamamoto (1923–24), and Tanaka (1927–29) cabinets as "low-intelligence" governments. Baba Tsunego attributes this condition to a single common denominator, namely, the idea entertained by the premier in each case, that the attainment of the premiership is the ultimate goal in one's search for fame and glory and nothing more. Consequently, they gave no thought to policy making and effective administration. Baba Tsunego, *Gendai Jimbutsu Hyoron*, pp. 211–212.

While most of them had served in the cabinet previously, their ex-periences had been confined pretty much to service portfolios where political acumen had little or no chance of developing.

Next to the military was the bureaucracy which furnished ten prime ministers. They were represented by diplomats, jurists, gov-ernment financial experts, and administrators. Six of them served as party presidents but these ex-bureaucrats were unable to rehabili-tate and reconstitute themselves into nonbureaucratic party men. Bureaucratic psychology and habits prevented them from developing into truly great political leaders.

During this same period of sixty years there were two members of the old nobility which traces its origin back to the seventh cen-tury.[37] But these two men were in public office all their lives. Prince Saionji was at one time president of the Seiyukai but was never a party man. Prince Konoe was an active member of the House of Peers serving as its president for some time and also was the president of the Imperial Rule Assistance Association, a totali-tarian organization which superseded the political parties.

There was actually only one person who could be called a party man in the true sense of the term. Inukai, who was assassinated by ultranationalistic young army cadets and navy officers on May 15, 1932, and with whom party government came to an end, was closest to being a simon-pure party politician untainted by bureaucratic ex-perience.

Surprising though it is, there was not even a single lawyer, that is, a practicing lawyer, who reached the premiership. There has been only one since the end of World War II.[38] This is due in part to the fact that the profession of law was not sufficiently well thought of nor was it particularly lucrative as compared with other countries like the United States, Great Britain, and France. Furthermore, the law has not been considered the logical stepping stone to a career in politics. Significantly, there have been several persons who at one time were engaged in journalistic endeavors though not for long.[39]

[37] From 1885 until 1918, every Prime Minister was titled but it was a title conferred in accordance with the Peerage Act of 1884.

[38] Premier Katayama, whose government extended from May 24, 1947, to March 10, 1948, was the first lawyer in Japan's constitutional history to become prime minister. There have been several legally trained bureaucrats who spent all or most of their lives in government service but never a private practitioner of law before.

[39] Among those distinguishing themselves in politics who had journalistic ex-perience were Hara, Kato, Okuma, Inukai, Saionji, and any number of others of lesser prominence.

With the exception of about seven persons, all the premiers came up from the ranks, that is from membership in the Cabinet. Almost every cabinet member dreams of becoming a prime minister some day. There is no doubt that a person who has served as a cabinet minister has a better chance than one who has not had the valuable experience and contacts that go with membership in the Cabinet.

There have been only a few ex-premiers who served subsequently in the government as ordinary cabinet ministers.[40] This is quite the opposite of what one finds in France where the government may include several ex-premiers.[41] In France not only do most ex-premiers come back into the government but, as has been said frequently, they never really leave the political scene except by death. As of April, 1952, there were sixteen of them alive and all except one were more or less active in politics.

The Prime Minister's Right-Hand Men

There are two men in the government who are the closest associates of the Prime Minister. One is the Vice-Premier who is the *alter ego* and the other is the Director of the Cabinet Secretariat, the confidant of the Prime Minister, who was known under the old system as the Chief Secretary of the Cabinet. His task has been and still is that of the Premier's Chief of Staff in the actual formation and operation of the cabinet. When the newly formed cabinet is announced, his name is always included in the lineup along with that of the Director of the Cabinet Bureau of Legislation. This practice developed because the former is the political strategist in the government[42] and the latter the chief architect and draftsman who translates government policies into specific blueprints of legislative program.

The Director of the Cabinet Secretariat is actually the Prime Minister's private secretary who not infrequently has the rank of minister and is always present at a cabinet meeting. Naturally he knows better than anyone else what is going on within the government. Moreover, he is the chief liasion with the outside and has contacts

[40] There are probably not more than half a dozen such instances. Among them were Yamagata, Kuroda, Matsukata, Takahashi, Yonai, and Shidehara.

[41] In the Antoine Pinay Government, in 1952, there were four ex-premiers: Foreign Minister Robert Schuman, Defense Minister René Pleven, Education Minister André Marie, and Vice Minister Henri Queuille.

[42] The Secretary-General of the government party is the party strategist who works closely with the Director of the Cabinet Secretariat, frequently issuing directives emanating from the party's inner circle.

with powerful persons outside of the government. As a result, he has tremendous power at his command, particularly if and when the Prime Minister is weak or too busy or when the cabinet itself is not particularly outstanding. For example, during the Sino-Japanese War, 1894–95, in the Ito Cabinet, the Chief Cabinet Secretary was more powerful than any of the Cabinet ministers.[43] In the government of General Tanaka, 1927–29, the man who ran the cabinet was Chief Cabinet Secretary Mori. It was he who directed cabinet activities and formulated policies. There has developed since World War II a high degree of interchangeability among the positions of the Director of the Cabinet Secretariat, Secretary General of the Government party, and Cabinet Minister.

The Vice-Premier who is the *alter ego* of the Prime Minister occupies a position somewhat analogous to that of the Vice-President of the United States but with greater prestige and influence. He is the top trouble-shooter and liaison man in the cabinet. He is the spokesman for the Prime Minister on a far more intimate and personal basis than the Director of the Cabinet Secretariat who is more the spokesman of the cabinet. In the absence of the Prime Minister, he is the acting head of the government and presides over the cabinet meetings and in other ways acts in the place of his superior. However, since he cannot succeed to the premiership automatically, his potential is perhaps not as great as the Vice-President of the United States who is in direct and immediate line of succession. However, in the influence he actually exerts upon the government, he is far more significant in policy making. Moreover, he is thoroughly informed on what is going on inside the government.[44] The Vice-Premier, having no department to administer can devote his entire time and energy to policy making. He is therefore the logical cabinet member to get the assignment to draft the addresses of the Prime Minister, especially the policy speech to the Diet.

[43] Ito Miyoji, who was the Chief Cabinet Secretary, was one of the closest friends of Prime Minister Ito for they had worked together closely in the drafting of the Meiji Constitution.

[44] In the United States, the Vice-President's position has not been as influential in spite of the fact that he succeeds to the presidency in the event of the death of the President. In 1945 when Vice-President Harry S. Truman succeeded Franklin Delano Roosevelt to the presidency he was woefully uninformed of what was going on in the government regarding policy making. Under the Eisenhower administration the Vice-President was given the task of presiding over a cabinet meeting in 1953 for the first time in American history. When President Eisenhower is unable to attend the National Security Council meeting, he turns over the chair to the Vice-President.

THE CABINET MINISTERS

It is a well-known fact that Japanese politicians have almost a consuming obsession to attain a ministerial post.[45] This is because it carries tremendous social prestige way out of proportion to the actual importance of the position. Once the position is held even for a few days, the holder benefits from it. Even the most pathetically ineffective minister will forever thereafter make use of the prestige of office in polite society though perhaps to a slightly lesser extent than in France where an ex-Minister is addressed as *Monsieur le Ministre* for the rest of his life to his everlasting benefit.

This condition gives rise to at least two significant consequences. In the first place it renders politicians quite amenable to the party leader's wishes since he can lure even his erstwhile antagonists into submission and compliance with the much desired post. Secondly, it tempts the prime minister to give as many persons as possible the chance to occupy even briefly the much desired cabinet post.[46]

The Size and Composition of the Cabinet

The Cabinet consists of the Prime Minister and sixteen other members. Eleven of them have departments of which they are administrative heads while the remaining five are ministers without portfolio and are usually referred to simply as state ministers. One of the ministers without portfolio is usually the Vice-Premier. All the members of the Cabinet are state ministers but the titles of those with portfolios are always identified by the names of the departments they head.[47]

According to the Constitution, all the ministers must be civilians and a majority of them must be members of the Diet. In practice, however, recent cabinets have been formed entirely of Diet members. For example, the Fifth Yoshida Government, formed in 1953, comprised thirteen members of the House of Representatives and four members of the House of Councillors.

[45] Political commentators describe those who have been bitten by the "ministerial bug" as being afflicted by *daijinbyo*.

[46] Prime Minister Yoshida holds the record for the frequency of reshuffling the Cabinet and for the tremendous turnover which resulted from constant reconstituting of membership.

[47] The eleven administrative departments as they are at present constituted are Foreign Affairs, Finance, Justice, International Trade and Industry, Agriculture and Forestry, Education, Postal Service, Transportation, Welfare, Labor, and Construction. Indications are that before long there will be added the twelfth, Defense.

All the members of the Cabinet are appointed by the Prime Minister. Actually it is not very often that an appointment can be regarded as the Prime Minister's free choice. In the selection of a cabinet minister, he consults his intimates, giving careful consideration to practical politics. Most of the leading party members in effect choose themselves so that the party's inner circle is well represented. Cabinet positions are the reward for faithful party men. At the same time, the premier must see to it that the economic interests are adequately represented. In the Fourth Yoshida Government six out of his sixteen ministers were representatives of business, industry, and finance.[48]   The Prime Minister can take on a ministry or ministries concurrently when this is necessary or helpful from the point of political strategy. However, he does not do this, as it is done in France, merely to strengthen his leadership for he already possesses ample power. He usually does it when in a hurry to complete the formation of a government and an appropriate person is not immediately available, or when he has a strong desire to run a ministry personally exactly the way he wants, or when for political or other reasons he does not wish to fill the post in a hurry. Sometimes the Prime Minister does concurrently assign a minister to head another ministry temporarily.

Role and Function of Ministers

There are two types of cabinet ministers, those who are without portfolio devoting all their time and energy to policy matters, and those who have administrative responsibilities of running a department in addition to policy making. But they are all members of the policy-making team working together under the direction of the Prime Minister. Thus, in a sense, they are simultaneously the advisers and assistants to the premier. They must determine policy in proposals for legislation falling within their allotted areas. It is also their responsibility to make decisions in many of the important

---

[48] The six cabinet members were:

Finance Minister Mukai Tadaharu, formerly of Mitsui and one of the leading figures in the financial world.

Education Minister Okano Kiyohide, President of Sanwa Bank.

Welfare Minister Yamagata Katsumi, President of Shin Nihon Steamship Company.

Agriculture and Forestry Minister Ogasawara Sankuro, President of Arctic Whaling Company and Pacific Marine Transportation Company.

State Minister Hayashiya Kamejiro, President of Dai Nihon Kikai Kogyo Company.

State Minister Ohnogi Hidejiro, President of Rakuto Textile Company.

matters lying in the wide field between high policy and purely administrative detail. They are responsible for the arduous process of conducting a highly contentious bill through committees of the Diet, frequently appearing in person to answer questions.

Next to the Prime Minister himself, the Vice-Premier who is the confidant and more often than not the *alter ego* of his superior is the most influential member of the Cabinet. He devotes his time exclusively to policy matters and functions as acting premier in the absence of his chief. That this position is of the highest trust can be seen by the fact that it has been said that Prime Minister Yoshida was deliberately grooming the Vice-Minister as "heir apparent" to succeed him. Actually succession is not possible so far as the premiership is concerned. Unlike the Vice-President of the United States, he cannot step into the position vacated by his chief. However, during his tenure of office, he exercises greater and more decisive power than the Vice-President of the United States.

Although in theory all ministers are equal, there are always a few who dominate the discussions and wield greater power and influence in decision making by reason of their seniority, personality, ability, political support, the position they occupy in the party councils, and the importance of the policy-making and administrative functions of their offices. From a purely functional point of view, for example, the Finance Minister has always been regarded as one of the key members of the Cabinet by reason of the control he has over fiscal affairs. Some prime ministers were of the belief that the Finance Minister should be the central figure in policy making. When the Ministry of Home Affairs was in existence, its head was regarded as the kingpin of national administration, with his control of the nation's police power. For a long period preceding the end of World War II, the Minister of the Army was the most powerful member of the Cabinet since, as the representative of the Army, he was able to make or break a Cabinet.

However, the times and especially the national exigencies determine which departments should play a major role in the shaping of policy. In the post-World War II period, because of the tremendous economic problems facing the nation, the three ministries whose functions are most important are Finance, International Trade and Industry, and Foreign Affairs.

There have been times of national crisis when policy making was carried out for the sake of speed and efficiency by a group of key cabinet ministers. This was especially common practice in the late 1930's when there were the "Four Ministers' Conference" and the

"Five Ministers' Conference" consisting of the Prime Minister and outstanding figures who by exceptional talent, wide experience, and personal and intimate relationship with the Prime Minister formed the inner council and gave direction to the policy of the cabinet.

There is no set of qualifications which apply equally to individual members of the cabinet. There is only one requirement which is at present mandatory, and that is they must be civilians. The Constitution also requires that a majority of the ministers must be Diet members. This permits one less than half of the ministers to be chosen from outside of the Diet. Despite this leeway, it has been the practice to appoint virtually all the ministers from among the Diet membership. Like the British rather than the French, the ministers in Japan are now usually amateurs in their fields of authority although some of them have become near-specialists through experience.

THE CABINET IN ACTION

The Office of the Prime Minister is the general staff headquarters of the cabinet. It is the office over which the Prime Minister has complete control as the Chief of General Staff and is the nerve center of the government. Its manager is the Director of the Cabinet Secretariat who handles the agenda for cabinet meetings and other business matters pertaining to the government. His position is comparable to that of the Executive Director of the Office of the President in the United States.

The business of the cabinet is conducted in the regular cabinet meetings which are held twice a week, Tuesday and Friday, usually in the premier's official residence beginning at 10 a.m. and which are executive sessions not open to the public. As in the British system, regulations forbid any official to report what goes on at cabinet meetings. When necessary, the Prime Minister can call special meetings any time. Secrecy is maintained rigidly with regard to the proceedings. All the ministers including those without portfolio attend the meetings. Unlike the British system, all the ministers are *ipso facto* members of the cabinet and none has to be made a member by the Prime Minister's note of request to attend a cabinet meeting.[49] It is also customary for the Director of the Cabinet Secretariat and the two Deputy Directors and the Director of the Bureau of Legislation to attend but they are not voting members of the meeting. Nor are those officials who appear from time to time to explain legislative proposals—such officials as Parliamentary Vice-Ministers, Vice-Ministers, Directors, and Bureau Chiefs.

[49] W. I. Jennings, *Cabinet Government,* pp. 68–71.

Cabinet meetings are presided over by the Prime Minister who enjoys great powers especially in an emergency. In his absence, however, the Vice-Premier takes the chair. There are no rules, customs, or precedents for the meetings. Nor is there a quorum, for business is known to have been transacted with less than half of the members present. The signatures of those absent could later be obtained for the decisions made. In emergencies when a cabinet meeting cannot be called, documents are circulated to cabinet members and acted upon individually and separately in the decision making.

The agenda is always fixed in advance in the Secretariat on the basis of the business submitted by the Ministers in the form of memoranda as well as drafts of bills to be submitted to the Diet. Members are given the opportunity to express their views. The practice is to talk around a subject until some agreement is reached or some compromise suggests itself. Unlike the British Cabinet, there is never a vote, no overriding of the minority by the majority. Decisions must always be unanimous. The Prime Minister sums up the results of the discussion and determines the consensus of the meeting. Securing agreement is very important, since the cabinet operates on the principle of joint responsibility. If a member is irreconcilably opposed to the decision there is only one alternative, to resign. Otherwise he would run the risk of being summarily dismissed by the Prime Minister.

There are two forms in which cabinet action is taken, namely, cabinet decision and cabinet understanding. The former is used for all matters on which cabinet decisions are required by law or the Constitution and also for policy matters of major importance. Matters within the exclusive competence of the minister in charge, matters in which the understanding of other ministers is desirable for the purpose of coordination between the administrative departments, and relatively minor matters take the latter form. In practical effect, there is not a great deal of difference although the latter may conceivably have matters of lesser legal significance.

Vice-Ministers' meetings have come to assume great importance in the operation of the cabinet. Since Vice-Ministers are career officials as opposed to the ministers who are more often than not amateurs and have a more direct hand in the administrative work of the departments and are their operational chiefs, they are in a far better position to make decisions, even high-level decisions which have no political implications. Moreover they have wide discretionary powers. Consequently, a great deal of the business which used to be taken up in the cabinet meetings are now disposed of in the Vice-Ministers' meetings, particularly those matters which are technical rather than political. They consider and decide details, for example the method of enforcement and administrative procedure. This relieves the cabinet ministers of the burden of details and technical matters and enables them to concentrate on problems requiring immediate action. The decisions of the Vice-Ministers must be approved in a cabinet meeting before they can be implemented.

Regular meetings of the Vice-Ministers are held twice a week, usually on Monday and Thursday, that is, a day before every regular cabinet meeting. All Vice-Ministers are members of the meeting. Attending in addition are the Director of the Cabinet Secretariat and the two Deputy Directors and the Director of the Bureau of Legislation. The Vice-Ministers' meeting is the highest administrative liaison conference in the government designed to achieve the highest degree of cooperation, coordination, and information. What it is entrusted with actually is preliminary decision of policies as well as legislative proposals which can safely be disposed of at this level without going to the very top.

Functionally it is like the "Little Cabinet" in the United States which is a subcabinet group consisting of the top deputy from each of the ten departments, plus the Bureau of the Budget, the Office of Defense Mobilization, the Foreign Operations Administration, and the Civil Service Commission, which meets formally every other Tuesday in the Cabinet room of the White House to perform the administrative functions of governing. The American counterpart, however, is a much larger group.

THE DURATION OF A GOVERNMENT

A government can continue as long as there is unity and it enjoys the confidence and support of the Diet which is the elected representative of the people. When the unity of the cabinet is impaired irreparably, there is no alternative for it but to resign en masse. Under the old Constitution this was the most frequent cause of the downfall of a government, largely attributable to the weakness of the Prime Minister. Although this weakness has been remedied to a large extent under the new Constitution, it is still possible for unity to be impaired sufficiently to bring about the fall of the government. Loss of confidence is the surest way to bring about the collapse of the government. Confidence in the government is often destroyed by the opposition by defeating major government bills and thereby preventing the government's legislative program from being carried out. It may be brought about by cabinet implication in political scandals which alienate public opinion and strengthen opposition attacks. However, the formal steps of a no-confidence vote in the Diet is a necessary procedure. If the House of Representatives passes a no-confidence resolution or rejects a confidence resolution the Cabinet has to resign unless it dissolves the Lower House within ten days of the censure vote.[50]

Dissolution, which is regarded as a powerful threat or a club held over the head of the Diet members, is just as much of a threat against the government itself because the majority, if not all of the members of the cabinet stand to lose their seats in the Diet. However, it is more of a tactical weapon which enables the government to select the most advantageous time for a general election. Since the question of dissolution is perhaps the most serious decision that a government has to make, it is always discussed in a cabinet meeting for final decision.

The death or resignation of the Prime Minister automatically brings about the end of a government because there is no provision for succession. Needless to say, the cabinet continues under an acting head, the Vice-Premier, until the new Prime Minister is designated by the Diet and formally appointed by the Emperor.

Procedurally, resignation en masse by the government is a relatively simple matter. When the decision is reached in a cabinet meeting the fact is communicated in writing to the presiding officers of both houses. Resignation is a unilateral action which requires merely the notification to the Diet. There is no official acceptance or approval or even an acknowledgement. The Diet then starts the process of selecting the candidate to head the next government. When the candidate is formally designated he starts lining up the team which he will captain. Immediately upon completion of a cabinet, he notifies the Diet and the outgoing Prime Minister who holds the last cabinet meeting at which it decides on advising the Emperor on the appointment of the new Prime Minister. Both the outgoing and incoming Prime Ministers and the cabinets proceed to the Imperial Palace for the ceremony of appointment and of attestation. After the ceremony the Diet is formally notified of the coming into being of a new government. Thus the cycle in the change of cabinet is completed.

In the period of sixty-nine years beginning in 1885 and ending in 1954, there has been a total of fifty-one separate cabinets. Statisti-

[50] Following the dissolution, the government must call a general election to elect the new members of the House of Representatives. After the convocation of the new Diet, the Cabinet must tender its resignation.

cally this gives an average of 1 year 4 months 7 days (1.35 yr.) per cabinet. This is much shorter than in Great Britain. In France, however, ten months is considered to be a pretty good tenure, for in the nine years since the end of World War II there have been twenty cabinets or an average life of 5 months 5 days per government. The longest-lived was the Henri Queuille government (September 10, 1948 to October 6, 1949) of 1 year 26 days. The average life expectancy of a government in France is seven months.[51]

The shortest-lived cabinet in Japan so far was the Higashikuni government which lasted only 1 month 20 days (August 17 to October 9, 1945) but this does not equal France's Albert Sarraut government which was in office less than a month in 1933 or Edgar Fauré government which lasted six weeks in early 1952.

The longest-lived government was the first Katsura Cabinet (June 2, 1901 to January 7, 1906) which lasted 4 years, 7 months, 5 days. Prime Minister Yoshida has set an all-time record of longest continuous tenure of over six years, this being the combined tenure of four separate but consecutive cabinets. Prime Minister Yoshida, however, established the record for the number of governments formed when he became Prime Minister in 1953 for the fifth time and four times consecutively. His nearest competitor was Ito who was Prime Minister four times, nonconsecutively, between 1885 and 1901. In point of durability, however, Ito was superior. The Japanese record does not come anywhere near that of Great Britain where the average is five years and general maximum seven years.[52]

[51] Robert G. Neumann, *European and Comparative Government*, p. 244.

[52] There is nothing in Japanese experience which can compare with such long tenures as those of Walpole, a continuous tenure of 21 years, of Younger Pitt of 18 years, of Lord Liverpool of 15 years, and of Asquith of 7 years.

8

The Diet:

Where Policies

Are Debated and Decided

In the center of Tokyo, the third largest city of the world and the capital of a nation which in the brief space of a century has become more Westernized than any other Asian country, stands conspicuously an impressive White Arabic structure unlike anything within miles of it. In this building which symbolizes the meeting of East and West sits the Diet, the lawmaking body of Japan. In comparison with the British Parliament or the Congress of the United States, Japan's national legislature is young, yet it is the oldest as well as the most experienced lawmaking body of the non-Western world. It is a parliamentary body which emerged as the inevitable result of the impact of Western civilization in the late nineteenth century.

As the highest organ of state power and the expression of the will of the people, the Diet is charged with the task of deliberating on national policies, making final decisions as to which ones are to be approved and enacted into laws. This parliamentary body is responsible to the people and specifically to the electorate in accordance with the principle of popular sovereignty which has been adopted since World War II. Although the Japanese Diet as a body of lawmakers does not even begin to compare with the French Assembly in its colorfulness, brilliance of eloquence and oratory, or in its demonstration of sentiment, it is nevertheless regarded by political commentators as "the greatest show in Tokyo,"[1] if not in the nation.

[1] In Tokyo at one of the theaters a play was presented in December, 1953, satirizing the behavior of the Diet members at work.

HISTORY OF THE DIET

It was almost a century ago, in 1860 to be exact, that the Japanese had the opportunity of observing at first hand and for the first time in history, a national legislative assembly in action when they visited the Congress of the United States in Washington, D.C.[2] The Japanese visitors witnessed the proceedings in both Houses with great interest and incredulous amazement although they were unable to fully understand or appreciate the significance of the process of lawmaking by a popularly elected representative assembly. One of the Japanese envoys noted in his diary that the entire proceedings reminded him of the activities in a fish market back home.

Exactly thirty years later, the Japanese set up their parliament to begin their deliberation and legislation on national affairs. In the period of more than sixty years which have proved exceedingly eventful, the Japanese lawmakers have recreated time and again, in the halls of the Diet, the atmosphere and scenes reminiscent of those which their predecessors had witnessed in the tense, emotion-charged atmosphere of the United States Congress on the eve of the Civil War. Even in the period since the end of World War II, the dignity of the Diet and its proceedings have been subjected to a severe test by less than commendable behavior characterized by rude, boisterous antics such as catcalls, heckling, calumny, name-calling, and open brawls. One of the most outrageous exhibitions ever to be witnessed on the floor of the Diet occurred on June 4, 1954, when the normally dignified meeting place was turned into a free-for-all in which fists as well as ash trays flew and pandemonium reigned.[3]

Japan's parliament came into existence in 1890 as a result of the successful movement for the establishment of a national representative assembly launched in 1874 by Itagaki Taisuke and a group of followers who were dissatisfied with the existing oligarchic control of national policy making. It took seven years of vigorous agitation on the part of political groups to induce the government leaders to take the final step toward constitutional representative government. In 1881, Emperor Meiji issued a rescript promising the nation a repre-

[2] For an account of this memorable event of far-reaching consequences, see the author's "The First Japanese Embassy to the United States," *Pacific Historical Review,* June, 1940.

[3] The press reported the Diet melee, which necessitated calling in 200 policemen from the outside and was quelled only after more than thirty persons had been injured, as the worst outbreak and the most disgraceful performance in the sixty-four-year history of the national legislature.

sentative assembly for 1890.   Political parties emerged on the heels of the announcement and began preparations for the launching of parliamentary government.

For the next ten years, the nation busied itself in the study and drafting of the Constitution.   Dozens of drafts were prepared by individuals, groups, and the government.   What finally emerged was the Meiji Constitution which was promulgated on February 11, 1889. Because of the strong German, or rather, Prussian, influence which made itself felt on the leaders in whose hands was vested the power of deciding the form of political structure, the Japanese Diet was modeled on the Prussian counterpart.   Consequently, the Diet was a lawmaking body in name and form, but in practice was little more than a body which rubber-stamped policies and enacted them into laws.   While it went through the motions of lawmaking, it merely gave formal consent and approval to the laws practically all of which had been drafted and submitted by the executive branch.

Although the period of World War I gave tremendous impetus to the cause of democracy and parliamentary government, actual achievements were not at all impressive until after the end of the conflict.   The fifteen years following the war witnessed a speedy awakening of the political consciousness of the people, thus opening the era of political activities by the masses.   Proletarian parties appeared on the scene for the first time in the early 1920's and universal manhood suffrage was achieved in 1925.   Party government had come to be accepted at least in principle by the major segments of society in the heyday of political parties.   But parliamentary government was still circumscribed by the rigid framework of the old political system.   Consequently, under existing conditions it was practically impossible for political democracy to develop even though the social democratic movement made considerable headway during the decade.

Internal crisis in the 1930's was brought on by the depression and by a series of unsavory political scandals aggravated by the international situation both economic and political.   This catapulted the military into power and, after 1932, responsible party government which had functioned all too briefly was superseded by supraparty coalition governments headed by military men or bureaucrats.   Then, in 1940, came the demise of political parties, bringing parliamentary government to an end after a none too successful trial period of exactly half a century.   Although the parliamentary body continued to exist and function, it was merely an ineffectual organ tolerated in a totalitarian political structure dominated by the military who did not dare abolish arbitrarily an institution provided for in the Constitution.

As a consequence of defeat came demilitarization and the barring of the military from participation in public affairs. A completely civilian dominated, democratically oriented political and governmental system was set up under the new Constitution with an overhauled parliament functioning as the supreme organ of the State.

FUNCTIONS AND POWERS OF THE DIET

General

Constitutionally, the Diet is the sole lawmaking organ of the State; as the highest organ of state power it enjoys a position of supremacy over the executive branch of the government. In spite of its designation as the sole lawmaking organ, the Diet's major function is not the planning of a legislative program which belongs to the Cabinet. Its role in legislation is to be seen rather in the selection, deliberation, and modification of the legislative proposals submitted to it with a view to giving legal effect to those it approves. In other words, its chief function is to provide a national forum where issues are debated and clarified and decisions reached so that, in the process, views are aired and differences threshed out and satisfactory compromises achieved. It also serves in part as a political safety valve permitting its members an opportunity to give vent to their feelings and expression to their ideas. The Diet in a sense is the modulator and adjustor of political issues.

The Diet is expected to serve as an effective link between the government and the people by establishing constant and extensive contacts. This function should be a two-way relationship since the wishes and views of the people should be made known clearly to the government, and at the same time the policies and actions of the government should be made clear and intelligible to the people.[4] In other words, the Diet must carry on political education by guiding and leading public opinion while at the same time reflecting it.

The powers of the Diet are not confined to legislative functions alone but extend to all aspects of governmental activity. Indeed, in the exercise of legislative powers, there are no constitutional limitations whatsoever on the Diet. Theoretically, all matters of State are regulated by laws enacted by the Diet or orders issued on the authority delegated by the Diet. Consequently they include such

---

[4] Mitsuchi Chuzo, "Seito no sekinin," *Chuo Koron,* June, 1939, p. 226.

matters as: (1) industries, (2) currency and banking, (3) weights and measures, (4) crime and punishment, (5) private law relationship of individuals, (6) foreign relations and foreign trade, (7) administrative system and the civil service, (8) judicial system, and (9) others.

Thus constitutionally legislative powers and the legislative activities of the Diet are virtually unlimited in theory. Yet the main task of the Diet, like that of the British Parliament, is to secure full discussion and airing of all questions of public policy as the necessary condition of giving assent to bills submitted to the body.

Powers pertaining to fiscal matters which the Diet exercises are great indeed. The most important of these is the power to act upon the budget bill which is drafted and submitted to it by the cabinet. Without the approval of the Diet, the budget cannot go into effect. In other words, the power of final decision over revenues and expenditures is firmly vested in the Diet. No taxes can be levied and no expenditures made without its approval. Needless to say, any changes in taxation must also have its approval. It examines the final accounts submitted by the government and also receives reports on the financial conditions of the nation. The Diet furthermore has control over the property of the Imperial Household.

The power to supervise the administration, which used to be indirect and weak under the old system, has now been greatly strengthened. It begins with the power to designate the Prime Minister, the head of the executive branch, together with the right to pass a no-confidence resolution or reject a confidence resolution. A no-confidence vote can be passed against a cabinet minister by the Diet, forcing him to resign.[5] As an integral part of the power to supervise the administration the Diet is now vested with the investigative power which it did not possess under the old Constitution. As in the United States, this power which must bear a direct relation to the lawmaking function enables the Diet to inquire into how existing laws are being administered, to seek facts for guidance in enacting wise laws, and to collect and disseminate facts for the information of the public. Investigations are conducted in the prefectures as well as in the national capital. The Diet has the power to demand administrative officers to submit records and reports and to subpoena witnesses, both officials and private citizens, to testify. Under the old system there was actually a ban on sending members of the Diet out to the prefectures and calling in people as witnesses.

[5] This actually happened to Finance Minister Ikeda in the Yoshida Cabinet in 1953.

The Diet's power of control over the conduct of foreign relations is new for under the old Constitution it had none. As part of the control of foreign relations the cabinet is required by law to report to the Diet on foreign relations. While the power to conclude treaties is vested in the government, the Constitution requires that it obtain either prior or subsequent approval of the legislative branch. Thus the ratification of treaties is possible only with its approval. It is also possible for the Diet to exercise some control over foreign relations, though more in a negative way, through the power of the purse.

Finally, the control it exercises over the judiciary takes the form of power of impeachment of judges. The Diet is empowered to set up an impeachment court consisting of an equal number of members from both Houses to try those judges against whom removal proceedings have been instituted by an indictment committee.

Differences in the Powers of the Two Houses

The degree and scope of powers enjoyed by the two houses of legislature necessarily differ because of the difference in the functions assigned them. Although the area of competence of the House of Councillors is as extensive as that of the House of Representatives, it is far less powerful[6] but, since it cannot be dissolved, one of its major functions is to give stability and continuity to the Diet. It is also a restraining, moderating, and dignifying influence upon the House of Representatives which is the real arena of political contests. It serves as an effective counterpoise to the spirited membership of the lower house where political pyrotechnics are common and actions are often impetuous and hasty, if not rash. The House of Councillors, however, is not a supreme court of appeal as is the British House of Lords. Nor is it as important as the United States Senate. However, in comparison with France's purely advisory and powerless Council of the Republic, it stands higher both in power and in prestige.

It is easy to see that the House of Representatives is really the more powerful of the two Houses since it is the repository of popular will. Still, it is by no means as all-powerful and uncontrollable as the French Assembly which is immune to dissolution. Actually, it closely resembles the United States House of Representatives in many ways. Because of its position of supremacy, its actions take precedence over, and even override, the decisions of the House of Councillors in the event of irreconcilable disagreements between the two Houses or

---

6 Under the old Constitution the House of Peers, which was never truly or directly representative of the people, could easily obstruct the enactment into law of any bill passed in the House of Representatives elected by the people.

delay or inaction on the part of the House of Councillors, and become the decisions of the Diet as a whole.   For example, a legislative bill which is passed by the House of Representatives and upon which the House of Councillors makes a decision different from that of the House of Representatives, becomes a law when passed a second time by the House of Representatives by a majority of two-thirds or more of the members present.   Normally this overriding action is not resorted to until a joint conference committee called to resolve the differences has failed.   Bills which have been killed by the House of Representatives cannot be reconsidered or revived by the House of Councillors.

In much the same manner the decisions of the House of Representatives takes precedence over those of the House of Councillors with regard to the budget, the conclusion of treaties, and the designation of the Prime Minister, except that in these matters the calling of a joint conference committee composed of an equal number of members from each House is mandatory.

Furthermore, as is the practice in the Congress of the United States, money bills must originate in the House of Representatives.   The budget bill is received first by the House of Representatives inasmuch as it has the control of the purse.   And this power of the purse is effectively used by the House of Representatives in the deliberation on national policies.   Yet, in spite of the power it enjoys it can be dissolved by the government.

THE HOUSE OF COUNCILLORS.   When the bicameral legislature was first established in 1890, the House of Peers was intended to serve as an effective counterpoise against the impetuosity of the House of Representatives.   It was designed by the framers of the Meiji Constitution as an instrumentality by which to maintain political equilibrium, to restrain the power of political parties, to check the evils of irresponsible discussion and action, to secure the stability of the Constitution, and to preserve harmony between the government and the people.   Its members were selected from among the experienced and the mature as well as the conservatives.

When the elective House of Councillors superseded the House of Peers in 1947, the membership ceased to represent special privilege in any form although it continued to include a wealth of experience and expertise in virtually every field.   Not harassed by the threat of dissolution or subjected to the kind of degree of political pressures which the Lower House has to contend with, the House of Councillors can take a broader, loftier, more detached, cautious, unhurried, long-term view in its policy deliberations.   Exercising greater judgment and acumen, it is in a position to give a measure of stability and continuity to the Diet and to forestall excesses as well as to rectify some of the errors made by the impulsive, impatient, and quick-acting House of Representatives. It is problematical, however, in view of the developments since the second election in April, 1953, whether the House of Councillors can actually carry out all these functions as expected.

Since the entire membership is elective, there has been an increasing awareness on the part of the members that unless they belong to a political party they are at a disadvantage when standing an election. This has resulted in the growing influence of the parties and decisions within the Chamber have come to be made by party caucuses.

STRUCTURE AND COMPOSITION

The legislative system is bicameral in its organization, as it has always been since its establishment in 1890. Under the old Constitution the Upper House which used to be known as the House of Peers with 416 members was a stronghold of special privilege for its membership was entirely appointive.[7] Under the new Constitution, it has been reconstituted into the House of Councillors with all elective membership. There have been no really appreciable changes in the composition or the method of election of the members of the House of Representatives.

Membership

The number of members in the House of Representatives totals 467[8] and all of them are elected by the voters of the election districts in the prefectures. Each prefecture constitutes anywhere from one to five election districts but Tokyo metropolitan prefecture has seven,

[7] As of 1945 the membership of the House of Peers was composed of the following:
   16 princes of the blood (hereditary)
   19 princes (hereditary)
   36 marquises (hereditary)
   18 counts ⎫
   66 barons ⎬ elected representatives of each rank (7 years)
   66 viscounts ⎭
  125 imperial appointees (life tenure) for erudition or meritorious service to the nation
   66 elected representatives of the highest taxpayers (7 years)
    4 elected representatives of the Imperial Academy (7 years)

[8] Until 1954 there were 466 seats as determined by the electoral law of 1925. However, when Amami-Oshima was restored to Japanese sovereignty it was given a representative, bringing the total number to 467.

which is the largest number of districts. This compares with the Congress of the United States with 435 members, British House of Commons with 625 members, and the French Assembly with 627 members. The House of Councillors is smaller in size with a membership of only 250,[9] of whom 150 are elected on a geographic basis, that is, from the prefectures which have from two to eight seats, while 100 are elected from the nation at large.

The term of office in the House of Representatives is four years but only rarely do the members serve out their full term because it is subject to dissolution by the government.[10] In the House of Councillors the term of office is six years, the same as in the United States Senate, with one-half of the membership standing election every three years. There is no dissolution in the upper house.

Qualifications for membership in the Diet are fixed by law and there must be no discrimination because of race, creed, sex, social status, family origin, education, property, or income. There are two essential requirements, one of age and the other of geography. The geographic requirements of elective offices, while stated legally, are actually more meaningful in a socio-political sense. Legal residence does not mean actual physical residence. It simply means having a legal domicile and being registered there. Unlike the practice in the United States, there is no requirement that one must live in the election district which he represents. The age qualification is 25 years for the House of Representatives and 30 years for the House of Councillors. All other qualifications are the same as those for ordinary voters.[11] The Constitution specifically prohibits anyone from holding membership simultaneously in both Houses. Nor can a member of the Diet hold any other office as in France where dual office holding is normal.[12] Disputes relating to qualifications of members are judged by each House. In order to deny a seat to any member, it is necessary to pass a resolution by a majority of two-thirds or more of the members present.[13]

[9] This compares with the United States Senate of 96 members, the French Council of the Republic of 320 members, and the British House of Peers of 862 members.

[10] The term of office in the French Assembly is five years, with no possibility of being dissolved as the government lacks the power of dissolution.

[11] See the chapter on the Electorate.

[12] In the French Assembly scores of deputies are concurrently mayors of their home towns. Edward Herriot for instance was Mayor of Lyons while President of the National Assembly. Premier Pinay was also a mayor of his home town.

[13] Although this is not an easy method of denying a seat to an elected representative of the people in the legislature, it has been carried out with greater frequency than in the United States.

There is considerable difference between the Houses in their actual composition. In spite of the fact that the Upper House enjoys less power than the Lower House it carries greater prestige for its members. This is largely the result of the carry-over into the new system of the prestige which attached to the old House of Peers. Because of the very nature of the functions assigned to it and the security of tenure, the proceedings in the House of Councillors are less hectic and stormy. Members are not only more dignified but much less ambitious politically than in the Lower House. They are as a rule a little older and more experienced in life, if not in politics. On the whole, they are better known nationally and a larger proportion of them have been specialists. The Lower House members are slightly younger, far more active and ambitious politically, and are frequently the local political leaders. In their educational backgrounds and the professions they follow, they seem to have much in common.

AGE. The age composition of the members of the Diet reveals that while the Japanese have the strong traditional respect for age, the members of the nation's lawmaking body are not any older than the members of the United States Congress. In the Diet which was constituted as the result of the general election of April, 1953, the average age of the members of the House of Representatives was 52.9 years while the average age in the House of Councillors was 53.4 years, or only a half year older. This compares favorably with the average of 52 years in the United States House of Representatives and 57 years in the United States Senate.

In the House of Representatives the age range was from 31 to 96 years with the 41–60 year range comprising 75 percent of the total membership. The ten-year span which had the largest proportion was 46–55, with 47 percent or nearly one-half of the total. In the House of Councillors the age range was 33–84 years with the 45–65 year range comprising 74.4 percent of the total. The ten-year span which made up the highest percentage of any was 49–58, with 43 percent of the total membership. Age composition indicates that there is almost no chance for a person under thirty to be elected to the House of Representatives even though it is permitted by law.[14]

[14] Age distribution, in the House of Representatives by political parties gives the following interesting picture:

Parties	Average Age	Range
Liberal	53.1	31–76
Progressive	51.6	34–70
Japan Liberal (Hatoyama)	54.4	37–70
Left Socialist	48.1	31–64
Right Socialist	51.4	35–67

EDUCATIONAL BACKGROUND. The educational background of the members of the House of Representatives shows that the college graduates and college educated comprise an overwhelming majority, since only 80 persons out of the 466 members either were secondary school graduates or made no mention of their educational background. In other words, 83 percent of the members had been to college. The graduates of Tokyo University, which is the leading government university, provided 113 M.P.'s or 24 percent of the total.[15]

The number and percentage of college graduate members of the House of Representatives by parties were as shown in Table III. The

TABLE III.   COLLEGE GRADUATES IN THE HOUSE OF REPRESENTATIVES

Election of April 1953

	Total Members	Number of College Graduates	Percentage of College Graduates
Liberal	199	176	88.4
Progressive	76	65	89.8
Japan Liberal (Hatoyama)	35	28	80.0
Left Socialist	72	52	72.2
Right Socialist	66	51	77.2

Left Socialist Party members had the lowest percentage of college graduates because there were many who had come up from the ranks of labor without the benefits of higher education while the conservative parties had a very high percentage because their membership was drawn from families which could afford higher education for their sons and daughters.

PROFESSIONAL BACKGROUND. The occupational statistics in Table IV pertaining to the members of the House of Representatives reflect the sources of political power and their relative strength.

Presiding Officers

The first step in the organization of the Diet is the election of the Speaker and Vice-Speaker in both Houses. Only after the presiding officer is chosen can business be transacted. Even the designation of the Prime Minister, urgent as it is, has to wait until after the Speaker and his deputy are chosen. Normally, the Speaker comes from the majority party which forms the government. However if the government does not command the absolute majority but only a

[15] After the election of October 1, 1952, the number and percentage were even higher for there were 122 graduates of Tokyo University which represented over 26 percent of the total. A total of 173, more than 37 percent, had come from government colleges and universities.

TABLE IV. OCCUPATIONAL COMPOSITION OF HOUSE OF
REPRESENTATIVES

Sept. 1, 1953

	Business, Finance, Industry	Law	Journalists, Writers, Teachers, Doctors, Social and Religious Workers	Party Officials	Agri- culture	Labor
Liberal	105	26	24	6	14	—
Progressive	41	6	9	9	7	—
Japan Liberal (Hatoyama)	19	6	4	2	2	—
Left Socialist	8	9	13	11	6	12
Right Socialist	19	15	5	16	2	3
	192	62	54	44	36	15
Percentage of membership	41.2	13.3	11.6	9.4	7.7	3.2

working majority with the help of some other party or parties, both the Speaker and the Vice-Speaker can come from parties other than the government party itself.[16]

The role of the presiding officer of the House of Representatives is very much like that of his counterpart in the United States Congress. Unlike the Speaker of the British House of Commons whose position is permanent and who transcends party interests, the Japanese Speaker holds his position only as long as he is a member of the Diet. He is usually elected from the majority party or the party which succeeds in forming a government,[17] though this is not mandatory. It is not necessary for the Speaker to resign from the party as is the case in Britain.[18]   However, an interesting development took place

[16] This happened in the Fifth Yoshida government after the elections of April, 1953, when the House of Representatives elected the Speaker and his deputy from outside Yoshida's own Liberal Party.

[17] In May, 1953, Premier Yoshida succeeded in forming a government for the fifth time and his Liberal Party had a plurality of 199 seats in the House of Representatives. However, the Speaker elected came from the Progressive Party and the Vice-Speaker from the Right Socialist Party.

[18] Before World War II, during a brief period of fifteen years from 1925 to 1940 (the 50th through the 75th Diet), both the Speaker and Vice-Speaker severed their connections with political parties as a result of a resolution passed in the House of Representatives. This practice was discontinued after 1940 and has not been revived since.

not long ago.   In the Sixteenth Special Diet Session during the Fifth Yoshida Government from May, 1953, to January, 1955, the Speaker of the House resigned from his party.[19]   He felt strongly that a Speaker should transcend party interests and function as a true representative of the highest organ of the state.   As a presiding officer of the highest lawmaking organ the Speaker is naturally expected to be as fair and impartial as possible, but he functions to advance the interests of the party and aids the government's legislative program.

The Speaker is entrusted with the responsibility of maintaining order in the Diet and seeing that proceedings are carried on smoothly and efficiently.   He is entrusted with a great deal of authority though not nearly as much as the Speaker of the House of Commons.   He functions as the official representative of the House in all its relations with the outside.   His authority includes among others the right to determine the order of business, refer bills to the appropriate committee, impose a time limit to interpellations and debates and apply cloture, propose executive sessions, approve the appointment of government members for the purpose of assisting cabinet ministers in the Diet, appear before any committee including the joint conference committee to express his views, and accept the resignation of a member of the Diet when it is not in session.   He gives permission to a member to interpellate.

Since the Speaker is responsible for the smooth functioning of the Diet, he has all the necessary police and disciplinary powers within the chamber to control the M.P.'s behavior on the floor.   He admonishes and censures disorderly conduct and speech unbecoming a member of the highest organ of state and may deny any member who disobeys the right to speak.   He is empowered to declare a recess or adjournment when order cannot be restored on the floor, to expel disorderly spectators and clear the entire gallery of visitors if disorderly.   He refers violations by M.P.'s to the Disciplinary Committee.   When necessary, as on the occasion of a melee in May, 1954, he can call in and direct the police from the outside.

Committees of the Diet

After the presiding officers have been selected, the next step is the selection of committee members.   The allocation of Diet members to the committees and their chairmanships is carried out strictly

---

[19] Yasujiro Tsutsumi resigned from the Progressive Party while Hara Hyo, the Vice-Speaker, resigned from the Left Socialist Party.

in accordance with party strength as represented in the legislative body.[20] According to the Law of the Diet, each member must serve on at least one standing committee and on not more than three committees. Assignments are formally made by the Diet's Ways and Means Committee but the selection of the individuals is carefully made by each party's inner circle to insure utmost effectiveness in the achievement of the party's objectives.

Since the operation of the Diet now centers around the committee system as in the United States, though not to the same extent,[21] the standing committees have become highly important organs of lawmaking. Under the Meiji Constitution there were only five committees in each of the Houses and these were not important since most of the business was transacted in the plenary sessions or the committee of the whole house. Under the new system there are twenty-two standing committees in each House as compared with nineteen in the United States House of Representatives and fifteen in the United States Senate.[22]

Representation of the political parties on the committees is carefully worked out according to their relative strength in the Diet and the members carry out the policies of their party's executive committee. Although the committee meetings are open to the public, the executive council (*rijikai*) which meets behind closed doors plans the strategy and conducts the meetings in a manner advantageous to the party in control of the Diet.

[20] This has been the case only since May, 1953, when a new precedent was established. Previously chairmanships were monopolized by the majority party or the government party.

[21] In the United States, critics contend that the Congress has surrendered control of legislative action to its standing committees whose chairmen are all-powerful and can expedite measures they favor and delay or pigeonhole those they dislike.

[22] As of September 1, 1953, the 22 standing committees which were identical in name in both Houses were:

1. Ways and Means	12. Education
2. Disciplinary	13. Welfare
3. Economic Stabilization	14. Agriculture and Forestry
4. Budget	15. Fisheries
5. Final Accounts	16. International Trade and Industry
6. Cabinet	17. Transportation
7. Personnel	18. Postal Affairs
8. Local Administration	19. Electrical Communications
9. Legal Affairs	20. Labor
10. Foreign Affairs	21. Construction
11. Finance	22. National Diet Library

Chairmanships of standing committees are allocated to the parties roughly in proportion to the number of seats held in the Diet.[23] The struggle as to which party is to have the chairmanship of which committee takes place in the Ways and Means Committee.   Perhaps the most powerful of the twenty-two standing committees is the thirty-member Ways and Means Committee which plays a major role in the political struggle which is carried on within the Diet.   Upon it devolves the responsibility of seeing that the Diet is run smoothly and efficiently.   The committee has jurisdiction over the rules of the Diet, their interpretation and application, impeachment, the Speaker, setting up of special committees, the assignment of bills to committees, and the extension of Diet sessions.   It is thought of as a "casting office" of the Diet since it determines the order of business, the speaking order of its members, the length of time they may speak, and passes upon the applications of those members who desire to go on junkets abroad as well as within the country.   Parties select for this committee experienced men with political acumen and proven skill and ability in negotiation and strategy.   Another committee which is of tremendous importance is the Budget Committee where the major policy battles are fought over appropriations and fiscal matters in general.   So far as the public is concerned the Budget Committee's activities are far better known.

Severe criticisms have been leveled at the committee system as it exists at present.   These criticisms have to do chiefly with the number of committees and their method of functioning.   There are altogether too many committees, resulting in the division of national affairs into small segments.   This is a serious obstacle to the development of an integrated and broad view of national problems.   Committees have been set up to correspond to the administrative departments.   Since they use the same names and identify themselves with the depart-

[23] As of September 1, 1953, chairmanships of the 22 standing committees in the House of Representatives were distributed as follows:

Liberal	11
Progressive	5
Left Socialist	3
Japan Liberal (Hatoyama)	2
Right Socialist	1

In the House of Councillors they were as follows:

Liberal	8
Ryokufukai	5
Left Socialist	4
Right Socialist	3
Progressives	2

ments, it has resulted in a serious confusion and obliteration of the functional distinction between the legislative and executive branches. Committees have thus become little more than branches and outposts of the administrative departments or agencies of business and special interests in the Diet.   Committee chairmen have become quite bureaucratic in their attitudes and functions for more often than not they are representatives and champions of the departments.   Consequently they tend to help increase the budget requests rather than curtail and slash them as they are expected to by the people. Ironically enough, the committees have encouraged the government to spend more money even when it was not actually asking for more funds.   Little wonder then that the committee system has been characterized sometimes as a "cancer of the Diet"[24] by political commentators.

In addition to these twenty-two standing committees, there are special committees which are for the most part *ad hoc* bodies appointed to investigate special problems as, for instance, a disaster, trade, repatriation, or a scandal. Actually, so far as the general public is concerned, it is the work of the special committees which attracts widespread attention and interest because of the emergency or sensational nature of most of the subject matter handled.

Over and above the two types of Diet committees, there is the Conference Committee of the two Houses which comes into being whenever the two Houses come into conflict over bills, budget, treaties, designation of the Prime Minister, or constitutional questions. It is the task of the Conference Committee, consisting of ten members from each House, to resolve these conflicts under a chairman of its own choosing. Actually there are three conditions under which a Conference Committee is mandatory:

(1) when the House of Councillors has revised or voted down the budget bill passed by the House of Representatives;
(2) when the views of the two Houses do not agree regarding the approval of a treaty;
(3) when the two Houses disagree over the designation of the Prime Minister.

There is yet another body which is very important not only for the effective operation of the Diet but also in maintaining a smooth working relationship between the two Houses. The Joint Legislative Committee, consisting of ten members from the House of Representatives and eight from the House of Councillors, is entrusted with

[24] *Seikai Orai,* March, 1953, pp. 111–112.

the responsibility of advising both Houses in advance regarding (1) those matters of national policy to be taken up by the Diet which could create problems, (2) proposals of new legislation as well as laws and cabinet orders in force, and (3) revision of laws and rules pertaining to the Diet. At every session of the Diet, the Joint Legislative Committee has to submit its report to the Speaker of the House of Representatives and the President of the House of Councillors.

Secretariats and Legislative Departments

Each House is provided with a secretariat under the direction of the Speaker for the purpose of managing its business affairs. The Chief Secretary who is appointed from outside the Diet membership and who is in charge of the office runs the business and signs official documents. There is also a Legislative Bureau in each House which exists for the purpose of assisting members in the work of drafting legislative bills.

National Diet Library

Closely patterned after the Library of Congress of the United States, the National Diet Library was set up for the purpose of aiding and facilitating the research and investigative activities of the members of the Diet. The usefulness of the Library has been more in the improvement of bibliographical facilities in the nation than in the facilitation of the work of the members of the Diet.

RIGHTS AND PRIVILEGES OF DIET MEMBERS

Members of the Diet enjoy complete freedom of speech vis-à-vis the public for they are not held liable outside the House for speeches, debates, or votes cast on the floor of the Diet. Moreover, except in cases provided by law (usually current criminal offenses), they are exempt from apprehension while the Diet is in session. Upon demand a member apprehended before the opening of the session must be freed for the duration of the session of the House. Such immunity is provided to insure the uninterrupted functioning of the legislative body. There is no guarantee however within the Diet against disciplinary action by the body for improper utterances or behavior deemed unbecoming a member that could result in expulsion.

They receive, in addition to the annual payment, per diem during the sessions of the Diet all of which total approximately ¥ 1,000,000 a year. Although they do not receive mileage allowance for traveling between Tokyo and their homes, they are given railway passes. Instead of the franking privilege such as members of the United States Congress enjoy, the Japanese lawmakers are given special allowances to defray the expenses of mailing public documents and carrying on correspondence during Diet session. There are provisions for retirement pensions for members. The chairmen of the standing committees, like the ministers and vice-ministers, have official automobiles placed at their disposal, making the chairmanship attractive in terms of prestige as well as financially.

9

The Diet in Action

The Lot of the Japanese M.P.

The political spectacle that is the Diet has become an overworked lawmaking factory. It is no longer the leisurely, part-time, deliberative body that it used to be in the days before World War II. Like their counterparts in Great Britain and the United States, the members of the Diet are under terrific pressure; they simply do not have the time to do well all the things they must attend to. Membership has become a very different occupation under the new Constitution in the postwar period. Members are expected to be at the House not only in the morning and afternoon but in the evening as well. The pace is gruelling, leaving little time for anything else and even families are neglected.[1]

That the profession of politics has become an all-year-round job is clear. The Thirteenth Diet set an all-time record of the longest continuous parliamentary session of 235 days. Convened in December, 1951, it finally came to a close on July 31, 1952, after it had been extended five times in succession. In 1953, the Diet held four separate sessions, keeping the lawmakers at their tasks for two thirds of the year. As if this were not enough, the government dissolved the Diet, forcing the members to stand an election in April.

[1] As an example, we may take July 28, 1953. On that day, according to the newspaper, *Asahi*, of the next day, there were a total of 33 separate meetings for members of the House of Representatives and 30 for the members of the House of Councillors in progress. These included the plenary session, committee and sub-committee meetings, party caucuses, etc.

187

To say that a member of the Diet is a harassed individual is to put it mildly. At times, the day-to-day life of a member becomes virtually unendurable but for the fact that he can hope that one day he may become a cabinet minister or, if fortunate, even a prime minister. For the first time in Japan's parliamentary history, the lawmaker is also under pressure of the ever increasing and exacting demands of his constituents. Until after World War II, the lawmakers paid almost no attention to the voters in their constituencies. Not only does a Diet member now have to spend his time during the recess and on weekends, but even while the Diet is in session, to receive his constituents who come to Tokyo. He must conduct them through the Diet, take them on sight-seeing tours, and even to the theater, as well as run all sorts of errands for them. In addition, he is called upon not infrequently to find jobs for constituents, serve as go-between in matrimonial match-making, attend public functions and make speeches, attend weddings and funerals, and do many other things to keep his political fences mended and in good shape. He receives grievances and complaints as well as all sorts of requests for assistance from his constituents. All these services not only consume a great deal of time and energy but have to be sandwiched in between the innumerable meetings he must attend. For those who take all these things seriously, it is exhausting work.

Financially, lawmakers the world over are underpaid and, for men of ability, politics is not a rewarding career. However, in the case of Japan, the members of the Diet have "never had it so good." There are two things which have improved since the end of World War II, according to a popular saying, and they are the train service and the treatment of M.P.'s. The ordinary members of the Diet receive a monthly salary of ¥ 78,000 ($216.66),[2] a per diem of ¥ 1,000 and ¥ 10,000 a month expenses for correspondence during the session, plus ¥ 20,000 a month for a private secretary and an office with a private telephone. The Speaker receives   110,000 ($305.55) per month which is the same as the Prime Minister and the Chief Justice of the Supreme Court, while the Vice-Speaker receives ¥ 88,000 ($244.44) which is the monthly salary of cabinet ministers.

In spite of the noticeable betterment in their economic position as compared with the conditions which obtained before World War II, the members of the Diet find it difficult to make ends meet. This is understandable in view of the fact that it is estimated that a minimum of ¥ 20,000,000 or roughly twenty times his annual salary is needed

---

[2] This compares with $374 (131,000 francs) of a French Deputy and $1,250 of a member of the United States Congress and $200 of a British M.P.

for a successful election campaign. Since the position is so demanding of time and energy, it is practically impossible for a member of the Diet to have any gainful employment on the side. This places him under the control of the party organization unless he happens to have his own means.

The Opening Ceremony

The ceremony opening the old Diet used to be a colorful pageant with all its members in attendance in full regalia and with decorations. The Emperor proceeded from the Imperial Palace to the Diet building where he appeared in the resplendent uniform of Grand Field Marshal, a rank which belonged exclusively to the reigning monarch. In a solemn and dignified palace language he read his message to the assembled M.P.'s, usually expressing in peacetime profound pleasure at the increasing amity and friendship with other nations and admonishing the lawmakers to discharge their duty of deliberating harmoniously upon the legislative proposals. Only the privileged few, along with high-ranking government officials and foreign diplomatic representatives and correspondents, were able to witness this solemn ceremony.

Since the end of the war all this has changed, much to the regret of those who look back with nostalgia to the days of imperial splendor. In keeping with the democratically inspired Constitution, there is no longer the pageantry and spectacle of former years. The Emperor now appears in a morning coat and reads his brief message written in ordinary everyday colloquial Japanese to the members of the Diet, who come dressed in plain business suits.

Interestingly enough, there has never been any ceremony connected with the opening of the daily session of the Diet. Nowhere in evidence are the robes, wigs, swords, mace, or any other symbols from the past such as one is accustomed to seeing in the British Parliament. Nor is there a chaplain or his counterpart to give an invocation before the opening of the day's proceedings. This is perhaps because, without a long history such as the British Parliament possesses, the Japanese have not yet been able to establish pomp and splendor in connection with the parliamentary process, much less to have developed any set of traditions surrounding it.

The Physical Arrangement

The seating of the members in the chamber of the House of Representatives is arranged in a semicircle like that of the Congress of the United States and the French Assembly. Seating is by parties, but is different from that of the United States where there is a two party system with the strength so evenly balanced that they are divided right down the middle of the center aisle. The two major parties occupy the greater part of the chamber with the Liberal Democratic Party on the right and the Socialist Party on the left.

In the front center of the chamber is a raised platform on which stands the rostrum where the members address the body. Right below the rostrum almost on the floor level in an enclosure is a team of four shorthand reporters, two of whom alternate at ten-minute intervals, taking verbatim notes of the proceedings. Back of the rostrum on the highest level sits the presiding officer. Flanking the presiding officer on practically the same level are seated the members of the Cabinet and their assistants who are known as government committee members. The Prime Minister occupies the first seat to the right of the Speaker and next to him is seated the Vice-Premier. Almost at the elbow of the Speaker, on a slightly lower level to the right, sits the expert parliamentarian, the chief secretary of the House, to help him in the smooth running of the proceedings.

This arrangement is in sharp contrast to that of the British House of Commons which not only is much smaller but has no raised platform from which to speak. Nor is there any elevated level on which Cabinet members can sit and look down on the rest of the membership. The British arrangement forces all the members including the Cabinet to sit on the same level and on the same uncomfortable benches under a condition of overcrowdedness. To this condition of slight discomfort but physical, if not spiritual, intimacy and equality has been attributed, partly at least, the nature and atmosphere of the British Parliament where oratory is discouraged while getting on with business is encouraged.[3]

THE SESSIONS

There are now, as there have always been since the beginning of the parliamentary system, three types of Diet sessions. The regular or ordinary session must be convoked once a year for a constitutionally required period of 150 days.[4] It usually opens ceremoniously in December in the presence of the Emperor who delivers a brief message to a joint session, following which it immediately goes into the

[3] H. Taine, *Notes on England* (1872), pp. 223–224.

[4] Under the old system an ordinary session of ninety days was held annually, subject to extensions when necessary.

work of organizing.[5]   After a few days, when the work of organizing the House is completed with the Speakers elected and standing committee assignments made and their chairmen chosen, the Diet goes into a recess which continues until about January 20 at the earliest, sometimes almost until the end of the month.

This year-end recess is designed to give the members an opportunity to prepare for the arduous task of deliberation.   It affords the parties the chance to organize themselves and adopt policies on the basis of which the struggle in the Diet is carried on.   The real work does not begin until after this recess.   The period of the regular session can be extended not only once but as many times as necessary. In 1951–52 the Thirteenth Diet session was extended five times for a total of 85 days, resulting in the longest ordinary session on record of 235 days or only a few days short of 8 months.

Extraordinary sessions are called by the government whenever necessary, to take up emergency matters which cannot wait until the next regular session in December.   Also, when one-fourth or more of the members of either House demand it, the government must call an extraordinary session.   The impending San Francisco Peace Conference necessitated the consideration of the treaty draft; so a three-day extraordinary session was convoked in August, 1951.   Following the conference another extraordinary session was called, this time to act upon the peace treaty which had been signed.   Extraordinary sessions have been held with great frequency in the postwar period although it was during the Pacific War itself from 1941 to 1945 that they were called most frequently.[6]   The shortest sessions, of two to three days' duration, are usually extraordinary or special sessions although an ordinary session is known to have lasted only three days because the Diet was suddenly dissolved.   This however can happen only rarely.

A special session is mandatory within thirty days of a general election following the dissolution of the Diet.   It has to come within seventy days of the dissolution since not more than forty days can elapse between dissolution and the general election.   The chief pur-

---

[5] More often than not, it opens in the latter part of December, though occasionally it has been convoked in the early part of the month.   In the post-World War II period, an ordinary session, the Tenth, was delayed until January 25, 1951, because the preceding extraordinary session could not adjourn until December 9, 1950.

[6] During this period, there were actually eleven extraordinary sessions as against five ordinary sessions.

pose of this type of session is to elect a Prime Minister to head a new government from among the membership of the new Diet and to dispose of the unfinished business which was left at the time of the dissolution.

PROCEDURAL RULES. Deliberations in the Diet are as a rule open to the public. In other words, all the sessions are open except when an executive session behind closed doors is voted for by a majority of two-thirds or more of the members present. Under the Meiji Constitution it was possible for the Cabinet to demand a closed session. However, under the new Constitution the Cabinet has no say whatsoever and only the House itself has the power to decide.

When important addresses are to be delivered or interesting debates are scheduled the public is given the opportunity to witness the proceedings through the media of electronic communication. Newsreel cameras, radio, and television carry the proceedings to millions of people who are unable to sit in the galleries to witness the Diet in action. Even committee meetings have been televised for the enlightenment if not the entertainment of the general public.

Each House is required to keep a record of its proceedings which must be published and made available to the general public, except such parts of the proceedings of closed sessions as require secrecy. Furthermore, whenever demanded by one-fifth or more of the members present, the votes of the Diet members on any matter must be recorded in the minutes.

No business can be transacted unless there is present a quorum which is one-third or more of the total membership of the body. All matters are decided by a majority vote of those present except as provided for in the Constitution. In case of a tie, the presiding officer casts the deciding vote.

Several methods of voting are used in the Diet. There is the standing vote and a show of hands. But the method which is different as well as time consuming is marching up to the rostrum and registering the vote by dropping a ballot into the box provided.

Each House selects its own presiding officer and other officials, makes its own rules pertaining to meetings, procedure, and internal discipline, and punishes members for disorderly conduct. In the operation of the Diet, precedents help to establish rules where none existed before.

In the event that the House of Representatives is dissolved, the House of Councillors must immediately go into adjournment. In times of national emergency, however, the Cabinet can call the House of Councillors into session to take action on urgent measures. However, measures adopted by the House of Councillors sitting alone are provisional and become null and void unless assent is given to them by the newly elected House of Representatives within a period of ten days after the opening of the next session which is usually a special session.

DAILY SCHEDULE. Normally the House of Representatives holds its plenary session in the afternoon beginning at one o'clock, leaving the morning for committee meetings which begin at ten o'clock. The House of Councillors reverses the schedule and holds its plenary session at ten o'clock in the morning, reserving the afternoon for committee meetings. Because of the large number of committees, it is inevitable that some committee meetings should conflict with the plenary session.[7]

DIET BEHAVIOR. In describing the French lawmakers, A. Lawrence Lowell[8] states: "Every large body of men is liable to occasional outbreaks, but the French Chamber of Deputies is especially tumultuous and in times of great excitement, sometimes breaks into a veritable uproar." This could have been written to characterize the Japanese Diet of today. A lawmaking body such as the Diet is a complex web of friendships, personalities, and issues. Individualism, idiosyncrasies, personal convictions, foibles, and animosities all become the ingredients in the discussion, molding, and adoption of policies. Nevertheless the Diet in action as seen by the public leaves much to be desired as far as behavior is concerned.

The first plenary session of the new postwar Diet broke up in confusion on June 21, 1946, after fist fights and general disorder resulted from uncontrolled heckling as the Speaker tried vainly to restore order on the floor. Heckling and name-calling have been rather common when feeling ran high. In late February of 1953, at a meeting of the Budget Committee, the Prime Minister indulged in name-calling and brought on himself a no-confidence vote which he countered with dissolution. On July 3, 1953, a Liberal Party member kicked the Left Socialist chairman of the House of Representatives

---

[7] On February 24, 1953, a typical day, the schedule for the Diet was as follows in the House of Representatives:

    1:00 p.m.   Plenary session

Committee meetings

    10:00 a.m.   Foreign Affairs, Finance, International Trade and Industry, Economic Stabilization, Budget

    10:30   Agriculture and Forestry

    11:00   Ways and Means

    1:00 p.m.   Electrical Communications, Final Accounts

[8] *Governments of France, Italy, and Germany*, p. 18.

Committee on Labor, and caused injury necessitating four days' medical care. This happened when the chairman adjourned the committee meeting ignoring a motion to take up the discussion of the controversial antistrike bill. On July 31, 1953, the House of Representatives Budget Committee meeting became the scene of fist fights and flying ash trays and later turned into a free-for-all among the committee members present.[9] But the high point of the outrageous incidents was the outbreak of June 3, 1954, which turned the floor of the Diet into a disorderly fracas. For the first time in the nation's parliamentary history, the police had to be called in by the Speaker to restore order. Such undignified antics as fisticuffs, hurling of ash trays and shouting of epithets by the members of the highest organ of the state power, outraged the public and caused their prestige considerable damage.

Attendance on the floor used to be excellent under the old system when business was transacted for the most part in plenary sessions. But now with important deliberations being carried on primarily though not exclusively in the committees as in the United States, attendance on the floor is poor during all but the final phases of the debate. Absenteeism has been a serious problem for the new Diet. This has been caused partly by the pressure on a member from the constituents and the need for utilizing every available opportunity to go back to his election district to mend the political fence.

As is an almost universal habit among lawmakers, the Japanese legislators begin their deliberations in a very leisurely manner without momentum until they get into the final stretch. The hectic last-minute rush to push legislation through in the final hours of the session is aggravated by the strategy of the government which carefully plans the timing of the introduction of every bill. Since the custom of stopping the clock has not been adopted by Japanese lawmakers, the alternative is the extension of the session which has been resorted to by the government time and again.

JUNKETS. One of the interesting postwar developments which constitutes a new departure is the popularity of junkets among the members of the Diet. This is reminiscent of the popularity of travel abroad among British M.P.'s who made no other use of holidays in the early 1870's than to "proceed to the Continent and institute an inquiry for a fortnight or for six weeks."[10] Members of Parliament went to France, Spain, Italy, and Germany for the purpose of refreshing, rectifying, and deepening their previous impressions and keep-

---

[9] See Tokyo newspapers of July 4 and August 1, 1953.

[10] H. Taine, *Notes on England* (1872), p. 202.

ing abreast of what was going on and following the fluctuations of public opinion.

Although the enthusiasm for trips abroad came eighty years later to the Japanese M.P.'s, they have been making excellent use of the opportunity afforded them by the new practice. Approval for the junkets is in the hands of the powerful Ways and Means Committee. While the junkets involve considerable expenditure of both time and money, they have undoubtedly served to heighten the M.P.'s awareness and understanding of international problems and bolstered their conviction that international cooperation and good will were basic to the nation's prosperity.[11]

THE COMMITTEE SYSTEM: CORE OF THE LEGISLATIVE PROCESS

As in the Congress of the United States, the Committee system forms the core of the legislative process in the Diet.[12] Consequently the committees determine both positively and negatively for the most part, if not entirely, the extent of the Diet's activities. They determine the question as to which legislative proposals should be brought up for deliberation and which may not be included in the legislative agenda. In other words, they have the power to block measures from consideration at all, unless wrested from them by specific and usually very difficult parliamentary procedures as well as political maneuvers. Upon the committees devolves the primary responsibility

[11] The year 1953 was one of great activity so far as foreign junkets of members of the Diet were concerned. Among them the more important ones included the following:

1. Ways and Means Committee trip to the United States and Europe to look into the functioning of the Congressional Committee system and the operation of the parliamentary system.

2. Six-week good-will mission to Brazil and Argentina to study at first hand the problems of Japanese immigrants.

3. Attendance at the Interparliamentary Union meeting in Washington, D.C.

4. Special Committee for the Repatriation of Nationals Abroad visit to the U.S.S.R. and Red China.

5. Fourth meeting of the U.N. Special Committee on Prisoners of War in Geneva.

6. Moral Rearmament meeting in Copenhagen and inspection tour of European nations.

7. Third International Students' Athletic meet in Germany.

8. Sixth meeting of the U.N. Conference on Social Security in Paris.

9. Special mission to the countries of Southeast Asia.

[12] Suzuki Takao, *Kokkai Un'ei no Riron*, pp. 10–12.

of selecting those legislative proposals submitted by the government and recommending them for approval and enactment by the Diet. The committee may function as a whole, a subcommittee, or a directorate which consists of the chairman and the key members representing the major parties.

By far the greater part of the work of deliberating on legislative proposals and other Diet business is carried on in the standing committees whose jurisdiction and competence are set forth in the rules of both Houses. The committees are organized to correspond to the administrative departments of government, an arrangement which is working to the detriment of legislative supremacy. Special committees as a rule are set up to deliberate upon matters which do not fall within the jurisdiction of the standing committees. Frequently, they are entrusted with matters of great political importance. Theoretically they are not supposed to come in conflict with standing committees over jurisdiction. In practice, however, conflicts do arise and the special committees are given precedence over the standing committees when functions overlap.[13]

Individual assignments to committees are determined by the parties although the formality of appointment is vested in the Ways and Means Committee. Training and experience rather than seniority of continuous service in the Diet are made the basis of assignment.[14] The needs of the party are more important than the wishes or preference of the individual member. Consequently, the members do not submit their names as applicants for membership in certain committees in the order of preference, a practice which is followed in the United States. Nor is there any serious consideration given to equitable geographical representation on the committees. This is natural since there do not exist the sort of geographic differences which are inevitable in a country the size of the United States.

A committee chairman is not selected on the basis of seniority as in the United States. The government party's high command normally has the power of selection, although the committee members elect him and the Speaker formally appoints him. Experience, training, and proven ability, as well as party loyalty are the qualifications for a committee chairman since his task is crucial, heavy, and onerous.

[13] Suzuki Takao, *Kokkai Un'ei no Riron*, pp. 44–45.

[14] This is in sharp contrast to the United States where the safe seats whose holders never lose seniority are invariably in the solid Republican or Democratic areas least affected by the movement of opinion that swings the doubtful areas and wins presidential elections as well as changes the balance of power in congressional politics.

Needless to say, his chief purpose is to guide legislation skillfully and safely to passage. In order to accomplish his primary responsibility, he must be able to preside over as colorful, temperamental, idiosyncratic, and ambitious a group of individuals as may be found anywhere in the country. He must be able to reconcile violent differences, forestall open clashes, mollify and humor the prima donnas, if there are any, influence and inspire a measure of cooperation and harmony, and even crack a whip, though only figuratively and without appearing high-handed, in order to get the legislation through.

Committee chairmanship is a position of power and is coveted by all politicians since it carries with it both prestige and power. Not only is a chairman able to influence the legislative program of the government but is able to enjoy the perquisites and compliments of his office which are considerable. As presiding officer, the chairman not only opens and closes the meetings of the committee but works out the agenda, determines the order of business and regulates the speed of deliberations. He is in control of the various stages of the committee's work, questioning, debate, and decision. In his capacity as the spokesman and representative of the committee in all its external relations and negotiations, he becomes a key figure. It is obvious why he is the person to be cultivated by groups and interests within and without the Diet and the government. The chairman of a special committee, however, is elected by its members without the formality necessary for the chairman of a standing committee.

In order that legislative proposals may be carefully examined and evaluated committees hold public hearings at which witnesses are called in and all kinds of materials and exhibits are made available. Through committee hearings the public is afforded the opportunity to participate, by expressing opinions, in the legislative process and at the same time to deepen its interest in national affairs. At the same time the hearings provide the means of adjusting private interests to the public interest. Witnesses are selected by committees with a view to giving the fullest possible representation to all segments of the public such as finance, business and industry, labor, agricultural interests, consumers, women, as well as experts both governmental and nongovernmental. Witnesses are subpoenaed and those who refuse to appear are subject to a contempt charge. Individuals who wish to volunteer as witnesses may apply and not infrequently they are actually chosen. Because the hearings as well as the committee deliberations are open, it often happens that pressure groups send well-known individuals whose presence alone would in effect be tantamount to lobbying.

CRITICISMS OF THE COMMITTEE SYSTEM. A great deal of criticism has been leveled at the effectiveness and appropriateness of the committee system now in operation. Actually the standing committee is not a permanent committee since it is appointed only for the duration of a session and its functions do not continue beyond the duration of the particular session. Its functions are not continuous for a committee has to be reactivated at the beginning of every session. Such loss of continuity and stability is not conducive to legislative efficiency.

Since much or most of the business is transacted in committees, many of the details of proposed legislation remain unknown to legislators who are not committee members. Moreover, the general membership does not show enough interest in the problem of general legislation.[15] This makes it difficult if not impossible to effectively dramatize the general debates on the floor of the House. In fact, it can often lead to the minimizing of the usefulness as well as the effectiveness of the general floor debate. It has also contributed to extremely poor attendance at plenary sessions except for very special occasions.

One of the most scathing criticisms leveled against the committee system as it actually operates is that the committees have degenerated into outposts of the government's administrative departments and that the powerful Ways and Means Committee has become a place for the political parties to bargain and make deals. Furthermore, it has been pointed out that because the members of the Diet have organized themselves into groups, which have intimate ties with special interests and special enterprises with regard to party and committee memberships, they have in many instances been functioning more as advocates of special interests than as representatives of the people and the general public interest.

SUPERVISION OF ADMINISTRATION. In both Great Britain and the United States investigations by the legislative branch into the administrative activities constitute an important and accepted part of the democratic governmental machinery and process. As a matter of fact, it is practically impossible for a legislative body to function properly without the use of investigative power which is necessary for obtaining information. The value of investigations lies not only in exposing official corruption and inefficiency, but in illuminating the facts and circumstances with which the lawmaking process is concerned. It is through the investigative process that the lawmakers can bring into their deliberations the facts and opinions which are in

15 Uehara Etsujiro, *Kokkai no Moten*, pp. 127–128.

possession of the people that otherwise would not be available to the Diet.

The investigative activities of the Diet are definitely a post-World War II innovation which originated with the setting up on December 11, 1947, of the Committee on Illegal Disposal of Government Property (Futo Zaisan Torihiki Iinkai) which probed deeply into national political affairs and exposed the unholy alliance between the party politicians under a democratic constitution and the newly risen post-war monopolistic capital. Sources of political party funds were divulged in a drive for the clean-up of political parties, officialdom, and financial circles.

The Special Committee for Investigation was set up on March 29, 1949, to continue the work of rooting out corruption in government.[16] From the very outset, however, the committee turned into an arena for the constant struggle for power between the Liberal Party and the Japan Communist Party. Its activities strongly inclined toward the investigation of obstructionist activities against the rebuilding of the Liberal Party. Thus, while on the surface it tried and appeared to be above party in its operation, the conflicting interests of the parties frequently clashed making it the battleground of party interests and the incubator of party conspiracies.

The Special Committee on Administrative Supervision superseded the Special Committee for Investigation and was entrusted with looking into the problems of lagging tax payments, obstacles to the rice quota system, labor disputes, and other serious problems. The committee is the Japanese counterpart of the United States Senate Government Operations Committee, the activities of which provided more excitement and held the limelight than any other committee in the United States Congress in 1954. Its chief responsibility is to ferret out corruption, inefficiency, and waste and keep watch over the general field of administrative operations. The authority it enjoys is extensive and ranges over practically all aspects of government. All matters which are the proper subject of legislation by the Diet come within its competence. All agencies operating under the appropriations of the Diet come under its scrutiny. Such matters as

[16] The committee of 30 members was composed as follows:

Liberal	17
Democratic	5
Socialist	3
Japan Communist Party	2
Cooperative	1
Kosei Club	1
Farmer-Labor	1

the functions of the Ministry of Justice, powers and duties of the Justice Minister, and functions of the procurator are legitimate subjects of investigation since it is entrusted with the duty of studying government operations at all levels with a view to determining its economy and efficiency. Although the Diet Committees are vested with independent authority vis-à-vis the higher offices, they do not go beyond the functions delegated by the Diet. There is a limit to the scope of the Committees' powers where the independence of the judiciary is concerned.

The function of supervising and investigating the administration of national affairs is thus a new principle that has been established in the Japanese political system since World War II. Under the old Constitution, the Diet had no power to issue notices to the people, to summon witnesses in connection with its deliberations, or even send its members out on investigative assignments. Under the new Constitution the exalted position of the legislature as the supreme organ of the state invests the Diet with virtually an unlimited power of supervision and investigation, at least in theory.[17] This investigative power actually extends over the judiciary as well as the executive branch. In most cases the committees investigating government operations assemble facts and submit reports on their findings and are content to stop there. However, in some cases they go a step further and pass judgment or make recommendations.

Standing committees too are entrusted with the investigation of government operations. This is in contrast to the practice in the United States where investigating committees are as a rule select and special committees. However, the activities of the standing committees are limited to the duration of the session and cannot go beyond it except by special Diet authorization.

Special committees are created by special resolution of the legislative body and are usually invested with special powers and functions. Their life may extend beyond the duration of the session which created them. They may conduct investigations while the Diet is not in session and subpoena witnesses and demand materials and reports without going through the Speaker of the House and may even request the appointment of necessary personnel and appropriate funds within certain limits. On the basis of their findings they may demand the government organ under investigation take suitable action deemed necessary by them.

[17] Suzuki Takao, *Kokkai Un'ei no Riron*, p. 312.

See Okada, Inosaburo, *Nihonkoku Kempo Shingi Yoroku*, p. 399, for the views of Kanamori Tokujiro who was the State Minister and expert on the Constitution.

THE DIET'S ROLE IN LAWMAKING

It is clear that legislation is necessitated by the demand for new policies as well as for modifications, amplifications or shifts in emphasis in existing laws deemed desirable and necessary in meeting new problems and changing conditions. It represents the final step in the formal process of policy making by the government in which the legislative branch gives its approval.

In theory, policies are first taken up in the cabinet meetings and discussed. Prior to this, of course, discussions are carried on by the government with its party. Once the policy decisions are reached by the cabinet, the task of concretizing the policy into the form of a bill is entrusted to the appropriate administrative department.

In actual practice, however, the legislative process works out quite differently. From the various administrative offices come suggestions and proposals which arise from or are based upon their actual day-to-day administrative experiences, general public opinion, and specific demands of the general public. These then are taken up by the cabinet for discussion at its meetings.

In drafting a particularly important piece of legislation, deliberative commissions composed of scholars, businessmen, experts, and administrative officials are consulted. In specific instances, this procedure is required by law. There are two ways in which this can be done. First, the draft outline prepared by a department may be submitted to a commission for its views and criticisms. The second method is to simply present the objectives and request a draft outline for their implementation. In recent years, the latter method has come to be used more generally especially when large-scale planning is involved. In exceptionally important legislation, the cabinet gives approval to the outline, but in most instances this is not regarded as a necessary preliminary.

DRAFTING OF A BILL. The drafting of a bill is normally the function of an administrative department. It originates at the section level and when it is finished the section chief sends it to his superior, the bureau chief, and it is circulated to other interested bureaus within the department. It then goes through the department's Documents Section Chief in the Secretariat, to the Parliamentary Vice-Minister, and finally to the Minister who acts on it.[18] After the bill is approved

[18] The Documents Section in the Secretariat serves as the "Bureau of Legislation" for each department and, in many of the departments, a legislative deliberative committee comprising key personnel is set up to consider the bills and even department-wide conferences are held to study them.

by the Minister, it is submitted in his name to the Prime Minister and placed on the agenda of the cabinet meeting for discussion and decision. If a bill involves matters touching upon more than one department, it is jointly sponsored and submitted by the ministers concerned.

The Cabinet Bureau of Legislation has the authority to draft a bill on any matter without any jurisdictional limitations and submit it for cabinet deliberation. However, its primary function is to study and scrutinize the draft bills that are submitted to it. All draft bills, wherever they may have originated, are delivered to the Cabinet Secretariat, but those submitted by the Bureau of Legislation are separated and readied for placing immediately on the Cabinet agenda for deliberation. The remaining bills are sent on to the Bureau of Legislation for careful study.

THE BUREAU OF LEGISLATION.[19] It used to be customary for the Bureau of Legislation to begin the study of draft bills only after they had been submitted by the Cabinet. But in recent years, it has become the usual practice to begin the study as soon as rough preliminary drafts are furnished by an administrative department. This has, in effect, made the drafting of the final bill a joint undertaking of the Bureau of Legislation and the administrative department concerned, thus expediting and speeding up the work and producing much more satisfactory results particularly in the case of complex and difficult bills.

The actual scrutiny and study of a bill is carried out as a rule by a group of Bureau officials although it is not unusual to have a bill in charge of two persons or even one person especially in the rush period.[20] However, on constitutional problems or matters involving difficult legal problems or legislative techniques which might set new precedents, the Bureau as a whole participates in the deliberation. The purpose of this careful study is to see clearly the relationship between the legislative proposal and existing legislation as well as the Constitution, to make sure that the purport of the proposed legislation is accurately stated in the document, that arrangement of the contents is proper, and that there are no errors or loopholes. Scrutiny is thorough and is made from various angles with special attention to

[19] There are twenty officials in the Bureau, of whom one is the Director and another the Deputy Director. See Sato Tatsuo, "Horitsu no Hiroba," *Horitsu Jiho*, November, 1952.

[20] In the Thirteenth Diet for instance, 249 pieces of legislation were submitted by the cabinet which gave each secretary in the Bureau 25 draft bills to go over.

legal and technical matters. Occasionally, it is necessary for a draft bill to be completely overhauled or rewritten by the Bureau.

Since the study is conducted like a hearing or conference with the officials of the department who drafted the bills as well as those from other interested departments, heated discussions and disagreements develop rather frequently. When jurisdictional disputes occur, the Bureau finds itself in the position of having to mediate and resolve the differences and restore harmony between the various departments.

The revisions and corrections on the draft bill made by the Bureau are written on separate sheets in red ink and tacked onto the draft submitted. However, this step is not necessary in the case of draft bills which the Bureau has followed through in the drafting process, from the beginning to its completion. The Bureau makes a notation to the effect that the draft bill has been carefully studied and is now ready to be submitted to the Diet after formal approval by the cabinet. This is routed to the Cabinet Secretariat from where it goes to the cabinet meeting itself.

THE CABINET. Before the draft bills are taken up in cabinet meetings, it is customary for the vice-ministers' meeting to discuss them first. This is a new procedure instituted after the end of World War II. The meetings of the vice-ministers which are held twice a week have become the highest liaison conference of the administrative officials of the cabinet.[21] Through this means, effective liaison is maintained so that no business taken up at a cabinet meeting comes as a surprise to any department as used to happen rather frequently in the past. As a rule, matters which are taken up at a vice-ministers' meeting are taken up at a cabinet meeting the next day. Decisions reached at the vice-ministers' meeting are usually approved as a matter of course by the cabinet since the vice-ministers do not deliberate upon high policy matters which are reserved for the cabinet ministers.

In a cabinet meeting, the Deputy Chief Secretary of the Cabinet gives a brief explanation of the item on the agenda. When necessary, the Minister concerned or the Director of the Bureau of Legislation, or both, may be called upon to give additional explanation. Except in special cases detailed discussions on the provisions of draft bills almost never take place. If the differences between the departments over the proposed legislation have not yet been resolved, they are

---

[21] The meetings which are held on Monday and Thursday are attended by all the vice-ministers and the Chief Cabinet Secretary, Deputy Chief Secretary, and the Director of the Bureau of Legislation.

settled at the cabinet meeting. All the original draft bills approved by the cabinet are deposited and preserved in the Cabinet Secretariat.[22]

PROCEDURE IN THE DIET. A few days after the Cabinet has taken action, draft bills are submitted in the name of the Prime Minister to either the Speaker of the House of Representatives or the President of the House of Councillors. Great deal of planning goes on in connection with timing and strategy of legislation. Money bills are always submitted to the lower chamber first. When a bill is submitted to one chamber, a copy is submitted to the other chamber within five days for preliminary study.

Upon receipt of a bill, the Speaker refers it to the proper committee on the recommendation of the Ways and Means Committee. The government not infrequently manages to steer a bill to the committee most sympathetic to it. However, in the case of extremely urgent bills, committee deliberation is omitted and decision reached in a plenary session. This procedure is employed especially in the case of a member's bill on which the understanding of the committee that would have deliberated on it has been obtained in advance. However, with government bills, instances are extremely rare of the omission of committee deliberation and study. A committee can pigeonhole any bill which it deems not worthy, necessary, or desirable and not report it out to the plenary session of the Diet.

Normally bills are not presented and explained to the plenary session and acted upon as was done under the old Diet. Only when the Ways and Means Committee decides that it is necessary is there an explanation in the plenary session preceding the referral of a bill to a committee. This was done, for example, in the case of such important items of legislation as the Subversive Activities Prevention Law, the National Civil Service Law, and the Police Law.

In the committee meetings, the Prime Minister, Ministers, and government representatives are required to attend to answer questions and make explanations on the bills. All the committees have the services of the Diet staff including experts and research personnel attached to them, to point up and explain the issues. In the course of the study, the committees frequently call on the Diet's Bureaus of Legislation for legal opinions. The Legislative Research Bureau of the National Diet Library is consulted for advice and assistance in the analysis and evaluation of the bills under study. Bills involving

[22] When an emergency situation calling for speedy action arises and there is no time for a cabinet meeting, the documents are taken around to the cabinet ministers separately and a cabinet decision is reached.

more than one committee are studied jointly, as in the case of the Subversive Activities Prevention Law which came under the jurisdiction of the Judiciary and Labor Committees. Such joint study may involve two committees in the two Houses.

Public hearings are usually held on important bills. As a matter of fact, in the case of major revenue bills, including the budget, hearings are required by law as part of regular procedure. Those witnesses who express their views before the committee at the public hearings are selected by the committee from among learned and experienced persons and those who ask for appearance at the hearings. Frequently, instead of a public hearing a much simpler method is used, namely, asking witnesses to appear before the committee to simply give information as well as their views.

Most of the time and energy is spent by the committee in questioning the sponsors of a bill. And this is the very first thing that is taken up by the committee. When all the questions have been answered the next stage of deliberation begins. Heated discussions can occur at this stage but what usually takes place is not a debate in the ordinary sense. Representatives of the different parties merely present their views in approving or disapproving the bill.

After the committee has acted on a bill, it is reported out and taken up in the plenary session of the Diet. The chairman of the committee gives a report on the course of the deliberation on the bill and the committee's decisions in the form of a recommendation to the Diet. The committee recommendation is always adopted by the Diet although amendments sometimes are made.

When the bill is passed by one chamber, it is sent immediately to the other. If it is defeated, the fact is reported to the other chamber. Until one chamber has passed a bill and sent it on to the other chamber, the second chamber can not proceed beyond the discussion stage in its committee. If the second chamber approves the bill without any changes, it becomes a law. However, if any changes have been made in the bill as approved, the second chamber must send it back to the first chamber which must approve the changes which have been made before it becomes a law. In the event that the first chamber disagrees, two methods of resolving the difficulty are available. A conference committee of the two Houses may decide the matter or the House of Representatives may override the House of Councillors by a two-thirds vote. Once a law is enacted by the Diet no veto is possible.

PROMULGATION OF LAW. When a law is enacted, the Speaker of the House of Representatives reports the fact to the Emperor through the

Cabinet. The Cabinet officially decides on its promulgation and submits to the Emperor the law with the signatures of the ministers. In the promulgation, the signature of the Prime Minister follows that of the Emperor and his sign manual. The law takes effect with the publication of this promulgation in the *Official Gazette* (Kampo) which must come within thirty days of the Speaker's report. In some instances, the date of taking effect is specified in the law itself. Each law is numbered in chronological order as it is promulgated.

MEMBER BILLS. Member bills, as opposed to government bills, are usually submitted to the Diet jointly by several members and differ considerably in their substance and in procedure. There are those motivated by individual beliefs or opinions, those based upon party policies, and those which represent demands transcending party interests. There are also bills introduced by members at the specific request of the government. These bills by government request deal with matters pertaining to the Diet, election, or electoral process. There has been an appreciable increase in the number of member bills introduced in the Diet, resulting in the clogging of the legislative machinery with matters that are not of major importance since most of them are designed to help the members in getting votes in their election campaign vis-à-vis their constituents. The party's high command in collaboration with the government has been reducing the number of private members' bills.

In the drafting of members' bills, the services of the Cabinet Bureau of Legislation are not available except that government bills in the guise of members' bills are its handiwork. However, the experts and research staff attached to the committees can be and are utilized along with the help of the Legislative Bureaus of both houses. Most valuable assistance comes from the Legislative Research Bureau of the National Diet Library.

Laws are, as we have seen, rarely if ever initiated by the members of the Diet. This is normally the practice which obtains in nearly every country and Japan is no exception. The lawmaking body aids in the formulation and development of policy. It simply affirms or disapproves solutions developed and presented by others, usually by the executive branch of the government. It is no reflection on the law-making body to say that its primary function is to scrutinize carefully the proposals in order that it may judiciously select, ratify, and validate those which are in the best interests of the nation and the people and enact them into laws. For after all, law is no more than the instrument or means of giving legal effect to the policy proposals of the government which have been derived from various sources.

The Diet and the Budget

It is impossible to overemphasize the importance of a nation's budget since it sets the framework and determines the course of national economy.   In the years since World War II the solution of the difficult problems of Japanese economy has had to rely almost exclusively on financial assistance from the State. Politically, the budget reflects the existing power relationship of those elements which constitute the nation's policy-making forces.   Consequently, in the course of its formulation and adoption it provides ammunition for some of the most interesting battles both inside and outside the Diet. The battle of the budget is fought with all the interested parties involved in varying degrees and in different ways, party politicians, government bureaucrats, financial and business interests, labor, and others.

The budget is the indispensable instrument by which policies are implemented by the government.   However, it is more than that.   It has been used by the government and its supporting party to make good their election promises.   Interestingly enough Japan may well claim the unique but dubious distinction of being perhaps the only country in the world where the lawmakers and the political parties, who are in reality the representatives of the people, strain themselves to the utmost in their efforts to increase the national budget.[23]   In their bid to win the support of their constituents and strengthen their positions, the parties vie with each other to include in the budget the largest possible amounts for subsidies and grants to be handed out to various governmental units for public works and food production increase.

Competition among department heads to get a larger slice of the budget than anyone else has become an intensive but a normal activity.   In fact the effectiveness of a cabinet minister is likely to be judged more on the basis of how large an appropriation he succeeds in getting than on his administrative or policy-making achievements. This situation arose from the fact that the department as well as the

---

[23] Premier Yoshida is said to have remarked to newspapermen that there is no other country in the world where the lawmakers and political parties worked so hard to boost the budget. See Arai Tatsuo "Yosan'an wa dono yo ni shite tsukurareta ka?" *Sekai*, April, 1953, p. 72.

minister with political power has always managed to get a sizeable portion of the budget.

BUDGET FORMULATION.   Budget making is a constitutional function which belongs to the Cabinet.   But it is exercised in conformity with the policies and demands of the party or parties supporting the government as well as the decisions of the Diet.   The brunt of the burden of preparing the budget falls on the Budget Bureau of the Finance Ministry.

Budget making is a continuous job.   The first step in the process is the adoption of a budget policy by the Cabinet in the month of July or August preceding the fiscal year.   This policy actually outlines the objectives and sets the framework within which the budget bill is to be drafted and is determined after a careful look into the future financial and economic prospects and in anticipation of the various requirements.   Both the domestic and international economic conditions must be taken into consideration.   While the budget policy is presented to the Cabinet by the Minister of Finance its adoption comes only after lengthy negotiations with the various government departments as well as the policy committees of the government and opposition parties.

The government's budget policy is announced as soon as it is adopted.   At the same time the Finance Ministry explains it in detail to the various departments and offices which subsequently submit, usually not later than August 31, their estimates of expenditures. Meanwhile the Finance Ministry proceeds to prepare a working budget on the basis of the current budget, deleting the items which are to be terminated, reducing those which have been agreed to, and adding on to those which must be increased in the new fiscal year.

The Finance Minister begins from about the middle of September the examination of the estimates submitted by the departments, which usually total two or three times the amount of the working budget. This necessitates a drastic trimming of the departmental budget requests.   The process of scrutinizing and paring down the estimates is completed during the latter part of October and the departments are notified of the resulting rough preliminary draft.   The departments vie with one another to get as large an amount as possible and demand the restoration of the slashes.   Occasionally the Finance Ministry accedes to their demands and restores some of the items. In the struggle, departments with political power are more likely to succeed in having their cuts restored.

The draft budget is then submitted early in January by the Finance

Ministry. Deliberations in the Cabinet usually extend over several cabinet meetings and when agreement is reached within the government and with the party it becomes the budget bill. The various departments now work out the details of their budgets and submit them to the Finance Minister who in turn works out a detailed budget of revenues and expenditures. This final draft budget is submitted for the last time to the cabinet meeting for the decision to transmit it to the Diet. The budget bill now goes to the House of Representatives. In an ordinary session this takes place in the latter part of January. The House of Councillors usually receives the budget bill the next day but not later than five days after submission to the first chamber.

BUDGET DELIBERATION AND APPROVAL BY THE DIET. The introduction of the budget bill in the regular session of the Diet is followed by the speeches of the Prime Minister on administrative policy, of the Foreign Minister on foreign policy, of the Finance Minister on financial policy, and of the Economic Policy Board Director on economic policy. All these addresses are given in the House of Representatives first and in the House of Councillors later.

The Finance Minister outlines the financial policy of the government along with an explanation of the policy followed in the formulation of the budget, its substance and special features, as well as money and banking, trade, international balance of payments, and prices. Party representatives immediately begin their interpellations.

As in the case of all bills, the budget bill is sent to a standing committee for careful deliberation. The Finance Minister explains to the Budget Committee the reasons for the budget bill and this is usually followed by a detailed explanation by a high official of the Finance Ministry. Members of the Committee examine the budget and question the government representatives on details. The deliberations of the Budget Committee are so important that, unlike the deliberations on legislative bills, the Prime Minister, and Finance Minister, and in fact all the cabinet ministers make their appearance. It is believed that of all the standing committees of the Diet, the Budget Committee is the most important and, with fifty-one members, it is also the largest. The Budget Committee meets as a whole for the most part, and also for a day or two in sections or subcommittees to deliberate on portions of the budget. Public hearings are mandatory in the deliberations on the budget and cannot be dispensed with.

When the deliberations of the Committee are finished, the chairman reports to the plenary session of the House what transpired in the Committee meetings and a vote is taken. The decision of the plenary session may or may not be the same as that of the Budget Committee. When the two Houses find themselves in disagreement, a joint conference committee is required by the Constitution.

Budget bills are passed as submitted or with revisions. The Diet may even refuse to approve the bill, in which case the refusal is equivalent to a no-confidence vote and will result either in the resignation of the Cabinet or the dissolution of the Diet.

There is no time limit as to the duration of the deliberations in the House of Representatives. Normally three to four weeks are consumed unless the Opposition happens to be very powerful. Budget Committee meetings have been the occasion for some of the liveliest political debates. In the House of Councillors, a time limit has been imposed since it must act upon the budget bill within thirty days after transmittal from the House of Representatives. If it should fail to act within that time, the decision of the House of Representatives will become the decision of the Diet.

If the budget bill is not enacted into law before the beginning of the fiscal year on April 1, it becomes necessary for the Diet to approve a provisional budget on a monthly basis until such time as it is finally approved.

FINAL ACCOUNTING. After the end of the fiscal year all the administrative departments submit their reports on final accounts to the Finance Minister not later than July 31 of the subsequent year. The Finance Minister in turn prepares the final accounts which are approved by the Cabinet before November 30 and submitted to the Board of Audit where they are carefully audited and scrutinized. The Board of Audit is charged with the task of examining the government's revenues and expenditures to see if there has been any contravention or violation of the budget or law. If everything is in order the Board of Audit gives the stamp of approval to the final accounts. The Cabinet submits the final accounts approved by the Board of Audit to the ordinary session of the Diet where the Final Accounts Committee goes over them. Unlike the budget bill, the House of Representatives does not have priority. Consequently, final accounts are submitted to both Houses at the same time. The Diet may and does submit its desires pertaining to the final accounts to the Cabinet in the form of a resolution. However, the two Houses need not concur in their decisions. If there have been any irregularities there is little that can be done about the *fait accompli*. Recourse can be had only in a political way.

10

The Development
and Nature
of Japanese Political Parties

After more than seventy years of varied experiences, the Japanese people have come to regard political parties as a necessary, if sometimes unpleasant, fact of their political life. They have come to see also that in practical politics the primary function of a political party is to win elections, that is, to get a majority and to form and run a government thereby putting into effect its program and policies in the management of national affairs. In Japan, as elsewhere, the political party has become the single most important instrument for the translation of social power into political power. And as such it is indispensable to the successful carrying out of responsible parliamentary government.

Political parties in Japan perform the function of formulating issues and reducing the choices or alternatives to manageable proportions for the electorate. They present their policies to the public with a view to influencing and leading public opinion on specific issues in a manner advantageous to themselves while at the same time trying not to lose sight of the broader interests of the public and nation. However, by and large, they have worked more for the advancement of their own interests than for the people as a whole.

Since the mobilization of the force of a majority becomes the primary function of a political party, it must appeal to general interests and promote accommodations and compromises among many interests, special and general. In Japan this has created multifarious problems involving the integration of special interests with public policy without yielding completely to the clamor of organized interests.

Traditional Attitude Toward Parties

Under the strong influence of both Buddhism and Confucianism the Japanese at an early period of their history developed a passion for harmony. In the Constitution of Seventeen Articles promulgated by Prince Shotoku in 604 A.D., government officials were strongly admonished against forming factions. Cleavages and functional struggles were abhorred and disparaged in the bureaucratic system established under Chinese influence. This attitude was further strengthened during the seven centuries of feudalism which followed when no political dissent or opposition was countenanced by the government.

When political parties appeared in 1881, the Japanese were without a terminology for them in their political vocabulary. What they had were such words as the Japanese equivalents of private factions or private cliques and gangs (junta or cabal) which had been banned by the authorities as dangerous. A new word therefore had to be coined to take care of the innovation. Unfortunately one of the ideographs which had been used for private cliques and cabals was taken and combined with another one which means government. It was necessary therefore to explain that a political party was not a private faction organized to serve private interests, but rather a public political organization to promote the public interest. The public found it difficult to accept the political parties as honest, respectable, unselfish organizations. There were some government officials who looked upon members of political parties as being no more respectable or trustworthy than burglars and arsonists.

Such an attitude of distrust, though extreme and unjustified, was quite natural in the 1880's, and perfectly understandable, in the light of Japanese traditional background. Even in the United States the advent of the political parties was not greeted with anything like enthusiasm. James Madison was of the opinion that parties were intrinsically bad while George Washington felt that the rise of political parties was responsible for subverting the Constitution. It had not occurred to either of the Founding Fathers that the parties might be used as effective and beneficent instruments of popular government.[1]

Distrust and hatred of political parties was inevitable since their very existence was a threat to the power of the government which

[1] Schattschneider, E., *Party Government*, p. 8.

was in the hands of a clan oligarchy. Even after the promulgation of the Constitution in 1889 the government continued to regard the political parties as its sworn enemy. A ruthless and relentless policy of suppression was directed at them. In his address of December 25, 1889, Prime Minister Yamagata stated that a party government would mean the destruction of the national polity because it would "degrade" the empire of Japan into a democracy. Yamagata's predecessor, Kuroda, had also taken a hostile stand against the political parties in his address to the conference of prefectural governors.

Prince Ito, the father of the Meiji Constitution, showed hostility toward political parties in the beginning and would have nothing to do with them. As head of the government, he managed to remain aloof and stand above the parties. However, he soon found himself trying to manipulate the parties though he was still not willing to concede their usefulness. By 1898, he was convinced that the affairs of state could not be managed without the support of political parties and had decided to try a hand at forming his own political party with the backing of the financial interests. Prince Yamagata, who was never reconciled to the idea of a political system in which parties were to play an important role, tried very hard at the meeting of the Elder Statesmen of June 24, 1898, to persuade Ito to abandon the idea of forming a political party, but to no avail. Two years later, Ito founded the Seiyukai which played a major role in Japanese politics until 1940 when all the political parties were disbanded.

The appearance of the first party government in 1898 was concrete evidence of the fact that political parties had succeeded in bringing the clan government to an end. While there were still diehards like Yamagata who would not admit that parties were here to stay, the fact was incontrovertible that they had become an indispensable part of politics.

In the upsurge of nationalism and the ascendancy of military power in the 1930's, the political parties suffered eclipse and were blamed for bringing on the economic depression which began with the panic of 1927 and the resultant unemployment and social insecurity. The political scandals of the 1920's were played up and exploited by the military to stir up the indignation of the public. Dissatisfaction at the outcome of the London Naval Treaty of 1930 caused the military to place the onus of this diplomatic defeat on the party politicians. Distrust of the parties had grown so by 1934 that public confidence in them all but disappeared. Matsuoka Yosuke, the erstwhile delegate to the League of Nations who had made a dramatic exit at a meeting in Geneva following his announcement of Japan's withdrawal from the world organization, seriously advocated the disbanding of political parties.[2]

Political parties continued even after party government came to an end in May, 1932, with the assassination of Premier Inukai but they lacked clear-cut policies and constructive programs. Moreover they dissipated their energies in a struggle for power in which they fought one another solely for their own narrow interests and advantages. They contributed thereby to the destruction of the party system itself. Under the strong pressure of the military which was now in control of national affairs and bent upon strengthening the political structure, the parties were abolished in 1940.

During the five-year period, 1940–45, the nation was organized into a single body, the Imperial Rule Assistance Association, under a totalitarian setup. With the end of World War II, however, political parties were revived; yet so far as the public was concerned, they were looked upon with distrust. This was rather natural for the Japanese who have, in times of emergency and especially in wartime, quite willingly suspended the normal operations of political parties by rallying around the government in response to the appeal for national unity and foregoing the duty of criticizing and providing loyal opposition to the Government. This happened in the Sino-Japanese War, 1894–95, and the Russo-Japanese War, 1904–05.

HISTORY OF POLITICAL PARTIES

Struggle Between the Clan Government and Political Parties 1881–1900

One may go all the way back to 552 A.D. for the first recorded instance of a major political struggle between two factions in Japanese historical development. The introduction of Buddhism provided the issue of whether or not to accept the alien religion. It was in reality not a religious issue which confronted the nation but a power struggle underlying the overt clash over Buddhism, with the faction in power opposing its adoption and the faction out of power favoring the new religion, which became an effective weapon in the power struggle. Factional struggles, however, did not end with the victory of the pro-Buddhist group. They continued for the next thirteen hundred years through the periods of court aristocracy and of feudalism and have come down to the present time.

2 Yosuke Matsuoka, "Dissolve the Political Parties," *Contemporary Japan,* March, 1934, pp. 661–667.

The reopening of Japan in 1854 to normal intercourse with the rest of the world after two centuries of isolation brought numerous problems to the nation that was confronted with the forces of nineteenth century European expansion. It was in response and submission to this external pressure that Japan opened her doors. She was in no position to resist or even forestall it. The only way to cope with the situation and preserve her integrity and independence, the leaders decided, was to build a strong nation as rapidly as possible.

In a bloodless "revolution" the feudal system which had lasted nearly seven centuries was quietly brought to an end and a new government was established in 1868. The newly organized government was of necessity oligarchic in leadership if not in organization. Its goal as expressed in the Charter Oath of Five Articles[3] and the national policy was to build a strong and efficient central government equal to the task of carrying on the work of modernization and industrialization.

In the process of erecting a strong political structure, differences of opinion developed among the oligarchy, which was made up of the powerful leaders of the four clans, namely, Satsuma, Choshu, Tosa, and Hizen. Political power of the new government was soon concentrated in the hands of a small group led by Okubo of Satsuma and Kido of Choshu, establishing in fact a sort of oligarchic despotism. The leaders of the two remaining clans[4] were left out of the important councils and policy decisions, and were given nominal posts. Inevitably a serious cleavage developed within the government itself. Thus, only five years after the Meiji government was established, the political struggle at the highest level came to a head in a violent split over the issue of the government's Korean policy.

On August 17, 1873, while Okubo and Kido were away on a mission to the United States and European countries, the stay-at-homes who had been consistently left out of important decisions, succeeded in securing imperial approval for a strong policy toward Korea which did not preclude the use of armed force in obtaining satisfaction for violence and outrages committed by her authorities against Japanese residents and diplomatic representatives.

However, upon the return of the Iwakura Mission, the decision which had already been made with imperial sanction was revoked

[3] For details on the Charter Oath of Five Articles, see Yanaga, *Japan Since Perry*, pp. 48–49.

[4] Itagaki Taisuke and Goto Shojiro of Tosa, Eto Shimpei and Soeshima Taneomi of Hizen were joined by Saigo Takamori of Satsuma.

through the efforts of Iwakura, Okubo, and Kido, who were convinced that priority should be given to internal improvements and developments inasmuch as foreign affairs could and should be deferred especially in view of the urgent need for building up national strength.

Indignant at the reversal of the policy at the instance of the "in" faction, the "out" faction headed by Saigo, Itagaki, Goto, Eto, Soeshima, and others resigned en masse from their government posts. This split the nation's leadership into two factions precipitating the country into a brief five-year period of internal strife in which resort to armed force was tried unsuccessfully.

Those who were frustrated by the defeat over the Korean issue left the government and went immediately into action to oppose the government but there developed two distinct approaches.   One group resorted to the use of armed force beginning in 1874 with the Saga Rebellion led by Eto and ending in the Satsuma Rebellion led by Saigo in 1877.   In this brief period there were four major rebellions which were all put down successfully by the government.   The new conscript army was put to the test in the largest and most serious armed opposition, the Satsuma Rebellion.   After this, there was no attempt made to oppose the government by force.

The second group led by Itagaki followed a different path, using peaceful means instead of armed force.   Early in January, 1874, Itagaki organized a political association called the Patriotic Public Party to carry on a movement for liberty and popular rights.   This was the first time an organization resembling a political party was founded in Japan.   As the name indicates, it was part of a nationalistic patriotic movement, an extension of the patriotic movement which got under way before the end of feudalism and the restoration of imperial authority.   It was Itagaki's aim to strengthen the nation by awakening the individual.   In other words, Itagaki's movement for popular rights and freedom had for its avowed goal the establishment of a strong nation.[5]

On January 18, 1874, Itagaki, Goto, and others presented to the government the famous "Memorial for the Establishment of a Popular Representative Assembly" which has become a prominent landmark in the constitutional and political development of the nation.[6]   It had a powerful and somewhat inflammatory effect on the nation, but the ruling oligarchy in the government not only refused to recognize it but undertook the suppression of the Patriotic Public Party.   As a

[5] Osadake Takeki, *Meiji Taisho Seijishi Kowa*, p. 175.
[6] See Yanaga, *op. cit.*, pp. 149–150.

result the first political association went out of existence in March after only two months.

In February, 1875, Itagaki organized the Patriotic Party (Aikokuto) but he soon joined the government and the organization expired. By October, however, he clashed with Okubo and Okuma over government reorganization and resigned from his government post. Thereupon he returned to his native province of Tosa and took up with vigor his fight for liberty and popular rights, using the Risshisha which he had set up in April, 1874, immediately after the Patriotic Party went out of existence. Thus Itagaki's popular rights movement was resumed at intervals when he was out of the government as a result of clash over policies. In April, 1878, the Patriotic Public Party was revived after a lapse of almost three years. In the following month, Okubo met an untimely death at the hands of assassins who accused him of obstructing public discussion, suppressing popular rights, abusing the powers of government, and bungling in the conduct of foreign relations. With all the Restoration triumvirate gone, political power now passed to younger second-echelon statesmen, Okuma, Ito, and Inoue.

Birth and Early Growth of Political Parties

Agitation for the establishment of a national assembly spread to all parts of the country. Alarmed at the intensity of the movement, the government passed suppressive measures regulating public meetings, associations, and newspapers. The government, realizing the futility of attempting to stop the movement that was rapidly gaining momentum, changed its policy and issued an imperial rescript on October 12, 1881, promising the opening of a national assembly in 1890. Against the government that had become completely the monopoly of the Satsuma and Choshu clans were arrayed the strong and determined opposition forces under the leadership of Itagaki, Eto, and Okuma.

Six days after the imperial rescript for the establishment of a national assembly was promulgated, the first political party, the Liberal Party, was organized in Tokyo with Itagaki as its president. In its manifesto were incorporated Rousseau's ideas taken right out of his *Social Contract*. The leadership of this party was inspired by Montesquieu, Rousseau, and Voltaire whose ideas provided the ideological foundation of the party. The Liberal Party formed the vanguard of the movement for popular representative government. In the vigorous agitation it carried on some segments of the party were guilty of excesses which gave a bad name to the party.

When Okuma was driven out of the government by the leaders of the Satsuma and Choshu clans for opposing their policies and exposing some of their shady deals, he gathered together men of like mind and launched the Reform Party on March 14, 1882.[7] The party advocated liberalism of the English type and the members followed the ideas of Adam Smith, Ricardo, Bentham, John Stuart Mill, and others. Fukuzawa and Keio University became the exponents of English utilitarianism and provided much of the leadership of the party. The party believed in moderation and gradual progress and eschewed direct action and violence.

Frightened by the challenge hurled at the government by the Liberal Party and the Reform Party, both of which advocated popular rights, Ito, Inoue, and Yamada sponsored the founding of the Imperial Party on March 18 only four days after Okuma's party was launched. This was a government-backed party and its ideological foundation was German political thought which stressed statism. It was intended by the government to be used in its counter-offensive against the Opposition parties. It was the instrument to implement its policy of fighting fire with fire.

These three parties were quite different in their ideas, attitudes, and make-up. The Liberal Party which emerged from the valleys of Tosa was influential in the rural areas, espoused radical French political ideas, and even imitated revolutionary tactics and included dissidents in its membership making it a heterogeneous grouping. Okuma's Reform Party emerged in an urban environment and its ideas and policies and means of implementing them were realistic and moderate, and gradual progress was its goal. The members were drawn from the educated class and also from the wealthy class. Because of the differences, these two parties were destined to be rivals from the very beginning in spite of the common objective of opposing the government.

Conservative in the extreme was the Imperial Party which was in effect an adjunct of the government. Its membership consisted of government officials, Shinto and Buddhist priests, nationalistic scholars

---

[7] Those who joined the ranks of the new party comprised the following:
1. Kono Togama group.
2. Yano Fumio group—Tōyō Giseisha
and Keio University graduates in the *Yubin Hochi* newspaper.
3. Ono Azusa group—Otokai
and Takata Sanae group—Daigakuha.
4. Numa Morikazu group—Omeisha
and those with the *Mainichi* Shimbun.

who were graduates of government schools. All three parties were engaged in a struggle for power with little or no thought whatever of such ideas as democracy or the rights or dignity of the individual. During the 1880's, they concentrated their attention on the pending Constitution with a view to getting as many of their ideas incorporated into the document as possible and thereby securing for themselves a stronger position in the new political system. At the same time the government carried on relentlessly its policy of suppression. Unable to tolerate this ruthless policy in which the police was used with devastating effect, the young hot-headed radical elements of the Liberal Party resorted to direct action in resisting the clan government. The years 1883–84 were characterized by serious outbreaks in widely scattered parts of the country.[8] These were acts of terrorism which spread consternation among the people. As a result the Liberal Party alienated the public support.

Itagaki returned from an extended tour of Europe and America in August, 1884, and tried vainly to restore order and unity within the Liberal Party. Finding it impossible to revitalize the party, he dissolved it in Osaka on October 29, 1884, three years after its founding. The Imperial Party had already been disbanded in September by Ito who had returned from Germany where he had been studying Western constitutional systems. Ito was strongly influenced by Bismarck and was now strongly opposed to political parties. The Reform Party, weary of government suppression and opposition from the Liberal Party, was willing to give up the struggle for the time being. But even more decisive was Okuma's feeling that continued struggle against the government might actually remove him further from the chances of securing political power and heading a government. Thus it was that Okuma reached the decision to disband the Reform Party in December, 1884, but it was not actually carried out. Instead he relinquished the leadership of the party. In three short years, the first stage of development of political parties that was eventful and turbulent came to an end. Two parties had disappeared from the scene and the third, the Reform Party, was leaderless.

The government run by the clan oligarchy of Choshu and Satsuma centering around Ito established a cabinet system in December, 1885. The first Ito government thus emerged. With the support of Foreign Minister Inoue, Prime Minister Ito pushed ahead the government's Westernization program. This strongly aroused the champions of popular rights as well as the nationalists and chauvinists. The will-

---

[8] Major outbreaks occurred in Osaka, Nagoya, Shizuoka, Chichibu, Iida, Takata, and Fukushima. See Yanaga, *op. cit.* for details.

ingness of Inoue in May, 1887, to make concessions in the negotiations for treaty revision brought upon the government severe criticism from various quarters and denunciation from Agriculture and Commerce Minister Tani. Attacks on the government were intensified and former members of the disbanded Liberal Party, the nationalists and conservatives, were all moved by Goto's strong appeal for the respect of popular rights and the joining of forces against the government in a "Great Coalition of Parties" which he had been urging for some time. The clan-dominated government saw this as an ominous development and, in a desperate move, issued on December 19, 1887, a peace preservation ordinance which ordered the expulsion of all those engaged in antigovernment activities from an area within a radius of seven and one-half miles from the capital. Although the ordinance affected something like 570 persons, it did not stop the movement which had spread into the outlying areas especially since Goto had gone on speaking tours throughout the country.

Prompted by failure in treaty negotiations and desiring to ease the tense domestic political situation, Premier Ito decided to bring into the government as Foreign Minister, Okuma, his former colleague, with whom he had parted political company in 1881. In this move Ito was successful, for Okuma was delighted that his political star was once more in the ascendancy. In the succeeding government headed by Kuroda, Okuma became the mainstay of the cabinet and actually came to lead if not dominate it.

Immediately after the Constitution was promulgated on February 11, 1889, Premier Kuroda asserted his determination to establish a supraparty government. Ito, then President of the Privy Council, declared publicly his faith in supraparty government and refused recognition of the political parties.[9] These were strong expressions of their support of oligarchic clan government and a challenge against the movement for popular rights and liberty. Disappointed but not discouraged, parties pushed ahead with firm resolve in their fight to overthrow the arbitrary rule of clan oligarchy.

In order to effectively parry the thrusts of the political parties Premier Kuroda brought Inoue into his government as Agriculture and Commerce Minister. Thereafter he worked out a scheme to bring into the fold of the government, Goto who had proved himself extremely popular as the moving spirit of the "Great Coalition." Confronted with Kuroda's offer, Goto seized the opportunity to become Minister of Postal Communications, forsaking his political associates without any hesitation or regret whatever. First it was Okuma, then

[9] Ten years later, however, Ito reversed his position.

Goto, who was soon followed by Itagaki. All these political leaders fought against the ruling oligarchy espousing the cause of liberalism and popular rights. Yet when lured with government posts of sufficient prestige, they gave up their fight and gladly joined the ranks of those in power. Their devotion to the ideal of responsible government or even to political parties was not only weak and expediential but easily purchasable. Their primary concern was to get themselves into a position of power rather than to work at personal sacrifice for the establishment of freedom and popular rights.

Confusion and Disunion of Political Parties, 1890–1900

The seven-year span preceding the first general election of July, 1890, was a period of trial and tribulation for the political parties because of the vigorous policy of suppression carried on by the government. Even the general election, the first ever to be held in Japan, had to be faced by the nation under a disorganized and ineffectual party system. Because of the strong need for a united party, the Constitutional Liberal Party was formed on August 25, 1890, as the result of a merger of several small parties. This new party was, in a sense, a revival of the old Liberal Party in that it brought together the various splinter groups which espoused liberalism and looked to the establishment of party government while advocating the reverence and prosperity of the imperial house as well as the extension of popular rights. In March, 1891, at a national conference in Osaka, Itagaki was elected president, and the name was simplified to Liberal Party.

General Yamagata, who was Prime Minister when the First Diet opened in 1890, saw the need for a government party to restrain and manipulate the popular parties which were opposing him. He and other clan oligarchs in the government devised the technique of keeping parties split into small ineffective groups and manipulating them in various ways. The technique of destroying opposition by encouraging internal strife and splitting it, came to be used by the government with increasing frequency and effectiveness.

During the First Diet, the government managed to work out a compromise with the Liberal Party through Agriculture Minister Mutsu's shrewd negotiation which won over its president Itagaki and his attitude became more and more amenable to the government. Unfortunately, however, this technique of manipulating the party and the Diet was to result in the corruption and degeneration of both the parties as well as parliamentary government itself.

The Liberal Party and the Progressive Party, which had been at odds except in their common opposition against the oligarchically-run government, buried their hatchets and formed a united front before the opening of the Second Diet. Because of the strenuous opposition of the parties the Second Diet was dissolved. The election which followed in February, 1892, was without doubt the most notorious one in that government interference was carried out on a large scale through the use of force as well as money, under the direction of the Minister of Home Affairs Shinagawa. Despite the ruthless interference, however, the government was unable to prevent the Opposition parties from winning a combined absolute majority.

In the first three years of parliamentary government, the Diet was dissolved three times creating the impression, for the outside world and especially for China, that Japan was hopelessly divided.[10] The government's repeated resort to dissolution was based on its belief that it was an instrument to be used at will to protect the government and its ruling oligarchy. The parties fought back at the government with all the strength and resources they could muster. But once the hostilities broke out with China in 1894 opposition against the government immediately ceased for the duration of the war.

After the Sino-Japanese War, the two leading opposition parties came to realize that for years they had been duped, bought, and exploited by the government and that it was imperative they abandon their useless and harmful struggle with each other and join forces in the fight against their common political enemy, the Satsuma-Choshu clique that was in control of the government. This realization took concrete form on June 22, 1898, with the founding of the Kenseito, achieved by the merger of the Liberal and Reform parties.

At the meeting of the Elder Statesmen in the Imperial Palace, two days later, Ito[11] tossed a bombshell by proposing that he either remain in the government to form a new political party to insure the smooth operation of the government or resign and form a new political party to support the government. If neither of these plans proved acceptable he believed that his government should resign and the newly organized Kenseito should be given the opportunity to form a new government. Needless to say the Elder Statesmen were flabbergasted. It was inconceivable that anyone should suggest making room for a party government which, in their minds, was not only contrary to the spirit of the Constitution but incompatible with the national polity. Ito dared the Elder Statesmen to show him the existence of a constitu-

---

[10] It was this fact that misled the Chinese statesman, Li Hung-chang, into believing that Japan was in no shape to start a war, much less to prosecute it, thereby permitting China to undertake a costly and disastrous war against Japan.

[11] See *Ito Hirobumi Den*, Vol. III, pp. 369–380.

tional provision forbidding a party government but this proposal was defeated and he resigned from the premiership.[12]

There were no takers among the Elder Statesmen who were asked to form the succeeding government for, while they were strongly opposed to party government, they did not care to be subjected to the withering attack of the Kenseito.[13]   As a result the task of forming a new government fell jointly on Okuma and Itagaki, who received the imperial command.   Circumstances forced the advocates of supra-party government to bow to the power of a political party.   Thus for the first time in Japan's constitutional development, a party government was formed on June 30, 1898.   Although in name and appearance it was a party government, it was still a long way from the kind of party government which was established twenty years later.   The merger proved to be extremely shaky when the selection of cabinet members began and even after the government was formed conflicts over policy matters could not be resolved.   Inevitably the Okuma-Itagaki government collapsed on October 30, after only four months, because of its inability to hold itself together notwithstanding the fact that the Kenseito party had captured an overwhelming majority of 80 percent or 266 seats in the Diet in the general election of August 10, 1898.

The split which began to develop within the Kenseito soon after the formation of the Okuma-Itagaki government widened rapidly and, even before the government resigned, the old Liberal Party faction passed a resolution for the liquidation of the party and simultaneously founded a new party which pre-empted the old name.   The old Reform Party faction formed their party on November 3, a few days after the government fell, assuming the name of Kenseihonto.   The two parties were now back where they were some half year earlier before the merger was effected, with the line of cleavage drawn exactly where it had been.

Yamagata followed Okuma to the premiership and, with effective tactics and the use of money, he reduced the Kenseito to the status of semisubserviency to the government.   His violent antipathy towards political parties was reflected in the many ordinances which he pushed through.   Among them were the revisions in civil service regulations, abolishing the liberal appointment policy and making it impossible for nonbureaucrats to enter government service.   He thereby insured the position of the bureaucrats and excluded party

[12] Suzuki Yasuzo, *Kindai Nihon no Seito to Gikai*, p. 104.
[13] Yamagata, Kuroda, Saigo, Inoue, and Oyama all declined the offer of premiership.

men from the civil service. Furthermore, he managed to put through an ordinance requiring that the Ministers of the Army and the Navy be generals and admirals on the active list. This had serious and far-reaching consequences on subsequent developments.

The Kenseito succeeded in breaking away from Yamagata's control and shifted its support to Ito who had come to the parting of the ways with Yamagata in June of 1898. The leaders of the Kenseito sought Ito's leadership by offering him the party presidency but he declined, as he himself had been thinking of founding a political party of his own. Ito finally recognized the principle of party government on February 13, 1899, in an address when he admitted that parties had become necessary to the proper functioning of the Diet.[14]

Clan Bureaucrats Form Political Parties, 1900–1918

The year 1900 occupies a special place in the history of political parties since it marks the founding of the Seiyukai, which not only established a record as the longest continuous party but also set a pattern for the party system. On August 25, 1900, Ito announced the purpose and manifesto of the Seiyukai. Ito had moved with caution and acted only after having secured imperial sanction as well as the assent of the Elder Statesmen whom he had consulted. The way in which the party was organized and the manner in which the manifesto was announced over his own signature indicated clearly that the party was as nearly the work of one man as has been seen in Japanese politics. As its president, Ito exercised dictatorial control over the affairs of the party after its formal launching on September 15. This was a highly significant event because it represented the organization, if not transformation, of a section of the clan bureaucracy led by Ito into a political party with the support of the business world.

Immediately thereafter, the Yamagata government resigned and recommended Ito, who, in his new capacity as President of the Seiyukai which commanded an absolute majority in the Diet, took over the reins of government for the fourth time.[15] Except for the Army and Navy ministers, the members of the Ito Cabinet were all from the Seiyukai. Early in May, 1901, the cabinet resigned en masse after admitting its inability to preserve unity because of disagreements in policy matters.

[14] Quoted in Suzuki Yasuzo, *Kindai Nihon no Seito to Gikai,* p. 100.

[15] This was the record number of times a Japanese premier had been called on to form a government until 1953 when Yoshida became Prime Minister for the fifth time.

Upon General Katsura, the protégé of Yamagata, fell the mantle of the premier and a new government was formed on June 2, 1901. From the beginning this government, which was made up largely of bureaucrats, was dubbed "second rate" and even referred to as "the vice-ministers' cabinet." However, it managed to survive much longer than most of the governments. In fact, it established a record in cabinet longevity largely by currying favor with the Elder Statesmen, businessmen, and politicians, and by resorting to compromises.

Although the Seiyukai captured an absolute majority in the election of August 10, 1902, the first instance of an election being held upon the expiration of a full four-year term, the unity of the party was shaken. Ito acceded to the compromise bid made by Katsura for Seiyukai support. Indignant at the compromise with Katsura as well as the high-handed manner in which Ito made the decision without consulting others in the party, some twenty members bolted. At this point, Katsura prevailed upon his mentor and protector Yamagata to kick Ito upstairs into the Privy Council. Ito in turn got Yamagata appointed to the same deliberative body, causing their removal from the arena of active politics. Following Ito's departure from the Seiyukai, those who belonged to his faction bolted causing a rapid decline although it managed to retain a majority in the Diet. Upon Ito's resignation Prince Saionji assumed the presidency.

The unfavorable terms of the Portsmouth Treaty which restored peace following the Russo-Japanese War inflamed public opinion since they were regarded as a national disgrace. Katsura, whose popularity was never great, had to bear the onus and resigned, recommending Saionji, who was selected to be Premier by the Elder Statesmen. Although the Seiyukai had a majority in the Diet, the Saionji government was not a party government, but rather a government made up of bureaucrats.

Opposition to the Seiyukai appeared when the Kokuminto was formed on March 14, 1910, by Inukai and others who were determined to hasten the establishment of responsible party government. Saionji had gone over to the support of the Katsura government in a political deal whereby the two men were to form the government in alternation, each recommending the other as his successor when relinquishing the premiership. Saionji's running of the Seiyukai party was just as arbitrary and dictatorial as that of Ito, its founder, and the members were dissatisfied.

The Katsura government, formed on December 22, 1912, inspired the concentrated attack of the political parties which succeeded

through the power of the press in mobilizing powerful public sentiment against the government and its behind-the-scenes supporters.
Yamagata was enjoying a virtual monopoly of political power since
Ito met an untimely death in Harbin at the hands of a Korean assassin
in October, 1908.   This assault on the power of clan government developed into the "Movement for the Protection of Constitutional
Government" and soon had the support of even the Elder Statesmen
and business leaders.   The irresistible force of public opinion left
Katsura no alternative but to resign after less than two months.

Katsura's successor was Admiral Yamamoto, the first Navy man to
become the head of a government.   He recognized the importance of
public opinion as an integral part of constitutional government, and
respected the role of political parties.   He reversed or revised several
of the regulations instituted by the Yamagata government among
which the most significant were the relaxation of civil service rules
and the revision of the requirement that only generals and admirals
on the active list were eligible for the posts of Army and Navy
Ministers.   By making those on the reserve list eligible for service
posts and throwing open high-level government positions to noncareer men, Yamamoto strengthened the position of the political
parties and officially recognized the principle of party government.

General Katsura, after being forced out of the premiership early in
1913, had begun preparations for a political party, but was stricken
by sudden illness and did not live to see its birth.   Katsura had thus
hoped to cope with the "Movement for the Protection of the Constitutional Government" by organizing the bureaucrats into a political
party.   The party actually emerged on December 23, 1913, as the
Rikken Doshikai with Kato Takaaki as its president.   This new party
was formed without the Katsura men although there were some who
had bolted the Kokuminto and had gone over to Katsura while
preparations were being made for the launching of a party.

The Yamamoto government fell as the upshot of the Siemens' affair,
a scandal in which the navy was involved, and was succeeded by
Okuma.   The Rikken Doshikai supported Prime Minister Okuma but
in spite of the majority support he had in the House of Representatives he was forced out by the bureaucrats in the Upper House who
engineered a successful plot.   This demonstrated clearly the need for
a stronger political party, resulting in the merger of the Rikken
Doshikai with the other groups which had been supporting Okuma.
The Kenseikai was thus born on October 10, 1915, under the presidency of Kato Takaaki.   Although in the basic policies it was a continuation of the Rikken Doshikai and Kokuminto, it was progressive

in envisaging and planning a realistic program of achieving responsible party government. With the establishment of the Kenseikai, it appeared as though a two-party system had come into existence. However, at the time of the collapse of the Okuma government in the fall of 1916, the Seiyukai was in such a weakened condition that General Terauchi was called upon to form a supraparty government which ran national affairs by manipulating the Seiyukai and other groups to support government policies.

By the spring of 1918 the nation felt the full impact of democracy and World War I as well as the Russian Revolution, producing an unsettled condition in national thought. Although the government was alarmed it was unable to suppress new and radical ideas. The adverse effects of the policies of the Terauchi government accumulated and resulted in the rice riots of the fall of 1918 shortly before the end of World War I and sealed the doom of the supraparty government. Thus came to an end a long period of clan dominance of Japanese politics.

The Supremacy of the Political Parties, 1918–1932

The advent of the government of Hara Takashi, the first "commoner" premier, on September 29, 1918, marked the beginning of party government in Japan in the real sense of the term. When General Terauchi's government resigned en masse in consequence of the rice riots, the Seiyukai commanded a majority in the Diet, but the three Elder Statesmen, Yamagata, Matsukata, and Saionji, were agreed that Saionji who was no longer head of the party should form the next government. However, Saionji recommended for the premiership, Hara, who had assumed the presidency of Seiyukai in June, 1914. Although it was Yamagata's desire that a coalition government be formed in collaboration with the bureaucratic forces, Hara rejected it in favor of a truly party government and all the cabinet posts, with the exception of the Army, the Navy, and the Foreign Ministers, went to members of the Seiyukai. Under Hara's leadership the party prospered and in the general election of May, 1920, it captured an overwhelming majority of 279 seats in the House of Representatives. Hara's ability as president brought power to the Seiyukai but it also created the impression that absolute power was being wielded by the party. As a result, strong resentment developed in some quarters and on November 5, 1921, Hara met an untimely death at the hands of an assassin at the pinnacle of his political career.

Hara's death seriously impaired the unity and strength of the Seiyukai but Takahashi, who had just succeeded to the presidency, was called on to head the government in a stop-gap arrangement which lasted only until June, 1922. This was followed by three successive supraparty governments which lasted until June, 1924. Although the Seiyukai was unable to form a government because of its weakness, yet, at the same time, it was fearful that the Kenseikai would gain control of the government. It had therefore given support willingly to the three nonparty governments organized mainly around the members of the House of Peers.[16]

Before the end of 1923, the cleavage within the Seiyukai had reached a point beyond repair. On January 29, 1924, the splinter faction headed by Tokonami formed the Seiyu-honto, becoming the government party supporting Premier Kiyoura. The Seiyukai, under Takahashi, was now only one-half of its former strength but managed to strengthen its unity and heighten its fighting spirit.

Opposition against the supraparty Kiyoura government developed into another movement for the protection of constitutional government sponsored by a three-party coalition of the Seiyukai, Kenseikai, and Kakushin Club. To this the government retaliated with dissolution but the general election which followed in May, 1924, gave the three-party coalition a majority and the Kenseikai emerged as the leading party.

Defeat in the general election forced the Kiyoura government out and the task of forming a new government fell upon Kato Takaaki, the president of the leading Kenseikai. This was a party government, to be sure, but it was based on a three-party coalition. Cleavages soon developed within the coalition and after a little more than a year it was forced to resign, largely through the maneuvers of the Seiyukai and particularly the refusal of its new president, Tanaka, to cooperate. But Kato was called on once again to form a government, this time by the Kenseikai alone. This second Kato government which came into being on August 2, 1925, unfortunately came to an end less than six months later because of the untimely death of the premier, without having the opportunity to prove itself.

Wakatsuki, who succeeded to the presidency of the Kenseikai upon Kato's death, was named Premier and another Kenseikai government was formed on January 30, 1926. Wakatsuki attempted unsuccessfully to reorganize the government by effecting a coalition with the Seiyu-honto. Political scandals almost brought forth a no-confidence vote on the government, but Wakatsuki forestalled it by calling on the opposition parties to suspend political struggles at the beginning

[16] The Kiyoura government was made up almost exclusively of the members of the Upper House.

of a new reign.[17] This temporary truce was of very brief duration, as the Kenseikai and the Seiyu-honto began to work together behind the scenes to direct their attacks upon the Seiyukai. Although the government's "soft" and ineffective diplomacy toward China under Foreign Minister Shidehara drew bitter criticisms, it was the government's handling of the panic of the spring of 1927 that brought its collapse. On June 1, 1927, the Seiyu-honto, headed by Tokonami, and the Kenseikai, headed by Wakatsuki, merged to form the Minseito with Hamaguchi as its president. The Seiyukai in the meantime had absorbed various segments of the little satellite parties. With these developments there came into existence, for all practical purposes, two major political parties and in a sense a two-party system, the Minseito with 219 seats and the Seiyukai with 190 seats in the Diet.

General Tanaka's government emerged on April 20, 1927, and lasted for over two years during which the first general election under the new universal manhood suffrage law of May 5, 1925, was held. Except for the Army, Navy, and Justice Ministers, the members of the cabinet were all from the Seiyukai. When the government fell as the result of the political conflict generated by the Kellogg-Briand Pact and the Chang Tso-lin murder, political power passed to the Minseito. For eight years, from 1924 to 1932, political power alternated back and forth between the two major parties, the Seiyukai and the Minseito and its predecessor, until the rise of the military to power sounded the death knell of party government.

Rise of Proletarian Parties

The mass proletarian party movement began with the founding of the Farmer-Labor Party in 1925. However, its antecedents may be traced as far back as 1882 to the founding of the Oriental Socialist Party which was ordered disbanded two months after it was organized and did not actually have the chance to begin any political activity. The party had for its goal not only opposition against arbitrary clan government but the achievement of equality and the greatest good of the social masses.

In the beginning the Socialists joined the Liberal Party and worked with the radical elements in carrying on political activities. In 1892 the radical faction of the Liberal Party founded the Oriental Liberal Party under the leadership of Oi Kentaro, and carried on until the outbreak of the Sino-Japanese War, but disappeared soon thereafter.

[17] This new era, Taishō, began in the year 1926 when Emperor Hirohito ascended the throne.

In May, 1901, the Social Democratic Party was launched, only to be banned on the same day.[18] Socialism was thereafter suppressed vigorously by the government and it was impossible to obtain permission to found a socialist party. By 1910 the government's ruthless suppression policy had all but driven the socialist movement out of existence. Even the labor movement had to be started with an innocuous sounding organization like the Friendly Society in 1912. This organization of very modest beginnings was greatly expanded in the wake of the Russian Revolution of 1917 and the rice riots of 1918 which contributed directly to the fall of the Terauchi government. In 1920, the League for Socialism was organized, but its life was brief for it was dissolved the following year as a consequence of government suppression and ideological clashes among its membership. Although it enjoyed only a brief existence it was nevertheless instrumental in bringing together the labor union movement and the political activities of the socialists. In 1922 the Japan Farmer's Union emerged as did the Japan Communist Party, though only as an underground movement.

The General Federation of Labor which was formed in 1921 passed through a whole gamut of ideological peregrinations, democracy, internationalism, syndicalism, Utopian revolutionism, Bolshevism, and finally came down to earth to pursue the realistic "return to trade unionism" policy. But in 1925 a split resulted from the opposition within the General Federation ranging the social democrats against the Communists. The splintered left wing organized the Council of Japanese Labor Unions.

The Farmer-Labor Party launched by the Japan Farmer's Union in December 1925, the first proletarian mass party in history, was allowed an existence of only 30 minutes. But a reorganization movement was begun immediately and the Labor-Farmer Party resulted in March, 1926 in Osaka with the General Federation becoming a part of it. The exclusion of the Communists from membership made it definitely a right-wing proletarian party.

The Japan Communist Party was disbanded in 1923 following a series of severe blows which fell on it, beginning with the arrest of June, the terrorism directed at it during the great earthquake of September, and the subsequent bolting by several members late in the year. However, it was revived in 1927 through the efforts of the Comintern but was subjected to wholesale roundup by the police in March, 1928. Arrest after arrest followed and the party organization

[18] Actually the party enjoyed a life of only two hours. Its sponsors were Abe, Katayama, Kawakami, Kinoshita, Kotoku, and Nishikawa.

was damaged beyond repair.   The final blow came with the climatic roundup at Atami in October, 1932, after which the central leadership of the Japan Communist Party was completely destroyed.

The split which came in the Labor-Farmer Party in October, 1926, determined the course of the General Federation and led to the formation of the Social Mass Party in December.   As the General Federation moved increasingly toward the right the Social Mass Party was once more split.   In December, 1928, the Japan Mass Party was formed by the merger of seven different parties but it was constantly harassed by internal divisive tendencies and difficulties of achieving party unity.   In July, 1930, the party combined with others to form the All-Japan Mass Party.

Proletarian parties succeeded in electing eight of their representatives to the Diet in the general election of February, 1928, the first to be held under universal manhood suffrage.   In the elections of 1930 and 1932 they won five seats each time, but in 1936 they increased their strength to eighteen seats.   They established a record in 1937 by winning thirty-seven seats, thereby becoming the third strongest party in the Diet.   The Socialists really gained strength in the post-World War II period.   In the election of February, 1955, they won a total of 156 seats,[19] thereby commanding more than one-third of the votes in the Diet.

The period of supremacy of political parties extending from 1918 to 1932 was not a healthy one although they found themselves in the heyday of affluence and power.   There was too much money to be had, something like six to seven billion yen in cash in the country, an unprecedented accumulation of gold in modern Japanese history. There was no opportunity for the development of democratic procedure within the parties. Presidents and members of the inner groups came to be selected more on the basis of their money-raising ability than on their character, wisdom, and acumen, which were pushed into the background in their struggle for power.   This led to arbitrary dictatorial management of the parties by a small number of bosses and an inevitable loss of public confidence in the political parties.   It was all too apparent now that parties had degenerated into mere cliques devoid of any well organized platforms or constructive programs, intent on the gratification of their own desires and advancement of their own personal interests, and paying little attention to the welfare of the nation or the people in general.   The heyday of political parties produced rampant corruption and re-

[19] Labor-Farmer Party won four seats, while the Japan Communist Party won two seats.

current political scandals to outrage the public and aid the military in its rise to power.

Decline and Disappearance of Parties, 1932–1945

With the assassination of Premier Inukai on May 15, 1932, party government in Japan came to an end before it had a chance to firmly establish itself. Reactionary elements came to the fore on the crest of a strong resurgence of nationalism amply supported by the chauvinistic elements of society. The military was given an opportunity to set out on its road to ascendancy. Militarists and "reformist" civilians taking advantage of their internal weakness attacked the political parties. All the difficulties of the nation were blamed upon the parties and the specially privileged classes. Japan's delegate to the League of Nations, Matsuoka, who made a dramatic exit from the Assembly meeting in Geneva in March, 1933, after announcing his nation's withdrawal, returned home and advocated in December the abolition of all political parties. Soon thereafter he bolted the Seiyukai. Meanwhile those who had been expelled from Seiyukai organized the Showakai. What remained of the original Seiyukai was now split three ways into the orthodox faction, the reform faction, and the neutral faction.

The Minseito was plagued by the same sort of difficulty that caused the weakening of the Seiyukai. Shortly after the Manchurian Incident of September, 1931, the Wakatsuki government fell as the result of the party's internal disunion. A group bolted the party and formed the Kokumin Domei under the leadership of Adachi while the remaining membership was divided into two opposing groups, the Nagai and Machida factions.

Although both the Seiyukai and Minseito parties were represented in the supraparty governments of Saito, Okada, and Hirota from 1932 to 1937, the government of General Hayashi formed in February, 1937, insisted that those who were asked to join the cabinet resign from their parties as a necessary condition of acceptance. This amounted to a complete denial of the role of political parties in the government. The Hayashi government was, in a sense, a coalition of the military, financial capital, and the bureaucracy. Naturally, it was strongly opposed by the political parties and industrial capital.

Developments of 1939 certainly did not enhance the position of the political parties.[20] The once powerful Seiyukai was split in the spring of that year, during the Hiranuma government, into two fac-

[20] See *Asahi* editorial of December 30, 1939.

tions forming two parties, the Reform Faction led by Nakajima, and the Orthodox Faction which named Kuhara its president.

The last desperate effort to save the political parties was started in the fall of 1936 during the Hirota government. Representatives of the parties met in what came to be known as the Ogikubo talks, to devise ways and means of resuscitating the parties. However, in every party there were those who favored the formation of a single new patriotic party. This movement gained momentum early in 1938 and what began as an effort to revive or rejuvenate the political parties actually ended up in their complete liquidation in 1940.

Even the socialist movement after the Manchurian Incident of 1931 had come under the strong influence of nationalism and by 1937 it had all but abandoned the united front of class struggle and veered strongly toward national or state socialism. At a general meeting on November 15, the Social Mass Party adopted a "wartime" program calling for the development of the nation "in accordance with the fundamental principles of national polity" and "to reform capitalism and establish a system of industrial management in order to stabilize the people's livelihood." It was quite apparent that the party had abandoned its original proletarian policies and principles. In 1939 the Social Mass Party was actually working seriously for a merger with Nakano's ultranationalistic party, Tohokai. Socialists were in many instances outdoing the members of conservative parties in enthusiastically supporting nationalistic policies. When the design for a new political order calling for the end of political parties was announced by Preimer Konoe, the Social Mass Party was the first to respond with its disbanding on July 3, 1940.

In the two-week period of July 16–30 all factions of the Seiyukai disbanded, followed by the Minseito on August 15. Thus after sixty years of stormy and eventful existence, the political parties came to an end in a concerted action of self-liquidation. The party system was superseded by a totalitarian structure euphemistically labeled "the new political structure" and known officially as the Imperial Rule Assistance Association. The I.R.A.A. with the Prime Minister as its president was designed as an all-inclusive structure which embraced all the Japanese people. This totalitarian structure never functioned with the kind of cold, ruthless efficiency characteristics of the Soviet monolithic system, nor did it even approach the effectiveness of the Nazi one-party system. In May, 1942, the Imperial Rule Assistance Political Society was organized around the members of both houses of the Diet with a Minister without portfolio as its head. For the greater part of the Pacific War, this was the sole political organization

in the country resembling a political party. Because of the ineffectiveness of the I.R.A.P.S. in coping with the problems the Japan
Political Association was organized in March, 1945, with General
Minami as its president. This was a desperate attempt to effectively
organize the nation to achieve closer cooperation between the armed
forces, the government, and the people. Structurally the J.P.A. was
organized exactly like a political party with a president, an executive
committee, a political affairs research committee, and various departments and bureaus. However, before it could go into operation, the
war came to an end and it was soon disbanded.

Reappearance of Political Parties, 1945

Political parties reappeared within a few weeks of the surrender.
The directive of October 4, 1945, issued by the Supreme Commander
for the Allied Powers abrogating and suspending all laws, orders, and
regulations restricting the freedom of thought, religion, assembly,
association, speech, and press was the green light for the resumption
of political activities which had been stifled if not actually forbidden
during the war.

First to reappear was the Social Democratic Party organized on
November 2. Right on its heels came the Japan Communist Party
which was legitimately and openly organized for the first time on
November 8, 1945. Then on the following day came the launching of
the Liberal Party and on the 16th came the Progressive Party. The
labels of these new postwar parties gave little indication of their
nature, policies, or principles. They were in reality a revival of the
old political forces and personalities and were the direct descendants
of the prewar parties. The Liberal Party comprised a number of old
familiar figures of the Seiyukai while the Progressive Party drew its
membership largely from the prewar Minseito. They were both
conservative in spite of their attractive labels. The ranks of the
Social Democratic Party were filled by many prominent socialists of
yesteryear drawn from the various factions representing ideas ranging
from the extreme right to the extreme left.

There was only one noteworthy change so far as party activities
were concerned. The new postwar Constitution made party government a normal and necessary condition of political life. However,
the manner in which the party, its leadership and membership
functioned showed little change from the prewar days. Personality
clashes and resultant splinters appeared just as common under the
new Constitution as they were under the old. Political ambitions as
well as the means for attaining them were still the same.

The Development and Nature of Political Parties   235

CHARACTERISTICS OF THE JAPANESE PARTY SYSTEM

One would search in vain for a definite provision for the role of political parties in the Japanese Constitution. In other words political parties are extraconstitutional just as they are in the American and British systems. There is to be found in the Constitution, however, a clear statement of cabinet responsibility to the Diet and also the provision that the premier must be chosen by the Diet from its own membership and that at least one-half of the cabinet ministers must be Diet members. While there is no mention of the party itself, the assumption of the Constitution is unmistakable, for responsible parliamentary government cannot exist or operate without political parties. There is definite statutory recognition of parties in that legislation is provided for the regulation of their activities.

The political parties are the natural result of the impact of Western civilization and a by-product of the program of modernization which was undertaken by the nation in the second half of the nineteenth century. However, they carry the unmistakable stamp of Japanese character and can be understood, analyzed, and appraised accurately only against the background of traditional socio-political and ethical ideas, values, attitudes, and institutions. Much of the folkways and mores of the people has influenced the activities of Japanese political parties.

As we have already seen, Japanese parties antedate the parliamentary system by a full decade, a development which is the converse of both Great Britain and the United States. This fact has an important bearing on their growth as well as the role they have played. Although they originally developed completely outside the framework of government as an instrument for the dislodging of the group in power, they formed at the same time an integral part of the nationalist movement which was being propelled by powerful royalist-patriotic sentiment. To them credit must be given for forcing the hand of the government in hastening the adoption of a parliamentary system. But their concern was not primarily or even remotely the achievement of liberty and popular rights. It was rather the achievement of a strong nation equal to the task of coping with its vexing problems and capable of assuming its rightful place in the world. To the parties as well as the government it appeared that a Constitution and a national assembly were the minimum political requirements on which a strong nation must be based. This sort of preoccupation with national strength has influenced the behavior of parties in times of national crises. Invariably in periods of stress the parties become nationalistic and abandon or suspend the normal functions of criticizing the government or its policies for the sake of national unity.

In the development of Japanese parties, geography has played a significant role and its influence is far from gone. The abolition of fiefs and the establishment in their place of prefectures as administrative units in 1871 served to de-emphasize at the time the strong sense of affinity that existed among individuals, by reason of a common geographic origin, that is, having the same home town or native province. However, when the new government was set up in 1868, political power was placed in the hands of a small group of men from four separate former feudal fiefs, or clans, Choshu, Satsuma, Tosa, and Hizen. By 1874 government had fallen into the hands of the oligarchy composed of Choshu and Satsuma men. Opposing them were the men from the two other clans of Tosa and Hizen who had been forced out. Thus a geographic line of cleavage or distinction was drawn in the political sphere. When the antioligarchy movement succeeded in forcing the government to accede to the demand for the establishment of a national assembly, and the Diet was opened in 1890, the prefectures became important since representation was based on this new geographic administrative unit. It was in the prefecture that candidates to the Diet had their friends and supporters and were known personally. Sectionalism or provincialism once more became important and the constituency as represented by the locality became an important asset in politics.

Ever since their inception, parties have had strong supporters in the native provinces of the founders. However, there has developed no regionalism in politics of the type which exists in the United States dividing the country into large sections as the South, East, Middle West, and Far West, because there are no marked sectional differences in economic interests. Until about the 1920's even the armed services had been affected by geographic tendencies, with the army control in the hands of Choshu men and the navy dominated by Satsuma. The geographic lines no longer exist in political alignments but home-town affinities are still an important fact which cannot be overlooked completely.

No political party in present-day Japan can exist except on a broad national basis, although in the early days of the parties there were strong geographic ties. The Liberal Party of Itagaki for example was the product of Tosa. For the last fifty years there has not been any local party that could be regarded as important. It is of great significance that there has been no party which truly represented any particular class in the country. This is simply because there have not developed strong enough class antagonisms. Nor has there been any racial issue in politics at any time in Japanese history. If anything there has been discrimination in favor of foreigners in different periods of national development.

Anticlericalism of the sort that has existed in France or elsewhere is not found in the alignment of political parties. Religion has not provided a basis of division or organization of parties as in European countries like France, Germany, or Italy where there are Catholic parties, or in some countries of Asia like India, Indonesia, and Pakistan where there are Hindu, Moslem, or Christian parties. This does not mean, however, that religion has not played an important role in the political development of Japan in the past particularly before the advent of the parties. Nor does it mean that religion is not a powerful force as a conditioning factor in politics. The significant fact is that parties cannot and do not use religion for political purposes. There are no religious blocs and no religiously dominated parties.

If politics springs inevitably and relentlessly out of economics it would seem that it is natural and even necessary that economic interests should constitute the most realistic basis of political alignments. While it is obvious that parties exist to serve the country and therefore must place its interests above those of any particular group, it is equally clear that in practical politics they cannot and do not represent the various interests evenly or equally. Since partisanship and factionalism are the stuff of which parties are made, clashes of economic interests are reflected and represented in the political arena that is the Diet. Cleavages of all sorts exist, capital against labor, rural versus urban interests, agriculture versus industry, but the lines are not always clearly drawn nor the issues crystal clear because of the complexity of a nation's economy and the intricate and interdependent economic relationships which exist between seemingly antagonistic groups. The party therefore has to function as a mediatory or conciliatory institution though it often intensifies conflicts among the people.

Multiplicity of parties has characterized the Japanese political scene since 1881 when they first appeared. At the time there were as many as 360 parties most of which were small independent local organizations not affiliated with any of the large parties of nationwide scope. Quite naturally they could not be based on principles, policies, ideas or interest of the nation as a whole but simply on geography and personalities. A somewhat similar situation arose in the period immediately following the end of the Pacific War. In the general election of April, 1946, there were more than 260 parties not counting scores of organizations which could not be legally recognized as parties.

Throughout history the Japanese people have shown great fondness for variety. Witness some aspects of their cultural developments: schools of painting, philosophy, poetry, flower arrangement, tea ceremony, archery, swordsmanship, swimming, and so on. Hardly anything remained untouched by this passion for a different style, form, or technique of doing things. In most instances the actual differences between the various schools were in substance very minor and even inconsequential.

Another trait which enters into the picture is the peculiar weakness for newness, something new, a new name, a new front, or even a rearrangement, if not a revamping or overhauling; but at the same time the tendency to easily tire of a "new toy" or even a "new experiment." Add to these traits the highly developed passion for action and especially for organizing in which the Japanese are perhaps second only to the Americans. They do not need much encouragement to go off and set up a competing organization, especially those who do not have their own way and feel aggrieved.

The existence of a large number of parties has been regarded by many politicians as unfortunate. Consequently the majority of party men have been looking to the eventual establishment of the two-party system as a means of achieving political stability. There is no doubt that the multiplicity of parties adds to the complexity and confusion of politics. But it is the product of national character and conditions just as is apparently the case with the French multiparty system. Consequently, it is perhaps not possible to develop a two-party system deliberately by design and conscious effort. The American two-party system represents a natural development rather than a deliberately planned and executed project. Before a truly two-party system could emerge and endure in Japan, it would be necessary to bring about other more basic changes in ideas and attitudes not only with regard to and in the parties but in the social milieu.

The existence of a multiparty system has greatly facilitated and even encouraged political peregrinations. In their attempts to strengthen their positions in the Diet, parties bid for new members by offering high prices. It has not been unusual for new members thus lured away from another party to be given far greater voice and role than they deserve and frequently given preferential treatment, generating strong resentment on the part of the constant and loyal members. This, of course, is not an aberrant behavior politically, socially, or economically. For it is almost customary in Japan for merchants, for instance, to be so eager to have new customers that they go out of their way to be accommodating and give the best possible service even at the expense of the old, steady customers who, they feel, will continue to do business out of sheer habit if not a sense of "loyalty."

Splits and mergers are going on constantly among the political parties. As a matter of fact there is not a single party in Japanese history, except for the Communists,[21] which has not been the result of a merger or a split of some kind. Most if not all of these mergers have been effected by incompatible groups for expediency and have been marriages of convenience. Even members who bolted the party, as well as splinter parties, have been readmitted without much ado into the parties. Political parties change their labels with the greatest of ease and without changing their policies. More often than not, names are changed merely to accommodate the newly won members or simply to give the psychological effect and illusion that the party is making a fresh start.

As a consequence of the multiparty system, coalition governments have been very common in the past and even in the period since World War II. Every single party government has of necessity been a coalition of intraparty factional forces. This has been true of the postwar Yoshida government which actually held an absolute majority in the Diet. When this intraparty coalition of the factions broke down there occurred a split which resulted in the founding of the Hatoyama Liberal Party in March, 1953, which became the Japan Democratic Party toward the end of 1954.

A genuine two-party system cannot emerge as long as parties remain "personality centered" and "leader centered" organizations in which loyalty is primarily to persons rather than to principles and policies. This is one of the legacies of feudalism which is very much alive not only in the political realm but in other spheres as well. Thus personalities influence decisions and actions to a far greater extent and with stronger impact than the issues involved. Personal loyalty provides the indispensable basis for bossism which pervades practically every level of politics from the lowest level of the village assembly to the highest level of the national Diet. It also contributes toward political corruption which raises its ugly head from time to time in spite of the existence of legislation designed to prevent corrupt practices. Ralph Waldo Emerson's observation that "a party is perpetually corrupted by personality" is quite apropos of Japanese politics. At this stage of

[21] Even the Communists have not been free of factional cleavages and troubles.

party growth in Japan there may be detected developments somewhat reminiscent of the conditions of party morality Emerson had in mind. Most, if not all, of the Japanese parties are parties of circumstances rather than of principles. Premier Yoshida's government was characterized by some critics as government by whims and fancies operated by high-handed, if not dictatorial, methods.

While Japanese parties are normally not as small as their French counterparts, there exists a striking resemblance between them in that they are split by internal cleavages. However, there is a difference in the fundamental basis of cleavage since the factionalization of Japanese parties is caused by personal clashes rather than by policy issues. Splintering of parties follows as a matter of course if and when the leader or "boss" of a faction bolts because his followers go along with him as surely as the loyal vassals cast their lot with their lords in feudal times. Thus a new splinter party is born. While there have been instances of "irreconcilable" disagreements developing over strategy, specific methods, or timing in the execution or implementation of policies, even in these instances they invariably involve personal sentiments.

Hypersensitivity to "public opinion" or extreme sensitivity to what the people would think or say coupled with an attitude of personal vindictiveness frequently make internal party struggles more intense and bitter than interparty fights. A factor which contributes to this sort of bitterness and spirit of vengeance is the fact that competition or rivalry in the pursuit of power or influence is an internal matter which takes precedence over interparty competition or rivalry in the realm of practical politics. But underlying this is the intensity of political ambitions among the party members. The supreme goal of a party politician, of course, is to achieve the premiership, which is far more attainable than the dream of an American youngster that he may one day be president. Moreover, the chances of a politician becoming a premier have been vastly increased since the war. But before he can aspire to the highest political office in the nation he must become a party leader. This position, too, has become much more easily attainable than previously.

Thus opportunism of the most naked and unabashed type can develop. Some party politicians are content to be cabinet minister even for "three days" only. Low morality has been attributed to party politicians and cited as one of the causes of internal cleavages of parties and the state of instability in the political sphere in general. Internal clashes of the parties at times remind political observers of brawls in gambling houses as more often than not they are caused not by legitimate differences over policies but by the sheer lust for power.[22]

The strong bond existing between "big business" or "monopolistic capitalism" and the parties was all but destroyed during the military occupation, but only temporarily, for it has been fairly well re-established since 1952. This intimate relationship originated first in the 1880's in the form of the government's paternalistic policy of starting modern enterprises and turning them over to private owner-ship and management after they had been placed on a profitable basis and with adequate guarantees on returns through generous govern-ment subsidies.

Business and industry were heavily dependent on government bounties and good will in the beginning. Policies were initiated, formulated, and enforced by the government originally. But by the turn of the century "big business" and "financial capitalism" had been established and the government began to look to them not only for financial support but for suggestions and advice in policy making. The influence of "big business" on politics reached a new high in the 1920's.

In spite of its eclipse during the war and in the period of military occupation, the structure of national economy and the economic needs of the country conspire to make the relationship between "big busi-ness" and the government, and hence the parties, even closer than it has ever been. Finance capitalism provides the parties with large contributions to help defray their political expenditures thereby insur-ing itself of the opportunity to make known its needs and desires with regard to policies. This is done by helping to elect members of the Diet who would represent its interests and by having its representa-tives in the high command of the party as well as in the government itself. Nothing short of a revolutionary change in the structure of national economy and politics can alter the basic relationship between "big business" and the parties.[23]

While the Occupation authorities endeavored to destroy the old bureaucratic forces which were rightly regarded as an obstacle to democratization of the country they were faced with a dilemma.[24] They had to depend to a large extent on the bureaucracy for the smooth running of the nation. Although they succeeded in destroying

---

[22] Maeda Tamon, "Seito no naifun," *Asahi,* February 25, 1953.

[23] Shinobu Seizaburo, "Shihon to kenryoku to no yuchaku," *1953 Seiji Gakkai Nempo* (Sengo Nihon no Seiji Katei), p. 63.

[24] Kinoshita Hanji, "Kyu shihaiso no kaitai to fukkatsu," *1953 Seijigaku Nempo* (Sengo Nihon no Seiji Katei), p. 75.

the Ministry of Home Affairs which was the stronghold of bureaucratic power and center of police as well, they actually did not divest
officialdom of the power and prestige it enjoyed. The bureaucrats
continued to grow in size and importance and even the parties began
to bring a number of them into their ranks, placing them in important
positions.

This steady influx of government officials, both past and present,
into the parties and into the Diet in the last few years has changed
both the political landscape and climate and introduced a new outlook and attitude in Japanese party politics. Bureaucratic mentality
and methods have permeated the parties and even the Diet to such a
degree that it would not be an exaggeration to say that Japanese
politics has undergone a kind of bureaucratization which was unknown in the country before the war and perhaps without parallel
anywhere else.

As the most serious consequence of this bureaucratization of politics
there has come into being an inordinate emphasis on, and concentration of, party activities in the Diet resulting virtually in the complete
ignoring of the importance and role of the extraparliamentary segment
of the party. According to this trend parliamentary government is no
more, no less, than party politics in the House of Representatives. In
a normal, responsible parliamentary system, the government should
have the power and ability to exercise control over the bureaucracy.
However, this is not the case with the Japanese political process, for
the bureaucracy is coordinate with, if not superior to, the parties in
the power exercised in practical politics.

Emergence of a Two-Party System

Toward the end of 1955, epoch-making developments took place
on the political scene. In October came the reunification of the
Socialists after four stormy years of conflict and separate existence.
This was brought on principally by their strong desire to lay a secure
foundation for a more effective struggle to achieve political power,
coupled with a growing feeling that they could do this in the not
too distant future. Then, little over a month later, on November 15,
the two conservative parties hurriedly merged and formed the Liberal-
Democratic Party in order to cope with the growing strength of the
Socialists. This gave the new party an overwhelming majority of
298 seats in the House of Representatives and 115 in the House of
Councillors for a total of 413 seats, the largest number of seats ever
commanded by a party in power. Thus, a two-party system emerged
at least in form, if not really in substance, with the conservatives and

radicals in opposition for the first time in Japan's constitutional history.[25] However, the structure and inner working of these parties showed few, if any, significant changes. In each case, it was a merger effected not primarily on the basis of political issues or goals but rather on the personal desires and ambitions of individual leaders whose real concern was to either capture or retain political power.

In the case of the Liberal-Democratic Party more than the Socialist Party, the choice of a new president became a crucial problem that could not be resolved in time for the merger and at one point appeared as though it might prove to be an insurmountable stumbling block. As a last-minute, desperate, stop-gap measure, presidential power and functions were delegated to a proxy committee of four key members including the presidents of the two parties that merged.[26] This situation, of course, did not bode well for the unity and solidarity of the party.[27] In March 1956, however, Hatoyama was elected as the first president of the new Liberal-Democratic Party.

The emergence of the two-party system occasioned expressions of sanguine hopes in various quarters both at home and abroad, and the financial circles indicated a degree of satisfaction that the long-waited merger of the conservative parties had come at last. However, no visible change in the substance and method of politics followed in the wake of the mergers that had been greeted with enthusiasm by all. The most immediately noticeable change was on the floor of the Diet where the division between the left and the right in the seating arrangement became very distinct for the first time. Also visible to observers was the difference in the atmosphere pervading the scene of lawmaking where two major parties now stand in clear opposition.

Both parties continue to be Diet-centered although efforts have been begun to remedy this situation through the strengthening of their

[25] In the 1920's, when there was a semblance of a two-party system, opposition was actually between two conservative parties with nearly identical political platforms and not between a radical and a conservative party.

[26] There was a precedent for this sort of temporary arrangement back in 1927 when the Seiyukai Party was unable to select its president because of internal strife which could not be resolved easily.

[27] There are at least half a dozen identifiable factions within the Liberal-Democratic Party, each of which is led by an influential figure of great ambition, as pointed out in "Gun'yu kakkyo no Jiyu-Minshuto," *Mainichi*, November 17, 1955. Kono Mitsu, one of the leaders of the Socialist Party, characterized the Liberal-Democratic Party as "a coalition of factions that knows the existence of factions but not the party, and the party but not the people." "Fugori no daikoiin sei," *Mainichi*, November 11, 1955.

local organizational basis. The Liberal-Democratic Party bolstered its internal organization somewhat at the central headquarters by increasing its high command from the "Big Three" to the "Big Five" through the elevation of two key officers, the chairmen of the Nationwide Organization Committee and the Party Rules Committee. This came in response to the strong need to broaden the base of party strength by building up its "grass roots" following, as well as to establish party rules which would insure smooth operation and effectiveness of its political activities. A new emphasis has been placed on the party's role in policymaking by the decision to entrust the function to the Political Research Committee composed of fifteen members of ministerial caliber. Stronger leadership is anticipated as a result of the setting up of a Central Political College in Tokyo for the training of party members. Under the new setup, the Liberal-Democratic Party management of political activities is entrusted to the Secretary-General, the Chairman of the Executive Committee, and the chairmen of the Political Research Committee, Nationwide Organization Committee, and the Party Rules Committee.

Political stability, which is regarded by a large number of Japanese almost as an inevitable sequel to the establishment of a two-party system, is still very much in the distant future. What is strongly desired by the public is something like the British political system where stability exists as a matter of course because the conservatives and the radicals are not at odds on every issue. Meanwhile, the conservatives are being strongly admonished to be more imaginative, idealistic, and forward looking and the Socialists are reminded that they need to be more realistic and practical in their approach to the various problems confronting the nation. There is ample evidence that both of the parties are exerting themselves in order to inject new blood, new ideas, and new leadership into their organizations to vitalize their programs.

11

How the Political
Parties Function

In spite of the growth of extraparliamentary organization of the parties in Japan, the importance as well as the autonomy of the parties in parliament has in no way been impaired or even lessened. Party organizations outside the Diet provide valuable channels of communication between the party presidents and their active supporters. However, since the arena of political struggle is the Diet, it is only natural that the parliamentary party has come to be the center of party activities and plays a decisive role in the determination of policies.

There is little doubt that local organizations are important as constituent bodies whose support cannot be dispensed with by the central national organization. On the local level the parties are organized on the prefectural, county, municipal, town, and village basis, with the prefectural governors and assemblymen and the mayors and assemblymen of the municipalities, towns, and villages playing prominent roles of leadership and influence in the running of these local organizations and their federated parent bodies.

Local party organizations are, as in England, not very much more than electioneering agencies without patronage and without power to control party policy. Furthermore, since there is no rigid geographical basis for the selection of candidates for the national legislature as exists in the residence requirement in the United States, the parties have no need to restrict themselves to the locality in the choice of candidates. As a matter of fact, local party organizations as a rule accept the candidates selected and assigned to their election districts by the national headquarters. Local party organizations thus have

very little if any initiative in policy making. Operationally, therefore, and particularly as regards the power structure of the party, the
focus of attention must necessarily be the central office which is in
the hands of the parliamentary party.

PARTY ORGANIZATION

Although it is impossible to determine exactly how power is
distributed within the party hierarchy operating in the management
of affairs, a general picture can be attempted since it will be helpful
in the understanding of party politics. The body which is vaguely
referred to as the executive is the core of the party of the central
office. This is the high command or the directorate, a part of which
comprises those who are close to the party president and known as the
inner circle (*sokkin*) which in turn contains a few, perhaps not more
than three or four, persons who make up the innermost circle or the
holy of holies.

Party Presidency

Party presidency was not always regarded as a sure route to the
premiership, the highest political office in the nation. The formation
of a government by Kato Takaaki in 1924 on the recommendation of
the Elder Statesmen set the precedent for the practice of automatically
recommending the president of a party for the premiership. As a
result the role of the party Leader in the parliamentary system came
to assume greater importance soon thereafter.

Until 1929 it was not possible to see the party Leaders representing
the government and the Opposition confronting each other on the
floor of the Diet. In that year, after the Hamaguchi government was
formed, the two Leaders, Inukai of the Opposition Seiyukai Party
and Hamaguchi of the Minseito, confronted each other in the House
of Representatives, achieving for the first time in Japanese politics
what has been the rule in Britain for a long time.[1]

The president of the party is internally the highest authority in
whom there resides enormous power and for whom the members have
great respect while externally he is the symbol of party power,
prestige, and popularity. If he is to be a true leader, he must risk
at times appearing to defy popular sentiment and act freely, for he
must not be a mere agent but an originator of new practices and institutions in spite of the countervailing force of tradition and majority
wishes. At the same time, it has been demonstrated that the Leader
of a party, however virtuous his private conduct, finds he could not in

[1] Yamaura Kan'ichi, *Mori Kaku wa Ikite Iru,* p. 102.

his political position fully exercise the common virtues of the honest man.

The responsibilities of the party Leader are both varied and heavy, for he must provide above all the kind of leadership which will command the respect of his followers and keep them reasonably satisfied and loyal while at the same time seeing to it that policies are formulated. He must determine the personnel of the party, especially its high command, to insure harmony and smooth functioning of the organization. He assumes final responsibility with regard to the election of party candidates and while he does not have to go out to collect party funds in person, he must ultimately bear the responsibility of fund-raising which is one of the biggest and most difficult of party activities. When his party wins a majority in the Diet he must carry the burden of directing the affairs of state as the head of the government.

HOW THE PARTY PRESIDENT IS CHOSEN. The practice at present is to elect the president publicly at an open party convention which is in theory the highest organ of the party. Actually, however, it is only a formality which gives a semblance of the democratic procedure of electing the Leader by popular vote. What really takes place at the convention is no more than a confirmation or announcement of the choice made by the party's directorate.

Immediately after the surrender when the parties reappeared, both the Liberal and Progressive parties selected their presidents on the recommendation of their executive committees. When Ito formed the Seiyukai in 1901, he became its president and upon his retirement designated his successor, Prince Saionji, who in turn designated Hara. This method of designating a party president continued until Tanaka became president. Beginning with him the practice was abandoned and the party convention became the scene of a formal election where a preselected candidate received confirmation by formal balloting. The Minseito, however, decided from the very beginning on the method of election at the convention but the president was actually selected in advance by the inner circle of the party, making the convention procedure merely a formality and more of an inauguration. Thus the party Leader has never been chosen openly by the general party membership. When the Progressive Party chose its president in June, 1952, the task of finding the man was entrusted to a Committee for the Selection of a President which recommended Shigemitsu who was unanimously elected by the five hundred party delegates assembled at the party's special convention.[2] The choice of

[2] See the author's article on Japan in the 1953 *Americana Annual*, p. 367.

Shigemitsu was in line with the well established practice of bringing in an outsider to be the party Leader, a method quite in keeping with the traditional practice of adoption in the Japanese family system.[3]

QUALIFICATIONS. In the early days of political parties heavy emphasis was placed on popularity and reputation, ability, capability, integrity, and acceptability of the candidate for the party presidency. But as the running of parties and especially elections became expensive, the ability to raise funds became an indispensable qualification. All through the 1920's, the choice of a party president was made primarily on the basis of his money-raising ability, for upon him rested the heavy responsibility of raising millions of yen during an election year for the party's "war chest." Ability to raise money is still a desideratum with very high priority. In the proletarian parties, however, a militant background or record was highly prized as one of the most important qualifications of a president.

As a natural consequence of the inordinate respect for the government and officialdom which has lasted for centuries, and due to the additional fact that all the conservative parties were founded and led by former government officials, it became an accepted practice to bring in from the outside prominent bureaucrats and even military men without any experience in party politics to head the parties. When parties first came into existence in 1881, the presidents of the two earliest parties, Itagaki and Okuma, were former government officials. This was before the establishment of the national assembly. Even Ito and Saionji who were presidents after 1900 were not members of the House of Representatives.

It was only after Hara became president of the Seiyukai in 1914 that the party Leader came to have a seat in the House of Representatives.[4] But even Hara who was by temperament suited for party politics had come to the position with a bureaucratic background. As a matter of fact, all through the 1920's and part of the 1930's, presidents of the two major parties were all one-time bureaucrats, the only exception being Inukai.[5]

[3] There are many "adopted son" presidents among whom were General Tanaka Giichi of the Seiyukai (1925), Shidehara Kijuro of the Progressives and Yoshida Shigeru of the Liberal Party in the postwar period.

[4] Between the opening of the Diet in 1890 and the liquidation of parties in 1940, there were only a few party presidents who had seats in the House of Representatives. They were Hara Takashi, Kato Takaaki, Takahashi Korekiyo, Tokonami Takejiro, Hamaguchi Yuko, Inukai Tsuyoshi, and Machida Chuji.

[5] Hara Takashi, Kato Takaaki, Hamaguchi Yuko, and Wakatsuki Reijiro were all former government officials and Tanaka Giichi was a general. All were supported by the financial power of the zaibatsu.

Many a party president had no experience whatever in party politics. Many of them joined a party only after they were assured of the presidency. Kato Takaaki, for example, had served for a long time as Foreign Minister in three governments before he became a party man. He made the decision with the very definite aim of becoming Prime Minister by way of a party presidency. Not being a party man by either training or inclination, he never developed into a party politician; he remained a bureaucrat to the last, playing the role of a party politician. General Tanaka was a glaring example of a party head who was completely devoid of political experience when he assumed the presidency and learned very little and very slowly while in office. There have been similar instances of inexperienced bureaucrats coming into the parties since the end of World War II. Shidehara, Yoshida, and Ashida came to the presidency of a party without any previous political experience in the period immediately following the end of the World War II. All three men were at one time career diplomats. In 1952 another career diplomat, Shigemitsu, "untainted" by experience in politics or in a party organization, was called upon to head the Progressive Party.

The Party Directorate: the Inner Core

In the performance of his duty and functions, the president is assisted by an inner core of party faithfuls who are in most cases hand-picked by him. This is a small group, kept down to manageable size, that runs the party. Practically all of them are members of the Diet, either present or past.[6] This body serves as the effective link between the party Leader and the rank and file membership. This group of elite within the party structure participates in policy planning, in the highest level convention machinery, and provides all the heads of the various departments of the party machinery. Included in this select company are the advisers[7] who comprise the Elder Statesmen of the party by reason of their long, meritorious service in the Diet and in the party. Many of them are ex-cabinet ministers and even a former premier may be found in this group of party veterans.

[6] This of course does not hold true for the Japan Communist Party which has only two members in the House of Representatives and the Directorate has disappeared into the underground and is not functioning as it used to.

[7] The number of advisers varies from party to party. As of September 1, 1953, the Liberal Party had five, Hatoyama Liberals six, the Progressives thirty-six, and the Right Socialists six. The Right Socialist Party had in addition to the regular advisers the highest adviser in the person of Katayama Tetsu, the only Socialist ever to form a government.

In addition, there are the confidants, consultants, and members of the executive committee and the political research committee.

The operational kingpin of this high command is the secretary-general who is the general manager of the party. He is the party's counterpart of the government's director of the cabinet secretariat. As the right-hand man, if not actually the *alter ego*, of the president, he is responsible for planning party strategy and operations while keeping unity within the party. He functions as a go-between in preserving and restoring harmony and unity within and in carrying on negotiations with the outside. He is the party's mouthpiece or spokesman. On him falls the onerous burden of seeing that the party coffers are kept full. Consequently, he must spend a great deal of his time and energy in raising party funds especially at election time. However, for a successful discharge of his duties, he is handsomely rewarded with an important post. So crucial is this position that the most experienced and the ablest available man, frequently with the experience of an ex-cabinet minister or ex-speaker of the House of Representatives, is appointed to the post. Often, however, the choice is more a result of compromise necessary to please all factions so that the widest acceptability rather than the greatest ability becomes the decisive factor in his selection. Because of the onerous duties of the office, as many as six deputy general secretaries are appointed to assist him. More often than not, the secretary is hand-picked by the party president himself.

Next comes the chairman of the Political Research Committee, which is in effect the brain trust, whose task it is to study, draft, and recommend policies. Assisted by several deputy chairmen[8] ranging in number from five to eight, he is responsible for studying policy problems and, if the party is in power, for proposing and even drafting bills for the government to submit to the Diet for enactment. When the party is in power, the Committee also assumes the responsibility of examining the draft budget and draft bills and even helps in their actual drafting.

The chairman of the Executive Committee is the third member of the party's "Big Three"[9] in the high command. It has been pointed out that in the selection of the chairman of the Liberal Party's executive committee, Miki Takeo, the decision was made in a four-man

---

[8] The Right Socialists had four, the Liberals and Hatoyama Liberals had five, while the Progressives had eight deputy chairmen.

[9] The "Big Three" of the Socialist Party are the secretary-general, the chairman of the policy committee, and the treasurer. In the new Liberal-Democratic Party the "Big Three" has been expanded into the "Big Five." See the section on "Emergence of a Two Party System" in Chapter 10.

conference of the innermost circle, namely, Premier Yoshida, Ogata Taketora, Hirokawa Kozen, and Sato Eisaku.[10]   In the executive committee deliberations are carried on and high-level decisions are reached on various matters including the selection of candidates for the Diet to be endorsed and supported by the party.   The size of the committee varies from party to party and from time to time.[11] In the Liberal Party, of the thirty members ten were appointees of the president and the remaining twenty were those selected from the nine geographic regions upon the recommendation of the local organizations.   All except one had seats in the Diet making it practically a Diet members' executive committee.[12]

In the Liberal Party, in particular, a great deal of criticism has been leveled against the executive committee by its own membership because of the practice of meeting behind closed doors, barring admission to the party's own Diet members.   It has thereby earned the stigma of being the hatching place of political plots and intrigues. This sort of secretiveness and exclusiveness, which is not confined to any single party, has given rise to the vociferous criticism that party leadership is not only undemocratic but actually disdainful of the wishes of the rank and file membership.

In addition to the "Big Three," there are other party officers who belong in the high command.   They are the chairmen of the Diet caucus, the Lower House caucus, the Upper House caucus, and the auditors.   Those officers who constitute the directorate are all elected for a term of one year.   Formerly, they were appointed directly by the president.   While election is stipulated, the actual process involves the selection or designation by the president and his staff after the choices have been made in the Diet members' caucus, followed by the confirmation of the slate of officers at a party convention by means of a formal voting procedure.

It is the duty of the party leaders to maintain the enthusiasm and loyalty of their followers, but the power to inspire enthusiasm in politics in Japan as elsewhere all too often does not go with an impartial mind and caution and prudence in both word and deed.   The tremendous power of the inner circle in the determination of party

[10] Gamo Kansuke, "Hoshu shinto no taido tsuyoshi," *Seikai Orai*, March, 1953, p. 47.

[11] Hatoyama Liberals had only ten members, the Progressives twenty-one, the Liberals thirty, the Left Socialists thirty-one, and the Right Socialists thirty-nine. Both Socialist parties had two women members each on the executive committee.

[12] Of the ten appointees of the president, eight were members of the House of Representatives, one was in the House of Councillors, and one was not a Diet member.   Of the remaining twenty who represented local organizations, eleven were in the Lower House and nine were in the Upper House.

policies is conducive to the generation of hostility particularly when that power operates visibly. It intensifies factional cleavage because those who are unable to get into this charmed circle find it necessary to join forces with others in an effort to checkmate its power.[13]

Membership

As has already been pointed out, political parties antedate the opening of the national assembly, inasmuch as its chief purpose was to fight the oligarchy which monopolized power and exercised it arbitrarily. Their chief goal was to establish a national assembly thereby opening the way for their participation in the exercise of political power. Consequently, their activities were predominantly, if not exclusively, in the nature of agitation until 1890 when the Diet was opened and the nation was provided with an excellent arena of political struggle.

In the early days of parliamentary government, a party was no more than a small group of Diet members banded together for the purpose of carrying on the fight for political power against the government. Naturally a party consisted of the party president and his high command, and not the large organization that it became subsequently. With the extension of the franchise and especially after the passage of the universal manhood suffrage law in 1925, parties enlarged their organizational base to include a large membership the majority of whom were outside of the Diet. Consequently they became more democratic at least in theory and some shift in emphasis from personalities to issues resulted. Political parties are coming to be looked upon as organizations of, for, and by their members but, in their actual operation, the presidents and their high commands run them pretty much as they see fit without worrying too much about the rank and file.

Although it has become quite natural to refer to the membership as a whole when thinking of political parties, their activities are concentrated in the Diet where the major battles against the government and between the parties are carried on. They are far more sensitive to the conditions and developments within the Diet than to what goes on the outside among the people. It is inevitable that the attention of the parties should be focussed on the marshaling of their strength in parliament.

Acquiring membership in a Japanese party is not as simple as in the United States where a legal voter decides on his own initiative

[13] Maeda Tamon, "Seito no naifun," *Asahi*, February 25, 1953.

and unilaterally declares himself a member of a party at the time he registers to vote. The party, of course, is not consulted nor does it even know about it until it is an accomplished fact. It cannot and does not accept or reject an application nor does it vote the applicant into the organization. Every Japanese party, however, requires a formal application for membership which must go through channels and the applicant's "credentials" are gone over carefully before he is accepted as a member. Normally, the recommendation of the local organization is the decisive factor in the processing of the application.

The Progressive Party required, as part of the application, introduction from at least two bona fide members. The Socialist Party has the same requirement of two or more "sponsors." The Japan Communist Party has the most rigid requirements, including a training and probationary period as well as a minimum specified lapse of time before an applicant is admitted to full membership. Even after admission, the Communists carry on their usual practice of purging those who are found to be unreliable or undesirable. All the parties require the payment of dues in advance at the time of the application as well as subscription to their principles and platforms.

Members are as free to withdraw from, as to join, a party. As a matter of fact, it is easier to quit than to join a party as can be seen by the constant change of party allegiance especially by the Diet members. The majority of the people are not party members, which means that the percentage of "floating votes" is far greater than in the United States, Great Britain, or even France. An interesting feature of Japanese party membership is that there is a considerable number of persons who have "multiple allegiance" in that they are members officially of more than one party. This is not considered unusual or aberrant by the public or by the politicians. It is not possible to predict on the basis of party membership the outcome of an election in Japan.

Party membership is still a long way from the prewar peak which for the Seiyukai was close to 3,000,000 while for the Minseito it was over 2,500,000. According to the figures for August, 1947, the membership of the various parties stood as follows:[14]

Liberal Party	21,365
Democratic Party	13,946
Socialist Party	90,679
National Cooperative Party	5,934
Japan Communist Party	14,427

[14] Inagaki Tatsuo, *Gendai Seito Ron*, p. 49.

In May, 1956, nearly ten years later, the parties showed a considerably larger membership. The estimated strength was as follows:[14a]

Liberal Democratic Party	1,500,000
Japan Socialist Party	50,000
Japan Communist Party	60,000

There are virtually no lowly positions in the parties normally open to those who want to work their way up from the very bottom on the precinct level doing menial party chores or working as ward heelers as is possible in American politics. This is due to the system which depends largely on bringing in promising young men from the outside who have possibilities and particularly good connections as evidenced by favorable introductions from those who count. Consequently, the inner core of the party is made up more often than not of those who came with connections and introductions but without a great deal of previous experience in practical politics.

Efforts to recruit new members are still inadequate except in the case of the radical parties, especially the Communists who more than any other party are fired with zeal and a sense of mission. Conservative parties which count their votes in millions do not seem interested in getting new party members. Instead at election time they concentrate their efforts in capturing the floating votes. Moreover, increasing party membership does not help to increase the party's political fund to any appreciable extent and therefore is not regarded as worth the effort. A major part of the effort of any party is devoted also to luring individuals away from another party, especially those who are in the Diet, in order to increase the party's parliamentary strength.

Practically no effort is made in the recruiting of new party members at the grass-roots level because the voters can be easily influenced or controlled by the local bosses and their assistants in such a way that votes can be delivered to the designated candidate. Consequently, there is no real need to have them registered as party members as there would be in a democratic system like that of the United States or Great Britain.

Because of the comparatively recent origin of political parties and the circumstances surrounding their development as well as the different traditional concepts which operate in Japan, there has not developed anything like "hereditary" allegiance to any party in the

[14a] Liberal Democratic Party figures represent official registration. While the Japan Communist Party figures are from Jiji Tsushinsha *Sekai Shubo*, June 21, 1955.

way that it exists in the United States.[15]   This condition undoubtedly adds to the fluidity and instability so characteristic of Japanese political parties.

Discipline

As in the British party system, Japanese party leaders have control of the careers of the members, especially of the parliamentary party, through appointments to responsible positions in the cabinet and in the standing committees of the Diet as well as to other key positions. This is in contrast to the American party system where there is no analogous control over the careers of the congressional party, giving rise to the system of seniority rule in committee appointments.

Party unity and solidarity are indispensable to the effective operation of a party.   Strenuous efforts therefore are made to keep the party members in line and not infrequently the obsession for unity backfires because high-handed methods are employed to preserve or even produce harmony.   In the internal management of a party, it is not unusual to attempt to bring about harmony through the use of coercion by the leadership.   This is, in a sense, a natural consequence of Japanese political development because of the conspicuous lack of party unity and solidarity and also the ease with which members have been lured away by another party or bought by the government.   This latter situation arises from the inordinate desire, an obsession, of every Diet member to become a cabinet minister.

Every important party move in the Diet is preceded by a caucus of the members and the decision of the caucus is binding upon a member.   Any deviation or intransigence can bring speedy political retribution which may take the form of expulsion.   Although expulsion is normally a decision of the Executive Committee it has also been carried out by the decision of a single man, the president.   Premier Yoshida expelled Ishibashi Tanzan and Kono Ichiro, two of the leading members of the Hatoyama faction of the Liberal Party, on the very eve of the general election of October 1, 1952, on the grounds of recalcitrance.[16]

In spite of the resort to drastic discipline available to the party leadership, members have demonstrated time and again that they are

[15] According to Merriam and Gosnell, approximately 75 percent of the American voters have a "hereditary allegiance" to one or the other of the major parties.   In other words, the family is the greatest formulator of political opinions and political loyalties in American society.   E. E. Schattschneider, *Party Government*, p. 21, and C. E. Merriam and Gosnell, *The American Party System*, 2nd ed., p. 28.

[16] See the author's article on "Japan" in the 1953 *Americana Annual*, p. 368.

quite adept at shifting and transferring their loyalties whenever they are offered an opportunity for advancement. Not many party men can successfully resist the lure of fame and fortune. Since Diet members enjoy power and influence and have a strong desire for position and honor as well as a strong fear of dissolution and frequent elections, the government in the past has been able to control and manipulate Diet members without much difficulty.

Political peregrinations of members have therefore not occasioned any surprise either among party men or the general public. Even those who were regarded as men of principle have indulged in the practice of frequently changing parties. For example, Ozaki Yukio who established the record of having won in twenty-five consecutive elections and served continuously without interruption for fifty-two years from the opening of the Diet in 1890 to the general election of October 1, 1952, changed his party allegiance many times during his long career.[17] He used to say that it was not he who changed but rather the political parties that kept on changing. There is an element of truth, of course, in his contention because the parties have always been in a state of flux, not knowing their own minds. Plagued with instability and internal bickerings, they were splintering, merging, disappearing, and re-emerging almost at regular intervals, making it impossible for even the experts to keep the lineage of any party straight.

Discipline in a Japanese party, however, is not as effective as it is in the British party system. This is because deep factional cleavages are ever present in the parties, splitting the high command into several groups. In the Liberal Party, for instance, there were at least four or five factions before the Hatoyama and Hirokawa factions splintered off and set up a new party in March, 1953.[18] A counterweapon which party members have at their disposal against a threat of disciplinary action is their own threat of bolting which is used against the leadership frequently with telling effect. Party discipline in Japan in practice is, therefore, somewhere in between the very effective control exercised in Britain and the American party system which has only a weak control over its membership because of the absence of any recognized and authoritative procedure by which the party may discipline its members by expulsion or other means.

[17] Ozaki began as a member of Okuma's Reform Party subsequently shifting to Ito's Seiyukai, to Doshikai, then back again the Seiyukai, then to Kato's Kenseikai, and over to the Kakushin Club.

[18] Among these were the "Entourage" (*sokkinha*), Hatoyama (*Mindoha*) Hirokawa, and "Neutral" (*chukanha*) factions, the last named group being formed of the Yokakai and the Hatsukakai.

PARTY FINANCES

Winning elections being the first goal in practical politics, a great deal of money is needed. So important is money as one of the means of insuring success in elections that effective fund-raising machinery and personnel are indispensable to a party. Political parties must have ample funds to take care of election expenditures as well as normal operating expenses. Yet in Japan, as in many other countries, no really satisfactory method of financing parties has been found.

So crucial is an adequate party war chest in the winning of elections that fund-raising calls for the best efforts of the leadership. In fact, between the two World Wars, one of the primary qualifications of a party president was the ability to raise money. However, since World War II, the job of raising money has become the responsibility of the inner core and particularly the "Big Three." If the party is in power, the Finance Minister usually plays an important role in fund-raising because of his prestige and the valuable connections he has with the financial world.[19] As a rule, those who have connections render valuable service in fund-raising and the individual best suited for the job is put in charge of the operations. It is not necessarily the official position occupied in the party that determines the choice. This can be seen from the fact that for the Diet elections of 1952 and 1953 the chief fund-raiser in the Liberal Party was its secretary-general, in the Hatoyama Liberal Party it was the chairman of the policy committee, while in the Progressive Party a large number pitched in including all the members of the election policy committee as well as the secretary-general, the ex-secretary-general, the chairman of the party affairs committee, and the head of the party funds bureau.[20] In the Right Socialist Party, the chairman of the executive committee, the treasurer, and the secretary-general who previously used to go only on speaking tours, assumed the responsibility of keeping the party's war chest replenished.[21]

Party funds come from various sources. Members contribute whatever they can except in the case of Diet members who must contribute a specified amount every year. Conservative parties as a rule do not rely on membership dues to take care of even the ordinary operating expenses of their national headquarters.[22] As a matter of

[19] In the third Yoshida government, Finance Minister Ikeda Hayato and in the fourth Yoshida government, Finance Minister Mukai Tadaharu were the principal fund-raisers.

[20] "Rusugachi no kambu," *Asahi*, Evening Edition, March 27, 1953.

[21] "Saihai wo furuu—usha no maki," *Asahi*, March 28, 1953.

fact, no attempt is made to force party members to pay their dues. Only radical parties enforce payment of membership dues. Although the members of the high command and well-to-do members contribute a great deal, membership dues can never provide more than a small fraction of the party's total expenditures.

Emergency funds from other sources which are not disclosed usually came before World War II from the zaibatsu and business, special banks, insurance companies, and securities firms, and sometimes even the government's slush funds were "borrowed." The old Seiyukai depended heavily on the support of the house of Mitsui while the old Minseito could always count on the Mitsubishi interests especially from the time of the presidency of Kato Takaaki who had married into the Iwasaki family. This Minseito tie with the Iwasaki family actually goes as far back as the late 1870's when Okuma was instrumental in getting the Mitsubishi enterprises started through government aid. When Saionji was president of the Seiyukai he could, in addition to the Mitsui, call on the Sumitomo banking interests which was headed by his older brother. Hara Takashi could tap the resources of the Furukawa mining interests of which he was an adviser.

In the period immediately following Japan's surrender, the parties were forced to seek new sources of political funds since the zaibatsu was liquidated as part of the Occupation policy of deconcentration of economic power, a preliminary step in the democratization of the country. As a result, a considerable portion of the financial support had to come from a new class of postwar rich, such as contractors and even black-marketeers. As industry was revived and business began to recover and economic conditions improved, party funds came increasingly from business firms and financial institutions. By 1951–52, political contributions were once again flowing into the party coffers from traditional sources.

There was a time, especially in the earlier part of this century, when contributions were made to parties with no strings attached. Things have changed, however, especially since the end of World War II and now contributions are made with the expectation, if not promise, of something in return, some special advantage or special consideration, or even a deal of some kind. As a result scandals

---

22 Operating expenses of the Liberal Party's national headquarters for 1952 amounted to ¥ 2,000,000 which was allocated as follows:

Contributions from the outside, ¥ 1,000,000
Party directorate's share   700,000
Diet members' share   300,000

have occurred frequently and on a grand scale, as for instance the Showa Denko case which shook the political world to its foundations and proved to be the undoing of the Ashida government.[23]

Significantly, all the conservative parties are getting contributions from firms which are wisely and calculatingly distributing their money in such a way as not to be left out on a political limb in the event of a change of government involving a shift in power from one party to another. They are playing safe by not putting all the political eggs in one basket. This is clearly reflected in the way three of the largest contributors of political funds distributed their aid to the three parties:

	Liberals	Progressives	Right Socialists
Kokusaku Pulp Company	¥ 4,000,000	¥ 1,000,000	¥ 1,000,000
Yawata Steel Works	3,000,000	1,000,000	500,000
Japan Steel Pipe Company	1,000,000	200,000	30 0,000

An examination of the sources of the Liberal Party's political funds for the period of May, 1951, through April, 1952,[24] indicates that the party does not depend on any single large source but on a number of sources, namely, large, medium, and small zaibatsu as well as business of all sorts and sizes.

[23] This was the case in which Premier Ashida received a political contribution of ¥ 1,500,000 in return for a large government loan to the Showa Denko Company, a fertilizer firm.

[24] Kokusaku Pulp Company	¥4,000,000
Yawata Steel Works	3,000,000
Japan Industrial (Kogyo) Association	2,000,000
Japan Beet Sugar Company	"
Tokiwa Sulphur Mining Company	1,500,000
Nitto Shosen Company	"
Japan Pharmaceutical Association (Yakuseikai)	1,000,000
Katakura Industrial Company	"
Japan Steel Pipe Company	"
Kobe Steel Works	"
Jujo Paper Company	"
Kawasaki Heavy Industries	"
Honshu Paper Company	"
San'yo Pulp Company	"
Japan Sake Brewers' Association	"
Japan Coal Mine Industry Federation	"
Japan Transportation Company	"
Iino Marine Transportation Company	700,000
Nippon Yusen Kaisha	500,000
Osaka Shosen Kaisha	"
Mitsui Shipping Company	"
Japan Mutual (Sogo) Bank Association	"
Tohoku Pulp Company	"

Radical parties are getting more from individual contributors than are the conservative parties. A considerable portion of the funds comes to the Right Socialist Party from labor unions, from the firms, and even from the Federation of Economic Organizations.[25] The Left Socialist Party gets the bulk of its financial support from the labor unions and from its membership and very little if any from business firms. The Communist Party gets its funds from labor unions, special publishing houses most of which handle leftist literature, street-corner collections, and profits derived from smuggling goods as well as from some sources outside Japan.

The zaibatsu came back to life shortly after the nation regained full sovereignty in 1952 and is again contributing to the party coffers. The Liberal Party has an intimate connection with Mitsui for Premier Yoshida's fund-raiser, former Finance Minister Mukai Tadaharu, is a former "chief of staff" who presided over the fortunes of the Mitsui financial empire. The intimate relationship which existed between the Mitsui interests and Seiyukai, the predecessor of the present Liberal Party, dates back to its beginning when Ito was president and his close friend and supporter, Inoue Kaoru, was adviser to the house of Mitsui.

Political contributions made by firms during the twelve-month period beginning May 1, 1951, and ending April 30, 1952, reveal the way the political parties depend on business for a considerable portion of their necessary funds.[26]

A special, though not a peculiar, feature of Japanese politics is the fact that the government party invariably has the advantage over the Opposition in fund-raising. This is because of the psychological advantage the party in power enjoys due to the burden of proof which rests on the Opposition if the government is to be thrown out and superseded by a new one formed by the Opposition.

The ease with which most of the party presidents have been able to raise funds can be attributed to one or both of two things. First is the fact that there exists some form of marital relationship which gives the president access to wealth which he can tap. Ex-Premier Yoshida has a daughter who is married to a wealthy coal mine owner in Fukuoka prefecture, a man who was also a Liberal Party member of the House of Representatives. Prime Minister Hatoyama, the president of the Liberal Democratic Party, and Ishibashi Shojiro, president of the Bridgestone Tire Company, are maritally related since their offsprings are married to each other. Shigemitsu Mamoru, ex-

[25] "Saihai wo furuu—usha no maki," *Asahi*, March 28, 1953.
[26] Daiyamondoshoa, *Gendai Seiji no Kiso Chishiki*, p. 141.

president of the Progressive Party, has access to Osaka financial circles through his father-in-law, Hayashi Ichizo, and also through a friend, Seki Keizo of the Toyo Spinning Company. Secondly, the president of the party utilizes every possible connection for fund-raising, officially if the party is in power, and unofficially through personal friendships of the party's high command.

PARTY ACTIVITIES AND OPERATIONS

Since every individual is torn by the diversity of his own interests, being a member of several groups, he finds himself divided and inconsistent in his attitudes. This situation makes it impossible to mobilize one hundred percent any particular interest which is a composite of many diverse individuals.[27] Add to this the complexity of society and the economy in which we live and all the innumerable ramifications, and we can begin to appreciate the fact that it is not a simple matter to analyze the economic representation within the political parties. Because of the plurality of interest that people have, it would be impossible for society to be neatly split into bitterly contending political parties based on clear-cut principles. Instead we have parties serving as agents for the multitude of interests which necessarily overlap at many points.

Political parties are therefore compelled to base their activities on common principles and interests which as a rule are greatly over-simplified. Policies are formulated with great flexibility and stated simply. But all their efforts would be of no avail unless they have smoothly running machinery equal to the task of performing such necessary functions as to hold members in line, recruit new members, formulate policies, select candidates for office, raise the funds necessary, and educate and attract the electorate to their policies in order to win elections. These are some of the activities which will now be taken up in the pages which follow.

Until and unless the whole story of party meetings is revealed, one cannot always be sure where the real decisions were made and where the real source of action lay. If this is true even in the case of British policy making where the party activities are more easily observable, it is doubly true in Japanese politics. Yet it is possible to discern the process of policy making.

It must be emphasized that policy cannot spring spontaneously from an unorganized inchoate mass. Initiative must usually come from above and direction too, especially in a crisis, must of necessity come from a small group. Pressure is incessant on parties in power

[27] E. Schattschneider, *Party Government*, p. 33.

to place the active phase of policy making in the hands of a few and
to reserve for the rank and file the passive roles of acceptance and to
a limited extent of criticism.

Party and Policies

The task of formulating policies and drafting platforms is entrusted
to the Political Affairs Research Committee, or the Policy Committee,
which is staffed to handle the research and planning that must
precede formulation. Stimulating and leading public opinion are
also legitimate functions of the policy committee. Some idea of a
party's policy committee can be gained by examining the Political
Research Committee of the Liberal Party, which is not by any means
typical but is indicative of its activities. Its chairman, who is one
of the "Big Three" of the party's directorate, is assisted by as many
as five to eight deputy chairmen. Below them are ten divisions—
public safety, administration, foreign relations, education, transportation and communications, industries, social problems, agriculture and
forestry, public finance and banking, and planning and development
—each headed by a chief.[28]

When the party is in power, before the draft bills and draft budget
are submitted to the Diet, they are sent first to the Political Research
Committee where its officers go over them hurriedly, after which they
are sent on to the Executive Committee where decisions are reached.
Although the organization at first glance appears impressive on paper,
as yet it is not as large or efficient a research section as is found in
many a business firm in terms of capacity for research or the avail-
ability of research materials on hand.

Party strategy not infrequently dictates the abandoning of con-
sistency and preciseness, at least in part, in response to political
exigencies and the harsh demands of compromise on any number of
fronts. The Liberal Party, for example, in 1953 found itself forced
to yield to the Progressive Party in exchange for badly needed support
to push through its legislative program. Refusal to make concessions
or to develop a many-sided program in a party simply reduces its
chances of winning votes and power. If politicians frequently appear
unprincipled, it is partly due to the fact that they must do business
with a great variety of people and interests and that they are forced
to constantly effect compromise.

It should be pointed out that even in the United States and Britian,
democratic formulation of party policy is limited by the need to win

[28] *Asahi*, May 27, 1953.

elections. Policy which is merely or entirely what the membership as a whole wants may fail to win many of the floating votes.

Conflicts are ever present in party affairs since realities often clash with theories and particularly with hopes and, since the future cannot be predicted, circumstances are bound to arise which will produce disagreements. Moreover, the path to power seems to deviate from the path of policy. Cleavages thus develop between intention and execution, program and performance, and rationalizations become inevitable just as much as the shifts and adjustments in the party line.

Party policies have a way of becoming merely means of advancing the *ad hoc* ideas conceived hastily, rather than carefully planned courses of action. Even the Liberal Party lacked long-term over-all policies. The fact is that Japanese parties have simply not developed into "policy" parties. They have not yet ceased to be "personality-centered" parties which operate on personal relations and sentiments and considerations.[29]

Although political parties all have their impressive manifestos, declarations, platforms, and all sorts of documents which purport to state their principles and policies, they are more often than not without much substance and with a great deal less of popular appeal. Conservative parties have shown a tendency to side-step thorny and difficult issues or to adopt a wait and see policy especially when confronted with vexing problems. Too often the issues at election time are reduced to simple slogans and neat cliches with little or no reference or relevance to the policies and principles of the parties.

In the present stage of party development, very little thought is given to providing means by which the people may actively participate in policy making. While there are such provisions for referendum and recall which bring the people into decision making at least partially, important issues of policy are not submitted to the electorate for their decision. There is still considerable reluctance on the part of political parties to allow the electorate to have a role in major policy decisions.

Policy differences between the conservative and radical parties are noticeable. However, differences among the conservative parties are actually not very great or significant. For instance, the Liberals and Progressives are both capitalists in their outlook as well as in the support they receive, and no cleavages exist between them with regard to principles or ideas that cannot be overcome. Differences are largely those of sentiment and personal relations. More often

[29] Maeda Tamon, "Seito no naifun," *Asahi*, February 25, 1953.

than not, they exist also in the tactics or strategy, the scope of action, that is, on the question of how far to go, and also in the timing.

A comparison of the platforms of the conservative parties demonstrates clearly the absence of real policy differences.[30] The Liberal, Progressive, and Democratic parties all advocated, in foreign relations, close cooperation with the free world and the United Nations, promotion of friendly relations with Asian, and especially Southeast Asian, countries and efforts toward the firm establishment of independence and promotion of international trade. On the rearmament issue, they were all agreed on the need for defensive force although this agreement was less apparent in the manner of expression used by the three parties. The Liberal Party showed a studied attitude of avoiding the word "rearmament" for political reasons until long after the election of April, 1953. On domestic policies they all declared the need for the rationalization and modernization of industry, rise in employment and real wages, reduction of the tax burden, aid to small and medium-scale enterprises, the accumulation of capital, and the regulation of strikes in the public interest.

Policy differences between the Left and Right Socialist parties have been so great, indeed, that the cleavages which have resulted are far deeper and more difficult to overcome than those which exist among conservative parties. This is due to the fact that radical parties, as in British politics, have taken policy matters far more seriously than the conservative parties. For example, the Left Socialist Party was unalterably opposed to armament in any form and it stands irrevocably for the complete disbanding of the national security force and returning its personnel to peaceful production, while the Right Socialist Party recognized the right of self-defense and simply placed limitations on the size of the force and the amount of expenditure which it felt was justified.

Political Education and Propaganda

It is the responsibility of the political parties as the most important instruments for the political education of the people to pursue certain activities. In order to discharge this responsibility, they must carry on research and inform the public accurately on such matters as the domestic political situation, national security, economic and industrial problems, diplomacy and world developments.[31] Nothing is more essential at the present stage of development than a constant and

[30] "Kakuto wa ko koyaku suru," *Asahi*, April 9, 1953. See also 1955 *Asahi Nenkan* for the platforms of all the parties.

[31] Mitsuchi Chuzo, "Seito no sekinin," *Chuo Koron*, June 1939, p. 227.

persistent year-round effort to educate and bring the electorate up to a high enough level of understanding of the national issues in order to make possible their intelligent participation in the political process. Unfortunately, however, so far very little is being done except at election time when feverish efforts are made by the parties to win votes by means of the extensive use of slogans and sterotypes and symbols which emphasize words but contribute little to the clarification of issues. Except for the Socialists and the Communists, the parties still concentrate most of their time and energies on merely supplying ammunition to the candidates for immediate use in their campaigns.

Educational and propaganda activities such as are carried on in Great Britain are still quite unknown in Japanese political parties. Parties do not tell the voters very clearly what they may expect from them. Nor do they succeed in reminding themselves of what they are and what they are for. As a result they tend to degenerate into mere agglomerations of ambitious power-seekers. Research aimed at long-term study of national problems is only now beginning to attract the serious attention of the party leaders who are far behind the business and industrial leaders. For years, economic organizations have been devoting a considerable amount of their time and energies to national problems.[32]

If political parties are to serve, as they must if the development of the democratic process is to be aided, as the agency through which new ideas are crystallized into institutions and practices and utilized in the solution of the nation's social and economic problems, the formidable task of creating favorable public opinion toward the parties and their leaders assumes peculiar urgency and should be given the highest priority.

Selection of Candidates

Winning elections, thereby capturing a majority of the House of Representatives, is the most important goal of a political party. If this goal is to be achieved, it is obvious that great care must be exercised in selecting the best available candidates to run under the party banner. The process of selecting candidates varies considerably as between the political parties in details but they all seem to follow a similar general pattern.

Each party sets up its election headquarters in the national office

[32] In the period before World War II such organizations as the Mitsubishi Institute of Economic Research and the Ohara Institute for Social Research carried on studies of great value.

with the secretary-general in command of a small group within the inner circle to map out election strategy and operations and select the party's candidates. The election general staff consisted, in the case of the Liberal party, of the secretary-general, the president's *alter ego* and heir apparent, the chairman of the executive committee, an ex-secretary-general, an ex-deputy secretary-general, and a party veteran strategist.[33] These six men went over the applications of candidates requesting party endorsement and not only selected those who met their approval but also assigned them to the election districts from which they could run most successfully. Those who were selected for endorsement received a sum of money labeled "endorsement money" from the party, which was used to defray the expenses of the campaign. They were also given all available assistance by way of campaign speakers who were sent out from the party's central headquarters. In the election of April, 1953, the Liberal Party handed out "endorsement money" to candidates according to the three categories which were established. Class A candidates received 1,000,000 yen; Class B, 800,000 and Class C, 500,000.

Patronage

The problem of patronage is not a major headache since it affects only a very small percentage of the party members directly. There is available only a handful of positions which are pre-empted by the party's inner core. As of December, 1953, there were estimated to be something like 2,900,000 national civil service positions in the country, which is far in excess of the number in the United States which was approximately 2,500,000. Although the percentage of highly professionalized personnel is no higher than in the United States, the civil service positions have been filled by career men almost exclusively since 1899 when party men were squeezed out and kept out thereafter.

Patronage is thus limited to positions at the very top. Cabinet and subcabinet posts always go to the party in power under the existing system. The members of the inner core become the cabinet members. There are practically no positions in the middle and lower echelons of the national civil service open to patronage seekers. The Japanese do not have counterparts of the American patronage positions such as postmasterships, federal and district judgeships, collectors of customs, United States district attorneys and marshals. In the United States there are approximately 170,000 "unprotected"

---

[33] "Rokunin de tama erabi," *Asahi,* Evening Edition, March 26, 1953.

federal jobs whereas in Japan a very small fraction of the number is available for distribution to deserving party men.

The party's inner core or the high command serves as the patronage bureau and appointments are decided at the national headquarters. There is no system of allocation or farming out appointments to local committees as in the United States, nor is there any need to keep in close touch with their equivalents of the Senators to guarantee confirmation.

In the period since the end of the war, the number of positions which may be filled by other than civil service appointees has been increased considerably through the liberalization of appointment policy. These positions are now available to party men whereas, in the years preceding World War II, hardly any "unprotected" policy positions existed.

Because of the large number of prestige positions on all sorts of advisory bodies, commissions, and deliberative councils, there are a great many more persons rewarded for their services than there are regular paid government positions. In many instances, these appointments which are in effect patronage positions prove satisfactory to the recipients of the honor. Indirectly, they are able to derive the kind of satisfaction they are after.

ACTIVITIES IN THE DIET

In the Diet, the party caucus, which is the center of practical party politics, is used constantly. For the Japanese who have a strong predilection for consultation in making decisions in any sphere or on any level, the party caucus is a natural procedure. Without it, it would be impossible to manage political affairs. Members of the Diet are rigidly bound by the decisions of the caucus and few dare to disregard them.

Diet members are organized by parties into working groups to insure smooth and efficient functioning. It is customary practice for the parties to have a separate organization for each of the houses as well as a joint or combined organization of their entire Diet membership. Both strategy and maneuvers are planned and directed by the party's Diet Policy and Strategy Committee and executed through the efforts of the whips who as "stage managers," "aides-de-camp," and intelligence department for the leader of the chamber, perform functions which strengthen the party's operation. They make sure the government party supporters are present when a decision is to be made; they keep the ministers informed on the state of feeling among the party's Diet members; they bring pressure to bear upon negligent or intransigent members; and they also act as intermediaries when making up committee membership lists.

When the Opposition is formed by a coalition of several parties, their policy and strategy committees work out plans of action separately first and then hold a joint caucus to map out their common strategy in an "opposition" caucus. This has no formal leaders but leadership is normally assumed by the party which has the strongest Diet representation. Veteran parliamentarians and proven fighters are chosen to carry out the joint strategy.

The party's directorate is constantly holding political "powwows" to discuss important matters. All the bargaining, compromises, concessions, deals, maneuvers and manipulations and negotiations which the political process involves in the party itself, in the Diet, and in interparty relations make the caucus an indispensable piece of machinery. Even in the selection of candidates, the caucus is a necessity. "Behind-the-scenes" moves are going on all the time.

Strategy for passing a no-confidence vote against the government has to be carefully planned and worked out to insure success, as was demonstrated in March, 1953. Interparty conferences are held to devise the plans in detail along with precise plans for their execution. To strengthen the forces of opposition the Left Socialist Party set up a "tactical conference" in its Diet Policy Committee in June, 1953. Opposition offensive within the Diet is often synchronized with demonstrations outside for maximum results. Labor unions in particular schedule their demonstrations on the very day the fight in the Diet is to reach its climax, thereby timing and synchronizing the activities within and without the Diet. This has been a characteristic postwar development.

Since most of the work of the Diet is done in committees, it becomes very important for the parties to make their strength felt by having as many as possible of the members assigned to important committees. The established practice now in the matter of committee assignments is to apportion seats in proportion to the strength of the party[34] in the Diet, with the chairmanship going to the majority party if there is one. If there is no majority party, chairmanships are usually allocated on the basis of party strength after negotiations and compromises. Unlike the Congress of the United States, no seniority rule operates in assignments to the important committees and committee chairmanships. If any sort of seniority preference exists, it is long and faithful service to the party which is rewarded before the length of service in the Diet.

[34] This practice originated during the first decade of the twentieth century. See *Hara Takashi Nikki*, entry of December 21, 1910.

Decision-making Process

Theoretically all decisions are made through authoritative party organs such as the caucus, the executive committee, and the annual conference. In practice, however, decisions are frequently arrived at outside of these organs or machinery, as for example by the president or a small informal group within the party's directorate powerful enough to prevail upon the executive committee or the president.

The utter informality with which decisions are often arrived at is indicated by the fact that the innermost circle of the directorate might even formulate policies and arrive at decisions at a teahouse meeting which has served as a Japanese counterpart of the smoke-filled back rooms which have become symbolic of the setting of caucuses in American politics. As a matter of fact, many of the teahouses of Tokyo are identified with leaders of Japanese politics who use them as their favorite rendezvous.[35]   Historically the teahouses of Shimbashi actually owe their origin to the patronage of the eminent statesmen of the early Meiji period. Some of Premier Yoshida's policies have been criticized as the fruits of teahouse politics, not without justification.

Differences of opinion over issues or policies are not discussed or aired thoroughly in the party caucuses before decisions are reached. All too frequently, and almost as a matter of course, decisions are imposed on the members from above even before the party members have been consulted or taken into confidence. The high command of the party does not take the trouble to convert or win them over by effective persuasion, but simply tells them what the decision is.

Party Convention

Regular annual conventions are usually held by the parties at the beginning of the year in January during the recess of the Diet. The convention which is held in Tokyo[36] lasts anywhere from a day to three days. The convention is actually little more than a jamboree but it is an indispensable adjunct to the party machinery because it adds color and gives publicity to the party's activities. As a national rally, it serves the necessary function of building up the party's morale by injecting a degree of enthusiasm into at least the new delegates

[35] "Seijika to machiai," *Seikai Orai*, March, 1953, p. 89.
[36] In 1953, the Right Socialist Party held its three-day convention at Asakusa Public Hall, January 18–20, the Left Socialist Party at Toyo University Auditorium, January 21–23, the Liberal Party at Hibiya Public Hall on January 25, and the Progressive Party at Hibiya Public Hall on February 9.

attending it for the first time. It affords the delegates from various parts of the country the opportunity of coming to the nation's capital to develop a feeling of belonging and a sense of importance, and returning to their homes to tell the folks back home what a wonderful time they had and what a grand reception they were given. The members of the directorates of the conservative parties actually make it a practice to thank the delegates for attending the convention. This sort of reception can give the delegates the incentive to work harder for the party.

The Socialist parties, however, do not regard attendance at the convention by the delegates as a favor to the central leadership. On the contrary, the convention is used as an attraction and special incentive for the members to whom attendance is a duty as well as a privilege. Only those members whose dues are fully paid up could qualify as delegates and they are not profusely thanked for attending either. On the whole the Socialist party conventions are held in a far more serious atmosphere than those of the conservative parties.

Attendance at the party conventions ranges all the way from several hundred to as many as one or two thousand persons. The plans for the convention and its agenda are carefully worked out months in advance by a preparatory committee whose members are chosen from the party's directorate. There is no doubt that the party convention attracts wide attention and the proceedings are reported in detail in the newspapers. Consequently, it provides the public with political education and party propaganda.

So far as decision making is concerned its role is still of relatively minor importance, for although the convention makes a show of adopting declarations, platforms, and policies, of voting for and electing officers, and of passing resolutions, it simply performs a rubber-stamp function of confirming the decisions made in advance by the party's directorate. Strong opposition seldom, if ever, develops against the decisions of the high command.

A more or less typical party convention opens with the singing of the national anthem after which the proceedings begin with a temporary chairman presiding. The first order of business is the election of the convention chairman of the Convention Preparatory Committee, the adoption of the party declaration, the party platform, resolutions and the like. Deliberation of policies and proposals of the central office and local organizations is then conducted but the entire procedure is characterized by shouts like "Let's make it simple," "Let's consider them in toto," "No objections," and so on, and amidst thundering applause and choruses of banzai, practically everything submitted for deliberation is approved in short order with hardly any discussion or debate. When the matter of election of officers came up at the Liberal Party Convention, for instance, in January, 1953, the motion was made and passed to the effect that, in accordance with the decision reached by the party's Executive Committee prior to the convention, the election of officers be entrusted to the Diet party caucus which was scheduled for January 29. The President of the party may or may not give an address before the convention. With rousing banzai for the party president, the convention comes to a close. Thus, although the convention as the most authoritative and important organ should have the power to decide matters of policy and election, it has not developed into much more than an announcement party which is, in Japanese social functions, always accompanied or followed by celebration and feasting.

PARTIES SINCE WORLD WAR II

There was a mushroom-like growth of parties immediately following the end of World War II. At one time there were more than 260 of them, not including countless additional political groupings or associations which could not qualify legally as parties. Most of them were transitory associations without any distinguishable ideas, principles, or policies. They were simply groups toying with ideas or concepts which were for the most part not even their own. These groups disappeared from the political scene through either natural death or absorption into the larger parties. By the end of 1953, more than a year after the restoration of full sovereignty and independence, the number of parties with seats in the Diet had been reduced to eight.[37] Two years later, the number decreased to five as the result of mergers.[37a]

[37] Their strength as of September 1, 1953, stood as follows:

House of Representatives		House of Councilors	
Liberal Party	201	Liberal Party	93
Progressive Party	76	Ryokufukai	48
Left Socialist Party	71	Left Socialist Party	43
Right Socialist Party	66	Right Socialist Party	26
Hatoyama Liberal Party	34	Progressive Party	17
Independents	10	Hatoyama Liberal	3
Labor-Farmer Party	5	Others	5
Japan Communist Party	1		
	466		250

[37a] The five parties are as follows:

Of these five parties, Ryokufukai exists only in the House of Councillors where it originated in 1947 as a political club whose membership comprised leading authorities in various fields of activity and whose emphasis was on "men rather than party."[38]   There are, in addition, the independents in both Houses who make up a surprisingly large proportion at times.   However, since the group is not organized, it is vulnerable to manipulations by the government party and many of them are lured in due course into the regular parties.

When these postwar parties were launched in the fall of 1945 they started out with new party names but with old familiar faces.   In a sense, however, even the party names were not altogether new for they had been used before in the 1880's at the very inception of the party system.[39]   As for their membership, the older ones came from the pre-World War II parties, the Seiyukai, Minseito, the different Socialist factions, and the Japan Communist Party which had not been legally recognized before the end of the war.

Few, if any, substantive changes could be detected in the "new" postwar parties for their emergence in effect was simply the resurrec-

---

Liberal Democratic Party
Japan Socialist Party
Labor-Farmer Party
Japan Communist Party
Ryokufukai

In December, the Diet seats were distributed* as follows:

House of Representatives		House of Councillors
Liberal Democratic Party	299	120
Japan Socialist Party	154	68
Ryokufukai	—	45
Labor-Farmer Party	4	2
Japan Communist Party	2	1
Others	2	5
Independents	3	4
Vacancy	3	5
	467	250

* *Asahi*, December 20, 1955.

[38] "Saihai wo furuu-Ryokufukai," *Asahi*, April 2, 1953.   In the prewar House of Peers, the upper house of the Diet, there were no political parties as such, only political clubs.

[39] The first Liberal Party (Jiyuto) was founded by Itagaki Taisuke in 1881 and the Reform Party (Kaishinto) was formed by Okuma Shigenobu in 1882. Yoshida's Liberal Party and even Hatoyama's Liberal Party use the name Jiyuto while Shigemitsu's Progressive Party is called Kaishinto.

tion or reassembling of the parties which had been disbanded in 1940. The Liberal Party provides an excellent case study for it was simply the coming together of the old members of the defunct Seiyukai of the Hatoyama faction. It is a party which was formed around the person of Hatoyama Ichiro with approximately ninety percent of the membership at the time of its founding on November 9, 1945, from the Seiyukai and the rest from the Minseito and others. The rebirth of the party was brought about not by first deciding upon the principles and policies and then finding like-minded persons who would support the party program under the president. Instead, old friends came together on the basis of personal acquaintance and for old time's sake. It was the regrouping and realignment of old political forces and elements which had lain dormant during World War II. Since it necessarily embraced individuals of all sorts, some of the members soon bolted and went off to set up a competing organization which later became the Progressive Party.

As for the policies which the parties have adopted in the postwar period, there have been no marked changes from the prewar period. The old wine has been poured into new bottles. This is particularly true of the conservative parties but applies also to the radical parties except the Communists who for the first time in history are enjoying legal existence and depending to a large extent on inspiration and direction from the outside.

One of the noteworthy developments in the postwar conservative parties is the rapidly increasing number of Diet members and party directors of bureaucratic training and experience. This is one of the conspicuous but unanticipated upshots of Occupation policies. When the program of political purge was carried out beginning in early January, 1946, practically all of the experienced party members were caught in the net and excluded from public activities. This left party affairs in the hands of inexperienced men and frequently men of small stature as well. Into the vacuum created in the directorate of the parties rushed the ambitious bureaucrats. These men were uninitiated in party politics but many of them managed to achieve high positions, even the presidency, in the hierarchy. Among those who achieved party presidency via this route and went on to the premiership are Shidehara Kijuro, Ashida Hitoshi, and Yoshida Shigeru. There are any number of others who have gone from amateur standing to leadership in party politics and the ranks of the Liberal Party in particular are full of ex-bureaucrats. Even the Socialists have brought bureaucrats into their party directorate. Only the Communists do not have ex-bureaucrats as rank and file members or in their directorate because they could not find any. The presence of a large number of bureaucrats in the parties affects party behavior since their ideas, attitudes, and biases and predilections are reflected in their actions and decisions, and particularly in their *modus operandi*.

As we have just seen, policy differences as between the different parties are slight and frequently indistinguishable. It would, therefore, be impossible to rely upon party labels or even to attempt an accurate classification of parties. However, for the sake of convenience it is possible to divide the parties into broad categories. Political observers have in practice established three categories: conservative, middle, and radical parties. For our purpose it would suffice to have only two, namely, the conservative and radical, the former representing and upholding the capitalistic system and interests and the latter anticapitalistic interests and attitudes. The Liberal, Democratic, Progressive, and Ryokufukai parties belong in the conservative fold while the Right Socialist, Left Socialist, Farmer-Labor, and the Japan Communist parties are in the radical camp. This general classification, however, must be qualified since the Right Socialist Party is clearly marginal in the sense that it can be included in either category with reference to policies or membership composition or voter support.

If it can be said, as it has been, that the Conservative Party in Great Britain is tending more and more to pass under the indirect but real and effective control of the organized economic interest of "big business," it is true that the conservative parties in Japan have long since passed under the control of "financial capitalism," although perhaps the period of the Occupation may be excepted. Before the war, and even during the period of the Allied military occupation of the country, the special interests which were served best by the conservative parties and the government were those of "big business."[40] The Liberal Party has come to be known, just as its immediate predecessor was known, as the party of big business although the landowners have always been an important element. This was true from the very beginning in 1881 when the original Liberal Party was founded. The Democratic Party is in fact no different from the Liberal Party. The Progressive Party is no less a party of big business although it has advocated adjustments and revisions in the capitalistic system. As a matter of fact, its predecessor strongly advocated what it termed "revised capitalism" as a

[40] See Nihon Shihon Shugi Koza, Vol. III, *Tochi Kiko to Seiji Undo*, pp. 178–180.

means of preserving and maintaining the capitalistic system but was hesitant to insist unconditionally on free economy or the complete abandonment of economic control. Such revision was regarded as a necessary recognition of and concession to the rising power of the laboring classes and also as a means of bringing the Socialists around to the party's viewpoint and even bringing them into its fold. In this respect, the Progressive Party appears to be in a position to effect compromise with some of the policies of both the Liberal and Right Socialist parties.

Although the conservative parties naturally look out more for the interests of big business and financial circles than any other group, their support comes from every class and stratum of society. As a matter of fact strong support, numerically speaking, comes from other than businessmen, industrialists, and financiers. In a poll conducted by the newspaper *Asahi*,[41] it was clearly brought out that a far higher percentage of industrial workers (ratio of 3:2) and farmers and fishermen (ratio of 4:1) indicated support of the conservative parties in preference to the Socialist Party. Even the unemployed preferred the conservative parties by a ratio of 5:1.[42]

Although the Liberal Party carried the "big business" label, the conservative rural populace continues to give solid support. Of all the parties, the Liberal Party has the support of the largest group of conservatives. This has been traditional with the predecessors of the present Liberal Party. It still derives strong support from the rural areas even in spite of the agricultural land reform program which modified the structure of agricultural land ownership. The most conservative voters in the country are still found in the rural agricultural communities. Because of this rural support, the Liberal Party still counts in its membership men who reflect the earthy, unsophisticated, rustic, and occasionally uncouth and blunt ways for which the Seiyukai used to be oustanding. It is impossible therefore to find a party which can be labeled a purely class party just as is the

[41] March 24, 1948.

[42] PARTY PREFERENCES OF ECONOMIC GROUPS

	Percentages Favoring		
Economic Groups	Liberal	Progressive	Socialist
Industrial laborers	32.4	12.2	30.1
Salaried persons	37.1	11.5	34.0
Businessmen-financiers	57.2	10.4	12.6
Farmers and fishermen	37.0	14.4	13.5
Unemployed persons	34.1	17.6	10.6
Others	38.0	16.6	13.7

case in the United States. An exception is the Japan Communist Party. However, even the Communists do not appeal exclusively to any particular class or classes for support in their movement although they believe in the idea and program of class struggle.

While the British Labor Party has definitely and formally passed under the control of the organized economic interest of the trade unions, the Japanese Socialist parties have not yet reached the same stage of development. The Socialists have been plagued constantly by dissensions, divisions, and vagaries of almost every conceivable sort, because of the heterogeneity of their membership and incessant, interminable clashes of views as well as of personalities. Since the ideas of the Socialists run the entire gamut of the ideological spectrum they have not been able to present a united front even for extremely short periods. There have been Marxists, Christian Socialists, and right-wing Socialists, to mention just a few. The cleavage which has developed between the Right and Left Socialists is so deep and wide that it seemed practically unbridgeable to many observers. However, they both have definitely urban working-class orientation.

Although the Right Socialist Party has made pronouncements to the effect that it rejects capitalism in order to win over the laboring classes, it has actually been working more towards "revised capitalism." It regards the Diet as the most important arena of struggle for political power and looks forward confidently to the day when it will again have a chance to form a government. It therefore looks for support wherever it can find it, big business and industry, small business, agriculture, labor, intellectuals. However, it is not a revolutionary party for it believes in nonviolent and gradual means.

The Left Socialists on the other hand are radical in their ideas and program and the party reflects in its crusading spirit the strong desire to realize the ideal of socialism. A socialist revolution is the goal, in the attainment of which members should not hesitate, if necessary, to sacrifice their seats in the Diet which is only one of the arenas of struggle. It is in the Left Socialist Party that the economic interests of the labor union receive the greatest attention and support because of the close working relationship with the General Council of Labor Unions. However, the labor unions do not have control of the party in spite of their constant efforts toward such an end.

Parliamentary Party Composition

A profile of the members of the Diet (based on the General Election of April, 1953) of the various parties with regard to age, education, and occupation or economic interests represented throws considerable light on the operational backdrop of the party system in the parliamentary sphere. Age is in Japanese politics an asset and can serve as an index of one's standing in a group. In the House of Representatives the age range was from 31 to 76 and there were two in each age. The average age was highest for the Hatoyama Liberals with 54.4, the Liberal Party next with 53.1, Progressive 51.6, Right Socialist 51.5 and the Left Socialist lowest with 48.1. The Left Socialists were the youngest group since exactly half of their members were in the 41–50 range and they had one-eighth of the entire membership in the 31–40 range. Only the Liberal Party had members over 70 years old although there were only 6 out of its 200 members.

The ten-year span 45–55 represented the highest concentration of combined party membership since 203 or 46.66 percent fell in this age group. However, the twenty-year span 41–60 must be regarded as the period of active participation of party men in the Diet, since 335 or slightly under 75 percent of the entire Diet membership fell in this age group.

Education

Educational background offers greater contrast between the various parties. In the Liberal Party there was no one with less than secondary education. College or university background was claimed by 170 and only 30 had secondary education. In the Hatoyama Liberal Party only 7 were with secondary education and the remaining 28 were college trained. Out of the 66 Right Socialist members only 7 were with secondary education, the remainder were college trained. The Left Socialist Party had the highest percentage of secondary school background, 14 persons out of 72 members or approximately 20 percent. The Progressive Party had 11 out of 76 members whose education did not go beyond secondary school. The over-all educational background was very high since in every party 80 percent or more of the members were college trained.[43]

The preponderance of Tokyo University graduates in the House of Representatives after the election of October 1, 1952, was amazing for there were at least 122 out of the 466 members or more than 1 out

[43] On the basis of the 1953 figures, the percentage of college-trained members of the House of Representatives in the different parties were as follows:

Liberal	85
Progressive	85
Right Socialist	84
Hatoyama Liberal	80
Left Socialist	80

of every 4.   This was 2.6 times the next largest group, Waseda University, which was represented by 47 members or 1 out of 10.   Even in the Socialist parties the Tokyo University group was the largest, with Waseda University coming second.[44]

There is a striking social disparity between the members of the Diet and the rank and file members of the party outside the parliament.   This is true of all the parties but is more clearly demonstrated in the conservative parties as can be seen by the educational background of the members who come from the upper and upper middle classes.   Within the parliamentary parties themselves, however, there is remarkable educational-level homogeneity.

As compared with the British Labor Party members of Parliament in 1950, of whom about 4 out of 11 or better than one-third had some kind of university education, the overwhelming majority of Socialist Party members of the Diet, to the extent of 80 to 84 percent, had some kind of college or university education.   This gives quite an intellectual flavor to the leadership in their activites.

Occupation

Occupational breakdown presents a difficult problem since accuracy in classification categories becomes almost impossible.   However, an analysis can provide a useful basis for understanding the bias of the Diet.   Table V represents the occupational distribution of the members of the House of Representatives who were elected in the General Election of April 19, 1953.

Several generalizations can be made from the figures given above. "Big business" has the biggest representation, taking up well over one-third of the entire House of Representatives membership on their side.   This compares with the conservative parties in which 3 in every

[44] The preponderance of Tokyo University graduates was maintained in the Diet as the result of the House of Representatives election of April 19, 1953, though there was a slight decrease in the total number.   The educational background of the newly elected members was as follows:

Tokyo University	113
Waseda University	50
Nippon University	34
Kyoto University	26
Chuo University	22
Other universities and colleges	141
Secondary education only	70
No mention	10
Total	466

TABLE V.   OCCUPATIONAL COMPOSITION OF THE HOUSE OF REPRE-
SENTATIVES ACCORDING TO POLITICAL PARTIES

Election of April 1953

	Liberal	Hatoyama	Progressive	S-R	S-L	Others	Total
Industry	38	11	18	8	5	2	82
Business	40	4	14	10	3	1	73
Banking	4	0	2	1	0	0	7
Lawyers	26	6	6	15	9	0	62
Party officials	6	2	9	16	11	5	49
Agriculture and fishery	23	3	10	4	7	3	50
Journalists, publishers, writers	14	3	5	1	6	2	31
Labor officials	0	0	0	3	12	0	15
Educators	5	2	1	2	3	1	14
Bureaucrats	14	0	0	0	0	0	14
Organization officials	3	0	2	3	5	2	13
Social work	6	0	2	1	1	1	11
Building and construction	9	0	1	0	0	0	10
Physicians	1	0	1	1	3	0	6
Business-firm employees	0	0	0	0	5	0	5
Religion	1	1	0	0	0	0	2
Artist	0	0	0	1	0	0	1
No gainful occupation	9	3	5	0	2	1	21
	199	35	76	66	72	18	466

8 M.P.'s were company directors. The lawyers comprise less than
12 percent of the House as compared with more than 50 percent of
the membership in the Congress of the United States.   This is a much
lower percentage than in the British House of Commons where in
1950 lawyers made up one-fourth of the Conservative M.P's and one-
seventh of the Labor M.P.'s.   Thus in general the legal profession
does not play as prominent a role in Japanese party affairs or in the
law-making process as it does in American government and politics.
However, in the Socialist parties the proportion of lawyers is much
higher than in the conservative parties.   In the Right Socialist Party
it is the largest single professional group although the party officials
outnumber the legal profession by only one.

12

Electing the Policy Makers

No political event can stand comparison with the election of the 467 *dramatis personae* of the Diet, which is looked upon as the greatest show in the land. It is not excelled by any political activity in its dramatic quality and the interest shown by the public. For the majority of the electorate, this affords the only opportunity to participate in the political process at the national level. National elections attract so much attention that they are given complete coverage by the press. On election day, newspapers and radio stations devote their entire energies to the election and little else receives much attention. They report the returns which come in practically by the minute. When the final returns are in, the leading newspapers with nation-wide circulation publish pictures of all the successful candidates together with their brief biographical sketches. The preoccupation of the newspapers with election campaigning is something which is difficult to visualize in countries where people have become accustomed to elections and take them in their stride. This can be attributed at least in part to the fact that the Japanese do not have such political spectacles as the presidential nominating conventions in which Americans participate quadrennially.

The Japanese people have had the longest experience of any Asian people in conducting their national affairs under a Western type of government. Their electoral experience actually dates back to 1890 when they chose their representatives for the national legislature for the first time.[1] Since the inception of parliamentary government Japan has held altogether twenty-seven general elections.[2]

As compared with that of the United States or Great Britain the number of elective officials in Japan is quite limited. Members of legislative bodies from the Diet on the national level down to the local assemblies on the township and village levels constitute by far the largest number of those elected. Among executive officials are the governors of the forty-six prefectures and the mayors of cities, towns, and villages. In addition, there is the referendum, a post-war innovation, which is employed to approve or disapprove the elected judges of the Supreme Court. Local elections as a rule do not attract nearly as much attention as the national elections, but the voting percentage is actually much higher.

THE RIGHT TO VOTE

In the first national election, held in July, 1890, to select representatives to the newly established Diet, there were only 450,000 eligible voters out of a total population of 40,000,000 or a little over 1.10 percent of the nation. The franchise was gradually extended by decreasing the tax qualification. In 1919, one year after Great Britain adopted universal suffrage, Japan's suffrage law lowered the tax qualification to three yen. This increased the number of eligible voters to more than 3,000,000. The greatest extension of the suffrage came with the enactment of the universal manhood suffrage law in 1925.[3] With the abolition of the tax qualification the number of eligible voters suddenly jumped to over 12,000,000, quadrupling the electorate. The number of voters increased thereafter in proportion to the natural increase in population. No appreciable increase in the percentage of voters took place in the next two decades.

Then came the final extension of the suffrage in 1946,[4] the year

---

[1] India held its first nationwide general election in 1952–53 since gaining independence. At the time she found it necessary to coin a word for "election," which was not in her vocabulary since it was unknown as a concept or practice. The Republic of the Philippines has had two general elections since independence, in 1949 and 1953.

[2] Twenty-one general elections were held under the old Constitution from 1890 to 1945 and six have been held since the end of World War II and under the new Constitution. The last one was on February 27, 1955.

[3] The amount of direct taxes paid as a requirement for voting was as follows: 1889, 15 yen; 1900, 10 yen; 1919, 3 yen; 1925 abolished.

[4] According to Government figures the percentage of eligible voters increased as follows:

after the end of World War II, when women were enfranchised, less than twenty years after British and American women had won the right to vote. Thus universal suffrage became an established fact even before the new Constitution went into effect on May 3, 1947.

The number of eligible voters at the time of the national election of February 27, 1955, was estimated to be close to 50,000,000. In the general election of April 19, 1953 there were 47,000,000[5] eligible voters out of a total population of 88,000,000. The percentage of voters had risen from 1.10 percent in 1890 to approximately 54 percent.[6] The number of eligible voters is increasing at the rate of about one million a year. An interesting fact in the composition of the Japanese electorate is the preponderance of women voters, one of the consequences of the Pacific War.[7]

QUALIFICATIONS FOR VOTING. The new Constitution confers on all Japanese citizens who have reached their twentieth birthday the right to vote. This represents a lowering of the age qualification by five years; along with Switzerland and West Germany it is the lowest age requirement for voting, except for the U.S.S.R.[8] Residence of three

Elections		Eligible Voters	Total Population	Percentage of Voters
July	1890	450,872	40,692,808 (est.)	1.10
May	1920	3,069,787	55,963,053	5.49
February	1928	12,405,056	59,763,822	20.76
April	1946	36,878,420	73,114,136	50.44

Jichicho Senkyobu, *Waga Kuni Senkyo no Hanashi*, p. 8.

[5] According to the figures of the Local Government Board the number of eligible voters on April 19, 1953, the date of the general election, was 47,090,167 of whom 19,976,369 were in urban areas and 27,113,798 were rural voters. See Jichicho Senkyobu, *Tokei ga Kataru Senkyo*, p. 3.

[6] This is approximately the percentage of the French electorate which numbers 25,000,000 out of a population of 45,000,000.

[7] Preponderance of women voters in the postwar elections is clearly revealed in the following figures prepared by the Government.

General Election	Men	Women	Total
22nd Apr. 10, 1946	16,320,752	20,557,668	36,878,420
23rd Apr. 25, 1947	19,577,766	21,329,727	40,907,493
24th Jan. 23, 1949	20,060,522	22,044,778	42,105,300
25th Oct. 1, 1952	22,312,761	25,459,823	46,772,584
26th Apr. 19, 1953	22,480,590	24,609,577	47,090,167

Jichicho Senkyobu, *Waga Kuni Senkyo no Hanashi*, p. 9 or *Shugiin Giin Sosenkyo Kekka Shirabe*, p. 5.

[8] In the United States, Great Britain, France, Italy, Belgium, Australia, and most other countries the age requirement is 21 years. In the Soviet Union, it is 18 years.

months, as opposed to the six months under the old law, in the election district in a city, town, or village is required. Under the old system literacy was a legal requirement for voting.[9] However, literacy was interpreted in the widest possible sense since the voter could write in any one of the several forms of writing, such as Chinese characters (*kanji*) or syllabary (*kana*), in either of the two styles and even in romanization as well as Korean writing. Under the present laws, there is no literacy requirement, and the extent of disability has been narrowed down. Those who are adjudged incompetent, those who have been sentenced to heavier than jail sentence, and those who are under conviction for election offenses are barred from voting.

A technical legal requirement of a voter is that he must be registered. Each year the local election supervision commission of the city, town, or village compiles by October 31 a list of eligible voters who had been residents in the election district for three months as of September 15. For a ten-day period, from November 5 to 15, the register is open for public inspection and on December 20 the voters' register is finalized. There is, however, provision for a supplementary list to be added after the basic register is finished.

QUALIFICATIONS FOR CANDIDACY. Only native-born citizens are eligible for membership in the Diet. Those who have acquired citizenship through naturalization are disqualified. The age requirement for candidacy is 25 years while the residence requirement of three months applies only to candidates for local assemblies. No residence requirement exists for candiates for the Diet whose members represent the nation as a whole and not geographical areas. This enables candidates to run from any election district in the country. The residence requirement is dispensed with also for candidates for prefectural governors and mayors of municipalities, towns, and villages since they are not primarily policy-making positions but administrative positions. This makes possible the securing of the best-qualified executives without being hampered by any residence requirement.

The Timing of a General Election

Constitutionally, the life of the Diet is set at four years. This has been so from the very inception of parliamentary government in 1890. In peacetime, a general election almost always occurs before the expiration of the four-year term.[10] Elections therefore do not come

---

[9] In the general election of April 19, 1953, there were 298,148 ballots cast by proxy for those who were completely or partially illiterate. See Jichicho Senkyobu, *Shugiin Giin Sosenkyo Kekka Shirabe*, p. 7.

[10] The fourth general election was held on September 1, 1894, a month after

with regularity as in the United States.   The first time that an election was held on the expiration of the Diet members' term of office was on August 10, 1902.

The Prime Minister has the authority to determine the timing of a general election.   He may decide on a sudden dissolution and call for a general election to reconstitute, reorganize, and strengthen his political power position.   Naturally, he would choose the time that would be most favorable to his own party, basing his action on an accurate reading of the signs of the times.   Sometimes, however, the Prime Minister is forced by the opposition into a position where he has no alternative but to call a general election.

The threat of dissolution is held as an effective club over the opposition inasmuch as an election is something which is dreaded by the members of parliament who do not care to go through one if it can possibly be avoided.   Even the most seasoned politicians do not relish the thought of standing an election after a dissolution.

The Constitution requires that a general election be held within thirty days of dissolution.   The decision regarding the actual date of the election is left to the Local Autonomy Board though it is formally announced by the government in an imperial rescript.   It has become the practice to hold a general election for the House of Representatives on a Sunday because it brings out a larger number of voters to the polls than on any other day.   The election of the members of the House of Councillors which does not normally bring out as many voters is held on a weekday as well as a Sunday.

Parliamentary Representation

There are 467 members in the House of Representatives who are the elected policy makers of the nearly 90,000,000 people.   This gives a member of the lower house a constituency of 190,000 persons, but an actual voting constituency of around 105,000 persons as compared with the 230,000 of a congressman in the United States.[11]

The administrative basis of representation is geographical with each prefecture comprising anywhere from one to seven election dis-

---

the outbreak of hostilities in the Sino-Japanese War.   The ninth general election took place on March 1, 1904, three weeks after the outbreak of the Russo-Japanese War.   During World War II, however, the Tojo Government extended the life of the Diet without going through a general election although the life of the lawmaking body had expired.

[11] A French deputy in the Assembly represents approximately 40,000 constituents while a British M.P. represents slightly less than 45,000 voters.

tricts depending on population.[12] The most populous, the Tokyo metropolitan prefecture, comprises seven districts with a total of twenty-seven seats. There are five prefectures which are populous enough to have five election districts each. The nine least populous prefectures each form a single election district. Each election district has from three to five seats in the Diet making it a medium sized unit.

Representation of the 250 members of the House of Councillors is on a different basis since the prefecture comprises a really large election district. Prefectures have anywhere from two to eight seats each for the 150 members who are elected geographically. The remaining 100 members are chosen from the nation at large.

Nomination of Candidates

Primaries are unknown in Japanese politics and have never been tried. Japan has nothing as colorful, dramatic, and spectacular as the party national conventions in the United States which enliven political activities quadrenially through the vicarious participation of the whole nation in the process of nominating presidential candidates. As in Great Britain, nominations are made informally, privately, and simply. Official party candidates are selected by the high command of the party and the decision is not arrived at in public meetings or conventions. This is in sharp contrast to the practice of American parties which have developed a variety of remarkably formal, public, and elaborate procedures for the selection of candidates.

As soon as a general election is called by the Government following dissolution of the Diet, political parties go into action. Party election headquarters are set up by the election high command which usually consists of anywhere from four to six members of the party's inner circle. These veteran election campaign strategists go over the candidates who have applied for official endorsement and financial support. The men who hand-pick candidates invariably include the party's secretary-general and business manager. The central office

---

[12] The 36 prefectures are divided as follows into 130 medium-sized election districts:

Election Districts	Number of Prefectures
1	9
2	18
3	9
4	4
5	5
7	1

of the party is in charge of election strategy and gives serious attention to finding suitable constituencies for aspiring and promising candidates who are selected. This system functions smoothly because of the prestige, influence, and authority of the central party organization and especially the power of the parliamentary party. Nomination contests are avoided without difficulty so that there is really no need for formal, public, or elaborate procedures to decide on the candidates.

The legal requirements for becoming a candidate are simple. Anyone who wishes to run for an elective office may file his candidacy papers with the head of the local election board, giving his name, legal residence (domicile), date of birth, occupation, as well as the political party or organization to which he belongs. This may be done by the candidate himself or by someone else in his behalf at any time from the official proclamation of the date of election until five, ten, fifteen, or twenty days before election day.[13] The papers must be accompanied by a deposit in varying amounts[14] as an indication of good faith. This is designed to discourage irresponsible candidature. The amount posted is returned if the candidate for the House of Representatives polls at least one fifth of the total number of votes cast, divided by the number of seats to be filled in the election district. The deposit is forfeited if the candidate declines to run or if he fails to poll the minimum number of votes specified by law.

ELECTION CAMPAIGNS

The government's formal announcement of the date of election signals the opening of the campaign. Candidates file their papers and the political parties swing into action. Unlike the United States

[13] The number of days before election varies with the electoral office being sought.

20 days for House of Councillors.

15 days for House of Representatives and prefectural governors.

10 days for mayors of municipalities and prefectural and municipal assemblymen.

5 days for town and village mayors and assemblymen.

[14] The amounts to be posted are as follows:

100,000 yen for the House of Representatives, House of Councillors, and prefectural governors.

25,000 yen for mayors of municipalities.

20,000 yen for prefectural assemblymen.

10,000 yen for municipal assemblymen.

None for town and village mayors and assemblymen.

where an election campaign can last more than three months, the period of electioneering in Japan is approximately three weeks. However, precampaign activities are becoming an accepted part of the politician's program. Public addresses on current issues and meetings to report the activities in the Diet are scheduled by members of the Diet to keep themselves before the constituents. Amazing ingenuity is exhibited by imaginative politicians who manage to engage in precampaign activities without actually violating the law. These tactics include the sending of telegrams back home to the constituents immediately upon the dissolution of the Diet, praying for their health and urging them on to "greater efforts." Postcards are sent with the season's greetings with the postscript explaining that the briefness of the Diet precluded the achievement of anticipated results and promising greater efforts in the future. Some distribute autographed photographs with season's greetings and best wishes while others prefer informal get-togethers at teahouses.[15]

It has become increasingly difficult to distinguish clearly between the year-round fence-mending activities of the members of the Diet and their electioneering, except perhaps that the latter is characterized by the intensity and the directness of the bid for votes. In the United States, a Congressional campaign could, in effect, be launched as early as fifteen months before election through the use of non-political devices.[16] Even in Japan politicians who are alert and clever manage to launch their campaign months in advance without running afoul of the law.[17]

The campaign is directed from the candidates' election headquarters which cannot exceed the maximum of five allowed by law. Normally only one is permitted to each candidate for the House of Representatives, House of Councillors, and prefectural governors. In the case of candidates for the House of Councillors running on a national ballot, up to fifteen election headquarters may be allowed. A candidate is required to have a campaign manager as well as a financial agent who assumes the responsibility of handling campaign funds and submitting a report of election expenditures to the government.

The Prime Minister, as party leader, stumps the country to help elect as many members of his party as possible since his own position depends upon the outcome of the election. In addition to the campaigning for their own reelection, members of the cabinet are

---

[15] *Asahi*, March 22, 1953.

[16] *New York Times* Magazine section, August 16, 1953.

[17] See Mori Naohiro, "Tsuji Masanobu wa kondo mo doshite tosen shita ka," *Chuo Koron*, June, 1953, pp. 167–172.

drafted to do their full stint for the party. College students sign up and participate as speakers for the parties in behalf of the candidates to add youthful zest to the campaign. Since it is impossible for the candidates and their supporters to speak in every little hamlet and village in the election district, resort to tape recordings has become quite common since they were first used in the election of October, 1952. Automobiles equipped with loud-speakers have become virtually standard equipment for candidates.

Campaign techniques vary a great deal from candidate to candidate. However, the successful candidates invariably exploit their popularity to the fullest extent, advocate ideas and issues with strong emotional appeal, employ dramatic effect to the greatest advantage, present themselves as selfless heroes championing the cause of the people, and give hope and confidence to the neglected and discouraged constituents.

Previous experience in any position of leadership is exploited to the fullest extent. Service in the local assemblies gives the prestige necessary to make the candidates' campaign more successful, especially if they have made the right contacts with the local political bigwigs. However, the percentage of those who go into national politics from local political activities is probably not nearly as high as in the United States.

The management of elections is in the hands of the Election Department of the Local Autonomy Board of the Prime Minister's Office. Efforts are made by this body to encourage voting and discourage nonvoting as well as election violations. In its efforts to give moral and material support to the election supervision commissions throughout the country, it mobilizes women and youth organizations, distributes handbills and posters using airplanes and helicopters, and makes broadcasts over radio. At the same time, it bombards voters with slogans and admonitions using every conceivable means of communication.

In order to insure fairness and equality of opportunity to the candidates during the election campaign, the government makes certain facilities available to them without charge. Each candidate is given free time over the network of the Japan Broadcasting Corporation to present a recording of his five-minute campaign speech for three separate broadcasts. In addition he is allowed a recorded broadcast over the radio ten times to present to the voters of his district his name, age, party affiliation and biographical, educational, and professional background and political views. No additional radio broadcasts are allowed beyond those furnished gratis by the government.

Candidates are required to participate in compulsory joint meetings held under the sponsorship of the local election supervision commission. This is a further effort to make the political views of the candidates known to the constituents. One of these meeting is required for cities, towns, and villages, for every 40,000 in the cities and for every 4,000 in towns and village. No more than sixty individual campaign speeches may be given during the period.

Each candidate for the Diet and prefectual governorship is entitled by law to have a 1500-word public statement, which includes his name, party, biographical data, and political views, published and distributed in the form of an election bulletin to all the constituents in his election district by the Prefectural Election Supervision Commission. He is also entitled to 10,000 government postal cards[18] free of charge, a 2″ x 2½″ newspaper advertisement of candidacy usually with a picture, 2,000 posters,[19] large stands with his name and party displayed at not less than three nor more than five places where they can be easily seen by the public, 1,200 tabloid-type posters to be used in notifying the public of his campaign speeches, fifteen railroad and bus passes for the duration of the campaign, and the use of a school or public hall for a campaign meeting free of charge once. All these are provided at government expense.

Certain legal restrictions are imposed on electioneering with regard to personnel, methods of campaigning, and expenditures. Officials who help to administer elections, judges, procurators, police and tax officials, and the Bureau of Audit officials are not allowed to take part in election campaigns. Nor can minors, civil service officials, and school teachers engage in political activities. Specific actions are forbidden such as door-to-door soliciting of votes, circulating and obtaining signatures on petitions, offering food, drink, or money, and holding parades and demonstrations. Although face-to-face personal individual vote soliciting is illegal, the use of the telephone for electioneering is unrestricted. The use of loud-speakers to announce political meetings and to publicize the names of the candidate as well as the parties is banned except for authorized vehicles or boats used exclusively for campaign purposes and so licensed. In their eagerness to make possible an inexpensive election, the lawmakers have imposed a number of restrictions on electioneering which cramp the style of the politicians without necessarily producing economy of expenditures.

Money and face are regarded as the two indispensable ingredients

18 50,000 for House of Councillors, nation at large.
19 20,000 for House of Councillors, nation at large.

of success in an election campaign. Those with money can conduct a vigorous campaign by enlisting the support of influential local leaders in their election districts, frequently employing assemblymen and mayors as campaign managers, workers, and supporters in getting out the votes. For those whose funds are limited, it becomes necessary to depend on their own physical stamina to stump their district, attend meetings of all sorts, and make speeches in order to make themselves well known and popular among the voters. It is no secret that many politicians operate on the thin borderline between legality and illegality in conducting their election campaigns.

Party leaders go on nation-wide campaign tours to help the party's candidates. As in the case with election campaigns everywhere, speeches are all too frequently characterized by clichés, balderdash, gibberish, double talk, and glittering generalities. A generous fare of clichés is fed the public and aptly-phrased slogans are kept before the voters throughout the campaign. Most political speeches tend to be very abstract and are only remotely, if at all, related to the realities of everyday life. Although attendance at political gatherings has been increasing, campaign speeches seem to attract middle-aged and older voters while young voters have not been showing a great deal of interest.

Campaign strategy is mapped out in a way calculated to produce the maximum results in the brief three- to four-week period. During the early and middle stages voters are inclined to, and actually do, exercise reason and judgment in listening to the election propaganda. In the final stage, however, the voters can easily be swept off their feet by the impassioned appeals of the campaign. Propaganda efforts are therefore intensified greatly and ideas are dinned into the ears of the voters by the repetitious use of slogans while maximum use is made of images and stereotypes. Appeals are made to the senses rather than to reason in the last-minute effort to capture the "floating votes."[20]

BALLOTING AND COUNTING. More than forty-three thousand polling places open simultaneously throughout the nation at 7 a.m. with fireworks signalling the beginning of balloting. The election of the members of the House of Representatives is held on a Sunday. However, if the election comes on a weekday, as does that of the House of Councillors, government offices, business houses, banks, and other places of work permit the voters to appear at work late to give them the necessary time to cast their votes.

The polling place is more often than not a school building and the voting procedure is very simple. After the voter's registration

---

[20] The Liberal Party carried out such a strategy in the general election of April 19, 1953. See "Rokunin de tama erabi," *Asahi*, March 26, 1953.

is verified, he is handed the official ballot which he takes to the booth and writes in the name of the single candidate of his choice and drops it in a ballot box in the presence of election watchers. The physically disabled and the blind are given assistance in voting. No voting machines have been introduced as yet. Even the printed ballot still remains to be tried out. Absentee voting is provided for those whose occupations or travels keep them away from their polling places as well as for those who are ill or incapacitated. In out-of-the-way places, such as remote islands, election day is moved up several days in order to permit the delivery of the ballot boxes to a central counting place.

After the polling places are closed, ballot boxes are sealed and taken to counting places—there are approximately 10,700—where they are opened in the presence of the counting overseer and witnesses. On a huge table the ballots are emptied and thoroughly mixed. Votes received by the candidates are read off in the presence of witnesses and voter-observers. Then they are counted and tied together in bundles of fifty and verified by the counting overseer. The work of counting is finished when the report of the counting is prepared. The ballots are then put back into the boxes and sealed and preserved for the term of office of the newly elected Diet. This is done to make the ballots available for recount in case there should be litigation over the election results.

In the process of counting the ballots a certain percentage is thrown out as invalid. These include ones cast on wrong ballots, and those with more than one candidate or names of persons who are not candidates, illegible or unrecognizable names, wrong characters, no names, and unnecessary remarks. In the House of Councillors election of April, 1953, as much as 8 percent of the total votes cast in the Tokyo metropolitan prefecture was invalidated.[21]

A vacancy resulting from resignation or death before a member has taken seat is usually filled without calling a new election except when absolutely necessary. The candidate with the next highest vote in the election is moved up into the vacancy.

In the general election of April, 1953, the successful candidates polled anywhere from 26,057 to 100,610 votes. Nearly 40 percent of them were elected by votes of between 40,000 and 50,000.[22] The largest number of votes captured was the Hatoyama Ichiro who received 100,610 votes. In the general election of February 27, 1955,

[21] In Nagano and Akita prefectures the percentage was higher, with 10 percent. In Kumamoto prefecture it was 9 percent.
[22] Kawarada Kakichi, a Liberal and former cabinet minister, was elected the last man in the five-seat Second District of Fukushima prefecture with 26,057 votes.

Hatoyama was elected by a grand total of 149,541 votes, the largest number ever garnered by a Diet candidate in the sixty-five-year history of parliamentary government.

Election Expenditures

There is no doubt that the most difficult and least effectively regulated aspect of the election laws is that pertaining to expenditures. The Political Fund-Regulating Law which is designed to prevent corrupt practices has not been altogether successful, although it requires the reporting of political donations and expenditures by the parties and candidates.

In the general election of October, 1952, the legal limit on campaign expenditures was set at between 300,000 and 400,000 yen.[23] Yet the actual minimum expenditure was something like 700,000 yen which was not enough to elect a candidate. Successful candidates actually had to spend 20,000,000 yen (about $55,555).[24] Maximum election expenditures allowed by law as amended in 1952 was 4 yen multiplied by the number obtained by dividing the number of registered voters by the number of seats in the election district. However, the enforcement of such limitation has been impossible. That election campaigns turn out to be expensive affairs can be seen by the fact that the cost to the candidates alone of the general election of October 1, 1952, the first one to be held since the regaining of independence, was estimated to be 8 billion yen[25] ($22,200,000 plus).

HOW CAMPAIGN FUNDS ARE RAISED AND DISBURSED. It is well known that business firms and economic organizations[26] constitute the major source of campaign funds of the political parties. Economic interests work out carefully their program of political contributions and see to it that most if not all of the political parties receive their contributions. This is to make certain that no matter which party wins they are not left out in the cold politically. By not putting all the eggs in one basket, the financial world as a whole has been able to insure its position as the "perennial government party" which never loses. In the distribution of political contributions preferences are shown by business interests for certain parties largely because of existing personal relationships rather than their policy orientation.

[23] At the current rate of exchange 360 yen equals one dollar.

[24] This gave rise to the expression in politics "nitō ichiraku" meaning 20,000,-000 will insure election while ¥10,000,000 defeat." See *Nippon Times* editorial, June 12, 1952.

[25] *Nippon Times*, April 6, 1953, p. 3.

[26] See Chapter X.

There are several ways in which the funds are given by business firms and organizations. They may go to the party treasury, to the members of the party's inner circle, or to the candidate directly. The Political Fund-Regulating Law of 1948 requires that the party treasurer report regularly, three times annually, the receipts and expenditures to the election supervision commission. Contributions of more than 500 yen by individuals and 1,000 yen by organizations are reported with the names and addresses of the donors. However, what is reported is the amount received openly by the party treasury and does not include the money given directly to the candidates or to the individual members of the party's high command but not turned over to the treasury. What this proves is the existence of a sizeable war chest that is not accounted for and is known as "unrecorded" funds.

There is a pattern which parties follow in the distribution of campaign funds. Those who are officially approved as party candidates receive endorsement fees along with additional campaign funds. In addition most candidates manage to get some money from their "bosses." However, all this is still inadequate to meet necessary expenses. Candidates therefore endeavor to obtain additional campaign money on their own, usually by going directly to business firms. In the final stages of the campaign, the parties provide additional funds to those candidates whose election appears doubtful but still with fairly good chances of winning.

VOTING BEHAVIOR

It is only recently that the voting behavior of the Japanese people has become a subject of study. Consequently, it is still too soon for anyone to attempt a definitive analysis particularly in the absence of adequate studies. However, some tentative conclusions can be safely attempted on the basis of what has been observed so far. There is one aspect in which a definitive conclusion seems warranted. This is in the matter of voting percentage for which reliable and accurate data can be found. On the basis of postwar experience, it seems quite reasonable to assume that voting percentage will remain pretty much where it is at present, that is, at about 75 percent of the eligible voters in general elections. The highest percentage was actually achieved in the first general election held on July 1, 1890, when 423,-400 out of 450,852 eligible voters cast their votes, giving a record of 93.91 percent. It is extremely unlikely that such a high voting percentage will ever be achieved again. The percentage has declined steadily since then as can be seen by the official figures compiled by the government.[27]

Statistics show that the voting percentage of male voters has been consistently higher than that of women.[27] While it is too soon to come to a definite conclusion, it is not unlikely that the voting percentage of women will lag slightly behind that of men until the social and economic position of women changes considerably. Not only has the voting percentage of women been lower than that of men but the actual number of those voting has been lower except for the first postwar general election of April 10, 1946, which was the first time women voted in Japan.[28] This has been the case in spite of the fact

[27] Voting Percentage in General Elections:

General Elections	Eligible Voters	Those Voting	Voting Percentage
1st　July　1, 1890	450,852	423,400	93.91
7th　Aug. 10, 1902	982,868	868,772	88.39
14th　May 10, 1920	3,064,590	2,657,870	86.73
16th　Feb. 20, 1928	12,405,056	9,968,162	80.36
17th　Feb. 20, 1930	12,651,785	10,544,128	83.34
18th　Feb. 20, 1932	12,014,963	9,813,542	81.68
19th　Feb. 20, 1936	14,303,780	11,249,662	78.65
20th　Apr. 30, 1937	14,074,888	10,317,789	73.31
21st　Apr. 30, 1942	14,594,287	12,137,228	83.16
22nd　Apr. 10, 1946	36,878,420	26,582,175	72.08
23rd　Apr. 25, 1947	40,907,493	27,797,748	67.95
24th　Jan. 23, 1949	42,105,300	31,175,895	74.04
25th　Oct.　1, 1952	46,772,584	35,749,723	76.43
26th　Apr. 19, 1953	47,090,167	34,948,008	74.22
27th　Feb. 27, 1955	49,235,242	37,014,332	75.84

Jichicho Senkyobu, *Shugiin Giin Sosenkyo Kekka Shirabe,* 1954, p. 34.

[27] A Comparison of Voting Percentage:

General Elections	Male	Female	Difference
April 10, 1946	78.52	66.97	11.55
April 25, 1947	74.87	61.60	13.27
Jan. 23, 1949	80.74	67.95	12.79
Oct.　1, 1952	80.46	72.76	7.70
April 19, 1953	78.35	70.44	7.91

Jichicho Senkyobu, *Shugiin Giin Senkyo Kekka Shirabe,* 1954, p. 5.

[28] The actual number of those voting for the five postwar general elections was as follows:

	Male	Female	Male over Female
April 10, 1946	12,814,875	13,767,300	−952,425
April 25, 1947	14,658,498	13,139,250	1,519,248
Jan. 23, 1949	16,196,844	14,979,051	1,219,793
Oct.　1, 1952	17,953,553	17,796,170	157,383
April 19, 1953	17,613,338	17,334,670	278,668

Jichicho Senkyobu, *Shugiin Senkyo Kekka Shirabe* (1954), p. 5.

that there have been more eligible women voters in every one of these elections.

As between urban and rural areas, the latter has shown a much higher voting percentage, as can be seen by the following comparison for the general election of October, 1953:

Urban Prefectures		Rural Prefectures	
Osaka	60.0	Saga	83.7
Kyoto	61.0	Tottori	83.7
Tokyo	61.8	Shimane	86.4
Hyogo	69.2	Gumma	87.4
Kanagawa	69.9	Yamagata	87.4

Since greater interest is shown in local elections, the voting percentage is noticeably higher than in national elections. In the elections of April 23, 1951, approximately 91 percent of the nation's eligible voters went to the polls to elect mayors and assemblymen in the municipalities, towns, and villages, establishing an all-time record for heavy voting.[28a] In three rural prefectures, Gumma, Tottori, and Yamanashi, there was an amazing turnout of 97 percent while in 38 other prefectures it was over 90 percent.

There is no doubt that there is a higher percentage of nonvoting among those who are having a difficult time in making a living, for not only do they lack adequate knowledge of candidates and political issues but also find they can ill afford even the time required for voting. It is also these same people who are more vulnerable to outside pressure, suggestions, and "vote buying."[29]

The political education and awareness of the voter in Japan has not yet reached the level of maturity found in the democratic nations of the West. Political consciousness and political action of the voter exists only within the framework of the nondemocratic social relationships of the community. His political as well as his social behavior is regulated, circumscribed, and restricted by the numerous obligations under which he lives. The result is that, even if he has his own political convictions, seldom does he act as an individualist.

How Choices Are Made

There is no question but that voters' choices are influenced, conditioned, and determined to some extent by their social status, income, family, occupation, religious affiliation, geographic location, as well as a good many other factors. However, no studies have yet been

[28a] *New York Times* April 24, 1951, and 1952 *Americana Annual,* Section on Japan.

[29] "Senkyo to fujinso wo miru." *Asahi,* Evening Edition, April 7, 1953.

made to determine just how they influence the voters or how they are actually reflected in the results of voting.

It is generally accepted that voters are more likely to vote for the familiar name and face and for the incumbent unless there is a strong and positive revulsion against the incumbent on the basis of his unsavory record or behavior coupled with a strong conviction that change is needed. Human nature prefers the familiar to the unfamiliar and untried. Furthermore affection or fondness can more easily be fixed on someone familiar. Change for the sake of change alone is not welcome to people who put a high value on stability and harmony.

Japanese voters are invariably attracted to name and face so that an obscure candidate stands a very small chance of winning even if he is able to put forth a worth-while political program.[30] This proclivity contributes to the political success of "local boys" who have made good as officials and have become the pride of the community. For these home-town heroes, the voters do not hesitate to cross their party line to vote. This explains in part why so many former officials, especially ex-cabinet ministers, are so successful in getting elected to the Diet. Moreover, experiences as cabinet ministers and members of the Diet put them in close touch with the bureaucratic structure, making them thoroughly familiar with the ropes and enabling them to take better care of the interests and needs of the constituents and constituencies by securing grants, subsidies, and loans.[31]

A feature of Japanese political behavior which reflects their voting psychology is their preference for a winner. This is by no means peculiar to the Japanese but it seems to be stronger than in other countries largely because of their conscious effort not to be out of step with the consensus of the community. It is not merely the desire to bet on the winner that makes the voter try to vote for a candidate who is likely to win. The average voter may not be vitally interested in the issues involved and yet he would like to feel that he was right in his choice. Furthermore, he hates to see his vote wasted on any candidate who has little chance of success. This is the reason why newspapers play such an important part in influencing the out-

[30] One of the major causes of the defeat suffered by the Japan Communist Party in the general election of October, 1952, was the fact that they simply could not put up candidates whose names were well known to the public because their prominent leaders had been driven underground or out of the country.

[31] See *Sekai*, December, 1952, p. 51.

come of an election. Japanese newspapers make a practice of forecasting election results on the eve of an election as part of their "public service." They classify candidates into such categories as those whose election appears to be certain, those whose election is possible, and those who are likely to be defeated and whose chances are very slim, if not hopeless. Such predictions seem to have very definite bearing on the success or failure of particular candidates as borne out by the fact that the forecasts have been surprisingly accurate.

Newspapers very likely would not have such influence if it were not for the fact that there is a rather large percentage of "floating votes." Not a few voters believe that the final choice of a candidate should be made at the polls, at the very last minute. One serious study points out that not an inconsiderable number of voters change their minds two or three times on their final choices between the time they enter the building where the voting booth is located and the actual casting of the ballot.[32] The influence of newspapers on women seems to be far greater than on men for the simple reason that many of them have little or no opportunity to discuss with others the bearing of politics on everyday life. It is with the purpose of capturing these "floating votes" that political parties intensify their efforts during the final lap of the electoral race. More money is spent toward the end of the campaign when the effectiveness of money is thought to be far greater than at any other time.

The question as to when voters actually make their choices has not yet been explored adequately. According to one study,[33] 30 percent of the laborers as well as voters in general have their minds made up within a week of election day. Even before the date of general election had been announced 28 percent of the laborers and 22 percent of the voters in general had reached their decisions as to whom they would vote for. It has been found that in the national elections for members of the House of Representatives and House of Councillors, a large proportion of the votes goes to radical party candidates because of the greater scope as well as the abstractness of the political issues involved.[34] In local elections, it is the reverse. The conservative vote predominates since the issues are concrete and direct pressure is brought to bear upon the voters by local political bosses.

---

[32] Kyodo Kenkyu, "Kokumin seikatsu to seiji ishiki," *Kaizo*, June, 1953, p. 86 ff.

[33] Nobushige Ukai, "Toshi kōjō rōdōsha no tōhyō kōdō," *Sekai*, December, 1952, p. 92.

[34] Kyodo Kenkyu, "Kokumin seikatsu to seiji ishiki," *Kaizo*, June, 1953, pp. 88, 91.

Politicians carry on their election campaigns on the assumption that women voters by and large follow their husbands or their fathers in their choice of candidates. It is generally believed that not more than 10 percent of the women actually make up their own minds and vote on the basis of their own judgment.

In rural areas the existence of primary social groups gives political bosses an effective means of mass control. People usually try to ascertain the majority opinion before they vote in order not to find themselves in a minority position. The political boss takes advantage of the strong desire to vote in conformity with the majority opinion in the community and offers "advice" on important political issues.[35] Members of the community usually do not dare violate the instructions of the powerful local boss especially in the rural areas, for retribution in the form of social ostracism can be swift for those individuals who act on their own judgment in disregard of the pattern of action laid down by the boss.[36] Although the influence of the old type of boss is far from gone, it is definitely on the decline.

It is quite likely that the farm worker or the tenant farmer would vote according to the wish of the employer or the landlord out of a strong sense of obligation.[37] Voting to a poor farmer who has to go to his landlord to borrow money to pay his taxes can mean no more than keeping a promise made to his benefactor and creditor. Quite frequently the employers and landlords make it a point to teach the farm hands and tenants the names of the candidates they favor, telling them that they have a way of finding out after election if they have actually voted for the ones suggested.

It has been noted that the influence of nonpolitical, private social groups was unexpectedly great in the election of October 1, 1952.[38] An interesting behavior reflected in an election was the support which many sympathetic voters gave those who missed being elected in the previous general election by the narrowest margin.[39]

[35] Nobushige Ukai, "Japanese Election Results Reconsidered," *Pacific Affairs*, June, 1953, p. 144.

[36] *Ibid.*, p. 145. There was a notorious case in Shizuoka prefecture in which the whole village of Ueno imposed social ostracism on the family of Ishikawa Satsuki, a high school girl, who reported an irregularity in the village election of October 1, 1952, involving the use of dummy ballots by a political boss.

[37] Kyodo Kenkyu, "Kokumin seikatsu to seiji ishiki," *Kaizo*, June, 1953, pp. 85–86.

[38] Royama Masamichi, "Seiji ishiki wa dō hyomei sareta ka," *Sekai*, December, 1952, p. 91.

[39] Kyodo Kenkyu, "Kokumin seikatsu to seiji ishiki," *Kaizo*, June, 1953, pp. 85–86.

ELECTION IRREGULARITIES

Election violations have been quite common in Japanese politics. Although this condition is undoubtedly attributable partly to the election law in force, the traditional social ideas, attitudes, and habits constitute the basic cause of offenses. By far the most serious as well as numerous offense is vote-buying with all its ramifications. In the April, 1951, election well over 80 percent of the violations fell in this category. The offering, receiving, and even promising of benefits, positions, employment, gifts of money and goods, entertainment, and refreshments for the purpose of electing or preventing the election of candidates constitute a typical vote-buying violation.[40] Another form is influencing constituents by promising in campaign speeches such public works as will benefit the locality.

Vote-buying through election brokers or by means of bribery has existed from the very outset of parliamentary government in Japan. Even the government has been guilty in the past of interfering in the elections in its own behalf almost as a matter of course, by a combination of intimidation and bribery. However, since the end of World War II this practice has disappeared completely. What still remains is the professional election broker whose illegal activity is to deliver votes and help to elect a candidate for a consideration. It is his existence which encourages corruption on the part of the individual voter and prevents the effective clean-up that is urgently needed in elections. Fraudulent registration, intimidation, violence, and actual interference with the freedom of election occur at every election but do not constitute the really serious violations.

There is a form of election violation in Japanese politics which does not come within the purview of the Corrupt Practices Act but is nonetheless a violation in spirit if not in form. There have been several instances, particularly in the election of October, 1952, of former and incumbent officials of the administrative departments such as the Finance, Agriculture and Forestry, and Railway ministries winning elections by utilizing the organization of the administrative agencies in their election campaigns.

Many candidates, by careful planning of precampaign activities, can carry on effective long-range electioneering by creating good

[40] In the mayoralty campaign in the city of Kawaguchi, Saitama prefecture not far from Tokyo, leaders of the local Women's Association (Fujinkai) made house-to-house calls and left money, food, cloth, and other items to influence the voters. See "Senkyo to fujinso no ugoki wo miru," *Asahi*, Evening Edition, April 6, 1953.

will and even manage to "buy votes" not with cash or directly but indirectly by presenting the voters with free luncheons, free rides, theater tickets, partially paid tours or pilgrimages and similar inexpensive favors.[41]

ELECTORAL REFORM. Electoral reforms with a view to establishing clean elections have been the perennial issue and problem of Japanese politics. Perhaps no law has undergone so many revisions as the election law and yet the problem of political corruption is still not anywhere near solution. Movements for clean elections have been carried on continuously since before World War II. In the forefront of the movement to achieve clean and fair election, is the League for Clean Elections (Komei Senkyo Remmei), which is made up of thirty-four cooperating organizations representing various interests and activities.[41a] In many respects Japan's problems are highly reminiscent of the corruption which obtained in England before the Reform Bill of 1832 was enacted when "bribery and corruption unblushingly controlled elections particularly in the boroughs."[42]

Corruption stems from several causes or conditions. One of them is the expensiveness of election campaigns. The weakness of the nation's economy causes business and industry to rely heavily upon loans and subsidies from the Government. Moreover, too often business and industry attempt to and succeed in exploiting governmental power for their own profit. Unless these conditions change, reforms in electoral laws in themselves will be of little avail.

Enactment of better election laws will help but the possibilities are that, however perfect or efficacious the legislation regulating elections may be, there will undoubtedly be politicians coming up with ingenious ways of circumventing some of the provisions of the law. There will also be a certain amount, perhaps an irreducible minimum, of financial transactions made under cover.[43]

---

[41] Nobushige Ukai, "Japanese Election Results Reconsidered," *Pacific Affairs,* June, 1953, p. 144.

[41a] See Komei Senkyo Remmei, *Komei Senkyo no Undo Jigyo Gaiyo* (1952).

[42] From two to twenty guineas per vote were figures commonly paid and there are innumerable stories of how the contemporary laws against bribery were circumvented. Porritt, *The Unreformed House of Commons,* p. 358.

[43] Paul R. Kent states in his *Political Behavior* (p. 226) that "in every campaign, whether national or state, there are invariably and inevitably certain financial transactions made under cover. There always have been and there probably always will be. No law has yet been devised that has stopped it. None is likely to be. Both sides do it. Both have to."

13

The Bureaucracy
in the Japanese Scheme

One of the interesting though by no means unexpected postwar developments is the fact that the bureaucracy emerged from defeat and the period of occupation not only unscathed and undaunted but with power and prestige greatly enhanced. This has come about in spite of the fact that the intent of the Constitution is distinctly anti-bureaucratic. As a matter of fact in Article 15 it actually repudiates the spirit of both the bureaucratic system and the bureaucrat. Yet the authoritarian tradition of centuries is still very much in evidence and the strengthening of executive power under the new Constitution has helped to enhance the position of prestige of the government official.

There has been such a tremendous expansion in the scope of governmental activities in the last several decades that only those who deal with them from day to day over a long period of time can hope to be familiar with their ramifications. The business of government has become much too complex for amateurs. This has led to an increasing dependence of the legislative branch as well as the government on the civil service. It has also led to the increase in the size of the civil service necessary for carrying on the expanded administrative functions. This development has not been viewed with equanimity in some quarters.[1]

---

[1] The newspaper *Asahi,* on December 19, 1953, advocated a drastic reform of the nation's bureaucratic system under the heading "National Ruin by the Bureaucracy is Not Impossible." Professor Suzuki Yasuzo attributes the ineffectiveness and confusion of Japanese politics to the bureaucracy.

The enormity and complexity of the government's administrative machinery can be gathered from the fact that in 1954 a force of 2,910,000 government workers was required to man the operations. Of these 1,540,000 were in national administration while 1,370,000 were in prefectural, town, and village administration.[2] The speed with which expansion in the size of the bureaucracy has taken place in the twenty years between 1931 and 1951 is startling, for on the national level it has been almost trebled while on the local level it has increased nearly fifteen fold as follows:

	National	Prefectural and Local
1931	591,000	90,000
1951	1,402,000	1,302,000

Governmental policies have brought about economic concentration which in turn has accelerated bureaucratization not only of government but of business as well. The facilitating of economic development for the nation by the government has had the effect of causing the growth of industrial concentration and administrative apparatus by proliferation.

In the modern state the bureaucracy occupies a strategic position[3] as its administrative instrument for the executive branch of government normally wields such power as is entrusted to it by the ruling class and often a little more. Bureaucracy is thus a body of government officials organized to execute the policy directives handed down from above and legally has no autonomous power of its own. Although much of the work it performs belongs in the category of routine which can be disposed of in accordance with existing rules and regulations, it frequently formulates policy or at least plays a part in the final crystallization of policy on the departmental and cabinet level as well as in the Diet. But more important perhaps is the fact that the bureaucracy not infrequently carries out the policy without any real control by either the Diet or the executive department.

While it is generally assumed that administration necessarily begins where politics leaves off and that policy determination is not considered the province of the bureaucracy, Japanese experience underscores the importance of the executive. Initiative in policy making

[2] Koga Juzo, "Yakunin no kuni Nihon no jittai," *Jitsugyo no Nihon*, March, 1954, p. 46.

[3] Yoshimura Tadashi, *Gendai Seiji ni Okeru Kanryo no Chii* (1950) gives a picture of the role the bureaucracy plays in Japanese politics.

has always been in the hands of the executive from the very beginning of the Japanese political system. It has been a tradition. The bureaucracy today is the main source of policy-making initiative and the chief function of the legislative branch has become one of encouraging or discouraging, publicizing, and approving or disapproving policy which springs from the agencies of administration. In order to see the important role of the bureaucracy in Japan's political structure, it is necessary to view hastily its historical development.

HISTORICAL BACKGROUND OF JAPANESE BUREAUCRACY

Until the seventh century A.D. Japan was without anything which even resembled a bureaucratic system. The patriarchal clan system in the meantime had produced abuses and conditions which threatened to upset the existing power structure and particularly the emperor system. To correct the situation, the leaders turned for inspiration to China whose civilization at the time was perhaps the most advanced in the world. These Japanese leaders were convinced that China's greatness and power under the T'ang dynasty (618–906) were the product of her highly developed administrative system. Naturally, China was taken as the model for the institutional framework of Japanese bureaucracy. Court ranks were adopted along with the civil service examination system and the administrative and penal codes.

Although the Japanese were at first dazzled by the brilliance of Chinese culture and became enamored of Chinese ideas and institutions, their eclecticism by and large prevented them from indulging in excesses. While they emulated Chinese achievements, they did not blindly imitate everything. Rather, they consciously adopted and adapted Chinese political ideas and institutions to suit their needs as well as peculiar conditions and proclivities. The civil service system for example was used to support and strengthen the new urban court aristocracy which formed the elite rather than to destroy it as was done in China. In the administration of the system, the scions of the aristocracy were given preferential treatment while commoners were for practical purposes excluded.

In adopting the Chinese bureaucratic system, the Japanese took its philosophical and ideological basis which was Confucianism and introduced modifications. They rejected the idea of revolution and subordinated filial piety to loyalty toward the sovereign. The borrowing of the Chinese bureaucratic system was motivated by the urgent need for a strong centralized administration with the emperor at the apex of the structure and supported by the urban aristocracy.

In China the civil service had been instituted to destroy the old power structure based on the aristocracy whereas in Japan it was used to strengthen the political structure dominated by the aristocracy. For well over five centuries, until the establishment of feudalism, the administration of national affairs was in the hands of a civilian aristocratic bureaucracy which operated out of the imperial court at the national capital. It is this traditional background which was reflected in the civil service system of Japan from the 1870's to the end of World War II.

The age of feudalism which historically constitutes the longest segment of Japan's development lasted nearly seven centuries. The administrative system which developed under feudalism was dominated by the military and the hierarchical organization was based on a strong bond of fealty existing between the lord and vassal. What really obtained was not strictly speaking a civil service system but a feudal bureaucracy based on status, and official posts were hereditary. However, the age of feudalism produced mutations and permutations partly as the result of the admixture and merger of Chinese ideas and practices with the indigenous practices.

By the seventeenth and eighteenth centuries the military bureaucracy had become a structure which was ordered by considerations of status, and key administrative positions, particularly those which were regarded as highly sensitive, went only to daimyos of lesser rank whose loyalty to the regime was beyond question. The larger and stronger daimyos, who were potential rivals of the Shogun, were not given administrative appointments but kept under constant surveillance.

Shortly after the collapse of feudalism and the establishment of the new Meiji Government a civil service system after the German pattern was established. But even before the system was officially instituted in 1887, a *de facto* bureaucracy had been formed by 1873 under Okubo, the Home Minister.[4] Since there were more samurai who were literate and in need of employment, they were integrated into the new bureaucracy monopolizing some of the activities such as teaching and law enforcement, and especially the police. The predominance of samurai in government positions gave special character to and molded the bureaucracy of the early Meiji period.

The overthrow of the feudal regime in 1868 would not have been possible without the yeoman service of the lesser samurai who came

---

[4] For an able historical treatment of the developments in the setting up of a bureaucratic system in the first few years of Meiji, see Sakada Yoshio, "Nihon ni okeru kindai kanryo no hassei," *Jimbun Gakuho*, III (1953), pp. 1–26.

from families who were for the most part retainers of the daimyos. With the establishment of the new Meiji Government, the former daimyos and the prominent officials of the Tokugawa regime receded into the background while the young and bright activists who were scions of retainers of the daimyos and the young officials of the Shogunate came to the fore as the new bureaucrats. Practically all the officials who achieved prominence in the early Meiji period were from these two groups.[5] Thus, the administrative class now came from the lower strata samurai than was the case during the period of feudalism.

The Imperial University Ordinance promulgated in March, 1886, was the cornerstone on which the new civil service system was erected. It not only formalized the new philosophy of higher education based upon a strongly nationalistic system patterned after that of Germany, but gave official sanction to the imperial university as the training school for the bureaucracy. The function of the imperial university was clearly defined as "the offering of instruction and carrying on thorough investigations in the arts and sciences to meet the needs of the State."[6]

Prince Ito, then Prime Minister, ruled that the graduates of the Tokyo Imperial University were eligible for appointment to the civil service without examination.[7] This preferential treatment was conceived by Ito as an effective method of building up a loyal following which he wanted as the underpinning and base of power for his political activities directed at the political parties. For the next sixty years or so, the ranks of the higher civil service were virtually monopolized by the graduates of the imperial universities with the Tokyo Imperial University supplying an overwhelmingly large number of government officials. Although the necessary groundwork for the Japanese civil service was laid by Ito, the task of nourishing and nurturing the bureaucracy into a fully developed system fell on a military man, General Yamagata, who served as Minister of Home Affairs without interruption from the inception of the cabinet system on December 22, 1885, until May 17, 1890, when under pressure of

[5] Civilian bureaucrats such as Okubo Toshimichi, Kido Koin, Yuri Kimmasa, Oki Takato, Kanda Kohei, Goto Shojiro, Mutsu Munemitsu, and Okuma Shigenobu, and military bureaucrats like Yamagata Aritomo, Saigo Tsugimichi, and Kuroda Kiyotaka are conspicuous examples of those who were of relatively low samurai status.

[6] Yanaga, *Japan Since Perry*, pp. 102–103

[7] This was promulgated as Bunkan Shiken oyobi Minarai Kisoku in July, 1887, at the same time the Civil Service Examination Committee was set up. See Tsuji Kiyoaki, *Nihon Kanryosei no Kenkyu*, pp. 120–121.

responsibilities as Prime Minister he relinquished the post. Thus in the formative years of the cabinet system he built the Home Ministry into the stronghold of Japanese bureaucracy to such a point that the term bureaucrats became practically synonymous with the officials of the Home Ministry. While Yamagata has been given the credit for the creation of the Japanese Army, his role in the development of the civil service system is no less significant. He has been rightly regarded as the "father of Japanese bureaucracy." Largely because of Yamagata's role and influence, the military has had more than its share in shaping the structure as well as the spirit of the bureaucracy during its formative years. For over twenty years from 1885 until after the Russo-Japanese War in 1906, the influence of military men over the Home Ministry was predominant.[8] Only from 1906 did it become an established practice for civilians to hold the Home Ministry portfolio.

In 1899, as Prime Minister, Yamagata managed to push through a number of imperial ordinances whereby he succeeded in making the bureaucratic system the bulwark against political parties which he hated and despised. Yamagata thus closed the door to government service to "outsiders," excluding them from such posts as vice-ministers and bureau chiefs which until then were not civil service positions.[9]

What developed under the Meiji Constitution stopped short of a truly modern civil service system. Although it had ceased to be a system based primarily on status, it nevertheless rested firmly on the sense of obligation and personal loyalty to the emperor. As officials of the emperor to whom they owed unquestioned and unquestioning loyalty and not as civil servants carrying out the will of the people and serving them, the bureaucrats were not concerned with the people and were even contemptuous of them. The bureaucratic system in time developed a position of independence and power and came to constitute a political force actually in opposition to the political parties as well as the Diet.[10]

In the 1930's, as the political parties declined, the bureaucrats began to assume increasingly crucial roles and toward the latter part of the decade, beginning with the Konoe cabinet, the operation of the government was taken over completely by them since the military

[8] The military men who held the post of Home Minister during the period virtually comprise the "Who's Who" of the army and navy: Generals Yamagata, Kodama, and Katsura; Admirals Saigo and Kabayama.

[9] See Nakamura Akira, *Chishiki Kaikyu no Seijiteki Tachiba*, p. 161.

[10] Royama Masamichi, "Nihon ni okeru kanryosei no mondaiten," *Kaizo*, September, 1952, p. 44.

lacked the necessary administrative know-how or skill and experience to manage national affairs. The bureaucracy could and did sabotage the operations of the government which was forever fearful of disaffection and desertion by the bureaucracy. A conspicuous example of this was the Foreign Ministry episode of the 1930's when the whole staff tendered resignation en masse in protest of the projected plan to establish a Ministry of Trade which threatened to take away those policy-making and administrative functions performed by the Foreign Office in the field of foreign trade.

The influence of the bureaucracy under the old system was pervasive and was felt far beyond the confines of administration. Former officials were in business, industry, and finance; they were in the House of Peers and the Privy Council; they held party presidencies and headed governments far more frequently than any other segment of Japanese society.

Defeat in 1945 brought in its wake the military occupation by the Allied Powers resulting in the heavy reliance on the bureaucracy by the Occupation for the administration of the country, thus actually enhancing instead of weakening its position and prestige. Although the civil service system was revamped along American lines, it did not appreciably alter the spirit or the substance of the bureaucracy.[11] It is not an overstatement to say that the change in the Constitution has not materially diminished the prestige or power of the bureaucracy.[12] Japan is still the bureaucrat's paradise and the "wonderland of bureaucracy."

THE BUREAUCRACY TODAY

In the period since the end of World War II, several attempts have been made by the government to carry out reduction in force and the simplification of administration through reorganization. However, every attempt so far has been an unqualified failure. Even a government commanding an absolute majority in the Diet was forced to back down by the united front of the bureaucracy, and the highly publicized program of administrative reform was completely emasculated.[13] The truth of the matter is that the politicians and Diet members are completely at the mercy of the bureaucracy since without the help and support of the career officials and ex-bureaucrats they are unable to operate at all.

[11] Nakamura Akira, *Chishiki Kaikyu no Seijiteki Tachiba*, p. 169.

[12] Professor Tabata Shinobu has gone so far as to say that absolutist bureaucratism in Japan remains stronger than in any of the advanced nations of the world. *Kaizo*, September, 1952, p. 52.

[13] See *Nippon Times*, editorial of August 2, 1952.

The position of the bureaucracy is strong because the Diet members in general are inexperienced in legislation as well as in negotiations. Experienced members are those with bureaucratic background and they quite naturally are prejudiced in favor of the bureaucracy. The number of those who have had administrative experience in the government has been increasing steadily both in the political parties and in the Diet. Such prominent political figures of the postwar period as Shidehara, Ashida, Yoshida, Shigemitsu, and Hatoyama are all men who have had a wealth of experience in the administrative activities of the government before becoming leaders of political parties. Because the functional organization of the Diet is still very inadequate and weak, the bureaucracy finds its position greatly enhanced. But far more basic than all these things is the fact that the entire Japanese political and social life is embedded in the authoritarian and bureaucratic traditions of the past.

Why has the bureaucratic structure been preserved and actually strengthened? Aside from the fact that the Occupation relied heavily if not exclusively on it, there is a deeply rooted feeling or perhaps strong faith on the part of the people in general that the bureaucracy is neutral, nonpartisan, and unbiased in its judgment and actions. Furthermore, the technical and social requirements and contents as well as methods of politics demand special competence, knowledge, and expertise such as possessed by the well trained, and experienced career officials place a high premium on their services.

Political parties are still weak in organization and short on operational efficiency. Consequently when a political party sets up a cabinet, it has to depend heavily on the bureaucrats for the formulating of government policies as well as the drafting of party platforms and policies. The party's inner circle consists of a large number, an unusually high percentage, of those with bureaucratic careers behind them. There has been a virtual infiltration of the parties by ex-bureaucrats. Invariably, the majority of the cabinet members come from the ranks of bureaucrats and ex-bureaucrats thereby causing the strengthening of the bureaucracy through the political parties. It is generally known that the bureaucracy, if left unrestrained, will in the course of its development continue to build up its own power position. Consequently, until there emerges a political force strong enough to control the bureaucracy, it will continue to wield considerable power. Only intelligent democratic public opinion can effectively check or offset the inordinate influence of the bureaucracy.

The power of the bureaucracy stems from the variety of functions it performs and is composed of a number of ingredients. Foremost among these is the administration and control of fiscal matters by bureaucrats. It has been said that taxes and bonds constitute their life blood.[14] Their management of state owned and operated enterprises such as railroads, communications, monopolies, and special banks, and their regulatory control over private enterprises give enormous powers to the officials. Moreover, the police powers in the hands of the bureaucracy together with discretionary powers can be exercised in a way that is not easily counteracted. With the development of technology and the increasing complexity of social and economic problems, the volume and variety of those which form the ingredients of policy have multiplied far beyond the ken and capacity of politicians to handle, thereby putting the bureaucracy in an indispensable position. Furthermore, they are at work continuously even when the legislative branch is not in session and frequently without direction or supervision.

At the higher levels, the officials are involved in both policy and operational activities. They are charged with seeing that certain things are done. However, no matter how explicitly the legislation may be worded, no matter how carefully and precisely the policy directives may be drafted, it becomes necessary to alter programs in the face of changing conditions and emergencies, especially when it is impossible to obtain the decision of a higher policy-determining authority. In a situation calling for the exercise of discretion, the administrator's interpretation of general policy can and does, in effect, redefine and modify the policy originally handed down from above. Organizational influences place only partial restrictions on the exercise of discretion inasmuch as subordinates are told what to do but are given considerable leeway as to how the task may be actually carried out.

Furthermore, the higher officials in the civil service are indispensable as links between successive governments and are the repository of principles and practices that endure while prime ministers come and go. Because of their security of tenure, they insure the continuity of the governmental process. Since under normal circumstances they stand aloof from the political parties, they have no personal motives for anything, but an impartial judgment on matters which come before them. However, in the period since the end of World War II, an increasing number of higher echelon civil servants has come to entertain political ambitions. As a result,

---

[14] "Nihon no Shihai Kozo," *Chuo Koron*, April, 1953, p. 45.

the relationship between government officials and members of the political parties is getting closer than ever before.

THE NATURE AND CHARACTERISTICS OF THE BUREAUCRACY[15]

Since institutions are but the products of the socio-cultural experiences of a people they conform to and reflect the existing social value system of society. In the socio-cultural value system of Japanese life, government officials have always enjoyed far greater prestige than in most Western countries. This was undoubtedly influenced by the Confucian political philosophy and statecraft which placed the ruling class in a position far superior to that of the ruled. The ruler was *ipso facto* virtuous and superior and his officials therefore had to be wise, moral, and superior, and by implication were paragons of virtue. They were the leaders of men.

The idea that government officials were leaders of superior ability and virtue has continued down to the present time and in the course of its development has given rise to the general public attitude which stresses the superiority of the officials and the inferiority of the people.[16] Such an attitude which is a legacy of feudalism has had the effect of boosting the prestige value of government positions to such a point that the achievement of a position in the government came to be a measure of one's success, particularly for people in the rural areas. As a matter of fact, becoming a government official is the only way open to a great many persons for the achievement of social recognition in the form of honor and material advantages as well as special privileges.[17] This accounts for the fact that, ever since the establishment of the civil service in 1886, the greater portion of the aspirants to government positions came from rural agricultural communities. For a time sons of rural landlords compromised a very high percentage of the recruits. These ambitious young men from the rural areas flocked to the law departments of the universities where they acquired legal education of a highly technical nature, almost to the exclusion of courses on politics or economics. This is in sharp contrast to the British civil servant who has a broad liberal background acquired in college. In order to pass the higher civil examination, they spent a large proportion of their time memorizing

---

[15] Perhaps the most candid and revealing work on the Japanese bureaucracy is Imai Kazuo, *Kanryo, Sono Seitai to Naimaku*, 1953.

One of the most valuable studies tracing the development of the Japanese bureaucracy is Tsuji Kiyoaki, *Nihon Kanryosei no Kenkyu*, 1952.

[16] Adachi Tadao, *Kindai Kanryosei to Shokkaisei*, p. 124.

[17] Tsuji Kiyoaki, *Nihon Kanryosei no Kenkyu*, p. 190.

the *Roppo Zensho*.[18] Trained as legal technicians and armed with the proper ideology of officials, they went into government service to form the bulwark of bureaucracy. Since most of them went through practically identical courses of study in the imperial universities and passed identical examinations made and graded by an examination committee composed of law professors of imperial universities, it was natural for the officials to be cast in the same mold.

The civil service is a step up the social ladder even in the postwar period particularly for the middle and lower class. That a large percentage of the recruits comes from these classes should therefore be regarded as almost inevitable.

It hardly needs to be emphasized that, while under the new Constitution it has been made very clear that Government officials are now public servants, it will be some time before the new legal status is accepted socially and psychologically by the officials themselves as well as the general public.[19]

Democratic control over bureaucracy is provided for legally, but it still remains to be firmly established in practice. Meanwhile, legislation strengthening the bureaucracy has been enacted in such fields as labor, police, national security, and antisubversive activities. These laws which strengthen bureaucratic power work inevitably toward the dimunition of individual freedom.

BUREAUCRATIC PSYCHOLOGY AND BEHAVIOR[20]

In a hierarchically arranged society, bureaucratic psychology and behavior are more likely to thrive than in an equalitarian atmosphere. Bureaucratism is widespread in Japan and is found outside of government circles such as in business firms, industrial establishments, and educational institutions. As a matter of fact, it is part of the feudal heritage which has survived the feudal political system and to a large extent is based on the strict observance of superior-subordinate relationships in society. Directors and high officials of business and industrial firms are regarded in the same light by the employees as

---

[18] Nakamura Akira, *Chishiki Kaikyu no Seijiteki Tachiba*, pp. 158–159. The *Roppo*, or six codes, consist of the Constitution, Civil Code, Commercial Code, Criminal Code, Code of Civil Procedure, and Code of Criminal Procedure.

[19] Under the new system according to the Civil Service Law (Article 96) (Kokka Komuinho) the officials must serve all the people, whereas under the Meiji Constitution they actually served the emperor and a privileged segment of the people but were not responsible to the Diet or the people.

[20] For a discussion of bureaucratic psychology, which is as realistic as it is severe, see Masaki Hiroshi, *Nihonjin no Ryoshin*, pp. 188–202.

the feudal lords and rulers were regarded by the loyal retainers and subjects.

Since it is the bureaucratic apparatus that gives the government a monopoly of power, it is quite natural that the administrative officials become highly conscious of the power they exercise. Their attitude toward the general public reflects this clearly. The officiousness of the bureaucrat is the natural corollary of his sense of importance which under the old system was buttressed by his status as an official of the emperor and not a servant of the people.[21]

Self-perpetuating and expansive tendencies are practically inherent characteristics of the bureaucratic machinery. It is perhaps the instinct of self-preservation applied to the administrative structure where it is axiomatic that if it does not grow and expand it will shrink and die. The bureaucrat is more interested in getting a raise than keeping the budget balanced.[22] This fact which is inextricably tied to the instinct of self-preservation on the part of the individual bureaucrat makes administrative simplification and retrenchment almost impossible. It is always the bureaucrats who emasculate and sabotage the government's program for trimming down the administrative structure.

While there is a loud and constant clamor for administrative efficiency and simplification by the bureaucracy itself, what has been taking place is just the opposite because the psychology, inclination, and *modus operandi* of the officials have actually brought about complication, duplication, inefficiency, and waste in government operations. Efficiency has remained the ideal rather than an accomplished fact.

As in the case of every known bureaucratic system, the Japanese administration is characterized by a high degree of red tape (*hambun jokurei*) which is the inevitable and natural consequence of excessive and rigid adherence to rules and regulations, forms, precedents, and procedures, coupled with a generous application of "gobbledygook" and circumlocution, "passing the buck," as well as a lack of imagination.

What obtains most conspicuously in government offices is what may well be described as "administration by government stamps and seals" for, indeed, a large proportion of the time of the officials is spent on affixing stamps and seals on documents. When official seals appear

---

[21] Adachi, Tadao, *Kindai Kanryosei to Shokkaisei*, p. 124.
Suzuki Yasuzo, "Nihon wa hatashite yakunin no kuni ka," *Jitsugyo no Nihon*, March, 1954, p. 48.
[22] See Ludwig von Mises, *Bureaucracy*, p. 80.

on documents, they give authority and validity not only in government but in business offices as well. Practically everything in Japan requires the use of seals—promissory notes, pay vouchers, withdrawal slips at a bank, applications for a position, and a thousand other things.

In Japanese thinking bureaucratic behavior is characterized most frequently by servility to power and authority. Bureaucrats have willingly made themselves subservient to whatever group happened to come to power. In the 1920's it was the political party, in the 1930's it was the military whom they served. Internally too, within the bureaucratic structure itself, this attitude of servility is in evidence. The superior is treated with awe, respect, and deference by the subordinate. Seniority is not forgotten even for a moment. Individuality and individualism are not only unnecessary but actually undesirable and incompatible with the "way of the bureaucrats." Loyalty to the superior and conscientious discharge of duties which loom so large are part of the feudal legacy of lord and vassal relationship. This leads to a modified form of flunkyism, if not sychophancy, which precludes even the offering of suggestions by subordinates to their superiors. It encourages the patient biding of time without getting into hot water by being branded a troublemaker or being accused of insubordination. This is, of course, not conducive to the encouragement of high efficiency or democratic process within the administrative structure.

Along with the attitude of servility, there is manifest a strong awareness of their role of leadership both in society and in politics. This consciousness is supported and bolstered by their attitude of self-righteousness that stems from their feeling that they know what is best and that they are always right. This not infrequently takes the form of haughtiness and disregard if not contempt of the populace. Fairness and concern for the needs, desires, and conveniences of the people have not yet been developed to any appreciable degree among the bureaucracy. More often than not indifference and callousness have characterized the attitude of officials.

Too often bureaucrats not only are far removed from the lives and wishes of the people but stand over them, turn their backs on them, and operate in a manner that removes them still further away from the people. A bureaucrat has been pictured as a peculiar breed who sits at his desk with a cigarette in his mouth and an official seal in his hand during office hours and attends mah jong parties in the afternoons and banquets at night.

It is not an attribute of bureaucrats to seek changes or innovations.

They have been trained and are thoroughly convinced that the safest course is to simply conform to time-honored practices and rely on precedents to discharge the duties of office if they wish to get ahead. Almost by instinct they carry out faithfully the orders or assignments handed down from above rather than follow their own convictions for fear they may lead to disastrous consequences.[23]　This dominant *status quo* mentality among officials tends to preserve and even nourish the legacies of feudalism in present-day political and social thinking and behavior not only of the bureaucrats themselves but of the public in general.

Their approach tends toward the negative rather than the positive. They have acquired the reputation of being evasive, secretive, and perfunctory in their ways of doing things. Their faith in the efficacy of laws is very strong, in fact, inordinately so. They are an embodiment of the cult of success and as a consequence would lose no opportunity to hang on to the coat tails of any group which comes into power.

Bureaucrats all strive for seniority, for the length of service alone is what really counts in the advancement of their careers. Rank, salary, and retirement pension depend on length of service. Consequently too rapid or too early promotion can actually work against an official's best interests since he may incur the jealousy, if not the ill-will, of his colleagues, and might well force his retirement too soon to earn maximum pension.[24]　In their overcautiousness to build up longevity too often initiative, imagination, and even thinking are stifled. Their passion for security, paucity of knowledge and broad cultural interests, and moving in the rather circumscribed world of officialdom tend to produce a unique kind of bureaucratic personality.

BUREAUCRACY AND POLITICS

Party politics in Japan today is still essentially bureaucratic-dominated politics. Since the end of World War II, there has literally been a steady procession of bureaucrats and ex-bureaucrats coming into the arena of politics.[25]　Under the new Constitution it has become necessary for most of the cabinet ministers to be members of the Diet. This forces those bureaucrats who aspire to membership in the cabinet to go into politics.

[23] Nakamura Akira, *Chishiki Kaikyu no Seijiteki Tachiba*, p. 150.

[24] *Ibid.*

[25] Kanda Mitsunobu, "Kanryo shusshin no seijika tachi," *Jitsugyo no Nihon*, March, 1954, pp. 52–55.

The presence in the Diet of bureaucrats became conspicuous following the general election of April, 1953, when more than one hundred were elected. These bureaucrat M.P.'s were mostly from departments handling money and materials and from offices in charge of various enterprises.[26] Most of them were elected on the strength of the support obtained from the bureaucrats whom they once supervised and now represent.

From the very beginning of Japanese party politics the leadership has come predominantly from the ranks of the bureaucracy. Leadership of the prewar Minseito party was in the hands of bureaucrats like Kato, Hamaguchi, and Wakatsuki. Few, indeed, are party presidents who were not in some way connected with the government as officials. As a matter of fact, a party man was made a party leader for the first time in Japan's political history when Inukai became president of the Seiyukai. Even in the period since World War II the influence of ex-bureaucrat members of the Diet within the political parties is great if not predominant. Those members of the Diet who are former or present government officials invariably prefer to be identified as ministers or vice-ministers rather than legislators. Some of the prefectural governors seem to regard themselves as occupying positions not unlike those of the feudal lords of the past and practically behave accordingly.

The twin constellations of the bureaucratic firmament have been the officials of the Home Ministry and those of the Finance Ministry. The Finance Ministry bureaucrats outrank the former since they go back to the 1870's when Okuma was the head of the original Ministry of Finance. The Home Ministry bureaucracy goes back to the 1880's when Yamagata presided over the Ministry. In the 1930's the Home Ministry officials comprised the most powerful segment of the bureaucracy as they were in control of the local government units as well as the national police power. In spite of the dissolution of the Ministry of Home Affairs after the war, the largest group of ex-bureaucrats who are members of the Diet are former Home Ministry officials. Next come the former officials of the Finance Ministry followed by those of the Ministries of Agriculture and Forestry, of International Trade and Industry, and of Transportation.

A disproportionately large number of former officials of the Foreign Ministry has achieved eminence in postwar politics. Four postwar party presidents have been former career diplomats—Shidehara, Ashida, Yoshida and Shigemitsu—and all but one have attained the

[26] Among the departments were Finance, Agriculture and Forestry, and Railway.

premiership. In the postwar period this group has occupied the limelight more than any other group, quite out of proportion to their numerical strength. This was due undoubtedly to the exigencies of the Occupation which unexpectedly brought those with diplomatic experience to the fore.

The Ministry of Home Affairs, until it was abolished, used to be the best possible training ground for a political career since all the officials who went through the prefectural governorship acquired valuable political experience in dealing with the prefectural assembly. The give-and-take that the prefectural governor has to master constitutes a valuable asset. Administrative skill such as a former Home Ministry official acquired was not as marketable in the world of business and industry as the knowledge and skill of an official in the ministries of Finance, Trade and Industry, Agriculture and Forestry, or Transportation. Consequently, a far greater number of them went into politics.

Bureaucrats and ex-bureaucrats with Finance Ministry background have gone into politics in smaller numbers than those of the Home Ministry. Yet those who have turned politicians have climbed rapidly because of their special skill which is indispensable to politics, as well as their excellent contacts with the business and financial world. For a long time, the brightest young imperial university graduates were brought into the Finance Ministry. This gave rise to the belief that the Finance Ministry offered the best opportunities for success. In time it became the stronghold of imperial university bureaucrats. It is also from the ranks of the Finance Ministry bureaucracy that the largest number of ex-officials have gone into business and industry to assume high executive positions.[27] The pipeline that the Finance Ministry maintains between industry and business gives it and its officials considerable political power.

BUREAUCRACY AND BUSINESS

It is a matter of historical record that the growth of Japanese capitalism was achieved largely through the guidance and direction of the bureaucrats and with the funds made available by the state. Business enterprises prospered through close ties with political power. The financial interests owed their prosperity and expansion to the bureaucracy and the military. The zaibatsu, or the financial clique, is the lineal descendant of the political businessman of the Meiji era

---

[27] Furuyama Fujio, "Yakunin shusshin no zaikaijin tachi," *Jitsugyo no Nihon*, March, 1954, pp. 56–59.

who prospered under the political aegis of the bureaucracy and the military.[27a]

Since business and industry must depend heavily on the government and the bureaucracy for their success, the best possible relationship is maintained at all times. The interchange of personnel between the government and business is taking place continuously. Government officials leave their posts to accept attractive positions in industry while leaders of finance and business join the government to assist in policy making. Favors received by business from the government are frequently repaid with parties and ex-officials as beneficiaries.

It is common knowledge that government officials in most of the departments who have reached a certain level and become well known to business and industry have no difficulty in finding attractive positions upon leaving government service. This is particularly true in the fields of finance, trade and industry, transportation, and construction. The effective vertical and horizontal organization that exists within the bureaucracy together with the bureaucratic *esprit de corps* enable the transfer from government to business with the greatest ease.

The professionalization of the bureaucracy makes the civil service subservient to political authority and subject to the official will. In theory, it is placed in the position of having to faithfully execute the duties of office regardless of personal sentiments and disagreements with the policies involved. It must be prepared to serve with the same competence whatever party is in power and observe strict professional neutrality and impartiality. Actually, however, any absolute dissociation of the bureaucrats from the realm of policy decisions and the sphere of political action is as unrealistic as it is impossible.

OFFICIAL CORRUPTION

One of the most conspicuous practices in Japanese official life is lavish and elaborate entertainment which has become the bane of political circles because it opens the way to corruption. Expensive banquets and receptions have come to be regarded by the bureaucrats as an indispensable part of the official procedure. Resort to padding payrolls is made to increase entertainment funds while entertainment money and even travel funds are frequently if not regularly used as

[27a] See Tsuchiya Takao, *Nihon no Seisho*, which is a study of businessmen who relied heavily on political connections in their successful enterprises during the early Meiji period.

bonuses for the staff members. No accurate figures are available though entertainment expenses constitute a standard budgetary item. One estimate, attributed to an American newspaper, placed the annual expenditure at ¥80,000,000,000 ($222 million).[28]

Even in government public works, 15 percent of the total amount appropriated is spent for the entertainment of local bigwigs and those involved in the contract.[29]

According to an observer of the political scene, there are five ways to corrupt officials, namely, to give them money, let them feel they are great, let them drink, give them food, and let them enjoy the geisha.[30]

The period following World War II saw the introduction of several new forms of corruption. These included the sending of gifts or presents to officials at their arrival and departure and on occasions like the birth of a child, mah jong parties at which officials were made to win large sums of money by those seeking favors, and providing lavish geisha entertainment.[31]

It has been a practice for the government to enable a firm or group to realize easy and quick profit, and collect a certain percentage for its political funds. This is done through tip-offs on government actions, such as the disposal of goods at a low price at the liquidation of an enterprise and repurchase later at a much higher price.[32]

THE CIVIL SERVICE

The civil service is based on Article 15 of the Constitution which provides that "the people have the inalienable right to choose their public officials and to dismiss them." It is emphatically stated that "public officials are servants of the whole community and not of any group thereof." This abolishes, at least legally, the old concept that an official is the emperor's servant and gives a new status, namely, that of a public servant, making it possible to achieve a civil service

[28] Quoted by Ariyama Tetsuo, "Fuhai seru Yoshida seiken wo tsuku," *Kaizo*, February, 1952, p. 59.

[29] According to Kimura Kihachiro, member of the House of Councillors, roughly 35 percent of government expenditure on public works is spent as follows:

15 percent for entertainment
10 percent for "consultations" (*hanashiai*)
10 percent profit for the contractors.

The remaining 65 percent becomes the actual cost of construction itself. See *Chuo Koron*, December, 1951.

[30] Takagi, "Kanjo genkei ki," *Kaizo*, September, 1952, pp. 63.

[31] *Ibid.*, pp. 64–65.

[32] Ariyama Tetsuo, "Fuhai seru Yoshida seiken wo tsuku," *Kaizo*, February, 1952, p. 61.

based on democratic concept and process. It recognizes and implements the principle that every one should have an equal opportunity to serve his government in those capacities for which he is qualified. What has been adopted is a classified service based on a merit system patterned after the American civil service with the administration of the system in the hands of the cabinet.[33] This new system is designed as an antithesis to the old system based upon subjective appraisal of the superiors combined with such factors as the school tie, marital tie, and factional affiliations.[34]

While the bulk of the civil service comes under the classified category there are also a considerable number of officials who are in the unclassified, exempt class. These officials are not subject to competitive or even noncompetitive examinations. Among those included in the exempt class are (a) the prime minister, cabinet ministers, and ambassadors, (b) parliamentary vice-ministers, counsellors, and private secretaries, (c) elective officials such as members of legislative bodies of commissions, (d) personnel officers and examiners of the Bureau of Audit, (e) officials of the Imperial Household Office, (f) judges and private secretaries in the Supreme Court, (g) officials and employees of public (government) corporations[35] designated by the National Personnel Authority, and (h) unemployed workers on government relief projects.

Under the newly instituted classified service[36] which is based on the United States civil service system, there are the following categories: (1) Professional and Scientific Service, (2) Subprofessional Service, (3) Clerical, Administrative, and Fiscal, (4) Crafts, Protective, and Custodial, and (5) Clerical and Mechanical. While in the United States there is a policy of geographic distribution in civil service appointments, similar arrangement does not obtain in Japan to effect such a distribution.

Civil Service Recruitment

The civil service in Japan has always attracted and still attracts those who are ambitious not only to become a part of the administrative service but also to eventually achieve the position of

[33] In Article 73 the Cabinet is empowered to administer the civil service in accordance with standards established by law. The basic law was enacted by the Diet as the National Public Officials Law in 1947.

[34] Adachi Tadao, *Kindai Kanryosei to Shokkaisei*, p. 123.

[35] These corporations are the Japanese equivalents of the Tennessee Valley Authority, Farm Credit Administration, Federal Deposit Insurance Corporation, and the like.

[36] Okabe Shiro, *Shokkaiho* (1950) gives a detailed discussion of the classified service.

cabinet minister and if possible the premiership. It differs therefore from the British or American civil service which attracts candidates whose thoughts and ambitions ordinarily do not turn readily to politics. Since the prestige enjoyed by government officials is considerable the civil service has more often than not claimed the cream of the annual crop of university graduates.

As a consequence of expanded educational opportunities of the past several decades, the upper ranks of the civil service are now open to social classes that had not been able to qualify before. At its inception the higher civil service was monopolized by the graduates of the Tokyo Imperial University because of the preferential treatment inaugurated by Prince Ito. As a matter of fact, the University was made into a training school for higher civil service officials. Graduates of other imperial universities did not have nearly as good a chance while graduates of private universities were virtually excluded from the higher civil service ranks. Slowly the monopoly by the Tokyo Imperial University graduates was reduced and by the 1930's graduates of other institutions had succeeded in breaking down the barrier. It is really since World War II that graduates of other universities, both government and private, began to go into the upper ranks of the civil service in increasing numbers.

Entrance into the service is by examinations which are a combination of two distinct types, one of which requires a broad cultural foundation though perhaps not to the extent of the British general cultural examination, and the other a specialized government examination which calls for specialized knowledge in one or more fields relating to government such as administrative law, public finance, or labor policy. Competition is so keen that only the very best will survive the examinations and in some years not more than three percent of those who take the examinations win appointment to the civil service.[37]

Japan has an extensive system of state examinations under which entrance to officialdom is achieved by the passing of examinations. Aside from administrative officials, diplomats, judges, procurators, and police officials, practically all professionals are required to take examinations. Lawyers, doctors, and nurses can practice only upon successfully passing state examinations. Even private firms have long made it a practice to give applicants examinations not very different

[37] For example, in late August of 1953, in fourteen different cities throughout the country, approximately 30,000 persons took the civil service examinations for appointment to administrative class six positions but only about one thousand actually were appointed.

from those given to candidates for the administrative service. Private firms frequently include psychological tests as well. In some instances, they have even introduced group discussions for the purpose of appraising the candidates.

From the kindergarten through the university a Japanese goes through a continuous succession of competitive examinations that are highlighted by those which are for entrance to the next higher level of education. These entrance examinations which are the bane of existence for parents and offspring alike have given rise to the expression, "examination hell." As the most important step marking the transition from college or university to a career in business or government, the graduate must go through the by no means final ordeal of entrance examinations which will admit him to the profession of his choice. Livelihood depends, indeed, on the successful passing of examinations.[38]

[38] Takagi Takeo, *Nihon to Yuu Na no Kuni,* pp. 177–178. The only ones who do not have to take examinations are cabinet ministers and beggars.

14

National Economy and General Welfare

The period since the end of the Second World War has witnessed in practically every country a spectacular expansion in the scope of governmental activity as a consequence of unexpected widening of the extent of public responsibilities. Social and economic services which are now the normal functions of government extend into virtually every area of national life. As a result few of us are alarmed to see that the state has become, in effect, a sort of "service" if not a "welfare" state responsible for creating and maintaining conditions favorable to the livelihood, living conditions, and happiness of the people in general.

THE STATE AND THE NATIONAL ECONOMY

It is patently clear in Japan today that economic problems constitute the most important substance of politics. The most serious aftermath of her defeat in World War II was the virtual collapse of national economy brought on by the destruction of productive power, and the loss of territory as well as sources of raw materials and markets. The impact on national economy was as immediate as it was disastrous. Moreover, it laid bare the inherent weaknesses of Japan's economic structure, namely, the paucity of raw materials, high population density, dependence on foreign markets, and obsolescent and inefficient industrial production facilities.

The loss of forty-five percent of her overseas territory was a severe blow to the economy since it forced Japan to pay in foreign currency for those materials she formerly obtained with her national currency, closed investment opportunities in her former colonies, terminated a condition of virtual monopoly in these special markets and, exposing her to the stiff competition of foreign manufactures, brought an end to advantageous industrial specialization in the manufacture of steel, sugar, salt, and major food products, and led to the loss of fishing grounds in the waters close to Soviet territory.

Japan emerged from her defeat not only with the complete destruction of military power but also with a severely crippled economy. Exclusive of the destruction of materials and equipment used for military purposes, direct war damages suffered amounted to thirty-five percent of the national wealth of 1935 or approximately $13,798,-000,000 which is the equivalent of the total national income of 1951.[1] Productive power in some industries had dropped to barely twenty percent of the capacity of the second half of 1944. The nation was actually in a state of economic prostration, the remaining productive capacity was totally inadequate, and most of the people were in rags and living either on a bare subsistence level or on the verge of starvation.

Needless to say, the reduction of territory by some forty-five percent was in itself a severe enough blow to the national economy. But to further aggravate the situation, the population of the country increased more rapidly during the postwar years than in any other period of Japanese history. In 1948, the natural increase reached the unheard of figure of a million and three-quarters. Since then, the increase has levelled off at slightly over a million a year. According to the estimates of the Economic Planning Board, the total population will reach 97,354,000 by 1965 with 74,760,000 in the working age group, giving an actual labor force of 46,350,000. It is this steadily mounting population pressure which is causing great apprehension among the nation's policy makers.[2] The rapid increase in population has been responsible in part for thwarting the rationalization of industry as well as the accumulation of capital so badly needed in the development of a self-sustaining national economy. A partial and temporary solution of the problem lies obviously in the development of a capacity to sustain an increasing population. However, the Malthusian theory seems to be in operation and the planners are fully aware that there is a limit to what can be achieved. In the long run, the only solution is the curtailment of population growth. The Population Policy Council of the Ministry of Welfare, composed of

[1] Daiyamondosha, *Gendai Seiji no Kiso Chishiki*, pp. 210–211.
[2] Japan's population density per arable square mile of 4,220, the highest in the world, is far more serious than the Netherlands' 2,577 and Belgium's 2,155.

representatives of business and industry, government agencies, and the public, made a definite recommendation to the government on August 24, 1954, urging the adoption of an over-all population policy in which family planning would be an integral part of the social security program. It underscored the fact that population pressure works against the social and economic welfare of the nation; therefore, it is imperative that positive action be taken to relieve it.[3] It would be impossible to assess accurately the impact and consequence of population pressure on a nation's policy, but there is no doubt that the fear of overpopulation was one of the factors which set Japan on the road to empire and war.[4] With a population of nearly 90,000,-000 and ranking as the world's fifth most populous nation, Japan finds her economic foundation far too shaky and inadequate to insure her national well-being and security. This condition has produced a sense of urgency which permeates the nation and propels it toward the achievement of a sound and stable economy. The problems of food, employment, health, education, and social security are thus directly affected. The primacy of economics in giving substance and shape to present-day Japanese politics thus becomes patently clear in the face of the serious problems confronting the nation. It is evident even to a casual observer that the preoccupation of the government and the political parties as well as business and industry is predominantly, if not exclusively, with economic problems.[5]

National Goals: Social and Economic

Stated simply and in the broadest terms, Japan's socio-economic goal is the achievement of a stable, self-sustaining national economy which would insure independence, security, and prosperity to the people individually as well as to the nation as a whole. A viable

[3] See a report by Okazaki Ayanori, Director of Population Research Institute of the Ministry of Welfare to the Twelfth International Conference of the Institute of Pacific Relations at Kyoto. *Sangyo Keizai*, Overseas Edition, December 1, 1954, pp. 4, 5, 8. The problem of population is dealt with concisely in a brief work, Minami Ryosaburo, *Meian no Nihon Jinko* (1955).

[4] See F. C. Jones, *Japan's New Order in East Asia, Its Rise and Fall, 1937–1945*. Overpopulation became a specter which hung over Japan from the late 1920's and policy makers became increasingly apprehensive in the face of paucity of raw materials and trade discrimination which was being directed against the nation.

[5] The importance of economic affairs is underscored by the fact that in the period since the war, the Direct General of the Economic Planning Board reports to the Diet on economic conditions and policies along with the Prime Minister, Foreign Minister, and Finance Minister.

national economy based on a carefully planned, national, and efficient production and profitable foreign trade must insure a decent and rising standard of living for all as well as a maximum degree of social security that is based on an enlightened and progressive labor policy, high level of employment, and adequate health and unemployment insurance. These are the goals toward which the government strives constantly through promotional, preventive, and remedial measures. The achievement of economic prosperity for all depends to a large extent on the maintenance of high-level, low-cost production, full employment, and adequate purchasing power as well as stable prices, sound financial policy, capital accumulation, and strong, mutually beneficial economic ties with the rest of the world.

Thus, the task faced by the nation involves to a large measure the building of a sound new economic structure rather than the mere patching up of old ideas, techniques, and organization. Innovation rather than renovation is required for the rationalization of the unstable economy. There must be increased output induced by higher productivity through the modernization of plants and techniques, development of domestic as well as foreign markets, and reduction in the cost of production to create a favorable balance of trade. The solution of economic problems must now be achieved on an entirely new basis and without the benefit of prewar methods and advantages such as cheap feudalistic methods, colonies, military power, and monopolistic capital, backed by the emperor system. The government's responsibility of insuring economic stability and promoting prosperity requires careful and astute planning coupled with bold and efficient execution in the best interests of the nation and the public.

Characteristics of Japanese Economic Development

Japan's emergence from more than two hundred years of isolation occurred at a time when European capitalism had already achieved phenomenal development with industrialization already in an advanced stage. It was clear to the leaders that the nation was far behind Western European countries in industrial development. Therefore, in order to achieve the speediest possible modernization of her industrial facilities, the government assumed the initiative and established up-to-date factories and workshops as models[6] and used

---

[6] Almost everything was started by the government: arsenals, chemical works, iron and steel mills, shipyards, machine factories, cement, brick, glass, and coke factories, silk filatures, cotton-spinning mills, power-loom weaving, carpet factories, paper mills, banks, trading companies, and mines.

practically every possible means to promote the growth and expansion of industries. For the key industries which were importations from the West, the Meiji government furnished everything necessary including capital, management, and operation. When the enterprises were developed sufficiently to insure their continuation with profit under their own power, they were turned over to private ownership by the government usually at cost and provided with generous subsidies for many more years. Industrialization was not only pushed at the expense of agriculture but actually financed by it through land taxes. Absence of antimonopoly laws and the constant support and encouragement by the government contributed to the growth of monopolistic capitalism. Intimate, if not inseparable, ties developed between the government and the zaibatsu or combines. Industrialists and financiers made handsome profits with the minimum effort in the name of national interests, if not patriotism, at a time when the attainment of national strength was placed above the interests and welfare of the individual and especially of the masses. This situation produced a type of businessmen who prospered under the aegis and patronage of the government and to whom political contacts or influence constituted the *sine qua non* of business success. They came to be known as *seisho* or merchants, who relied on political support or favors.

Japanese capitalism, which was forced to undergo rapid and perhaps unduly accelerated development under terrific pressure and protected by the strong paternalistic attitude of the government, failed to develop independence and self-reliance. Since it grew under the aegis of feudalistic, bureaucratic forces, the legacies of feudalism not only did not disappear but were actually preserved. Although after 1883 the government increasingly withdrew from direct ownership or management except in fields where the national policy requirements made it unwise to do so, as in iron and steel, railroads, and communications, subsidies became an important part of the government's policy toward industry. This resulted in the protection and subsidization of enterprises, particularly the larger ones, at the expense of the small ones as well as the taxpayers. Consequently, small scale business and industry have not fared well. There was a deliberate and systematic dovetailing of the power requirements of the army and navy and economic development so that it catered to the rapidly mounting needs of monopolistic industrial, commercial, and financial capitalism.[7] Thus the structure of industry was shaped by the efforts and influence of the military whose primary concern

[7] Brady, Robert A., *Business as a System of Power*, p. 104.

was to direct the development of the country's resources along lines dictated by strategic and military needs.[8]

Because of the manner in which Japan's economy was developed during the last one hundred years, there has been no really serious policy struggle between the government and the business interests. As a matter of fact, partnership between business and government has been the pattern of the growth of capitalism in Japan. Rather than having to fight the government, business found itself actually allied to it, receiving protection and aid from the government.

In recent years, especially in the period following World War II, the lack of private capital has brought about a situation where business and industry rely upon state capital, that is, government funds collected through taxation. The financial world depends on the government regularly for loans and subsidies. In order to do this effectively, business and industry have to work with the government and its officials and leave no stone unturned to remain in their favor.

Furthermore, from the very outset, Japan's industrialization was strongly dependent on foreign countries both as sources of necessary raw materials and as markets for her manufactured products. In other words, her economic prosperity has been vulnerable to world price fluctuations from the beginning and to a much greater extent than in most of the modern industrialized nations. This dependence on world conditions and prices for the nation's prosperity was accentuated by the commercialization of agricultural production which took place in the late nineteenth century.

Economic Planning

The havoc wrought on Japanese industry by the war was so great that planning became imperative for the reconstruction and rehabilitation of national economy. It was not a question of choice but of dire necessity. The idea of planning as such, however, was by no means new for the decade of the 1930's was one of active efforts at planning, although it could well be argued that what actually took place was more in the nature of control than planning.

Economic planning can be said to have first begun with the creation of the Bureau of Resources which exercised jurisdiction over all the plans that were concerned with the regulation and disposition of raw materials as well as human and material resources. Then, in June, 1930, the Industrial Rationalization Bureau was established in the Ministry of Commerce and Industry to carry out an ambitious but vaguely conceived plan for the reorganization of the entire economic

[8] Allen, George C., *Japanese Industry*, p. 15.

system of the country.[9] Its function was to devise as well as direct measures that might lead to the coordination of both control and policy within the various industries and at the same time increase efficiency. It was given the responsibility of supervising the enforcement of the Major Industries Control Law designed to create for every large scale industry a cartel for the control of production, sale, and price. Planning commissions were set up for all major industries in the 1930's. Under a quasi-wartime economic structure after 1936, planning and control became a major government activity especially under the National Mobilization Law, and the newly established Planning Board concentrated its efforts on pushing ahead its policy of government ownership and operation of industries. Resources were diverted to industries which were regarded necessary for military and strategic purposes. This was achieved largely through the cooperation of the newly risen industrialists who emerged with the support of the military. The new economic structure instituted in 1940 as part of the totalitarian governmental setup was new only in name for its substance was several years old. Under the exigencies of the Pacific War, the General Planning Bureau was set up on November 1, 1944, under the direct control and supervision of the Prime Minister, for the planning, operation, and expansion of national war production and for the adjustment, unification, and coordination as well as the supervision of the administrative activities of government agencies involved in war production work.

NATURE AND ORGANIZATION. In its simplest form, national economic planning involves the determination of policies by the government usually with the help of public or private organizations and the outlining of a course of action in order to achieve certain economic objectives for the nation. Several steps are involved in the process of planning: research and analysis which are the prerequisites for the understanding and appraisal of the problems to be solved; the determination of objectives; the discovery of alternative solutions; decision-making, involving the formulation of policies; and finally the execution of the plans through effective organization, procedure, and work schedule.

Economic planning is largely, though not by any means exclusively, in the hands of the government. Private economic organizations participate actively and quite conspicuously in policy-making not only in economic matters but in all aspects of national affairs. Best known among such economic organizations are the Federation of

[9] Allen, George C., *Japanese Industry: Its Recent Development and Present Condition*, p. 17.

Economic Organizations, Japan Federation of Employers' Associations, Japan Chamber of Commerce and Industry, and the Japan Management Association. These are the peak associations for the closer coordination of networks of business organizations. The cumulative power of business as reflected in and applied through these associations shapes the forms and determines the content of economic policies in Japan. Their influence is all the more significant since popular restraints are still not developed to any appreciable degree. Until toward the end of World War I, there was no formal economic organization for the purpose of influencing the government's policy-making or proposing specific policies. It was in 1917 that the Japan Industry Club[10] was formed as a private organization of large industrialists to facilitate intimate relations among its membership, to study economic policies from the viewpoint of the large industries, to promote harmonious relationship between capital and labor, and to represent Japanese industry in dealing with foreign businessmen.

In 1922, the Japan Economic Federation was established by business leaders[11] as a representative organ of Japanese business interests. Although it was ostensibly devoted to the formulation of economic policies for the Japanese business community as a whole, this compact coordinating body of a limited number of business establishments was dominated by a few of the giant concerns like the Mitsui and Mitsubishi interests. Until the end of World War II, it was this organization that aided the government in the formulation and execution of major national policies. It possessed its own blueprint for the full and complete coordination of the economic, financial, and commercial policies of Japan. In the postwar reorganization, it became the Federation of Economic Organizations in August, 1946, and, unlike its prewar predecessor which protected the interests of zaibatsu concerns, it became the voice of various business and industrial enterprises. The roster of officers reads like a "Who's Who" of Japanese business,

---

[10] The Kogyo Club, as it is known in Japanese, has its own building which not only houses the Federation of Economic Organizations and the Japan Federation of Employers' Associations but constitutes the most important meeting place for all sorts of policy-making groups.

[11] Baron Dan Takuma, the head of Mitsui interests, was greatly impressed by the activities of the International Chamber of Commerce and wanted to see Japan participate in it. However, there was no body that was representative of the business world for the purpose of joining the world organization. After discussing the problem with Inoue Junnosuke, Governor of the Bank of Japan, Ogura Masatsune, head of the Sumitomo interests, Ikeda Seihin, director of the Mitsui Bank, and Kodama Kenji, president of the Yokohama Specie Bank, he undertook the founding of the Japan Economic Federation (Nihon Keizai Remmeikai).

finance, and industry. The Federation of Economic Organizations whose membership is institutional rather than individual is concerned with the broader aspects of economic problems and policies and is interested in the development of the national economy as a whole as well as individual enterprises. Its work is carried on by its nineteen standing committees and the results of its studies are made available through pamphlets and other publications. It keeps the public and the government as well as its membership informed through a monthly periodical and a weekly newsletter. As the most powerful peak organization of Japanese business and industry it virtually presides over the nation's economic destiny by playing a decisive role in national policy-making.[12]

The Japan Federation of Employers' Associations which came into being in April, 1948, is the unified headquarters of national employers' groups and concerns itself exclusively with labor problems. Its origin goes back to the Federation of Industrial Organizations (Zenkoku Sangyo Dantai Rengokai) first formed in 1931 for the formulation and execution of important national labor policies for the upper reaches of Japan's big business. Its organization is based on prefectural and regional employers' as well as industry-wide employers' associations. Its institutional membership overlaps to a considerable extent that of the Federation of Economic Organizations which has only industry-wide associations and no local organizations. Although the two are clearly distinct and separate entities, the relationship is so intimate that they represent in a sense the two sides of one coin. However, the Japan Federation of Employers' Associations is regarded as the right wing organization of business and finance since it has been active in resisting the demands of labor whereas the Federation of Economic Organizations has on the whole evinced a greater degree of interest in and sympathy for the problems of labor and agrarian population.

The Japan Chamber of Commerce and Industry, first set up in 1928 under legislative sanction as the legally competent and officially recognized central federation of all chambers of commerce and industry in the nation, carries great weight in policy-making. It is entrusted with such major functions as the making of representations to proper authorities on commercial and industrial matters, issuing of reports and statistical information on commerce and industry, organizing and supervising commercial and industrial bodies and arbitrating disputes.

---

[12] Keizai Dantai Rengokai, *Keidanren Jigyo Hokoku* (1954), gives a comprehensive picture of the multifarious activities of the organization. See also its report, *Dai Jugokai Teiji Sokai Yoroku* (1955).

Its officers are also drawn from among the prominent leaders of business and industry.

A newcomer in the field without the antecedents comparable to those of the three other economic organizations already discussed, the Japan Management Association (Keizai Doyukai) which was launched in 1946 is nevertheless an influential body of some 700 individual members. It is organized into four regional units, namely, Central, Kansai, Kyushu, and Hokkaido, and is by far the most liberal of the four major economic organizations as can be seen by the fact that at its Eighth National Convention held on November 10, 1955, one of its managers strongly advocated the acceptance by business and industry of the view that an enterprise is a public trust and should be managed for the good of all.[13]

All these economic organizations are strictly nonpartisan in their purpose and activities. They transcend party differences inasmuch as they are concerned first and last with the protection and advancement of their economic interests. In practice, they function as organs cooperating with the government in the proposing and formulating of important policies, drafting plans for their execution, and presenting views and recommendations either on their own initiative or at the request of the government. They carry on research in the problems of production, distribution, management, finance, and trade, and publish their results. Even individual firms have excellent research organizations which are frequently superior to those in the government itself. One of the best known is the Mitsubishi Institute of Economic Research which carries on the kind of research which rates high even by Western standards. The economic organizations also arrange, from time to time, informal discussions with the Prime Minister as well as the members of the cabinet and the policy committees of the political parties to express and exchange views and make policy recommendations on political matters and economic problems. The four leading economic organizations frequently issue joint statements or make joint policy recommendations which receive the serious consideration of the government. They also give leadership and guidance to subordinate and subsidiary economic organizations on policy matters and course of action.

Economic Planning Machinery

In the postwar period, unified general economic planning has become almost an obsession with the government and its policy makers.

---

[13] *Keizai Doyu*, December 1, 1955, pp. 11–12.

The General National Resources Development Law which was enacted in May, 1950, forms the basis of the government's efforts to find a way to make the national economy self-sustaining. The Economic Planning Board, which first began as the Economic Stabilization Board and then became the Economic Policy Board before assuming its present name and functions, is an extraministerial agency attached to the Office of the Prime Minister and constitutes the highest authority in over-all economic planning. Its Director General who is state minister and member of the cabinet wields enormous influence in the nation's policy making. The Board is assisted by the Economic Deliberation Council, which is a statutory advisory body in the Prime Minister's Office, and the informal Financial Policy Deliberation Committee set up in the Ministry of Finance. It is made up of influential representatives of business, finance, and industry as well as professors and others who represent experience and expertise, and is primarily an advisory body to help the Minister of Finance in his policy making. The former is entrusted with the huge task of working out an over-all multiple-purpose development policy which would insure maximum utilization of all available national resources both human and natural. Its responsibility extends to everything except defense problems in the narrowest technical sense. It studies and formulates policies on food, agriculture, forestry and fisheries, population, labor, employment, housing, health, social security, hydroelectric power, fuels, construction, public works, business and industry, foreign trade, and production and consumption goals. In short, nothing escapes its scrutiny.

The National Over-all Development Law of 1950 which is the brain child of the Economic Planning Board is designed with a view to attaining economic self-sustenance through the conservation and utilization of land, development of resources, and creation and promotion of industries. It envisages a ten-year plan for the development of nine specially designated areas in the nation through the joint efforts of the Ministries of International Trade and Industry, Transportation, and Construction, with one half of the cost coming from the national government and the other half from electric power companies and other interested parties. Included in the multipurpose development program are the construction of dams for flood control and irrigation as well as for electric power, efficient exploitation of agricultural, forest and mineral resources, extensive public works, land development and forestation, and the construction of railroads and bridges.

Another example of national economic planning is provided by the

Hokkaido development program which is in the hands of the Hokkaido Development Board in the Prime Minister's Office. The northern frontier island of Hokkaido close to Soviet territory has been regarded traditionally as the vulnerable area of the nation. Although it comprises over twenty percent of the nation's total land area, its population density per square mile is only one fourth that of the nation as a whole. Industrial production represents only four percent of the national total and the total income of the population is not more than five percent of the national total. The over-all development scheme for this underdeveloped area of Japan operates as a ten-year plan beginning in 1952. At the end of the first five-year period, that is, in 1956, Hokkaido is expected to support a population of 6,000,000 through the fuller utilization of its natural resources, namely, land, water and forest. This first phase is devoted to the construction of basic facilities necessary for the establishment of new industries. In the second phase, efforts will be concentrated on advanced industrial development. The plan envisages the development of Hokkaido to the point of supporting a population of 10,000,000 by 1961.

The Economic Planning Board cannot and does not work alone. It works together with and through the executive departments and independent agencies which are concerned with various aspects of the economic problem. The Bank of Japan, the center of the nation's financial policy formulation, carries on research and gives assistance through its Policy Committee[14] which has the final say in the determination of interest rates. It also has the power to render final decision in credit matters and serves as a go-between in the joint financing of enterprises by commercial banks and also as a clearing house in foreign exchange. No economic policy can be formulated or carried out without the participation of the Ministry of Finance which has control over revenues and expenditures as well as the budget of the nation. The Ministry of International Trade and Industry is entrusted with the formulation and execution of policies pertaining to industry as well as domestic and foreign trade. Both the Ministries of Agriculture and Forestry and Transportation assume important roles in the over-all planning of both domestic and international economic policies. It is the responsibility of the government to coordinate trade and industrial policy and also to coordinate and integrate

[14] This policy-making committee was established in June, 1949, to formulate the financial policy of the Bank of Japan which must operate within the framework set. An excellent discussion of the role of the Bank of Japan is Yoshino Toshihiko, *Waga Kuni Kin'yu Seido to Kin'yu Seisaku.*

it with all aspects of economic policy including finance, credit, agriculture, and labor.

In discharging its responsibility of recommending comprehensive national development plans to the government, the Economic Planning Board obtains the advice of the Economic Deliberative Council[15] and conducts surveys, carries on the problems and needs of business and industry and publishes a "White Paper" which is an annual report analyzing the state of the nation's economy. It also gathers and assesses economic intelligence, prepares forecasts, frames economic plans, advises Ministers regarding these plans, and offers assistance in their implementation.

The Industrial Rationalization Council in the Ministry of International Trade and Industry, the largest deliberative body in the government with 122 members, studies and recommends ways and means of achieving modernization of plant and equipment, improvement of technology, increase of labor productivity, reduction of unit cost, and rationalization of management. Since rationalization is one of the most pressing needs today, efforts are constantly being made by the government though apparently with limited success so far.[16] With increasing interest shown by industry in the problem of the peaceful use of atomic energy, the newly created Atomic Energy Council is attracting the attention of the public. Planning and policymaking in the newest field of science and technology are being watched with a great deal of excitement as a possible means of solving Japan's ever present economic problems.

As part of the responsibility of the state to insure the social and economic well-being of the people and the nation, the government finds itself becoming increasingly and inextricably involved in various forms of activities, not only economic, social, and political but scientific and technological as well. In its efforts to achieve economic stability and prosperity, the government is forced to play the multiple role of manager-operator, regulator, promoter, conserver, and educator.

[15] How well financial and business interests are represented in this official governmental advisory body can be seen from the fact that its membership included among others, the President of the Shipowners' Association, President of the Federation of Economic Organizations, President of Fuji Trading Company, President of Daiichi Bussan Company, President of Yawata Steel Works, President of the Industrial Bank, President of the Japan Development Bank, Chairman of the Board of Central Bank for Agriculture, and President of the Cotton Manufacturers' Association. These members were appointed on December 26, 1952, when the Economic Policy Board was established. *Asahi*, December 27, 1952.

[16] The problems of rationalization in Japanese industry are brought out clearly in Tsusansho, *Kigyo Gorika no Shomondai*.

Government as Manager and Operator

At the inception of the long-range program of modernization and industrialization in the last quarter of the nineteenth century, Japan embarked upon a program of nationalization. The services which were nationalized included the postal service, telephone and telegraph, and the railways.[17] Nationalization was prompted chiefly by national crisis brought on by the war and subsequent depression as well as by strategic military considerations. Tobacco, salt, and camphor were made government monopolies primarily for the purpose of deriving a part of the national revenues from them. All these monopolistic enterprises with the exception of the postal services have been reorganized since World War II into public corporations, namely, the Japan National Railways Corporation, Japan Telegraph and Telephone Corporation, and the Japan Monopolies Corporation which has exclusive charge of the manufacture and sale of tobacco and the sale of salt and camphor.[18] This change was effected to preclude direct government management, red tape, and possible political bias in its management as well as to relieve the cabinet ministers, under whose control they came, of the inordinate burden. The public corporation, however, is in effect a monopoly with all the power of the state behind it, but the final decision as to what is in the best public interest cannot be left in the hands of a small group of men. It is therefore through the Diet, which is the only body which can express and safeguard the public interest, that control is exercised over these public corporations.

In addition to the Japan National Railways Corporation, Japan Telegraph and Telephone Corporation, and the Japan Monopolies Corporation, there are several other public corporations. These are the Japan Development Bank which provides funds for economic development, the Japan Export-Import Bank which finances export and import transactions as well as investment activities abroad by Japanese nationals, the Middle and Small Scale Enterprises Fund, Agriculture, Forestry and Fisheries Fund, Home Loan Fund, and the National Loan Fund, which derive their entire working capital from the government. It is not difficult to see how far reaching their in-

---

[17] All the railways were in private hands until 1907 when the main railroad lines were nationalized for strategic reasons and 2,823 miles were transferred to government ownership. Those lines which were less important strategically continued under private ownership.

[18] During the Pacific War, alcohol attained the status of government monopoly and has continued to be so but its administration is now placed in the hands of the Ministry of International Trade and Industry. See Ouchi Hyoe, *Kokka Shikin*, pp. 108–121.

fluence may be on the economic development of the country for they have vast sums at their disposal along with the power to decide when, where, how, to whom and for what purposes loans may be made.

Government Control and Regulation

It is impossible in the nature of things for the government to regulate everything or to leave anything completely alone. Ideally, the government should do what can most effectively be done through political agencies and instrumentalities for the benefit of the community. Under the traditional Japanese political system, practically everything came within the purview of government concern and therefore was subject to regulation and control by it. The Confucian philosophy and idea of statecraft, though modified to some extent by centuries of Japanese environment, produced a highly authoritarian and paternalistic pattern of government. It is therefore generally accepted by the Japanese people that increasingly government surveillance, if not control, must be extended to economic activities.

Control in various forms is exercised over economic activities for different purposes, namely, preventive, promotional and remedial. Combinations and cartels have been permitted and reintroduced to effect the elimination of the wastes of undue domestic competition. Taxation may be and has been employed to control the supply of capital, the development of industries, and the distribution of wealth among individuals and classes. Interest rates are adjusted to affect trade and influence industrial policy. Public utilities are controlled and regulated through the limitation of profits and supervision of accounts and management. Production, distribution, consumption, price and wage controls are instituted for the social and economic well-being of the industries and the consumers.

REGULATION OF TRADE AND INDUSTRY. From the very beginning of Japan's advent into the arena of world commerce, manufacturing has been geared to the demands of foreign trade. Goods were manufactured primarily, if not exclusively, for the export market and not for domestic consumption. Consequently, her economic prosperity was extremely vulnerable to the fluctuations in the foreign market. This feature of the Japanese economy was in no way altered or mitigated by the period of military occupation after the end of the war. On the contrary, this condition was recognized and re-emphasized through the creation of the Ministry of International Trade and Industry. This subordination and subservience of industry to the demands of international trade is an open recognition of the vital and indispensable role of foreign trade in the nation's economy.

In the postwar period, the Allied Powers attempted the democratization of the country through the revamping of its economic structure. Deconcentration of economic power was made the cornerstone of the new economic order. Holding companies were liquidated while antimonopoly and antitrust laws were passed to force the breakup of the big zaibatsu or combines. In spite of adequate legislation and elaborate administrative machinery provided for its execution, the antimonopoly program instituted in 1945 was never given full opportunity to become firmly established. Even before it was given a fair trial, a gradual relaxation of the provisions was begun. Legislation to force the deconcentration of economic power was abandoned and the zaibatsu was permitted to revive itself. The shift in the policy of the Occupation from democratization as the primary objective to the development of the nation into a bastion against Communist aggression in the Far East made the revival of the zaibatsu inevitable. Cartels were revived in the face of deteriorating economic conditions with the hope of strengthening the economic structure.

The Fair Trade Commission which is the Japanese counterpart of the Federal Trade Commission in the United States is the watchdog of business whose function it is to keep surveillance over every nook and cranny of commercial activity. Set up in July, 1947, it endeavors to protect the interests of the consumers and small and medium business enterprises against the power of big business which if left unchecked would operate to their detriment and in restraint of fair competition. The Commission of five members, is the policy and decision making authority whose principal task is the promotion of free competition. It keeps close watch over the activities of business firms, investigates possible violations, holds hearings, hands down decisions, issues cease-and-desist orders, and brings suits against violators who refuse to heed its orders. Although the Commission is the custodian of the antimonopoly laws, it has been a consistent advocate of the relaxation of certain features in the enforcement of the legislation.

While the achievements of the Commission have by no means been spectacular, it has through its rulings championed the cause of the consumers and small business and has brought the activities of the government much closer to the lives of the people than was the case before. In the work of preventing unfair trade competition, the Commission is assisted by the Ministry of International Trade and Industry and the Medium and Small Enterprises Board. The Fair Trade Commission exercises vigilance over any action which may impair healthy economic competition, such as undue pressure on or interference in the management of enterprises by the commercial banks. Price-fixing, false deceptive advertising, offering of expensive prizes to induce purchases, and unwarranted price discounts are some of the things which come under the special surveillance of the Commission. It also sponsors bills in the Diet and proposes revisions in existing legislation when the need arises.

Upon the Ministry of International Trade and Industry devolves the heavy responsibility of strengthening the nation's competitive position while keeping to the minimum harmful or wasteful domestic competition. This has to be achieved in such a way as to preclude the oppression of small and medium scale business and industrial enterprises by giant corporations. Small and medium scale enterprises are at a tremendous disadvantage; consequently they need not only capital which is difficult to obtain but also every possible assistance and guidance in management as well as in technology. The Small and Medium Enterprises Board which was set up in August, 1948, is charged with the responsibility of protecting and promoting the interests of small enterprises. With the Small and Medium Enterprises Fund, it works to effectively utilize the productive power of those enterprises not only for the two million persons engaged in them but as a means of strengthening the national economy and improving the standard of living in general. This is in harmony with the responsibility of the Ministry of International Trade and Industry to promote national economic well-being without producing any accentuation of class cleavage between big and small business interests and between capital and labor.

The regulation of currency, credit, and exchange rests jointly in the hands of the Ministry of Finance, the Bank of Japan, and the Securities and Exchange Commission. Between them, they regulate interest rates, the amount of money in circulation, and other matters pertaining to financial and fiscal policies. The Bank of Japan which came into existence in 1882 is a central bank which serves as the sole bank of issue, a bank of banks, that is, as a central clearing house to settle accounts for all bill transactions in the country, and the government bank entrusted with the handling of receipts and disbursements of the state treasury and issuance and redemption of national bonds. Its Policy Committee, which was created in 1949 and designed to democratize the central bank system and insure the bank's independence from government control, consists of seven members presided over by the Governor. The two government representatives from the Finance Ministry and the Economic Planning Board have no voice in the committee's decisions. The five members representing the commercial banks both urban and rural, commerce, industry, and agriculture, form the top-decision-making body of the Bank.

The regulation of supply and demand as well as prices is shared by the Ministry of Trade and Industry and the Ministry of Agriculture and Forestry while that of wages is the primary responsibility of the Ministry of Labor. In every sphere of policy-making, whether economic or political, the Ministry of Finance plays a prominent role. It is involved in the lowering of commodity prices and cost of production as well as in keeping trade deficits as low as possible. It takes a hand in the settlement of labor disputes. But most important of all, it distributes government capital[19] for investment purposes, giving priority to industrial rationalization projects which contribute toward the building up of economic strength through a more rational and efficient use of productive power.

Government Promotion of Economic Activities

There has been in Japan a tradition of government protection of industries in the form of direct legislation and indirect aid through special financial privileges, subsidies, and government loans at low interest rates. Liberal government subsidies have always played a major role in the development of the nation's economic system in the last three-quarters of a century. Practically every major industry in existence today owes its prosperity to government bounty which made it possible to lay a solid foundation for growth. Moreover, loans at reasonable interest rates have been and are now available to business and industry through government supported banks.

The Japan Development Bank was established by the government in April, 1951, for the purpose of supplying long-term capital funds for the promotion of economic reconstruction and industrial development. Its predecessor was the Reconstruction Finance Bank set up in 1947 to provide funds for the rehabilitation of war-damaged national economy. While its chief function is to assist in the nation's economic recovery and stabilization, it also aims to bolster the nation's banking system by supplementing the ordinary banks and easing their financial burdens. It has now become by far the largest supplier of long-term industrial capital. Through the Japan Export-Import Bank established in December, 1950, long-term operating funds are supplied to export and import activities, especially for the export of plant facilities and other products of heavy and chemical

[19] Government funds which can easily be converted into commercial and industrial capital are derived from three main sources, namely, taxes, postal savings, and small life insurance operated by the government.

industries. Government aid to foreign trade activities is furnished through this bank which also encourages commercial banks to provide funds for foreign trade purposes.

Small and medium scale enterprises have been receiving special attention in recent years for they have always suffered from adverse conditions, especially the lack of capital since loans are not readily available to them in the regular commercial banks. In order to help them, the Medium and Small Enterprises Fund makes available funds not exceeding 10,000,000 yen for long-term operating capital and for equipment. The Central Fund for Agriculture, Forestry and Fisheries also provides capital to those engaged in these particular activities.

Technical assistance in different forms is given to the various industries. Every possible assistance and encouragement is willingly given by the government as part of the program of rationalization. In manufacturing as well as in agriculture, aid is given through research institutes, experiment stations, and laboratories. Standards are established for products, particularly in foreign trade commodities, and testing facilities are made available in laboratories. Trade promotion is carried on by means of fairs and trade centers both at home and abroad. Market surveys, price indices, all sorts of reports and services are made easily available to business and industry.

Fairly typical of the kind of promotional and rationalization planning that is carried on by the Ministry of International Trade and Industry is its plan to stabilize the coal industry through a program of price reduction. The Ministry has estimated the demand for coal and mapped out production plans to meet it. The plans include the improvement of pit operations, finding ways of effectively utilizing low grade coal, devising consumption policy to balance or equalize supply and demand, production priority, proper disposition of surplus labor resulting from rationalization, and devising of tax measures which would facilitate investment in the rationalization of the coal industry.

THE STATE AND GENERAL WELFARE

In the years since the restoration of independence and sovereignty in 1952, social security has become virtually a household word providing a major political issue which the conservatives and the radicals alike are supporting. The public as well as the policy makers are "social security" conscious to a degree totally unknown in the prewar era.[20] Interestingly enough the concept of social security is very

[20] Suetaka Shin, "Shakai hosho to toshi," *Shisei*, October, 1955, p. 1. See also 1954 *Shakai Hosho Nenkan*, pp. 18–20.

new, having been introduced into Japan in the period following the war. The term itself is the literal translation of the borrowed concept derived from the United States Social Security Act of 1935.

Social security was not regarded as a public responsibility until the New Constitution guaranteed individuals the right to live. This was the traditional attitude, for through the centuries it was the family system which had assumed the responsibility of looking after the social and economic welfare of all its members with no help whatsoever from the government. Only recently has the solution of social problems come to be looked upon as the responsibility of society rather than of the family or of individuals. This has resulted from the recognition that social conditions produce poverty, ignorance, illness, disease, unemployment, delinquency, and crime, and that they should be dealt with as social ills. No longer is poverty regarded as something attributable entirely to the incapability, shiftlessness, or unwillingness of the individual to work.

Japan's social security system[21] reflects many of the features of the American system after which it was patterned. However, it is built upon the experiences of the Japanese people dating back to the prewar period. The notable change that has taken place is in the philosophy as well as the scope of the program which now sets as its goal the achievement of a minimum standard of living for all. While the system at this point is still not adequate, it represents a definite advance. The administration of social welfare activities is vested in the Welfare and Labor Ministries.[22] The highest advisory body charged with the responsibility of firmly establishing social security is the Social Security Policy Council of forty members representing the Diet, government agencies, interested groups including employers, doctors, dentists, and pharmacists, and the public. The Council which is attached directly to the Office of Prime Minister carries on studies and deliberations, recommends legislation, approves draft laws, and gives advice regarding the implementation and execution of the social security program. Its actual work is handled by a staff of thirty fulltime secretaries appointed by the Prime Minister from among government officials and learned persons of experience who are vitally concerned with the problem of social security. In its broadest sense, the successful carrying out of the social security program actually

---

[21] For the most recent and comprehensive discussion and evaluation of the social security system, see Shimizu Kinjiro, *Shakai Hosho Seido* (1954).

[22] From about the middle of 1951 there have been several proposals to consolidate the Welfare and Labor Ministries into a single department of social affairs in the interests of greater efficiency in the administration of social welfare and social security.

requires the combined efforts of the National Diet, the Office of the Prime Minister as well as the Ministries of Labor, Welfare, Transportation, Construction, and Finance.[23]

An ambitious program of social security legislation was undertaken by the Diet during its sessions from December, 1951, to July, 1952, when a large number of laws was passed. The program which has since been growing steadily aims not so much at the protection and assistance of the poor as the improvement of conditions for the people in general and particularly those in the low income groups so that they would not fall into a condition of poverty and dependence. In other words, it is conceived as a positive program that is an integral part of the larger effort to increase the social and economic welfare of the people. During the fiscal year 1952, social security expenditures comprised 6.7 percent of the national budget; in 1953 it increased to 7.5 percent, and in 1954 to 8.2 percent, showing a steady increase from year to year as the need for social security receives greater emphasis.[24]

Public assistance plays a very important role in the Japanese social security scheme. As a postwar innovation, it is not administered as a charitable handout but as a form of assistance which constitutes an integral part of the individual's right to the security of livelihood guaranteed by the Constitution. Far reaching in its implications, therefore, was the enactment of the Livelihood Protection Law in 1946 which is the cornerstone of the public assistance program which insures a minimum standard of living. Under this legislation, public assistance is given to the poor,[25] the sick, and the aged in such forms as minimum cost of living allowance for food, clothing, rental, com-

---

[23] In the National Diet are two standing Committees on Welfare, one in the House of Representatives and the other in the House of Councillors. Central policy planning rests in the Office of the Prime Minister where the Social Security Policy Council as well as the Unemployment Measures Council is situated. The Welfare Ministry, which is the agency primarily responsible for the administration of social security, claims no less than thirteen different councils entrusted with advisory functions relating to all aspects of social welfare. Councils entrusted with matters relating to wages, employment, unemployment, and workmen's compensation exist in the Ministry of Labor, while the Ministry of Transportation has a policy council on the employment security of seamen. Matters relating to housing are in the hands of the Housing Policy Council in the Ministry of Construction. Finally, the Ministry of Finance plays an indispensable role in the carrying out of the over-all security program through its Budget Bureau and the Government Funds Investment Council.

[24] 1955 *Shakai Hosho Nenkan*, p. 33.

[25] According to the Ministry of Welfare survey of April, 1953, more than

pulsory education expenses, medical and hospital expenses, child-birth expenses including prenatal and postnatal care, funeral expenses, and occupational needs including equipment, funds, and rehabilitation training for the acquisition of necessary skills.

In principle, assistance is given in money, but is also furnished in kind, such as the use of different facilities like the home for the aged, relief agencies, hospitals, health centers, occupational training centers, and public lodging houses. For the administration of the program which is in the hands of the prefectural governors and mayors of cities, there are welfare offices[26] staffed with social workers. A peculiarly Japanese institution, the People's Livelihood Committees with a total nationwide membership of some 125,000 persons, provide invaluable assistance in the administration of the livelihood security program in the localities.

The coming into effect of the Child Welfare Law on January 1, 1948, marked a notable advance in the promotion of the welfare of children. While the welfare of children in general is the main objective of the legislation, special attention is directed at orphans and homeless children, and to the helping and rehabilitation of juvenile delinquents as well as the physically weak, mentally deficient, the deaf, and the blind. Most of the work of giving protection and guidance to children is done in the more than one hundred Child Welfare Consultation Offices located in the principal centers of the nation. The general health of children and pregnant mothers is protected through the numerous health clinics. The child welfare program is administered by the Children's Bureau of the Ministry of Welfare and the Children's Sections and the Mother and Child Health Sections in the prefectural governments. They carry out the policy determined by the Central Child Welfare Council of the national government and the prefectural child welfare councils, both of which carry on studies, make recommendations, and give advice.

Since the end of the war, special attention is being given to the care of the physically handicapped. The care of both military and civilian casualties of war as well as the naturally handicapped is provided in the law which has been in force since 1950. Medical care and other forms of aid as well as occupational rehabilitation are avail-

---

9,000,000 persons or more than ten percent of the entire population were found to be in a condition of poverty. Of these 2,200,000 were eligible for and actually receiving public assistance while 7,000,000 were borderline cases. 1955 *Shakai Hosho Nenkan,* p. 121.

[26] There were 835 welfare offices throughout the nation as of January, 1954.

able so that those whose earning power has been reduced or destroyed by impaired sight or hearing, speech impediment, damaged nervous system, loss of limbs, and other handicaps may be helped to become partially or entirely self-supporting and useful members of society.

Social security has to rely a great deal on various forms of social insurance. The oldest of these is the health insurance which dates back to the original legislation which was enacted in 1922 but did not go into full effect until January 1, 1927, due to the interruption caused by the great earthquake. Health insurance for workers, which provides medical, surgical, hospital, childbirth, and funeral expenses, is now compulsory in enterprises where five or more persons are employed. Its purpose is to give medical care and contribute toward the restoration of earning power lost through illness or injury.[27] Health insurance for day laborers was set up separately in 1954. The approximately 150,000 seamen are covered separately under the Seamen's Insurance Law that was enacted to meet the special needs of this particular occupational group. Their insurance system is unique in that its coverage is comprehensive with health, unemployment, old age annuity, and workmen's compensation all rolled into one.[28]

For the people in general, the National Health Insurance Law which went into effect in 1938 provides the same sort of benefits as those provided in the workers' health insurance. This insurance is set up on a geographic basis while the workers' insurance is administered through the various enterprises. In spite of these two systems of insurance, there are still some 30,000,000 persons in the low income group who are left out as ineligible since they do not fall in the specified categories. Still excluded are those employed in small enterprises with less than five workers as well as the farmers and fishermen.

The workers are protected by unemployment insurance which insures security of livelihood to the unemployed for a maximum period of six months with benefits amounting to sixty percent of their wages. In 1953, approximately 8,000,000 workers were protected. Since 1951 unemployment insurance has been extended to some half million day-laborers who now enjoy security of the sort that was not even dreamed of during or before World War II. Through the Workmen's Compensation Law, workers receive compensation for illness,

[27] A detailed discussion of the Health Insurance Law is found in Koyama Shinjiro, *Shakai Hosho Kankeiho*, Vol. I, p. 15–200.

[28] Suetaka Shin, "Shakai hosho to toshi," *Shisei*, October, 1955, p. 7.

injury, disability, or death caused while on their jobs. The compensation takes the form of medical expenses, wage loss, disability payments, survivor benefits, and funeral expenses.

Public servants are in a special social security category of their own. They come under a system of health, unemployment, and workmen's compensation insurance set up exclusively for them under separate legislation. Moreover, they come under a pension system which has been in existence since 1923 when it was first instituted.

Illness being the major cause of unemployment and insecurity of livelihood which in turn force people to seek public assistance, the government in its social security program places heavy emphasis on its prevention.[29] Since tuberculosis has always been the greatest killer in Japan with nearly 3,000,000 sufferers at present, major efforts are being concentrated on the control and eradication of the disease.[30] The Tuberculosis Prevention Law provides not only for the care of patients, which is still far from adequate, but also facilities for research. Mental illness, which in recent years has assumed alarming proportions with an estimated 3,500,000 persons mentally ill, is receiving the concentrated attention of the government through the Mental Hygiene Law. Leprosy, though no longer the dreaded disease that it once was, is still the object of vigorous efforts. Public health and sanitation have made such progress in the postwar years that mortality rates have fallen to the lowest point ever reached in Japan's history. The reduction of infant mortality in particular has been almost beyond belief.

The Eugenics Protection Law which first came into existence in the years preceding the Second World War now forms the basis of birth control which is accepted as part of the long-range social security program. Family planning and legalized abortion for economic as well as health reasons have been accepted as necessary for the economic and social welfare of individuals and families and in the long run of the entire nation.

[29] Of those who receive public assistance, sixty percent attribute their plight to illness. *Asahi*, November 20, 1955.

[30] According to the survey made by the Ministry of Welfare in 1953, there were 2,920,000 tuberculosis patients of whom 1,379,000 required hospitalization.

15 ————————

The Citizen, Law,

and the Courts

Undoubtedly the post-World War II period has witnessed the greatest changes in the legal system of the country since constitutional government was first instituted in 1889. In accordance with the avowed objectives of the Potsdam Declaration, the Allied occupation authorities initiated legislation of a very advanced character in the hope that it would supply the framework for future growth along democratic lines. This resulted in the infusion of alien concepts at a furious tempo for the purpose of achieving speedy reforms. Such frantic and determined efforts at legislation were reminiscent of the assiduous efforts made in the last quarter of the nineteenth century by an enlightened and realistic group of Japanese statesmen under terrific pressure to modernize and strengthen the nation in order to preserve its independence against Western encroachment and exploitation.[1]

It is quite apparent that a considerable portion of the new Constitution reflects much that does not yet exist in Japanese society. Some of the provisions are meant to be no more than a blueprint of things yet to be achieved. Some things will never materialize while many others must and will be modified to fit the needs or even the predilections of the Japanese people and society.

BACKGROUND OF JAPANESE LAW

If one were to trace back historically the lineage of Japanese law, he would find that before the seventh century A.D. there was nothing

[1] Thomas L. Blakemore, "Post-war Developments in Japanese Law," *Wisconsin Law Review* (July, 1947), pp. 633–653, gives an excellent summary of the changes which took place under the new Constitution.

that could be regarded as a legal system. It was only after frequent contacts were established with her continental neighbor that Japan instituted a legal system. However, since the laws were so closely modeled on the Chinese legal codes it soon turned out that the system was not very well suited to Japanese needs. The establishment of feudalism toward the end of the twelfth century caused the abandoning of the borrowed legal system which was elaborate and impressive enough but very inadequate. Feudalism developed its own kind of customary law which superseded Chinese law, since the problems of feudal society could not be dealt with effectively by an alien legal system. The laws of the feudatories, which developed in the century of internecine warfare roughly from 1475 to 1575 A.D. as house laws of the feudal barons, became the basis of feudal legal development for nearly three centuries.

The overthrow of the feudal system in 1868 and the establishment of the new Meiji government called for a new legal system which would effectively destroy the laws and practices of the past which stood in the way of progress. Codes patterned after those of France and Germany were enacted with the advice of French and German jurists. Naturally Japanese jurisprudence took on a marked continental appearance. Thus the Westernization of Japanese law has left very few visible reminders of earlier indigenous concepts, practices, and institutions. Yet in the spirit of the law and its application as well as interpretation, a great deal of the traditional is still preserved. The surviving old attitudes and concepts which are not always discernible to the casual observer lead to unexpected results when Westernized statutes are applied. Westernization of Japanese law was necessitated not only by the urgent need to unify and strengthen domestic law in such a way as to aid the nation's modernization but also by the fact that Western powers were reluctant to relinquish extraterritorial rights so long as unfamiliar, non-Western, and "barbarian" patterns of law continued to exist. In other words, legal reform was the result of international demands rather than of internal pressures. It was to make the nation strong and to preserve its independence that the reform was undertaken. Consequently, the establishment of a democratic government or the rights of individuals was not the primary objective, and not the concern of the leaders. It was perhaps not envisaged even as a by product of the new legal system.

CHANGES IN LEGAL SYSTEM AND CONCEPTS

Under the Constitution of 1947 noticeable changes have occurred in both the form and substance of the law. For the first time, common-law principles have been introduced with the result that the influence of Anglo-American legal system is now quite evident. Even the oath has been introduced in both form and language very much like that which obtains in the United States.

The stilted and often well-nigh unintelligible legal language has been discarded in favor of the easily understandable vernacular language appropriate for the general public. Judicial decisions are now rendered in simple, everyday colloquial language. The most conspicuous of all is the Constitution which is now intelligible to the average Japanese since it is no longer in the semiarchaic classical language of the imperial court but in plain, everyday vernacular. This should help to dissipate the general and widespread attitude that law is something beyond comprehension for most people and that it has little, if any, bearing on one's everyday activities.

New concepts have been introduced which are radical departures from traditional attitudes. The concept of citizenship which had been alien to the Japanese system is now accepted though not yet firmly established. Virtually gone is the idea that the people are the emperor's subjects, not only subservient to the ruler but without independence to assert their rights against him. The dignity of the individual is stressed to an extent previously not known. Individual rights are clearly and unequivocably established so that the individual worth of the person has become a basic principle supported by law. This is indeed a far cry from the authoritarianism which completely submerged individual rights to the collective good of the nation making possible the development of a police state which was easily controlled by the privileged few.

To enhance the dignity of the individual the new Constitution provides that there shall be no discrimination in political, economic, or social relations because of sex or family origin. This has resulted in radical changes in the family system. The revised Civil Code has entirely eliminated the prerogative powers of the head of a house and for practical purposes abolished the house as a legal institution. It permits children to freely establish their own households. Furthermore, the parents are to respect the individuality of their children. The law of inheritance has been changed so as to confer equal rights on all the children regardless of sex, and the right of inheritance of husband and wife has been greatly strengthened. Primogeniture as a system of inheritance has been abandoned. Adoption has been liberalized to the extent of permitting parents to adopt a son even where there is already a son in the family. It has removed all restrictions upon the financial independence and rights of inheritance of the

wife and has given her equality as well as initiative in divorce proceedings and she now enjoys parity with her husband in the exercise
of parental authority.

In the implementation of the principle of equality of the sexes, a
serious problem was encountered in how to handle legally the question of adultery. Under the old system which followed the traditional feudal concept and practice supported by Confucianism, the
wife was liable to punishment while the husband was not. In resolving the dilemma of how equality could be carried out, adultery was
removed as a criminal offense. The legalization of the equality of
the sexes thus removes from the Japanese social pattern the Confucian
roles traditionally assigned to women in various stages of life in the
form of "three obediences," namely, subservience to the father while
a child, to the husband as a wife, and finally to the son as a widowed
mother.[2] By not recognizing it as a criminal offense, adultery was
made a subject for settlement within the family between the husband
and wife, without dragging it out into public view. Because of the
way in which it was handled under the old criminal code, the abolition of the crime actually had the effect of legally liberating women
from injustice. At the same time it also indirectly removed the stigma
of illegitimacy.

In the matter of marriage, a woman can no longer be forced into it
against her will since mutual consent by both parties is now a necessary condition. At the same time, there has been a liberalization and
simplification of divorce procedure to the extent that only mutual
consent is necessary and that the only legal requirements to effectuate
divorce is the reporting of the divorce agreement to the town or city
hall. The responsibility of mutual support between husband and
wife and between close relatives is in no way weakened in the revised
family system.

Habeas corpus, which is alien to Asian countries, is now an integral
part of the legal system as is the common-law principle that a person
is presumed to be innocent until proved guilty. In the administration of justice, even the once serious offense of lèse majesté is no
longer on the law books. This of course destroys the traditional
legal doctrine of the sanctity of the sovereign and makes it impossible
to use the emperor as a shield against or instrument for power struggle. There has been a very considerable extension in the use of suspended sentences as an application of the principle of the dignity of
the individual. The reform and rehabilitation of the individual now
receives greater emphasis than ever.

[2] See Masaki Hiroshi, *Nihonjin no Ryoshin*, pp. 81–90.

The establishment of the rule of law is a highly significant innovation which negates the Confucian political ideal, the government of men, which gave rise to so much abuse even in the recent political history of Japan. Since this is a new principle which is completely devoid of traditional base or roots in the Japanese scheme, it would require persistent effort to establish it firmly, especially in view of the concept that laws are but temporary expressions of opinion or policy of the government as to what is best at any given time and therefore are neither permanent nor sacrosanct. That laws constitute therefore a convenient embodiment of certain principles and policies is a view that is difficult to square off with the idea that the rule of law is of overwhelming importance in orderly political life.

The doctrine of judicial review has also been made an integral part of the Japanese Constitution which vests the Supreme Court with the supreme judicial power to interpret laws and pass upon their constitutionality. Although this follows the American instead of the British practice, it goes a step further than the United States where is exists not as a constitutional provision but rather as an established custom. Under the old Meiji Constitution, a law enacted by the Diet was never unconstitutional and the courts did not have the function of ruling on its constitutionality.[3]

NATIONALITY. While a new concept of a citizen was introduced as part of the democratization of the country, there has been very little change in the concept of nationality. Japanese nationality may be acquired in several ways. The most common and natural method is by birth. It may be acquired also by the creation of family relationships such as marriage or adoption. It is also possible to obtain nationality by the process of naturalization. The basic nationality legislation is the Nationality Law enacted by the Diet on March 16, 1899, in force from April 1, which follows the principle of *jus sanguinis* without completely excluding *jus soli*. Normally the child wherever born takes the nationality of his parents.

Foreign women acquire nationality when they become wives of Japanese; foreign men when they marry Japanese women and become members of their wives' families or when adopted as sons. Normally, an adult alone is eligible for naturalization in his own right, although a minor child derives Japanese nationality through the acquisition of nationality of the parent and a wife acquires it through the act of her

---

[3] Under the old system the watchdog of the Constitution was the Privy Council which had the power to interpret and declare laws unconstitutional and even succeeded in preventing the enactment of statutes by clearly indicating its disapproval in advance.

husband. Naturalization is a process that is effectuated by the issuance of a grant of nationality by the Minister of Justice. Long residence is normally required although certain categories of aliens, such as those born in Japan or closely related to a Japanese national, receive preferential treatment. In the case of those who have rendered meritorious service to Japan, normal requirements may be waived and naturalization may be effectuated speedily. The Nationality Law denies certain political rights to persons whose nationality is derived by the process of naturalization.

Voluntary renunciation of nationality was provided for by the revision of the Nationality Law in 1924. Until expatriation was authorized in that year, all children born of Japanese parents in foreign countries whose births were reported to Japanese consular authorities possessed dual nationality; they were nationals of the country of their birth as well as of their parents' country. There was no way to avoid the legal complications arising from the conflicting claims of two countries. Expatriation made it possible for individuals to keep one nationality and renounce the other but it required initiative on the part of the individuals. The revision of 1947 simplified expatriation by making it almost automatic. Thus the present Nationality Law with the 1950 revision provides that Japanese born in the United States, Canada, Mexico, Argentina, Brazil, Chile, and Peru are regarded as nationals of those countries only, unless they indicate their desire to retain Japanese nationality. Those born in countries other than the seven mentioned above, must go through the formal procedure of expatriation to renounce Japanese nationality.

CIVIL LIBERTIES

Perhaps no other area of law reflects as much advance as that of civil liberties. Japan, like other Asian nations, has not in the past developed liberal traditions which the Western democracies take for granted as part of their political heritage. As a legacy of the long authoritarian tradition the populace still betray a fear of officials and there is a general reluctance on the part of individuals to challenge administrative actions or even question the wisdom of executive judgments. The bill of rights as contained in the new Constitution could, when understood and applied properly, go a long way toward rectifying the conditions and the psychology which stand in the way of democratization.

Even a cursory reading of the bill of rights will leave no doubt in the reader's mind that this portion of the Constitution is the crux of the new political system. Actually the chapter which sets forth the rights and duties of the individual constitutes far and away the longest and the most important portion of the entire document, with thirty-one out of a total of 103 articles, and represents the most radical departure. The enumeration of individual rights is more specific and detailed than can be found even in the older constitutions of the democracies such as the United States. This was necessary in order not to take anything for granted and to preclude the possibility of misinterpretation or underinterpretation of the rights of a people who do not have the benefit of liberal traditions. The old Constitution provided for civil liberties but not unconditionally since they could be abridged or curtailed by statutory enactments. Violations of personal freedoms resulted not only from statutory provisions but through loopholes in the law and legal fictions which were developed.

The new Constitution provides that all the people will be respected as individuals and that their right to life, liberty, and the pursuit of happiness must be the supreme consideration in legislation and in the administration of governmental affairs. That these fundamental human rights are eternal and inviolable is clearly stated in the guarantee that they "shall be conferred upon the people of this and future generations as eternal and inviolate rights."

Equality before the law is expressed in the provision forbidding discrimination in political, economic, or social relations because of race, creed, sex, social status, or family origin. Special privilege has been abolished by discontinuing the system of peerage and excluding any privilege from any award of honor or any distinction which will be limited in validity to only the lifetime of the recipient.

Never before has the individual citizen enjoyed such extensive rights and freedoms which have been made an integral part of the legal system to protect and enhance his position in society. All the freedoms guaranteed to individuals in democracies are provided for. The freedom of thought, worship, assembly, and association as well as speech, press, and all other forms of expression are guaranteed along with the freedom of residence and movement, choice of occupation, choice of nationality, academic freedom, and freedom from servitude, self-incriminating testimony, forced confession, double jeopardy and *ex post facto* legislation.

Included in the political and civil rights enjoyed by the people are the following:

1. Right to choose their public officials and to dismiss them.
2. Right of peaceful petition for the
   (a) redress of damage
   (b) removal of public officials

(c) enactment, repeal, or amendment of laws, ordinances, regulations, and other matters.

3. Right to sue and be indemnified by the government for any damages
resulting from the administrative actions of officials.

4. Equal rights of husband and wife.

5. Right to a decent standard of living, namely, "the right to maintain
the minimum standards of wholesome and cultural living."

6. Right to receive an equal education corresponding to their ability.

7. Right and the obligation to work.

8. Right of workers to organize and bargain and act collectively.

9. Right to own or to hold property.

10. Right to life and liberty.

11. Right of due process.

12. Right of access to the courts.

13. Right of counsel.

14. Right to be secure in their homes—freedom from illegal search,
seizure, detention, and arrest.

15. Right to speedy, impartial, public trial.

16. Right to habeas corpus.

It is clear from the reading of the Constitution that far greater
emphasis has been placed on the rights than on the duties of the
people. The traditional attitude has for centuries been to emphasize
duties practically to the exclusion of rights; this was especially the
case under feudalism. For the purpose of encouraging democratic
development it was imperative that individual rights be stressed to
effectively counteract the altogether too powerful influence of the
authoritarian tradition and its legacies in Japanese society. The
result has been the inclusion of only a few basic obligations of citizenship such as the liability to taxation, the obligation to work, and the
responsibility of preserving and maintaining by constant endeavor
the freedoms and rights guaranteed by the Constitution and of
utilizing them for the public welfare. The obligation to receive an
education, while not specifically stated, has been a responsibility of
citizenship which has long since gained complete acceptance.

The constant threat of curtailment of civil liberties hangs over the
head of the people as a result of the government's inability to devise
effective measures to cope with subversive activities as well as non-
subversive but highly critical activities of opposition forces. The
Subversive Activities Prevention Law which went into effect on July
4, 1952, only a few months after the restoration of independence and
full sovereignty was without doubt one of the most controversial
pieces of legislation to be enacted in postwar Japan. It met with the
powerful opposition of labor unions, political parties, and liberal
groups who were apprehensive that the government in its eagerness

to curb, if not stamp out, the subversive activities of the Communists may overstep its bounds and terrorize and victimize innocent citizens.[4]

As an aftermath of the abominable behavior of Communists and their sympathizers in the courtroom while trials were in progress and as an integral part of the government's antisubversive program, the Law for the Maintenance of Order in Court was enacted on July 7, 1952. This law, which was inspired and necessitated by the obstructionist dilatory tactics of leftists on trial, enables the Japanese court to prevent using the courts as a place to wage political contests or carry on propaganda or publicity. Any person who interferes with the exercise of court functions or seriously prejudices the dignity of justice by disobeying orders issued or measures taken by the court for the maintenance of order will be liable to noncriminal confinement not exceeding twenty days or a noncriminal fine not exceeding 30,000 yen or both.

THE NEW ROLE OF THE JUDICIARY

There has been such a complete revamping of the judiciary that the courts are actually cast in an entirely new role. Under the new system the judiciary has achieved independence in the true sense of the word. It is no longer the strong arm of the executive branch that it was under the old Constitution; it is completely independent of executive control, intervention, or pressure.

Independence and dignity of the judiciary have been insured by entrusting the administration of justice to the Supreme Court and subordinate courts of law. In recognition of the new status of the judiciary, the Chief Justice of the Supreme Court has been accorded a rank equivalent to that of the Prime Minister. The fifteen-member Supreme Court has complete control over the administration of the judicial affairs, not only exercising powers of nomination and supervision over all subordinate judicial personnel but also assuming administrative responsibility for the operations of the entire judicial branch. It also assumes responsibility for the recruiting, training, and assignment of judicial personnel as well as the preparation of the judicial budget. Nonjudicial administrative functions have been taken over by the Justice Ministry or transferred to other administrative agencies.

A complete separation of judicial administration from criminal investigation has been achieved with the procurator's offices being placed under the control of the Ministry of Justice but in such a

[4] The scope of the Subversive Activities Prevention Law is discussed in detail in Tokunaga Masaji, *Nihon Kyosanto to Bohaho* (1952).

manner as to enable them to develop a degree of independence of action. Consequently, the judges and procurators work independently and not together as under the old system when they were both under the supervision of the Justice Ministry and the latter were actually attached to the courts. Functionally the judges and procurators are separate and distinct. Yet, they actually start out with identical training though years later they may differ noticeably in experience. Unlike the French system which does not permit interchange between the judiciary and the legal profession, the Japanese system allows lawyers to become judges or procurators without much difficulty.

The expansion of the judicial function has been achieved also by the abolition of extraordinary courts which were auxiliary to administrative power and, further, by the denial of final judicial power to any organ or agency of the executive branch. The Court of Administrative Litigation under the old system, patterned after its French counterpart, was abolished.[5] Administrative litigation is now placed within the jurisdiction of the regular courts. The so-called "maritime courts" and "patent courts" have become administrative tribunals and while the processes resemble those of regular courts their decisions are administrative in nature and therefore subject to judicial review.

The revamped codes of civil and criminal procedure assign a far greater role to the courts than was the case previously. Warrants for arrest and detention can be issued only by the judges; procurators and police officials no longer have the right to issue warrants. The presumption of innocence on the part of the defendant on trial places a heavier burden on the courts which are responsible for the impartial administration of justice. Preliminary investigations which were a prominent feature of the old system are gone, as are forced confessions. Moreover, the legal validity of confessions has been greatly limited.

ORGANIZATION AND FUNCTION OF THE COURTS

SUPREME COURT. At the apex of the judicial structure is the Supreme Court located in Tokyo which is composed of fifteen judges

---

[5] When the Court of Administrative Litigation was first set up, it was based on Prince Ito's belief that, if administrative activities were placed under the scrutiny and control of the judicature, and if courts of law were given the power to review and invalidate administrative acts, the executive would be subordinated to the judiciary thereby impairing the integrity and effectiveness of the executive branch.

no younger than forty years of age, of whom ten must have been legal experts of not less than twenty years' professional standing while the remaining five may be learned persons of experience but not necessarily in the field of law. This is designed to permit a more democratic and varied representation of expertise on the highest tribunal of the nation. The Chief Judge of the Supreme Court is appointed by the Emperor on the recommendation of the Cabinet while the other justices are appointed by the Cabinet. Safeguards are provided to uphold their independence in the exercise of their conscience by guaranteeing adequate compensation which cannot be decreased during their terms of office. The Supreme Court operates through a Grand Bench of all fifteen justices (nine constituting a quorum) which hears all cases involving the question of constitutionality, and petty benches of five justices (three being a quorum). In the consideration of appeals, the highest tribunal in the land limits itself to issues of law.

The Supreme Court is the court of last resort with power to determine the constitutionality of any law, order, regulation, or official act. It is vested with the rule-making power by virtue of which it determines rules of procedure and of practice and of matters relating to attorneys, the internal discipline of the courts, and the administration of judicial affairs. Even the public procurators are subject to the rule-making power of the highest tribunal. This rule-making power, however, may be delegated to inferior courts in so far as their own regulation is concerned.

A unique feature of the new judicial system is the device of recall that has been introduced for the first time for the popular determination of the fitness of the justices of the highest tribunal. On the theory that the justices of the Supreme Court must reflect the collective will of the people, the Constitution specifically provides for their review "by the people at the first general election of the members of the House of Representatives following their appointment, and shall be reviewed again at the first general election of the House of Representatives after a lapse of ten years and in the same manner thereafter." Should the majority of the voters favor the dismissal of a justice, the popular mandate must be carried out.

THE LOWER COURTS. Next to the Supreme Court are the eight High Courts of regional jurisdiction whose function, with minor exceptions, is purely appellate and for a great many cases its decisions are final. Judges must have had at least ten years of experience in a judicial or procuratorial capacity or as practicing attorneys. The court normally operates through panels of three judges but for crimes to overthrow the government, for which it becomes a court of first instance, it employs panels of five judges instead. The number of judges comprising the court from which trial panels are drawn ranges anywhere from sixty-four in Tokyo which is the largest down to seven in Sapporo.[6]

On the next lower level are forty-nine District Courts, one in each of the forty-six prefectures plus Hokkaido which covers a larger area than any prefecture and has three. These courts constitute the principal trial courts and exercise a general jurisdiction over all civil actions not specifically given to other courts. Trial is ordinarily by a single judge but in more serious cases by a collegiate court of three judges.

On the lowest rung of the judicial ladder are the Summary Courts which number about six thousand. These courts superseded the old police courts and operate at a level slightly above that of the justice of the peace in America, handling civil actions involving less than 5,000 yen and criminal actions involving offenses subject to imprisonment for less than a month. These courts represent an innovation designed to simplify the judicial procedure at the lowest level and to overcome the public attitude of awe, if not distrust, toward the courts as well as to do away with the stigma attached to litigation by encouraging the use of courts. The single judge of a summary court has a broad latitude in the conduct of trials.

COURTS OF DOMESTIC RELATIONS. The Civil Code which is based on the dignity of the individual and the equality of the sexes must rely heavily for its smooth operation on the Courts of Domestic Relations which are branches of the District Courts designed to promote harmonious relationship within the family and among relatives. The 276 courts, which in reality are half-arbitral, half-judicial tribunals composed of judges and laymen, operate informally in the probate and domestic relations field, handling such matters as divorce, alimony, breach of promise, inheritance, property division, adoption, guardianship, mutual-support, and similar matters. Normal judicial procedure is not followed in every case since there are instances where arbitral actions are more appropriate. At the inception of the system, the courts were swamped with work since many people came

[6] According to the 1953 *Zenkankocho Binran,* the number of judges attached to the eight High Courts was as follows:

Tokyo	64	Takamatsu	13
Osaka	35	Hiroshima	11
Fukuoka	22	Sendai	11
Nagoya	16	Sapporo	7

with domestic problems with the idea that they could be solved simply and speedily according to their desires. Since the establishment of these courts the number of cases brought in by women increased noticeably.

THE PROCURATORS. Criminal prosecution is the function of the procurators who come under the jurisdiction and control of the Ministry of Justice. Because of the nature of their functions which are clearly administrative, they have been separated from the judiciary. In their capacity as public prosecutors, they perform functions paralleling those of the district attorneys in the United States. Although the system at its inception in the 1880's was based on the French model, appreciable modifications were effected. Under the present setup, it represents more of a combination and merger of the features of the French, British, and American systems.

JURY TRIAL. The jury system was tried and abandoned and has not been revived. Legislation establishing the jury system was enacted in 1923 providing for trial by jury in criminal cases. It was not until October 1, 1928, that the jury was used for the first time. Jury trial was mandatory unless waived by the accused in all cases in which the accused was liable to the death penalty or to life imprisonment except when provided otherwise. A jury consisted of twelve persons who decided on the questions of fact and who rendered their verdict by a simple majority. The verdict however was not binding upon the court. There was a very small demand for jury trials for several reasons. In the absence of a common-law tradition of trial by jury, the average accused person did not have confidence in a jury made up of ordinary individuals and felt that he would be no worse off and perhaps better off if he entrusted his fate to the judge who was trained and experienced in the administration of justice. Another deterrent to the use of the jury was its high cost to the defendant.

QUALIFICATIONS OF JUDICIAL PERSONNEL. The ideal of the unification of the bench and bar is the goal which underlies the method of recruitment employed in the judiciary. Those who seek careers as judges, procurators, and lawyers all must pass the same examinations and go through the same training required by law. In order to be admitted to special judicial training that is prescribed, candidates must pass the state judicial examinations.

These state judicial examinations consist of three parts. The first part is a written examination designed to test the general cultural background of the candidates on the college graduation level, while the second, also written, tests specialized knowledge of law in seven

fields of which five are required and two are electives.[7] The third
and final part consists of oral examinations on the five required fields.

Those who successfully pass the examinations are designated
judicial trainees by the Judicial Examination Committee and are
enrolled in a two-year training program at the Institute of Judicial
Training of the Supreme Court.[8] During the training period eight
months are devoted to the courts, four months to the procurator's
office, and four months to the bar association for the purpose of
becoming thoroughly familiar with their activities, routine, and
operations as well as problems. Upon the successful completion of
the two-year course of study and the passing of examinations, the
trainees become eligible for appointment as assistant judges (*hanjiho*)
or procurators, or for private practice as lawyers. The Japanese
method of selecting the judges is in sharp contrast to the practice
which obtains in the United States and Great Britain. In the United
States they are appointed or elected after they have established their
reputation as practicing attorneys and often after they have rendered
important political service to the party in power. In Britain the
appointees are in all instances drawn entirely from one branch of the
legal profession, the barristers who practice before the courts. In
the continental countries of Europe, judges are regarded as a specialized body of the bureaucracy headed by the Minister of Justice.

The method of recruiting and training judges has been under
criticism for several reasons. It is felt in some quarters and particularly by the bar that by and large the judges are the product of
the judicial "hot house" and consequently are not familiar with the
realities of life, especially when compared with the lawyers who are
in private practice. Moreover, the training in the Judicial Training
Institute is more in the order of bureaucratic training in which the
government or official point of view predominates. It has been
proposed that judges be recruited mainly from among practicing
lawyers as is done in the United States, and with the endorsement of
the bar associations.

Extraordinary measures and efforts are perhaps necessary in providing judicial personnel with the kind of training and background

---

[7] Required fields of the examination are the Constitution, Civil Code, Criminal
Code, Code of Civil Procedure, and Code of Criminal Procedure. Elective fields
are the Commercial Code, Administrative Law, Labor Law, Bankruptcy Law,
Conflict of Laws, etc.

[8] Although as trainees they are not government employees, they receive allowances from the government during the period of training.

which would give them the broadest possible outlook and appreciation of social problems instead of highly competent technical legal knowledge devoid of liberal views. For a country like Japan the need is, indeed, crucial, if a solid popular foundation of justice is to be created.

It is generally known even in the democracies of the West that courts, through their practice of following precedent in interpreting a particular law, very often have resisted change. In many instances the courts have been regarded as instruments of special resistance to change.[9] Members of the bench often have little sympathy with the new social policies that are needed. The preservation of the *status quo* certainly would not be in the best interests of Japan since she is in need of changes and readjustments as much as, if not more than, most of the countries of the West. The judiciary cannot therefore knowingly serve as a brake to hold back the constant readjustments that have to be effected in the workable *modus vivendi* of the Japanese people.

Once they are appointed to official positions in the judiciary and pass beyond the probationary stage, judges are assured tenure for life although many of the appointments are for a legally specified term. There is not a single elective judgeship in the entire system. Promotion is virtually automatic.

However, in spite of the independence of the judiciary and freedom from control by the executive branch, it has not been entirely removed from the range of various pressures. While the integrity of the judges and the independence of their thought and action are regarded with the highest respect, there is no doubt that they must reflect a point of view morally and even socially acceptable to the majority of the community. In so far as they must be in consonance or harmony with public opinion their independence is of a relative nature. Consequently the judiciary cannot be completely impervious to political pressure. In the final analysis, even the judiciary itself is in a broad sense a form of political action and there can be no law or judiciary without politics.[10] While the members of the judiciary enjoy security of tenure, the system of control exercised over them particularly in regard to their discipline has undergone radical

[9] William F. Ogburn, "Technology and Governmental Change," *Journal of Business*, January, 1936.

[10] Professor Ono Seijiro while arguing that the courts should not be turned into arenas of political struggle recognizes the fact that the judiciary cannot be entirely free of political influences. See "Hotei no chitsujo wo tattobe," *Asahi*, August 9, 1953.

changes. The disciplinary committee composed of their own numbers has been abolished and a system of impeachment has been set up.[11] Impeachment proceedings are in the hands of an impeachment court composed of the members of the House of Representatives. Dismissals can be on grounds of neglect or dereliction of duties or violation of obligations of office or conduct unbecoming a judge which impairs the dignity of office.

THE CITIZEN AND THE LAW

The fact that the Japanese people are law-abiding and obedient to authority almost to a fault is not necessarily the reflection of a deep understanding and appreciation of the relationship of law to everyday life.[12] In general the substance of legislation is much less known among the Japanese than among Americans due largely to the fact that the means used for announcing statutory enactments are wholly inadequate. Actually the *Official Gazette* published by the government is the only channel employed by the government to publicize the laws enacted.

In spite of the conscious effort to simplify the language of law, the substance becomes more complex and difficult to understand. To complicate matters further, the volume of legislation is increasing at such a rate that it becomes almost impossible for all but the specialists and the lawyers to keep abreast of new laws and constant revisions. This is indeed a distressing state of affairs though it is not limited to Japan alone. Yet it complicates matters terribly, especially for a people whose experience is relatively brief and limited so far as legislative matters are concerned.

However, there are encouraging signs which augur well for the future. There has been developing in recent years a growing interest in the protection of the rights of citizens. In the vanguard of the movement is the Japanese Civil Liberties Union organized during the occupation period. While its emphasis at the outset was on the discussion of new legislation, it has increasingly devoted its efforts to giving protection to individuals who need but cannot afford it.

Also aiding the citizens' activities is the Civil Liberties Bureau of the Ministry of Justice whose function is to protect the rights of individuals. As the counterpart of the Civil Liberties Unit of the United States Department of Justice, this bureau not only channels and focusses criticism of governmental agencies but comments in-

---

[11] Saito Hideo, *Kokkai to Shihoken no Dokuritsu*, pp. 229–270.

[12] See Kaino Michitaka, "Nihonjin no ho ishiki" in Nihon Jimbun Kagakukai, *Hōken Isei*, pp. 44–73.

dependently upon situations in which the rights of individuals may have been abused by government officials. It also takes vigorous action against employers who are guilty or suspected of infringing upon the rights of workers.

Individuals and groups concerned with civil liberties are now better equipped than ever before, since they have at their disposal new procedures and techniques for the defense of individual rights. Every person is guaranteed right of access to the court by the Constitution. The Code of Criminal Procedure puts the defendant or the suspect on an equal footing with the prosecution and does not place the burden of proof on him. The Administrative Procedure Law facilitates the challenge of administrative acts while the State Redress Law fixes liability for the illegal acts of government employees. The Habeas Corpus Law gives relief to persons illegally detained. These legal weapons are a tremendous aid to the advancement of civil liberties but they are of little avail unless they are used. There must of course be a desire on the part of individuals to put them to use whenever the occasion demands. But the desire to use legal weapons cannot be developed so long as the servile attitude toward authority persists as the legacy of the feudal past.

It has been observed by students of law, both native and foreign, that there is an amazing lack of litigation in Japan.[13] This is a phenomenon which results in part from the traditional attitude that differences in social relations should be settled without resort to legal means and that something is wrong with individuals who cannot compose differences and live harmoniously. The natural reaction of an individual has been, and still is, to try to settle disputes out of court. Furthermore, Japanese law has permitted extensive recourse to conciliation procedures even after actions have been instituted. There is conspicuously lacking among the people a contentious spirit while at the same time there are innumerable pressures for settlements such as are provided by intermediaries of all sorts. While the sluggishness as well as the expensiveness of judicial process undoubtedly contribute to the nonutilization of the courts, these are not the important reasons. There has been a tendency to look upon judges as cold, indifferent, unsympathetic, and even difficult persons rather than as defenders and champions of citizens' rights. This sort of attitude was inevitable during the feudal period since judges were administrators representing the government rather than impartial dispensers of justice, and impartial and enlightened judges were very rare.

[13] Thomas L. Blakemore, *op cit.*, p. 649.

The people do not as yet seem to show any particular enthusiasm for the courts. Actually the great majority are still indifferent if not averse to the litigative process partly because the role of the courts is not adequately and favorably dramatized to impress the people. No serious efforts have been made as yet to bring the courts closer to the people and to win their confidence and support. Consequently the prevailing attitude of the people is that the less they have to do with the law and the courts the better inasmuch as the court is a place frequented by wrongdoers, the procurator's office is the enemy of the people, and the lawyers are friends and defenders of evil men.[14] Aware of this situation, the Civil Liberties Committee of the Japan Bar Association and local units of the association have been rendering yoeman service in awakening the interest of the public in the courts through their civil liberties activities.

[14] Iwata Chuzo, "Shihoken no arikata," *Asahi*, April 26, 1953.

16

Relations with
the Outside World

A CENTURY OF DIPLOMACY

For more than two hundred years beginning in the 1630's Japan managed to pursue a self-imposed policy of isolation permitting only the Dutch and the Chinese to carry on trade at Nagasaki while forbidding her own nationals to set foot on foreign soil. This policy which has no parallel in the world was motivated by the fear of European aggression. With amazing effectiveness the seclusion decree was enforced by the authorities. Yet, once the policy proved untenable in the face of pressure brought to bear upon her by the overwhelming power of the West, she "voluntarily" opened her doors to diplomatic and commercial intercourse. Security was no longer to be sought through isolation; it had to be achieved now through diplomacy and trade as well as national strength. But two centuries of nonintercourse with the rest of the world had stifled the nation's full economic development and prevented the acquisition of much-needed skill in the art of diplomacy.

As a matter of fact, she had not learned even the rudiments of international law or the simple ground rules of Western diplomacy. Upon the New York merchant, Townsend Harris, the first diplomatic representative of the United States, therefore, fell the onerous but fruitful task of explaining to the Japanese officials the rules and techniques of diplomacy. Thus in 1856 began the American tutelage of the Japanese in the art of diplomacy which continued for more than a half century. Several Americans served as legal advisers during this period in the Foreign Office where most of the Japanese diplomats who achieved prominence in the twentieth century came under their tutelage and training.[1] By far the strongest and most lasting influence on Japanese diplomacy and diplomatists was exerted by the least known of these American advisers, Henry Willard Denison, a self-effacing New Englander whose passion for anonymity was exceeded only by his single-minded devotion to the cause of Japanese diplomacy.[1a] Through his incessant efforts Japanese diplomacy was raised to a high level comparable to that of the Western nations. This period of tutelage saw the shaping of the pattern and character of Japanese diplomacy. The struggle for diplomatic equality was carried on vigorously and won, thanks to the combined efforts and tutelage of exceptionally able American advisers like Erasmus P. Smith, Henry Willard Denison, and Durham White Stevens.

The treaties which Japan signed beginning in 1858 threw the country open to diplomatic and commercial intercourse with the powers under unfavorable conditions, for the advantages which accrued were one-sided, that is, all on the side of the West. In the treaties Japan conceded extraterritoriality and surrendered tariff autonomy. This distressed Townsend Harris who was strongly opposed to extraterritoriality but he knew only too well that a treaty without such a provision stood no chance of approval in the United States Senate or, for that matter, in any country of the West. With great reluctance he accepted the inevitable since it was clearly a choice between a commercial treaty which was not entirely satisfactory yet served the chief purpose, and no treaty at all.

After the treaty was signed, Harris made every effort to help the Japanese to get rid of the unequal treaties. It was chiefly through his efforts that the first Japanese diplomatic mission to the West was dispatched in 1860[2] to the United States rather than to Britain. The knowledge brought back by the Embassy of 1860 opened a new era of progress for the nation. In the United States interest in Japan was greatly heightened as the result of the visit of the Japanese. The visit of former Secretary of State William H. Seward in the fall of 1870 was soon followed by the dispatch of the Iwakura Mission to the

[1] Diplomats like Komura, Kato, Makino, Ishii, Shidehara, and Yoshida were among those who came under the influence of American advisers.

[1a] Although it is not possible to accurately evaluate the over-all influence of Denison on Japanese diplomacy and diplomats, the extent to which he influenced Shidehara is clearly revealed in a recent biographical work, Shidehara Heiwa Zaidan, *Shidehara Kijuro* (1955).

[2] See Chitoshi Yanaga, "The First Japanese Embassy to the United States," *The Pacific Historical Review*, June, 1940, pp. 113–138.

United States and European countries avowedly for the renewal of treaties but actually for the study of conditions in the countries of the West.[3] The return of the Iwakura Mission was the opening signal for assiduous efforts to modernize the nation and bring about treaty revision through vigorous diplomacy. The unremitting efforts were crowned with success only after twenty years of persistent negotiations by the Foreign Office with the help of American advisers. With the signing of a new treaty with Great Britain in 1894, Japan finally achieved her goal of equality in diplomacy.

As an integral part of the program to achieve recognition as an equal in her diplomatic relations with the West, Japan made her debut as a participant in international agreements, organizations, and conferences. Beginning with her joining of the International Postal Union in 1876, she adhered to the International Telegraphic Union (1879) and the International Red Cross Convention (1886), and by the eve of World War I she had become an active participant in all major international organizations and agreements.

Japan's first opportunity to become a diplomatic cynosure of the world came in 1895 when she engaged in negotiations for a treaty of peace after her victory over China. Behind the Treaty of Shimon-oseki which ended the Sino-Japanese War was the guiding hand of the able American adviser, Henry Willard Denison.[4] The Triple Intervention that was master-minded by the Czar and the Kaiser to wrest the Liaotung peninsula from the Japanese in 1895, even before the ink was dry on the treaty that had ceded the territory to Japan, was a diplomatic lesson of far-reaching consequences. In its wake, the nation found itself in the vortex of European power politics in the Far East. The intervention by the European entente paved the way for the Anglo-Japanese Alliance in 1902[5] and enabled her to prosecute the Russo-Japanese War as the result of which she became a world power. In 1899, the year extraterritoriality came to an end, she had found the first opportunity to participate with the Western nations in an international conference, the Hague Conference, which was summoned by the Czar with whom the Japanese were to find themselves locked in a military contest only five years later. At the second Hague Conference of 1907, which contributed greatly to the

[3] Behind the sending of the Iwakura Mission was an American, Dr. Guido Verbeck, who was then educational adviser to the Japanese government. For details, see Yanaga, *Japan Since Perry*, pp. 176–179.

[4] The Chinese government had as its adviser, John W. Foster, one-time United States Secretary of State.

[5] Yanaga, *op. cit.*, pp. 290–304.

advancement of the rules of warfare, Japan was represented by American advisers.[6]

Japan gained recognition as a major world power when she won a seat at the Versailles Peace Conference following World War I as one of the "Big Five" and became one of the charter members of the League of Nations. The decade following the end of the war was one of active and wholehearted international cooperation such as had not been seen before. This short-lived internationalism was superseded by aggressive nationalism of the 1930's, aggravated by worldwide economic nationalism, which culminated in the Pacific War in 1941. Defeat brought Japan under the control of the Allied Powers under whom the rehabilitation and democratization of the nation were undertaken with vigor in accordance with the Potsdam Declaration. With the readmission of the country into the comity of nations, cooperation with the free world and democratic nations have brought about a reorientation of diplomacy.

GOALS OF JAPANESE DIPLOMACY

The existence of a powerful neighbor, China, in the seventh century, drew Japan's attention to the great achievements of the T'ang Empire. Understandably, the leaders were determined to import the civilization which contributed so much to China's greatness. To achieve a level of culture that would merit China's recognition and lead to equality with her neighbor became the consuming passion of Japan's leaders. The relentless and conscious struggle for equality with China continued for the next twelve centuries though with diminishing vigor until in the nineteenth century it was superseded by the struggle for equality with the Western powers.

When the nation was reopened to Western intercourse in 1854 the preservation of independence was given the highest priority. Every other objective was subordinated and made subservient to this single most important goal. Economic and industrial development, education, defense organization, and diplomacy were all motivated by the instinct of self-preservation and were directed toward the strengthening of the country. National prosperity and national strength became the twin goals of national policy and have been clearly reflected in Japanese diplomacy of the past one hundred years.

After the first few decades of the Meiji era (1868–1912), the national obsession for independence and security gave way to the intensive desire for racial equality. Having emerged as a victor in

[6] Henry Willard Denison and Durham White Stevens were Japan's delegates to the conference.

three foreign wars, the last being a world war, the demand for racial equality at Versailles in 1918 was the natural sequel to her achievement of diplomatic equality. Rebuffed by the West at Versailles and at the Washington Conference, the Japanese gradually drifted away from the Western democracies as the military exploited the economically and politically deteriorating conditions in the country.

Economic difficulties began to plague the nation beginning in the 1920's and domestic conditions went from bad to worse in the 1930's as the world found itself in the grip of economic nationalism as well as totalitarian philosophies. The political and economic impasse for the solution of which the military resorted to the use of force led the nation down the road to disastrous war and ultimately to defeat.

With the loss of territories, Japan's land area was reduced by some forty-five percent. Her primary concern in the postwar period shifted to the problem of how to survive as a nation economically. Efforts to achieve economic viability have been receiving the highest priority. Diplomacy has in effect become the indispensable handmaiden in the search for national economic well-being. Its primary responsibility has shifted from political matters to trade promotion for trade is the indispensable lifeblood of national economy. Even the problem of security does not have nearly the urgency that economic self-sustenance does. It cannot be overemphasized that Japan's diplomacy is geared primarily to the problem of finding ways and means of meeting the nation's dire economic needs.

Japan's diplomacy must operate within the framework provided more by world conditions than by the developments within her own boundaries. Though the nation is sovereign and independent politically, the initiative in foreign relations is not yet entirely her own and probably will not be for years to come. The success of her foreign policy naturally will be affected profoundly by the conditions and developments on the international scene. In other words, her foreign policy will, more often than not, be at the mercy of external forces over which she may have little or no control.

Yet her goals are quite clear and can be simply summarized as independence, security, equality, self-respect, and a self-sustaining national economy. The methods for achieving these goals constitute the crux of her foreign policy. With the clearly enunciated disavowal in the Constitution of the use of force as a method of settling international disputes and problems, Japan is pledged to resolve international differences through peaceful means.[7] Her only recourse is

---

[7] The preamble to the Constitution is in fact a declaration to the world that the Japanese people desire peace for all time.

to diplomacy of peace and cooperation. A good-neighbor policy of broadest implications but with particular emphasis on relations with the Asian nations whom she victimized in the last war is a *sine qua non* for the regaining of the trust and confidence of the Asians. It has become a matter of great imperativeness to work in partnership with Asian countries in helping to develop their economy in order to build up trade which will insure economic prosperity and political stability for Japan as well as for the Asian countries. International cooperation and collaboration for peaceful change and healthy economic development do not constitute an altruistic policy dreamed up by starry-eyed visionaries but rather an imperative condition for survival in the face of clear and present danger of Communist international conspiracy.

MANAGEMENT OF FOREIGN AFFAIRS

It can actually be said that in the management of foreign affairs, the Prime Minister proposes and the Diet disposes. As Chief of State, the Prime Minister alone can negotiate treaties but the Diet must approve them. Unless a treaty receives prior or subsequent approval by the Diet it cannot become the law of the land. Usually the approval of both houses is obtained, although in case of disagreement between the two the decision of the House of Representatives prevails.

The scope of the matters which should go into the making of decisions and judgments is so vast, complex, and interrelated and requires such depth of specialized knowledge as well as synthesis that no single person or small group of persons would be adequate for the thinking and planning involved. In the management of foreign affairs, the final responsibility for foreign policy rests with the Prime Minister who is the constitutional authority entrusted with the management of foreign affairs.

Presiding over the department is the Minister of Foreign Affairs who is the principal adviser to the Prime Minister. He is the counterpart of the American Secretary of State and the British Foreign Secretary. As such he has perhaps the second most difficult assignment in the government. His role in making foreign policy is that of the formulator, "activator," and leader whose chief responsibility is to direct the conduct of foreign relations. It is also his responsibility to interpret and explain its temporary nuances as well as its long-range trends and implications to the Diet, the nation, and the world at large. He must not only conduct diplomacy abroad but must also always practice diplomacy at home in dealing with other departments. He must be a skilled tactician both at home and abroad. His interests must range widely over the world for his responsibilities are on a global scale.

To function effectively, the Foreign Minister must not only have ready access to all available information but must be privy to all the thoughts of the Prime Minister and should be given the last chance to offer advice before final action is taken. Upon him devolves the difficult if not onerous task of eliciting the inspired efforts as well as the loyalty of his staff. His success depends to a large degree on his effectiveness in protecting, criticizing, and appreciating the work of his subordinates. One of the most difficult tasks of the Foreign Minister is to draw them out and utilize their capacity to reflect boldly and candidly on the facts as they see them, and to make them offer advice without regard to the popularity of that advice.

Needless to say, the formulation of foreign policies depends heavily on information gathered and made available by diplomatic representatives stationed abroad. The importance of accurate information and evaluation of persons and events abroad therefore can hardly be overemphasized. To provide the Foreign Minister with such data, all the available facilities of the Foreign Office must be mobilized to maximum advantage.

Constitutionally, treaty-making power is vested in the Cabinet and the Prime Minister entrusts the Foreign Minister with diplomatic negotiations which are conducted under the latter's direction after approval is given by the Cabinet. Diplomatic representatives do not have the authority to start negotiations on their own initiative; they must await instructions from the Foreign Office. When a tentative agreement is reached a draft treaty is drawn up and submitted to the Cabinet for decision. When Cabinet approval is obtained, the negotiator is instructed to sign the agreement. If prior approval had not already been obtained, the treaty is then submitted to the Diet for approval. It is then formally promulgated by the Emperor following the exchange of ratifications. For nontreaty agreements which usually take the form of executive agreements, the procedure is far less complicated and the approval of the Diet is not required.

The administrative arrangement of the Foreign Office is quite simple and it is organized very much like the British Foreign Office and the United States Department of State. Assisting the Foreign Minister is the parliamentary vice-minister and the administrative vice-minister. The former is normally appointed from among the members of the Diet and participates in policy and planning matters, and on important policies serves as a liaison between the department and the Diet as well as the political party; the latter occupies the most important position within the department and as the Foreign Minister's *alter ego* he actually runs the department and is responsible to his superior for all policy matters.

Unlike the United States Department of State, there are no positions corresponding to the undersecretaries and assistant secretaries. The Foreign Office is divided into a secretariat and six bureaus, in charge of directors. Two of them, the Asia Bureau and the Europe-America Bureau, are geographical units while the remaining four are functional units dealing with economic affairs, treaties, information and cultural affairs, and international cooperation. It is in these bureaus that the day-to-day problems of the world are handled. The geographical units deal with country and area problems while the functional units furnish materials on specialized and technical problems from legal and economic matters to international organization and cooperation.

The geographical division of the world is carried out with utmost simplicity between two bureaus. The Asia Bureau divides its functions among its five sections as follows: (1) general over-all planning, implementation, and control of Asian policy as well as the coordination of business within the bureau; (2) Northeast Asia; (3) Southeast Asia, namely, the Philippines, Malaya, Indo-China and Indonesia; (4) Asian countries outside of the Middle East, Northeast Asia, and Southeast Asia; (5) Korea, Taiwan (Formosa), Karafuto (Sahkalin), South Seas, and other areas as well as repatriation matters. In the Europe-America Bureau are also five sections: (1) general planning and coordination of the bureau together with the two North American nations, the United States and Canada; (2) Central and South America; (3) Commonwealth Nations and Eire; (4) Western Europe, the Middle East, and Africa; and (5) Eastern Europe, Turkey, Iran, and Afghanistan.

Perhaps the largest and most important of all the units at present is the Economic Affairs Bureau which consists of six sections and a research division. This is quite natural for postwar Japan inasmuch as economic problems comprise the most important single ingredient of foreign policy today. The organization of this bureau is quite different from that of other bureaus in that it is a combination of geographical and functional arrangements embracing the following: (1) general affairs of the bureau in addition to trade policy, trade agreements, commercial treaties, trade promotion, foreign exchange and the attracting of foreign capitals; (2) multilateral commercial pacts and trade agreements, international economic conferences, economic cooperation pertaining to underdeveloped areas, customs, maritime transportation and protection of shipping; (3) planning and execution of trade policies relating to the Americas, economic cooperation, protection, and promotion of economic interests, trade agreements and international payments agreements; (4) Commonwealth Nations; (5) Asian countries, and (6) European, Middle Eastern, and African countries.

The Treaty Bureau with its four sections handles (1) the coordination and planning in the concluding of treaties and agreements; (2) treaties pertaining to international organization and administration; (3) international law problems, dual nationality and expatriation cases, and protection of Japanese nationals abroad; and (4) drafting of treaties, study of treaties and international law theory and precedents, and domestic and foreign law with implications on international relations.

In the Information and Culture Bureau, the four sections carry on the following activities: (1) planning and coordination, collection and dissemination of information, publication, and collection of foreign materials; (2) the dissemination of information abroad and the study of foreign media of communication; (3) international cultural exchange; and (4) UNESCO affairs. In addition, the Foreign Office Training Institute is operated as a part of this bureau.

The International Cooperation Bureau is in charge of a wide variety of special problems among which are (1) matters pertaining to the United States, (2) international organizations and conferences, (3) administrative agreements based on the United States-Japan Security Pact, and (4) custody and return of seized Allied property, war indemnities, and validation of prewar national bonds and indebtedness.

The housekeeping functions of the department are vested in the Secretariat which has charge of matters pertaining to personnel, protocol, documents, telegraphic communication, finance, and welfare, as well as planning, coordination, and research relating to the administration of the department, with the General Affairs Section serving as the department's nerve center. Also located in the Secretariat is the Policy Planning Staff. The consultants and counsellors who are not burdened with the day-to-day operations of foreign policy as well as administrative responsibilities advise the Foreign Minister on policy matters. It is the responsibility of the Policy Planning Staff to anticipate developments on the basis of accurate intelligence estimates and be ready with appropriate measures and countermeasures.

Foreign policy may originate almost anywhere within or without the Foreign Office. The suggestion or inspiration may come from the Prime Minister, the Foreign Minister, any cabinet minister, an ambassador, any official in the department, a private economic organization, chamber of commerce, the Economic Planning Board, the Bank of Japan, or even a newspaper editorial. The "germ" of a policy wherever found is seized upon and developed by an alert, imaginative individual on the staff. The main task for the Foreign Minister and his advisers is to apply creative thinking to arrive at a decision after relating all existing and proposed policies to one another. In addition to the Foreign Minister, those officials who are regarded as heavy contributors to policy making are the Ministers and International Trade and Industry, the head of the Economic Planning Board, and the governor of the Bank of Japan. The Foreign Office has always jealously guarded its prerogatives and has seldom brooked any interference. It has been quite successful in keeping it on a strictly career basis, permitting no invasion of the department by outsiders. This policy of keeping the department as an exclusive preserve for career foreign service officials held its ground even at the height of power of the military in the 1930's. In policy making the Foreign Office has not been as successful for the military was able to completely by-pass the department to give rise to what was known as "dual diplomacy."

The Diet and Foreign Policy

The chief function of the Diet so far as foreign policy is concerned is consultative. It aids the government in the formulation and development of policy through discussions and chiefly debates which take place in the committees and less frequently in plenary sessions. Liaison is maintained by the Foreign Office through its parliamentary vice-minister and, at the beginning of every session, the Prime Minister informs the Diet on the state of foreign relations, through the Foreign Minister's foreign policy address. Almost always the Diet accepts the recommendations of the Prime Minister and approves the treaties concluded. The Diet, of course, has no part in the international negotiations carried on by the government. Thus the role constitutionally assigned to the Diet is more impressive in theory than in practice. However, there is nothing in the way of a legal obstacle to prevent the legislative branch from assuming a more active part in the formulating of foreign policy. At the present time the Diet's role in foreign affairs is far less important than that of the United States Senate. This is due to the fact that executive leadership has almost invariably overshadowed legislative leadership partly as a result of tradition and partly because of lack of experience. There is still a strong tendency to regard foreign policy as the special preserve of the government experts who endeavor so far as possible to keep it out of reach of parliamentary debate. This is true to some extent even in the democracies but is far more applicable to Japan.[8] To deal effectively with the interpellations and questioning of the opposition in the Diet, the Foreign Office frequently holds staff conferences of key officials to discuss ways and means of coping with the members of the Diet. These meetings are designed to present a "united front" when confronted by Diet members as well as to map out strategy. Questions which are likely to come up, particularly those issues which are expected to produce heated debates in the Diet, are discussed in advance among key officials of the Foreign Office.

Popular control of foreign policy is possible within the existing constitutional framework. However, the mechanics necessary for the exercise of such a control as well as sufficient popular interest in and desire for effectuating it are still lacking. Public opinion is still not influential enough to exercise appreciable control over the thinking or actions of the foreign policy makers.

FOREIGN SERVICE PERSONNEL

Entrance into foreign service is by successful passing of examinations and the completion of a training course at the Foreign Office Training Institute. Examinations which are held once a year are open to those under thirty years of age who have been adjudged eligible by the authorities. The first part which is written and is given in eight different cities[9] tests general cultural knowledge and special knowledge of the Constitution, Economics, International Public Law, International Private Law, and Modern Diplomatic History as well as one of the seven languages, English, French, German, Russian, Chinese, Spanish, and Portuguese. The second part which is given only in Tokyo consists of tests in dictation as well as conversational ability in the foreign language selected in the written examination, an oral "character" examination and physical examination. In addi-

---

[8] With regard to the Canadian House of Commons, Vincent Massey states: "Foreign Affairs traditionally have been presented to the House as a mystery into which the uninitiated should not venture; in moments of crises the members have been cautioned to leave such explosive matters alone." *On Being Canadian*, p. 90.

[9] The eight cities are Tokyo, Osaka, Nagoya, Sendai, Sapporo, Hiroshima, Takamatsu, and Fukuoka.

tion, a security and character check is made before the results of the examination are announced. Appointments to the foreign service are made in the order of the grades achieved in the examinations.

Immediately upon appointment they are admitted to the Foreign Office Training Institute where they receive instruction in language and other fields with strong emphasis on preparation for practical duties. There are four different levels of instruction or curricula. Section One has for its goal the training of grade-two foreign service officers destined to be the core and leaders of the diplomatic corps. The emphasis is therefore on the study of the theory of diplomatic relations and functions, diplomatic history and conditions both at home and abroad. Section Two is tailored to the needs of the new appointees who have just passed the examinations and therefore stresses the study of the languages and conditions of the countries to which the neophytes are being assigned. Section Three specializes in the training of grade-three Foreign Service officers, while Section Four has for its aim the training of the staff for specialized language assignments.

With rare exceptions, those who go into the diplomatic service are university or college graduates. Although the law does not specify that applicants should be college or university graduates, it is virtually impossible for those without higher education to pass the diplomatic examinations. There was a time when the diplomatic service was practically the monopoly of the graduates of the Tokyo Imperial University with only a feeble competition coming from the graduates of the Tokyo Higher Commercial School (the present Hitotsubashi University).[10] In recent years there has been an influx into the service of successful candidates whose education has been obtained in a variety of colleges and universities. Yet the influence of the school tie is still quite appreciable as is the case in Britain. The Japanese counterpart of the American characterization of a diplomat as a "cookie pusher in striped pants" is revealed in the kind of stereotype created, especially regarding his qualifications.[11]

As of July 1, 1955, Japan's diplomatic establishments included

[10] It used to be said that in order to succeed and reach the top in the foreign service one must be a graduate of the First Higher School (Daiichi Koto Gakko) and the Law Department of Tokyo Imperial University and then marry into an influential family with political or business connections.

[11] One observer lists as the necessary equipment of a diplomat the following: a foreign language, Western etiquette, social dancing, a tuxedo, knowledge of memorized international law, and money either his own or his wife's. Takagi Takeo, *Nihon to Yuu Na no Kuni*, p. 190.

twenty-one embassies and eighteen legations.[12]   From these outposts the ambassadors and ministers send in their detailed reports periodically on the political, economic, and military conditions as well as the state of public opinion and sentiment of the countries where they are stationed, thus providing the raw materials out of which the nation's foreign policy must be fashioned.   These representatives are responsible for carrying on diplomatic negotiations as well as for the protection of nationals abroad.   Most important of all the functions assigned to them at present is the promotion of friendly relations and the development of commercial opportunities which, when achieved in combination, can go a long way toward the amelioration of the desperate plight of Japan's national economy.

In the postwar period following the restoration of independence and sovereignty a considerable number of noncareer ambassadors were appointed to important posts.   This was a radical departure since in normal times the ambassadors were always career men who had risen to their positions from the ranks.[13]   Because of the change in the political system and the urgent need of finding solutions to dire economic problems not a few of the ambassadors were chosen from among financial experts.[14]   The liberalization of the policy of appointment to ambassadorial posts by admitting noncareer men represented a step toward the debureaucratization of the foreign service.   However, the policy which was more in the nature of an experiment forced by necessity is no longer being actively carried out and reversion to the old pattern appears to be in the cards.

NEW ROLE IN INTERNATIONAL RELATIONS

World War II helped to release pent-up revolutionary forces in Asian lands.   The effective reins which held nationalism in check over a long period were destroyed under the impact of war.   Japan's early successes in defeating the forces trained and led by Europeans

[12] The U.S.S.R. has not terminated the state of war while Indonesia and the Philippines have not concluded a peace treaty.   These countries would normally receive ambassadors bringing the total number of Japanese embassies abroad to twenty-four.

[13] The appointment of a general as ambassador to Nazi Germany in 1936 broke the well-established practice of assigning only career men as ambassadors, which had been in existence for some time.

[14] The most outstanding example of this was the first postwar Ambassador to the United States, Araki Eikichi, who was at the time of appointment Governor of the Bank of Japan and has returned to the same post upon relinquishing the ambassadorship.

in Asia at the start of the war sparked the intense nationalism and inspired the Asians to fight on for their freedom. In its full fury Asian nationalism forced Britain to withdraw from India, Pakistan, Ceylon, and Burma, and brought an end to Dutch rule in Indonesia. Thus, in the wake of the war, Asian peoples who had for centuries submitted themselves to the rule of Western powers won their freedom practically overnight and in the brief space of a few years established their newly independent states.

The vast expanse of Asia from the Mediterranean to the Pacific where more than half of the world's population must eke out their insecure living is in violent convulsion and is enveloped in the consuming passion of anti-Westernism. The Asian revolt is directed against inequality, injustice, and oppression, that is, against all the conditions and forces, both internal and external, that are keeping the people down and preventing them from improving their lot, socially, economically, and politically. The hopes and fears and aspirations of more than half of the human race thus impinge upon, and clash with, those of the Western world. Japan is caught in the middle of these powerful forces of Asia and of the West which are all too frequently pulling in opposite directions.

The violent stirrings of Asia activated by abject poverty, unrest, and general insecurity are aggravated by woefully underdeveloped economic conditions and distressing political instability, inefficiency, and even corruption. Resultant tensions and anxieties have made the newly independent states easy prey to subversive activities. As the power struggle between the Free World and Communist imperialism rages in Asia, the continent is being turned into a battleground in a fight to win the minds of men. Aggressive Communism has missed no opportunity in exploiting existing conditions to foment trouble and instigate subversion even while brazenly posing as the champion of Asian hopes and aspirations and identifying itself with the powerful nationalist movements and anticolonial and anti-Western feelings of Asian peoples.

In the wake of World War II, Japan has suddenly found herself in the role of the Free World's bastion against Communist aggression in the Far East. It is one of the poignant ironies of history that, in defeat, Japan has this role thrust upon her by the very powers who brought about her defeat. She is now a welcome partner and ally of the democracies in the struggle to preserve freedom in the world. In this new and unanticipated role, she is to the democratic nations a symbol of Asia's hope, no less than a symbol of Western capitalism to the Soviet Union and Communist China. The turn of events has thus placed Japan in a position to contribute her mite in frustrating Communist ambitions to dominate the world.

Clearly, there have been basic changes in Japan's role in international relations. In her relations with the countries of both Asia and the West, she no longer pursues a unilateral course of noncooperation that would disregard the interests of others. Her policy is based firmly on the conviction that there can be no security for her so long as insecurity plagues Asia. She is thoroughly convinced that no nation, however powerful and determined, can go it alone, and least of all Japan whose national existence and prosperity depend heavily, if not entirely, on the mutual understanding, cooperation, and good will of nations.

Japan's eagerness to get back into the fold of international cooperation is reflected in the speed with which she has resumed her place in world organizations. Starting with her re-entry into the International Postal Convention in July, 1948, she had by 1952, that is, in the brief space of barely four years, achieved membership in practically all the major international organizations and agreements.[15] Membership in the United Nations, however, has been consistently vetoed by the Soviet Union.

In the existing bipolarized power structure which divides the world into the Communist World and the Free World, there are three possibilities open to Japan as far as her international position is concerned. The first is to ally herself with the free nations under the leadership of the Western democracies. This is the course she has chosen to follow. The second is to fall behind the Iron Curtain and become a part of the Communist bloc. This cannot and will not happen by choice. It can only happen, though this is not very likely, under irresistible pressure of an overwhelming combination of eco-

[15] Among those Japan rejoined or joined for the first time are:

> International Postal Convention, July, 1948
> International Telecommunications Convention, July, 1948
> International Whaling Convention, April, 1951
> World Health Organization, May, 1951
> International Wheat Council, May, 1951
> International Materials Conference, June, 1951
> United Nations Educational, Scientific, and Cultural Conference, June, 1951
> International Labor Organization, June, 1951
> International Convention for the Safety of Life at Sea, August, 1951
> Food and Agriculture Organization, November, 1951
> North Pacific Tripartite Fisheries Convention, May, 1952
> International Monetary Fund, May, 1952
> International Bank for Reconstruction and Development, May, 1952.

nomic, political, and military power of the Communist bloc. The third course is neutrality and noninvolvement in the power struggle between the Communist and non-Communist world. The adoption of elements or ingredients of this third alternative is apparently regarded as feasible by a considerable number of Japan's political leaders even though the nation has already chosen the first alternative and aligned herself firmly with the Western powers. Without actually aspiring to the role of a third force, Japan entertains hopes of working out mutually satisfactory arrangements with the Communist bloc. Japan sees, through her Oriental eyes, coexistence with the Communist world as not only feasible but necessary and inevitable so long as she adheres to the policy of adjusting and settling international problems and issues without resort to war.

Politically and diplomatically, Japan is gradually regaining the position of influence she once occupied in international affairs. However, before she can effectively play a major role in Asian affairs, the considerable residue of distrust, suspicion, and even hatred which exists in some of the Asian nations which she victimized during the war needs to be dissipated and superseded by confidence and trust. This task conceivably will be aided to some extent by the fact that there still exists among Asian peoples a healthy respect for the Japanese for having dispelled their feeling of inferiority vis-à-vis the nations of the West, and for having played a direct role in hastening the end of European colonialism in Asia.

In the field of industry and technology, Japan has already begun to offer guidance and assistance to her neighbors for technologically she is the most advanced nation in Asia, her experience in industrialization extending over a period of nearly a century. It is because her technical know-how, productive capacity, and skilled manpower resources exceed those of other Asian countries that Japan has become the acknowledged workshop of Asia for the Free World in its struggle against Communism. Japan's resources are necessary for the building of Asian security which in turn benefits her economically. Consequently the role assigned by the Free World to Japan is one that is benefiting her as much as the other Asian countries which receive her assistance.

Various forms of technical assistance have already been given by Japan to India, Pakistan, Ceylon, Burma, the Philippines, and Thailand. Different types of machinery and equipment, such as cotton spinning and weaving machines, electric motors and generators, locomotives, rolling stock, merchant ships, freighters, oil tankers, steam turbines, and boilers have been exported, along with technicians to install them and give instruction in their operation and maintenance. Japanese agricultural methods, especially in the cultivation of rice, have been introduced with phenomenal results. Japanese fishing and mining methods have also been introduced with equally satisfactory results. In exchange for these exports of goods and services, Japan receives raw materials which she desperately needs. The role which Japan is playing in stimulating and aiding technical and economic development of the underdeveloped areas of Asia is in cooperation and conformity with such programs as the United Nations Technical Assistance and the United States Point Four programs and the Colombo Plan.

By virtue of her experience of more than a century, Japan is in an advantageous position to function as a purveyor of Western ideas and particularly Western techniques of production which have gone through a process of screening, modification, and adaptation, if not Asianization. After being subjected to such a process of selection, adaptation, and assimilation by Japan, ideas and techniques of the West would appear much less alien and far less repugnant to those Asian peoples who are still strongly anti-Western in their orientation.

Since Japan is the only country in Asia which voluntarily embarked upon a carefully and deliberately planned program of Westernization and modernization in the nineteenth century and adopted and adapted to her special needs Western techniques of production, finance, and government administrations as well as Western educational and national defense systems, her experiences provide invaluable lessons to other Asian nations which are at present undergoing the difficult process of adjustment. It is generally recognized that in Japan both Eastern and Western cultures have met and merged to a greater extent than anywhere else in the world. This qualifies Japan peculiarly for the role of an intermediary in the harmonization of the elements of the East and the West.

Politically, no other nation of the non-Western world has had the experience of being an ally on an equal footing with the world's greatest power of the time in a bilateral alliance. For two decades, from 1902 to 1922, Japan and Great Britain were bound closely together in intimate friendship by the Anglo-Japanese Alliance which was designed originally to check the expansion of Czarist Russia in Asia. Moreover, Japan has never really developed a deep-rooted antipathy toward the West. This fact has not changed in spite of the disastrous defeat she suffered at the hands of the Western powers. Neither has she developed any real xenophobia in the entire course of her national development for her progress has been achieved mainly through the adoption and adaptation of the desirable features of alien cultures both Oriental and Occidental. Even the Japanese themselves regard their nation as being something of "the West in the East." Yet for all the mastery of Western science, technology, and methods of doing things, she has preserved the spirit and heritage of the Orient and continues to cherish her age-old traditions.

Is postwar Japan really equal to the heavy responsibilities entrusted to her in a period of increasing tension in international relations? Will she play her role carefully and wisely? There seems to be little doubt in the minds of responsible Japanese leaders that the future of the country lies only in responsible action through the pursuit of a peaceful policy of cooperation with the countries of Asia and the West. Nor is there any doubt that, with the longest history of independence combined with the longest period of political experience under a constitutional government of any country in Asia, she faces the severest test in the struggle to firmly re-establish herself and assume her rightful place in the affairs of the world.

Appendix A

Imperial Rescript

Promulgating the Constitution[1]

I rejoice that the foundation for the construction of a new Japan has been laid according to the will of the Japanese people, and hereby sanction and promulgate the amendments of the Imperial Japanese Constitution effected following the consultation with the Privy Council and the decisions of the Imperial Diet made in accordance with Article 73 of the said Constitution.

Signed: Hirohito (Seal of the Emperor)

This third day of the eleventh month of the twenty-first year of Showa (November 3, 1946).

Countersigned:

Prime Minister and concurrently Minister for Foreign Affairs, YOSHIDA Shigeru.
Minister of State, Baron SHIDEHARA Kijuro.
Minister of Justice, KIMURA Tokutaro.
Minister of Home Affairs, OMURA Seiichi.
Minister of Education, TANAKA Kotaro.
Minister of Agriculture and Forestry, WADA Hiroo.
Minister of State, SAITO Takao.
Minister of Communications, HITOTSUMATSU Sadayoshi.
Minister of Commerce and Industry, HOSHIJIMA Niro.
Minister of Welfare, KAWAI Yoshinari.
Minister of State, UEHARA Etsujiro.
Minister of Transportation, HIRATSUKA Tsunejiro.
Minister of Finance, ISHIBASHI Tanzan.
Minister of State, KANAMORI Tokujiro.
Minister of State, ZEN Keinosuke.

[1] Official version taken from Report of Government Section, Supreme Commander for Allied Powers, *Political Reorientation of Japan*, p. 670.

Appendix B

"The Constitution of Japan"

We, the Japanese people, acting through our duly elected representatives in the National Diet, determined that we shall secure for ourselves and our posterity the fruits of peaceful cooperation with all nations and the blessings of liberty throughout this land, and resolved that never again shall we be visited with the horrors of war through the action of government, do proclaim that sovereign power resides with the people and do firmly establish this Constitution.   Government is a sacred trust of the people, the authority for which is derived from the people, the powers of which are exercised by the representatives of the people, and the benefits of which are enjoyed by the people.   This is a universal principle of mankind upon which this Constitution is founded.   We reject and revoke all constitutions, laws, ordinances, and rescripts in conflict herewith.

We, the Japanese people, desire peace for all time and are deeply conscious of the high ideals controlling human relationship, and we have determined to preserve our security and existence, trusting in the justice and faith of the peace-loving peoples of the world.   We desire to occupy an honored place in an international society striving for the preservation of peace, and the banishment of tyranny and slavery, oppression and intolerance for all time from the earth.   We recognize that all peoples of the world have the right to live in peace, free from fear and want.

We believe that no nation is responsible to itself alone, but that laws of political morality are universal; and that obedience to such laws is incumbent upon all nations who would sustain their own sovereignty and justify their sovereign relationship with other nations.

We, the Japanese people, pledge our national honor to accomplish these high ideals and purposes with all our resources.

CHAPTER 1.   THE EMPEROR

ARTICLE 1.   The Emperor shall be the symbol of the State and of the unity of the people, deriving his position from the will of the people with whom resides sovereign power.

ARTICLE 2.   The Imperial Throne shall be dynastic and succeeded to in accordance with the Imperial House Law passed by the Diet.

[1] *Ibid.*, pp. 671–677.

ARTICLE 3. The advice and approval of the Cabinet shall be required for all acts of the Emperor in matters of state, and the Cabinet shall be responsible therefor.

ARTICLE 4. The Emperor shall perform only such acts in matters of state as are provided for in this Constitution and he shall not have powers related to government.

The Emperor may delegate the performance of his acts in matters of state as may be provided by law.

ARTICLE 5. When, in accordance with the Imperial House Law, a Regency is established, the Regent shall perform his acts in matters of state in the Emperor's name. In this case, paragraph one of the preceding article will be applicable.

ARTICLE 6. The Emperor shall appoint the Prime Minister as designated by the Diet.

The Emperor shall appoint the Chief Justice of the Supreme Court as designated by the Cabinet.

ARTICLE 7. The Emperor, with the advice and approval of the Cabinet, shall perform the following acts in matters of state on behalf of the people.

Promulgation of amendments of the constitution, laws, cabinet orders and treaties.

Convocation of the Diet.

Dissolution of the House of Representatives.

Proclamation of general election of members of the Diet.

Attestation of the appointment and dismissal of Ministers of State and other officials as provided for by law, and of full powers and credentials of Ambassadors and Ministers.

Attestation of general and special amnesty, commutation of punishment, reprieve, and restoration of rights.

Awarding of honors.

Attestation of instruments of ratification and other diplomatic documents as provided for by the law.

Receiving foreign ambassadors and ministers.

Performance of ceremonial functions.

ARTICLE 8. No property can be given to, or received by, the Imperial House, nor can any gifts be made therefrom, without the authorization of the Diet.

CHAPTER II. RENUNCIATION OF WAR

ARTICLE 9. Aspiring sincerely to an international peace based on justice and order, the Japanese people forever renounce war as a sovereign right of the nation and the threat or use of force as a means of settling international disputes.

In order to accomplish the aim of the preceding paragraph, land, sea, and air forces, as well as other war potential, will never be maintained. The right of belligerency of the state will not be recognized.

CHAPTER III. RIGHTS AND DUTIES OF THE PEOPLE

ARTICLE 10. The conditions necessary for being a Japanese national shall be determined by law.

ARTICLE 11. The people shall not be prevented from enjoying any of the fundamental human rights. These fundamental human rights guaranteed to the people by this Constitution shall be conferred upon the people of this and future generations as eternal and inviolate rights.

ARTICLE 12.   The freedoms and rights guaranteed to the people by this Constitution shall be maintained by the constant endeavor of the people, who shall refrain from any abuse of these freedoms and rights and shall always be responsible for utilizing them for the public welfare.

ARTICLE 13.   All of the people shall be respected as individuals.   Their right to life, liberty, and the pursuit of happiness shall, to the extent that it does not interfere with the public welfare, be the supreme consideration in legislation and in other governmental affairs.

ARTICLE 14.   All of the people are equal under the law and there shall be no discrimination in political, economic or social relations because of race, creed, sex, social status or family origin.
  Peers and peerage shall not be recognized.
  No privilege shall accompany any award of honor, decoration or any distinction, nor shall any such award be valid beyond the lifetime of the individual who now holds or hereafter may receive it.

ARTICLE 15.   The people have the inalienable right to choose their public officials and to dismiss them.
  All public officials are servants of the whole community and not any group thereof.
  Universal adult suffrage is guaranteed with regard to the election of public officials.
  In all elections, secrecy of the ballot shall not be violated.   A voter shall not be answerable, publicly or privately, for the choice he has made.

ARTICLE 16.   Every person shall have the right of peaceful petition for the redress of damage, for the removal of public officials, for the enactment, repeal or amendment of laws, ordinances or regulations and for other matters; nor shall any person be in any way discriminated against for sponsoring such a petition.

ARTICLE 17.   Every person may sue for redress as provided by law from the State or a public entity, in case he has suffered damage through illegal act of any public official.

ARTICLE 18.   No person shall be held in bondage of any kind.   Involuntary servitude, except as punishment for crime, is prohibited.

ARTICLE 19.   Freedom of thought and conscience shall not be violated.

ARTICLE 20.   Freedom of religion is guaranteed to all.   No religious organization shall receive any privileges from the State, nor exercise any political authority.
  No person shall be compelled to take part in any religious act, celebration, rite or practice.
  The State and its organs shall refrain from religious education or any other religious activity.

ARTICLE 21. Freedom of assembly and association as well as speech, press and all other forms of expression are guaranteed.

No censorship shall be maintained, nor shall the secrecy of any means of communication be violated.

ARTICLE 22. Every person shall have freedom to choose and change his residence and to choose his occupation to the extent that it does not interfere with the public welfare.

Freedom of all persons to move to a foreign country and to divest themselves of their nationality shall be inviolate.

ARTICLE 23. Academic freedom is guaranteed.

ARTICLE 24. Marriage shall be based only on the mutual consent of both sexes and it shall be maintained through mutual cooperation with the equal rights of husband and wife as a basis.

With regard to choice of spouse, property rights, inheritance, choice of domicile, divorce and other matters pertaining to marriage and the family, laws shall be enacted from the standpoint of individual dignity and the essential equality of the sexes.

ARTICLE 25. All people shall have the right to maintain the minimum standards of wholesome and cultural living.

In all spheres of life, the State shall use its endeavors for the promotion and extension of social welfare and security, and of public health.

ARTICLE 26. All people shall have the right to receive an equal education correspondent to their ability, as provided by law.

All people shall be obligated to have all boys and girls under their protection receive ordinary education as provided for by law. Such compulsory education shall be free.

ARTICLE 27. All people shall have the right and the obligation to work.

Standards for wages, hours, rest and other working conditions shall be fixed by law.

Children shall not be exploited.

ARTICLE 28. The right of workers to organize and bargain and act collectively is guaranteed.

ARTICLE 29. The right to own or to hold property is inviolable.

Property rights shall be defined by law, in conformity with the public welfare.

Private property may be taken for public use upon just compensation therefor.

ARTICLE 30. The people shall be liable to taxation as provided by law.

ARTICLE 31. No person shall be deprived of life or liberty, nor shall any other criminal penalty be imposed, except according to procedure established by law.

ARTICLE 32. No person shall be denied the right of access to the courts.

ARTICLE 33. No person shall be apprehended except upon warrant issued by a competent judicial officer which specifies the offense with which the person is charged, unless he is apprehended, the offense being committed.

ARTICLE 34. No person shall be arrested or detained without being at once informed of the charges against him or without the immediate privilege of counsel; nor shall he be detained without adequate cause; and upon demand of any person such cause must be immediately shown in open court in his presence and the presence of his counsel.

ARTICLE 35. The right of all persons to be secure in their homes, papers and effects against entries, searches and seizures shall not be impaired except upon warrant issued for adequate cause and particularly describing the place to be searched and things to be seized, or except as provided by Article 33.

Each search and seizure shall be made upon separate warrant issued by a competent judicial officer.

ARTICLE 36. The infliction of torture by any public officer and cruel punishments are absolutely forbidden.

ARTICLE 37. In all criminal cases the accused shall enjoy the right to a speedy and public trial by an impartial tribunal.

He shall be permitted full opportunity to examine all witnesses, and he shall have the right of compulsory process for obtaining witnesses on his behalf at public expense.

At all times the accused shall have the assistance of competent counsel who shall, if the accused is unable to secure the same by his own efforts, be assigned to his use by the State.

ARTICLE 38. No person shall be compelled to testify against himself.

Confession made under compulsion, torture or threat, or after prolonged arrest or detention shall not be admitted in evidence.

No person shall be convicted or punished in cases where the only proof against him is his own confession.

ARTICLE 39. No person shall be held criminally liable for an act which was lawful at the time it was committed, or of which he has been acquitted, nor shall he be placed in double jeopardy.

ARTICLE 40. Any person, in case he is acquitted after he has been arrested or detained, may sue the State for redress as provided by law.

CHAPTER IV. THE DIET

ARTICLE 41. The Diet shall be the highest organ of state power, and shall be the sole law-making organ of the State.

ARTICLE 42. The Diet shall consist of two Houses, namely the House of Representatives and the House of Councillors.

ARTICLE 43.　Both Houses shall consist of elected members, representative of all the people.

The number of the members of each House shall be fixed by law.

ARTICLE 44.　The qualifications of members of both Houses and their electors shall be fixed by law.　However, there shall be no discrimination because of race, creed, sex, social status, family origin, education, property or income.

ARTICLE 45.　The term of office of members of the House of Representatives shall be four years.　However, the term shall be terminated before the full term is up in case the House of Representatives is dissolved.

ARTICLE 46.　The term of office of members of the House of Councillors shall be six years, and election for half the members shall take place every three years.

ARTICLE 47.　Electoral districts, method of voting and other matters pertaining to the method of election of members of both Houses shall be fixed by law.

ARTICLE 48.　No person shall be permitted to be a member of both Houses simultaneously.

ARTICLE 49.　Members of both Houses shall receive appropriate annual payment from the national treasury in accordance with law.

ARTICLE 50.　Except in cases provided by law, members of both Houses shall be exempt from apprehension while the Diet is in session, and any members apprehended before the opening of the session shall be freed during the term of the session upon demand of the House.

ARTICLE 51.　Members of both Houses shall not be held liable outside the House for speeches, debates or votes cast inside the House.

ARTICLE 52.　An ordinary session of the Diet shall be convoked once per year.

ARTICLE 53.　The Cabinet may determine to convoke extraordinary sessions of the Diet.　When a quarter or more of the total members of either House makes the demand, the Cabinet must determine on such convocation.

ARTICLE 54.　When the House of Representatives is dissolved, there must be a general election of members of the House of Representatives within forty (40) days from the date of dissolution, and the Diet must be convoked within thirty (30) days from the date of the election.

When the House of Representatives is dissolved, the House of Councillors is closed at the same time.　However, the Cabinet may in time of national emergency convoke the House of Councillors in emergency session.

Measures taken at such session as mentioned in the proviso of the preceding paragraph shall be provisional and shall become null and void unless agreed to by the House of Representatives within a period of ten (10) days after the opening of the next session of the Diet.

ARTICLE 55. Each House shall judge disputes related to qualifications of its members. However, in order to deny a seat to any member, it is necessary to pass a resolution by a majority of two-thirds or more of the members present.

ARTICLE 56. Business cannot be transacted in either House unless one-third or more of total membership is present.

All matters shall be decided, in each House, by a majority of those present, except as elsewhere provided in the Constitution, and in case of a tie, the presiding officer shall decide the issue.

ARTICLE 57. Deliberation in each House shall be public. However, a secret meeting may be held where a majority of two-thirds or more of those present passes a resolution therefor.

Each House shall keep a record of proceedings. This record shall be published and given general circulation, excepting such parts of proceedings of secret session as may be deemed to require secrecy.

Upon demand of one-fifth or more of the members present, votes of the members on any matter shall be recorded in the minutes.

ARTICLE 58. Each House shall select its own president and other officials.

Each House shall establish its rules pertaining to meetings, proceedings and internal discipline, and may punish members for disorderly conduct. However, in order to expel a member, a majority of two-thirds or more of those members present must pass a resolution thereon.

ARTICLE 59. A bill becomes a law on passage by both Houses, except as otherwise provided by the Constitution.

A bill which is passed by the House of Representatives, and upon which the House of Councillors makes a decision different from that of the House of Representatives, becomes a law when passed a second time by the House of Representatives by a majority of two-thirds or more of the members present.

The provision of the preceding paragraph does not preclude the House of Representatives from calling for the meeting of a joint committee of both Houses, provided for by law.

Failure by the House of Councillors to take final action within sixty (60) days after receipt of a bill passed by the House of Representatives, time in recess excepted, may be determined by the House of Representatives to constitute a rejection of the said bill by the House of Councillors.

ARTICLE 60. The budget must first be submitted to the House of Representatives.

Upon consideration of the budget, when the House of Councillors makes a decision different from that of the House of Representatives, and when no agreement can be reached even through a joint committee of both Houses, provided for by law, or in the case of failure by the House of Councillors to take final action within thirty (30) days, the period of recess excluded, after the receipt of the budget passed by the House of Representatives, the decision of the House of Representatives shall be the decision of the Diet.

ARTICLE 61. The second paragraph of the preceding article applies also to the Diet approval required for the conclusion of treaties.

ARTICLE 62. Each House may conduct investigations in relation to government, and may demand the presence and testimony of witnesses, and the production of records.

ARTICLE 63. The Prime Minister and other Ministers of State may, at any time, appear in either House for the purpose of speaking on bills, regardless of whether they are members of the House or not. They must appear when their presence is required in order to give answers or explanations.

ARTICLE 64. The Diet shall set up an impeachment court from among the members of both Houses for the purpose of trying those judges against whom removal proceedings have been instituted.

Matters relating to impeachment shall be provided by law.

CHAPTER V. THE CABINET

ARTICLE 65. Executive power shall be vested in the Cabinet.

ARTICLE 66. The Cabinet shall consist of the Prime Minister, who shall be its head, and other Ministers of State, as provided for by law.

The Prime Minister and other Ministers of State must be civilians.

The Cabinet, in the exercise of executive power, shall be collectively responsible to the Diet.

ARTICLE 67. The Prime Minister shall be designated from among the members of the Diet by a resolution of the Diet. This designation shall precede all other business.

If the House of Representatives and the House of Councillors disagree and if no agreement can be reached even through a joint committee of both Houses, provided by law, or the House of Councillors fails to make designation within ten (10) days, exclusive of the period of recess, after the House of Representatives has made designation, the decision of the House of Representatives shall be the decision of the Diet.

ARTICLE 68. The Prime Minister shall appoint the Ministers of State. However, a majority of their number must be chosen from among the members of the Diet.

The Prime Minister may remove the Ministers of State as he chooses.

ARTICLE 69. If the House of Representatives passes a non-confidence resolution, or rejects a confidence resolution, the Cabinet shall resign en masse, unless the House of Representatives is dissolved within ten (10) days.

ARTICLE 70. When there is a vacancy in the post of Prime Minister, or upon the first convocation of the Diet after a general election of members of the House of Representatives, the Cabinet shall resign en masse.

ARTICLE 71. In the cases mentioned in the two preceding articles, the Cabinet shall continue its functions until the time when a new Prime Minister is appointed.

ARTICLE 72. The Prime Minister, representing the Cabinet, submits bills, reports on general national affairs and foreign relations to the Diet and exercises control and supervision over various administrative branches.

ARTICLE 73. The Cabinet, in addition to other general administrative functions, shall perform the following functions:

Administer the law faithfully; conduct affairs of state.

Manage foreign affairs.

Conclude treaties. However, it shall obtain prior or, depending on circumstances, subsequent approval of the Diet.

Administer the civil service, in accordance with standards established by law.

Prepare the budget, and present it to the Diet.

Enact cabinet orders in order to execute the provisions of this Constitution and of the law. However, it cannot include penal provisions in such cabinet orders unless authorized by such law.

Decide on general amnesty, special amnesty, commutation of punishment, reprieve, and restoration of rights.

ARTICLE 74. All laws and cabinet orders shall be signed by the competent Minister of State and countersigned by the Prime Minister.

ARTICLE 75. The Ministers of State, during their tenure of office, shall not be subject to legal action without the consent of the Prime Minister. However, the right to take that action is not impaired hereby.

CHAPTER VI. JUDICIARY

ARTICLE 76. The whole judicial power is vested in a Supreme Court and in such inferior courts as are established by law.

No extraordinary tribunal shall be established, nor shall any organ or agency of the Executive be given final judicial power.

All judges shall be independent in the exercise of their conscience and shall be bound only by this Constitution and the laws.

ARTICLE 77. The Supreme Court is vested with the rule-making power under which it determines the rules of procedure and of practice, and of matters relating to attorneys, the internal discipline of the courts and the administration of judicial affairs.

Public procurators shall be subject to the rule-making power of the Supreme Court.

The Supreme Court may delegate the power to make rules for inferior courts to such courts.

ARTICLE 78. Judges shall not be removed except by public impeachment unless judicially declared mentally or physically incompetent to perform official duties. No disciplinary action against judges shall be administered by any executive organ or agency.

ARTICLE 79. The Supreme Court shall consist of a Chief Judge and such number of judges as may be determined by law; all such judges excepting the Chief Judge shall be appointed by the Cabinet.

The appointment of the judges of the Supreme Court shall be reviewed by the people at the first general election of members of the House of Representatives following their appointment, and shall be reviewed again at the first general election of members of the House of Representatives after a lapse of ten (10) years, and in the same manner thereafter.

In cases mentioned in the foregoing paragraph, when the majority of the voters favors the dismissal of a judge, he shall be dismissed.

Matters pertaining to review shall be prescribed by law.

The judges of the Supreme Court shall be retired upon the attainment of the age as fixed by law.

All such judges shall receive, at regular stated intervals, adequate compensation which shall not be decreased during their terms of office.

ARTICLE 80.   The judges of the inferior courts shall be appointed by the Cabinet from a list of persons nominated by the Supreme Court. All such judges shall hold office for a term of ten (10) years with privilege of reappointment, provided that they shall be retired upon the attainment of the age as fixed by law.

The judges of the inferior courts shall receive, at regular stated intervals, adequate compensation which shall not be decreased during their terms of office.

ARTICLE 81.   The Supreme Court is the court of last resort with power to determine the constitutionality of any law, order, regulation or official act.

ARTICLE 82.   Trials shall be conducted and judgment declared publicly.

Where a court unanimously determines publicity to be dangerous to public order or morals, a trial may be conducted privately, but trials of political offenses, offenses involving the press or cases wherein the rights of people as guaranteed in Chapter III of this Constitution are in question shall always be conducted publicly.

CHAPTER VII.   FINANCE

ARTICLE 83.   The power to administer national finances shall be exercised as the Diet shall determine.

ARTICLE 84.   No new taxes shall be imposed or existing ones modified except by law or under such conditions as law may prescribe.

ARTICLE 85.   No money shall be expended, nor shall the State obligate itself, except as authorized by the Diet.

ARTICLE 86.   The Cabinet shall prepare and submit to the Diet for its consideration and decision a budget for each fiscal year.

ARTICLE 87.   In order to provide for unforeseen deficiencies in the budget, a reserve fund may be authorized by the Diet to be expended upon the responsibility of the Cabinet.

The Cabinet must get subsequent approval of the Diet for all payments, from the reserve fund.

ARTICLE 88.   All property of the Imperial Household shall belong to the State. All expenses of the Imperial Household shall be appropriated by the Diet in the budget.

ARTICLE 89. No public money or other property shall be expended or appropriated for the use, benefit or maintenance of any religious institution or association, or for any charitable, educational, or benevolent enterprises not under the control of public authority.

ARTICLE 90. Final accounts of the expenditures and revenues of the State shall be audited annually by a Board of Audit and submitted by the Cabinet to the Diet, together with the statement of audit, during the fiscal year immediately following the period covered.

The organization and competency of the Board of Audit shall be determined by law.

ARTICLE 91. At regular intervals and at least annually the Cabinet shall report to the Diet and the people on the state of national finances.

CHAPTER VIII. LOCAL SELF GOVERNMENT

ARTICLE 92. Regulations concerning organization and operations of local public entities shall be fixed by law in accordance with the principle of local autonomy.

ARTICLE 93. The local public entities shall establish assemblies as their deliberative organs, in accordance with law.

The chief executive officers of all local public entities, the members of their assemblies, and such other local officials as may be determined by law shall be elected by direct popular vote within their several communities.

ARTICLE 94. Local public entities shall have the right to manage their property, affairs and administration and to enact their own regulations within law.

ARTICLE 95. A special law, applicable only to one local public entity, cannot be enacted by the Diet without the consent of the majority of the voters of the local public entity concerned, obtained in accordance with law.

CHAPTER IX. AMENDMENTS

ARTICLE 96. Amendments to the Constitution shall be initiated by the Diet, through a concurring vote of two-thirds or more of all the members of each House and shall thereupon be submitted to the people for ratification, which shall require the affirmative vote of a majority of all votes cast thereon, at a special referendum or at such election as the Diet shall specify.

Amendments when so ratified shall immediately be promulgated by the Emperor in the name of the people, as an integral part of this Constitution.

CHAPTER X. SUPREME LAW

ARTICLE 97. The fundamental human rights by this Constitution guaranteed to the people of Japan are fruits of the age-old struggle of man to be free; they have survived the many exacting tests for durability and are conferred upon this and future generations in trust, to be held for all time inviolate.

ARTICLE 98. This Constitution shall be the supreme law of the nation and no law, ordinance, imperial rescript or other act of government, or part thereof, contrary to the provisions hereof, shall have legal force or validity.

The treaties concluded by Japan and established laws of nations shall be faithfully observed.

ARTICLE 99. The Emperor or the Regent as well as Ministers of State, members of the Diet, judges, and all other public officials have the obligation to respect and uphold this Constitution.

CHAPTER XI. SUPPLEMENTARY PROVISIONS

ARTICLE 100. This Constitution shall be enforced as from the day when the period of six months will have elapsed counting from the day of its promulgation.

The enactment of laws necessary for the enforcement of this Constitution, the election of members of the House of Councillors and the procedure for the convocation of the Diet and other preparatory procedures necessary for the enforcement of this Constitution may be executed before the day prescribed in the preceding paragraph.

ARTICLE 101. If the House of Councillors is not constituted before the effective date of this Constitution, the House of Representatives shall function as the Diet until such time as the House of Councillors shall be constituted.

ARTICLE 102. The term of office for half the members of the House of Councillors serving in the first term under this Constitution shall be three years. Members falling under this category shall be determined in accordance with law.

ARTICLE 103. The Ministers of State, members of the House of Representatives and judges in office on the effective date of this Constitution, and all other public officials who occupy positions corresponding to such positions as are recognized by this Constitution shall not forfeit their positions automatically on account of the enforcement of this Constitution unless otherwise specified by law. When, however, successors are elected or appointed under the provisions of this Constitution, they shall forfeit their positions as a matter of course.

Appendix $\mathcal{C}$

Japanese Cabinets During the Last Seventy Years, 1885–1955[1]

Cabinet	Duration Yr.-Mo.-Da.	Dates
1. Ito, Hirobumi (I)	2- 4- 8	Dec. 22, 1885–Apr. 30, 1888
2. Kuroda, General Kiyotaka	1- 7- 4	Apr. 30, 1888–Dec. 24, 1889
3. Yamagata, General Aritomo (I)	1- 4-12	Dec. 24, 1889–May 6, 1891
4. Matsukata, Masayoshi (I)	1- 3- 3	May 6, 1891–Aug. 8, 1892
5. Ito, Hirobumi (II)	4- 1-10	Aug. 8, 1892–Sep. 18, 1896
6. Matsukata, Masayoshi (II)	1- 4-25	Sep. 18, 1896–Jan. 12, 1898
7. Ito, Hirobumi (III)	0- 5-18	Jan. 12, 1898–Jun. 30, 1898
8. Okuma, Shigenobu (I)	0- 4- 1	Jun. 30, 1898–Nov. 8, 1898
9. Yamagata, General Aritomo (II)	1-11-11	Nov. 8, 1898–Oct. 19, 1900
10. Ito, Hirobumi (IV)	0- 7- 5	Oct. 19, 1900–Jun. 2, 1901
11. Katsura, General Taro (I)	4- 7- 5	Jun. 2, 1901–Jan. 7, 1906
12. Saionji, Prince Kimmochi (I)	2- 6- 7	Jan. 7, 1906–Jul. 14, 1908
13. Katsura, General Taro (II)	3-11-16	Jul. 14, 1908–Aug. 30, 1911
14. Saionji, Prince Kimmochi (II)	1- 3-10	Aug. 30, 1911–Dec. 21, 1912
15. Katsura, General Taro (III)	0- 2- 0	Dec. 21, 1912–Feb. 20, 1913
16. Yamamoto, Admiral Gombei (I)	1- 1-17	Feb. 20, 1913–Apr. 16, 1914
17. Okuma, Shigenobu (II)	2- 5-23	Apr. 16, 1914–Oct. 9, 1916
18. Terauchi, General Masatake	1-10-20	Oct. 9, 1916–Sep. 29, 1918
19. Hara, Takashi	3- 1-14	Sep. 29, 1918–Nov. 13, 1921
20. Takahashi, Korekiyo	0- 6-29	Nov. 13, 1921–Jun. 12, 1922
21. Kato, Admiral Tomosaburo	1- 2-23	Jun. 12, 1922–Sep. 2, 1923
22. Yamamoto, Admiral Gombei (II)	0- 4- 5	Sep. 2, 1923–Jan. 7, 1924

[1] Naikaku Kambo, *Naikaku Seido Shichijunen Shi* (1955), pp. 641–678, lists the Kato Takaaki cabinet as the 24th and a single continuous government whereas most other sources list two separate and distinct cabinets, that is, as the first and second Kato Cabinets.   See 1954 *Jiji Nenkan*, pp. 466–468 and Amano Yoshikazu *Seiji no Jiten*, pp. 446–461.

Cabinet	Duration Yr.-Mo.-Da.	Dates
23. Kiyoura, Keigo	0- 5- 4	Jan. 7, 1924–Jun. 11, 1924
24. Kato, Takaaki (I)	1- 1-20	Jun. 11, 1924–Aug. 2, 1925
25. Kato Takaaki (II)	0- 5-26	Aug. 2, 1925–Jan. 30, 1926
26. Wakatsuki, Reijiro (I)	1- 2-18	Jan. 30, 1926–Apr. 20, 1927
27. Tanaka, General Giichi	2- 2-13	Apr. 20, 1927–Jul. 2, 1929
28. Hamaguchi, Yuko	1- 9-13	Jul. 2, 1929–Apr. 14, 1931
29. Wakatsuki, Reijiro (II)	0- 8- 0	Apr. 14, 1931–Dec. 13, 1931
30. Inukai, Tsuyoshi	0- 5-15	Dec. 13, 1931–May 26, 1932
31. Saito, Admiral Makoto	2- 1-12	May 26, 1932–Jul. 8, 1934
32. Okada, Admiral Keisuke	1- 8- 2	Jul. 8, 1934–Mar. 9, 1936
33. Hirota, Koki	0-10-20	Mar. 9, 1936–Feb. 2, 1937
34. Hayashi, General Senjuro	0- 4- 0	Feb. 2, 1937–Jun. 4, 1937
35. Konoe, Prince Fumimaro (I)	1- 7- 1	Jun. 4, 1937–Jan. 5, 1939
36. Hiranuma, Kiichiro	0- 7-27	Jan. 5, 1939–Aug. 30, 1939
37. Abe, General Nobuyuki	0- 4-17	Aug. 30, 1939–Jan. 16, 1940
38. Yonai, Admiral Mitsumasa	0- 6- 6	Jan. 16, 1940–Jul. 22, 1940
39. Konoe, Prince Fumimaro (II)	0-11-26	Jul. 22, 1940–Jul. 18, 1941
40. Konoe, Prince Fumimaro (III)	0- 3- 0	Jul. 18, 1941–Oct. 18, 1941
41. Tojo, General Hideki	2- 9- 5	Oct. 18, 1941–Jul. 22, 1944
42. Koiso, General Kuniaki	0- 8-12	Jul. 22, 1944–Apr. 7, 1945
43. Suzuki, Admiral Kantaro	0- 4-10	Apr. 7, 1945–Aug. 17, 1945
44. Higashikuni, Prince Naruhiko	0- 1-23	Aug. 17, 1945–Oct. 9, 1945
45. Shidehara, Kijuro	0- 7-13	Oct. 9, 1945–May 22, 1946
46. Yoshida, Shigeru (I)	1- 0- 3	May 22, 1946–May 24, 1947
47. Katayama, Tetsu	0- 9-15	May 24, 1947–Mar. 10, 1948
48. Ashida, Hitoshi	0- 7- 10	Mar. 10, 1948–Oct. 19, 1948
49. Yoshida, Shigeru (II)	0- 4- 1	Oct. 19, 1948–Feb. 16, 1949
50. Yoshida, Shigeru (III)	3- 8-15	Feb. 16, 1949–Oct. 30, 1952
51. Yoshida, Shigeru (IV)	0- 6-22	Oct. 30, 1952–May 21, 1953
52. Yoshida, Shigeru (V)	1- 6-20	May 21, 1953–Dec. 10, 1954
53. Hatoyama, Ichiro (I)	0- 3-10	Dec. 10, 1954–Mar. 19, 1955
54. Hatoyama, Ichiro (II)	0- 8- 4	Mar. 19, 1955–Nov. 22, 1955
55. Hatoyama, Ichiro (III)		Nov. 22, 1955–

Index